Neoliberalism, Accountability, and Reform
Failures in Emerging Markets

Neoliberalism, Accountability, and Reform Failures in Emerging Markets

Eastern Europe, Russia, Argentina, and Chile in Comparative Perspective

LUIGI MANZETTI

the pennsylvania state university press
university park, pennsylvania

LIBRARY OF CONGRESS
CATALOGING-IN-PUBLICATION DATA

Manzetti, Luigi.
Neoliberalism, accountability, and reform failures in emerging markets: Eastern Europe, Russia,
Argentina, and Chile in comparative perspective / Luigi Manzetti.
p.   cm.
Includes bibliographical references and index.
Summary: "An analysis of the failure of neoliberal market reforms in producing sustained growth
in emerging markets. Focuses on problems with weak accountability institutions, and collusion
between government and business, political patronage, and corruption"—Provided by publisher.
ISBN 978-0-271-03574-1 (cloth : alk. paper)
1. Developing countries—Economic policy.
2. Neoliberalism—Developing countries.
3. Structural adjustment (Economic policy)—Developing countries.
4. Government accountability—Developing countries.
5. Europe, Eastern—Economic policy—1989–
6. Russia (Federation)—Economic policy—1991–
7. Argentina—Economic policy.
8. Chile—Economic policy.
I. Title.

HC59.7.M2865 2009
338.9—dc22
2009042714

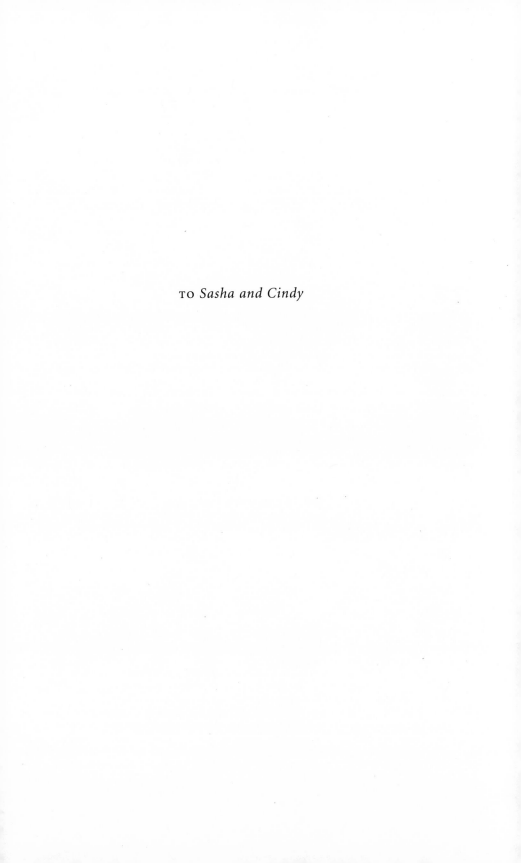

TO *Sasha and Cindy*

contents

preface

My interest in the relationship between market reforms and accountability started in 1990, when I was working on a related project on privatization policy in South America. Having lived through two bouts of hyperinflation spirals and witnessed firsthand how it had destroyed people's lives and savings, I came to the conclusion that market-oriented reforms were the only way out in that part of the world. However, as my field research progressed, I realized fairly quickly that theory was not meeting reality. Worse yet, reforms were steamrolled through undemocratic means, and in the process the political elites in charge were enriching themselves and those business groups willing to bankroll them. In 1993, while I was a researcher at the North-South Center of the University of Miami, I wrote a short paper pointing to these problems and their possible consequences. To the best of my knowledge, nothing in English had been published on that subject matter at the time. Later that year the Wilson Center invited me to give a presentation as part of a conference on market reforms in Latin America where I exposed my misgivings. I did not get many questions, but at the end of the talk a senior staffer of the World Bank came to me and said, "So it's you who is writing these things! You know, you should be careful. We are trying to help these countries and what you write can be used by those vested interests which are trying to stop the reform process." In 1995 a high-level officer of the U.S. State Department gave me the same warning. His line of thought was the following: Some presidents have engaged in corruption and crony capitalism, but they will change their ways, and if they do not, people will vote them out of office. However, three years later the tune had changed considerably. The same person approached me to give a talk co-sponsored by the U.S. State Department to discuss how corruption was detrimental to foreign investments. As U.S. companies were losing business in lucrative privatization bids, the Clinton administration began to change its earlier views. The sad thing is that the problem was not limited to Latin America. At the end of a presentation that I gave at a conference sponsored by the World Bank, an eastern European gentleman approached me and said, "What you just described about crony market reforms in Latin America could have applied just as well to my own country." It was a sobering realization that things were going astray globally. In the aftermath of Argentina's collapse in 2002, I began to notice that what drove that country to disaster shared many similar patterns with early financial crises in East Asia and Russia. From that point on I became hooked. I first published the original theoretical argument of the book in *World Politics* in 2003, and by 2006 I completed most of the field research.

During the gestation of the project I received help and advice from many people and institutions in so many ways. Surely, this book could not have been written without the generous financial assistance of the North-South Center (NSC) at the University of Miami where I spent most of the 1992–95 period researching on the chapters dealing with Argentina and Chile. The NSC proved to be a once-in-a-lifetime opportunity for a project of this kind. This was due to the direct linkage that the NSC had with the U.S. State Department, which allowed me to travel to Latin America on many occasions and receive the full cooperation of U.S. Embassy staffs in setting up interviews with more than three hundred and fifty policy makers, economists, bankers, politicians, diplomats, and so forth, who would have been impossible to contact as a simple academician. To this end, I would like to personally thank the U.S. Information Agency personnel in Miami (Louis Falino), Argentina (Alexander Almasov), Brazil (Lane Cubstead), and Chile (Barbara Moore). Back in Miami, I took full advantage of the large number of scholars in residence who provided important suggestions and intellectual support. More specifically, I am indebted to my good friend Jeff Stark, whose good humor kept us all sane, and Robin Rosenberg, Ambler Moss, and Tony Maingot. My graduate assistants in Miami, María Eugenia Mujica and María Gloria Cano, did a great job in carrying out their research assignments and giving me plenty of suggestions.

In Argentina, Roberto de Michele not only spent considerable time helping with the field research but in the process became one of my most trusted friends, whose hospitality made Buenos Aires like a second home for me. Similarly, Mirta Detrizio at the U.S. Information System office turned out to be a one-person army as she did an incredible job in setting up interviews on my behalf and taught me a great deal about Argentina.

Luis Moreno Ocampo, Kevin O'Reilly, Roberto Saba, and Ernesto Calvo were of invaluable help as well while I was in Buenos Aires. I am deeply indebted to my friends in St. Petersburg, Moscow, and Prague who helped out with my research trips in Russia and the Czech Republic. Moreover, I would like to thank Silvana Malle, the former Head of Division of Non-member Economies at the Economics Department at the Organization of Economic Cooperation and Development, and now at the University of Verona, for her comments and suggestions regarding the Eastern European and Russian cases.

In the United States, the John Goodwin Tower Center at Southern Methodist University provided additional financial assistance through travel and research grants from 2001 to 2007. At Southern Methodist University quite a few people helped me in so many ways, particularly Nöelle McAlpine, Jimmeca Dorsey, and Beth McKnigh, while Howard H. Geoghegan spent a considerable amount of time editing the whole book. I owe a large debt to many officials at the U.S. State Department, the World Bank, the Inter-American Development Bank, and the Organization of Economic Cooperation and Development whose interviews were critical in allowing me to get a better picture about the role of the international community in the implementation of market reforms.

I am also grateful for the comments I received from colleagues and students at seminars held at the University of Ancona, the University of Cincinnati, the Copenhagen Business School, Duke University, the London School of Economics, Oxford University (Nuffield College), Ohio State University, the University of Pittsburgh, the University of Siena, and the University of Texas at Austin. Several colleagues were also very kind in taking the time to make valuable suggestions on earlier drafts of the manuscript, including Alan Angell, Marcus Kurtz, Peter Siavelis, Eduardo Silva, Carole Wilson, Charles Blake, Kurt Weyland, and Steve Wegren. I also would like to thank Sandy Thatcher at Penn State University Press for taking an interest in the project, as well as the three anonymous reviewers he solicited to comment on the book. I naturally take full responsibility for any errors that remain.

Lastly, and most of all, I want to thank my wife, Cindy, whose love and support never ceased even during the most difficult times, and to my son, Sasha, who was deprived of his best playmate due to a seemingly endless travel schedule. To all concerned goes my deepest gratitude.

one

ACCOUNTABILITY AND MARKET REFORMS

Introduction

Since the early 1980s, market reforms have been considered indispensable for reviving the ailing economies of developing and postcommunist countries. Inspired by neoliberal economic theory, these reforms were adopted, in varying degrees, throughout many countries of the world during the 1990s. One of the pivotal contentions that their proponents made from a broad political standpoint was that free markets are the best agents for bringing about individual freedom and, therefore, democracy. Rolling back the state, according to free-market advocates, would lead to sustained growth and strengthen individual rights in the economic and political realm. Thus, the message that the most industrialized nations sent struggling countries worldwide was straightforward. Free markets and democracy go hand in hand, and if a country wanted to become part of the democratic capitalist system, market reforms were in order.[1] By the early 1990s, lacking an alternative credible strategy, and often with a dire need to obtain international financial aid, many less developed countries around the globe (now dubbed "emerging markets") joined the bandwagon.[2]

Indeed, the 1990s marked the heyday of market reforms, but their results were at best disappointing (World Bank 2005). After some progress in the first part of the 1990s, many Latin American countries suffered serious economic downturns. In the former Soviet republics the transition from the

1. The most famous proponents of this view were British prime minister Margaret Thatcher and U.S. president Ronald Reagan (Busch 2001).
2. "Emerging markets" is a term that Antoine W. van Agtmael, of the International Finance Corporation at the World Bank, coined in 1981. It describes an emerging, or developing, market economy characterized by low to middle per capita income.

command economy to markets was traumatic and associated with sharp declines in output and living standards, whereas some Eastern European countries, including the Czech Republic, Hungary, Slovenia, and Poland, showed good progress after going through painful adjustments. Success stories were also the exception in the sub-Saharan region. Substantial growth and poverty reduction were primarily confined to East and Southeast Asia, but its star performers, China and India, applied the market reform agenda very selectively. On the one hand, they created incentives to export, but on the other, they ignored core policies such as privatization, labor reform, and fiscal reform and retained strong industrial policies and high trade barriers (World Bank 2005; Rodrik 2006).

Equally troubling was the fact that, as time went on, some of the largest emerging markets to have adopted market reforms were crushed under waves of unprecedented financial crises. Chile, which pioneered such reforms beginning in the mid-1970s, had already provided an early warning that when policies were implemented in a nontransparent way they were self-destructive, as its financial meltdown of 1982 proved. The trend continued with greater ramifications starting with Mexico (1995), to be followed by Thailand (1997), South Korea (1997), Indonesia (1997), Russia (1998), Turkey (2001), and Argentina (2001/2002).

While economic policies played an important role in the collapse of these economies, observers increasingly began to notice that they often shared disturbing similarities in the political realm; namely, that the lack of transparency exposed repeated instances of moral hazard. On many occasions, policy makers' behavior raised suspicion that they exploited their positions of power to reward political clienteles, thereby enriching themselves at the expense of their own people, the national coffers, investors, multilateral aid agencies, and foreign governments. For instance, privatization, which symbolized market reforms in the former Soviet bloc and Latin America, was marred by charges of corruption and crony capitalism that undermined its many successes (IDB 2007, 1). By 2008 these factors heavily contributed to the popular rejection of state divestiture in that region of the world and gave a pretext for populist leaders such as presidents Hugo Chávez in Venezuela, Nestor Kirchner in Argentina, and Evo Morales in Bolivia to return several key industries and public utility companies that had been privatized in the 1990s to government ownership ("Populism for a Price," *Washington Post*, August 3, 2007).

The danger that market reforms pursued in a political system lacking accountability opened up opportunities for old-style politics, threatening their sustainability and the legitimacy of the democratic process associated with them. Discussing the Argentine crisis of 2001/2002, the then U.S. secretary of state, Colin Powell, warned that serious political and institutional changes were needed to bring transparency and accountability to Argentine government action ("Going South: Old Demons Return to Haunt Latin America Progress," *Wall Street Journal,* July 25, 2002). Months later, the then U.S. treasury department secretary, Paul O'Neill, was even more explicit as he added that his government was reluctant to bail out Latin American countries if aid would end up in Swiss bank accounts ("The U.S. Pumps $1.5 Billion into Uruguay to Avert Latin American Crisis," *The Independent,* August 5, 2002).

As noted, some of the most important countries that took the path of market reforms ended up in severe financial crises with negative socioeconomic consequences that, in some cases, linger on to this day. Other countries avoided financial meltdowns but struggled, while a few instead met with success. Why have some countries succeeded and others failed? What went wrong in countries that experienced major financial crises?

An extensive literature in economics has tried to address these questions. In justifying so many "disappointments," the International Monetary Fund (IMF) and many economists supporting market reforms have contended that political leaders lacked the necessary commitment and tried too little, and, even when the commitment was there, the breadth and scope of reforms was uneven and policies were implemented in a piecemeal fashion (Shleifer and Treisman 2000, Åslund 2002; Kuczynski and Williamson 2003; Krueger 2004; Singh et al. 2005). According to this line of thinking, the soundness of the theory behind market reforms is not the issue since the problem arose from a mix of lack of political will and poor execution.

Critics of this point of view, however, argue instead that such policies were theoretically flawed and created more problems than those that they were attempting to solve, which often ended in the worst of both worlds as they impoverished many countries while keeping corrupt politicians in power (Stiglitz 2002).[3]

---

3. For an overview of this debate from the IMF's perspective, see Zettelmeyer (2006).

Institutions and Growth

Both sides of the argument just described contain elements of truth and have made important contributions to the scholarly debate, but they both downplay the question of how politics, and particularly political institutions, shaped the reform processes that ushered market reforms in emerging markets. This book will try to fill this gap in the literature from the vantage point of political science. This is not to imply that macroeconomic factors did not matter. On the contrary, my goal is to *complement* the insights that economists have developed so far by focusing on theoretical and institutional factors that contributed significantly to the design and implementation of reform policies, thus shaping their outcomes. Institutional explanations about economic performance stem from the early theoretical works of North and Thomas (1973), North (1990), and Olson (1965, 1982). While some studies have dismissed the importance of institutions (Sachs 2003; Goldsmith 2005), other empirical works have shown the importance of institutional factors in determining economic performance (Krusell and Ríos-Rull 1996; Parente and Prescott 1999; Hall and Jones 1999; Acemoglu and Robinson 2000, 2001; Easterly and Levine 2003). Dollar and Kraay (2003) also found that when institutions are treated as exogenous, there is significant partial association between trade and growth even after the inclusion of a variety of proxies for institutional quality. However, their model leads to inconclusive results once institutions are treated as endogenous.

Some studies have focused specifically on the role of democracy in promoting economic growth. For his part, Barro (1996) argued that low levels of democracy positively affect growth, but as democracy becomes more mature, its impact turns negative, whereas Rodrik (1997, 1999, 2007) concluded that democracy produces less randomness and economic volatility, is better suited to manage shocks, and produces more equitable distributional outcomes. In yet another study, Rivera-Batiz's (2007) results suggested that democracy does have a direct influence in total factor productivity but only when democratic institutions are associated with greater quality of governance. Conversely, when democratic institutions do not result in enhanced governance, then democracy has a negligible effect on growth. For Keech (2009), instead, the impact of democracy in the short term is mixed at best. It is in the long run that democratic institutions, once consolidated, are instrumental in the sustainability of good economic performance.

However, only a handful of studies have focused on the relationship between institutions and economic crises, and the results have run counter to conventional wisdom. The most important of such works concluded that "distortionary macroeconomic policies are more likely to be symptoms of underlying institutional problems rather than the main causes of economic volatility, and also that the effects of institutional differences on volatility do not appear to be primarily mediated by any of the standard macroeconomic variables. Instead, it appears that weak institutions cause volatility through a number of microeconomic, as well as macroeconomic, channels" (Acemoglu et al. 2003, 49).

Moreover, and just as important, Acemoglu et al. (2003) asserted that the economic instability of institutionally weak societies is not particularly the result of external shocks (such as a world recession) but is caused by their inability to deal with their own political problems in the first place. Further works (Addison and Baliamoune-Lutz 2006, 1030) pointed out that the economic literature "has less to say about the relationship between economic reform and institutions, and how that relationship can differ at different stages in the process of improving institutional quality." Indeed, when institutions do not conform to policy reforms (either because they are in the process of being reformed themselves or are obsolete), it is not surprising then that "donor-sponsored reforms break down and . . . have unintended results" (Addison and Baliamoune-Lutz 2006, 1030). Consistent with previous findings by Acemoglu, Johnson, and Robinson (2001), Dollar and Kraay (2003), and Rodrik, Subramanian, and Trebbi (2004), Addison and Baliamoune-Lutz (2006, 1040) found evidence that institutions play a crucial role, but their impact is not linear. In fact, countries in the middle range of institutional quality (measured by using Freedom House's indexes on political rights and liberties), and moving only slowly toward a free society, may experience weak or even negative economic results. In other words, not only do institutions matter for successful reforms but their quality matters even more.

However, while economists have been interested in explaining growth and/or economic crises using broad measurements of institutional capacity, my focus in this book centers on the logic behind market reforms and how their success or failure has been influenced by democratic institutions of political accountability in emerging markets. Accordingly, the first goal of the book is to show how market-oriented economic theory, despite its strong belief in individual freedom when it comes to the economic realm, is rather ambivalent about the virtues of the democratic process. As I will argue later, this partly explains why market-oriented reforms once put into concrete policy action in emerging markets were often used to undermine political accountability and the due process associated with democratic governance. The logic vis-à-vis the practice of conservative economic theories is an aspect of the market-reform agenda that has been usually scarcely examined in the economic literature but is of fundamental importance if we want to understand why by the early 2000s such theories fell in disrepute in so many emerging markets as they became associated with corruption, crony capitalism, and patronage politics. Focusing on the theory and practice of conservative economic thinking will also shed light into the reasons why the United States and the international financial institutions (IFIS) often condoned, and on occasions even blessed, policies that they knew were marred by all kinds of irregularities and deliberately ignored or even dismantled the checks and balances of the democratic process.[4]

The second goal of the book is to support its core argument. My thesis, which I will develop in greater detail later in this chapter, is that if market reforms are implemented without accountability, then they are likely to be manipulated in a way that creates opportunity for corruption, crony capitalism, and political patronage—all factors that are conducive to large fiscal deficits and costly rent-seeking behavior. Consistent with previous works on Russia and Eastern Europe (Stark and Bruszt 1998; Orenstein 2001; and Gould 2003), I will argue that governments that implement market reforms without being bound in their action by accountability institutions are likely to experience financial crises. Conversely, those countries whose executives are held in check through a variety of accountability institutions are more likely to avoid financial crises and put into place market-friendly policies that yield positive results as the proponents of market reforms envisioned.

The Rise of Neoliberal Economic Theory

Market reforms have been inspired by the theories of Friedrich von Hayek (1944) and Milton Friedman (1962). These scholars have usually been

---

4. The most important IFIS are the IMF and the World Bank, but regional development banks such as the African Development Bank, the Asian Development Bank, the Bank for International Settlements, the European Bank for Reconstruction and Development, and the Inter-American Development Bank play an important role.

dubbed as "neoliberal" because their writings are modern adaptations of the "liberal" or "laissez faire" economic thinking pioneered by Adam Smith, who postulated that capitalism performs best when left to its own devices and unhindered by government regulation. While economists have written much about the pros and cons of Hayek's and Friedman's theories, analysts have paid relatively little attention to the role that these two scholars have assigned to politics and the role of government institutions in a capitalist economy.

Consistent with the teachings of Ludwig von Mises and the Austrian school of economics, of which he was a member, Hayek (1944) contended that the best way to coordinate people's economic activity is to promote free markets and foster competition whenever possible. In Hayek's view, competition is at the heart of economic growth as it functions as a voluntary social control mechanism by allowing individuals to pursue their self-interest. In so doing, competition is a much more efficient tool to organize an economy than government regulation, which he regarded as cumbersome, wasteful, and prone to arbitrary and coercive decision-making processes. Far from advocating the status quo benefiting vested interests, Hayek argued that where competition does not exist, it should be created. He also believed that democracy is an important safeguard against tyranny but can only exist if there is first freedom of contract. Thus, democracy is a means to strengthen economic freedom, not an end in itself. Moreover, to prevent democracy from becoming captive to special interests and totalitarian legislative majorities, it must be bounded by the "rule of law" (Bellamy 1994). In this regard, Hayek believed that the best means to accomplish effective democracy and healthy competition was by having government establish a legal framework that protected individuals' rights and the contract obligations of the parties involved. These measures would, on the one hand, restrict the coercive powers of government vis-à-vis its citizens and, on the other, discourage collusion and entry barriers.

Friedman (1962) later argued much of the same, but at times in a more radical fashion. For Friedman economic freedom is an end in itself and a prerequisite for the establishment of political freedom. Thus, the freer individuals are from government regulation in economic transactions, the freer they would be in the polity. Friedman believed that because government regulation allows politicians to abuse their power to pursue their own interests, it is a universal culprit impinging on individual freedoms. Therefore, if politicians are to be deprived of the authority to curtail individual freedom, government intervention must be reduced to only the most basic tasks, including national defense and the definition and enforcement of property rights. This last point was particularly important in Friedman's theory, as it was meant to create a level playing field that would prevent noncompetitive behavior. Like Hayek, Friedman believed that competition in the marketplace is the best means to promote freedom and, at the same time, the best antidote to prevent monopolistic behavior from private agents. Within this context, Friedman assigned to government the role of establishing antitrust legislation and institutions to deter collusion. Everything else, Friedman contended, could be handled much more efficiently by the private sector.

In the mid-twentieth century Hayek and Friedman played a pivotal role in sharpening and keeping alive economic liberalism, which had dominated economic policy in the United Kingdom, the United States, and Latin America until 1929 but had fallen in disrepute as it was identified as the main cause behind the Great Depression. In fact, from the 1930s until the early 1980s, policies in industrialized nations abided to the principles enunciated by John Maynard Keynes, which created welfare states and granted government extensive regulatory powers along with the control of key industries in what Lenin called the "commanding heights" of the economy. In a similar vein, after World War II the most important developing countries, in their attempt to become more self-sufficient and less exposed to commodity fluctuations, adopted import substitution industrialization (ISI) and economic protectionism (Prebisch 1950). Yet, the most radical rejection of economic liberalism came from Marxism-Leninism. As the Soviet Union influence increased tremendously after World War II in Eastern Europe and developing countries, so did its model based on a command economy.[5]

However, by the mid-1970s the theoretical ideas of Hayek, Friedman, and their colleagues at the University of Chicago began to achieve greater acceptance not just among economists but, most important, among conservative leaders such as General Augusto Pinochet, Margaret Thatcher, and Ronald Reagan who embraced parts of their theories and turned them into policies.[6] This is why economic neoliberalism has usually been identified

---

5. In the Soviet model the state owned all means of production and was responsible for making all decisions about production and investments.

6. In 1950 Hayek left the London School of Economics to join the faculty of the University of Chicago, where he remained until 1962. In 1974 he received the Nobel Prize for economics.

with conservative (if not authoritarian) political agendas. For instance, Chile was the first country to experiment extensively with many of Friedman's principles, but, due to the brutal nature of the Pinochet's dictatorship (1973–90), its accomplishments were usually dismissed. For her part, Thatcher proudly admitted that her controversial reforms, which overhauled the United Kingdom between 1979 and 1990, were deeply influenced by Hayek's ideas. However, it was only after President Reagan (1981–89) assumed power and reshaped the U.S. economy according to Hayek's and Friedman's theories that the neoliberal economic view began to shape the policies of the U.S. Treasury (Stiglitz 2002).

By the mid-1980s the policy cycle had come full circle. Keynesianism and isi had produced on many occasions stagflation, whereas the Soviet economic system was rapidly crumbling. In sharp contrast to these events, the Chilean, British and U.S. economies, with their emphasis on free markets, were on the rebound and, by either default or true change of heart, world leaders began to look to neoliberalism as the only way out to jump-start their troubled economies (Yergin and Stanislaw 1998).

As a direct consequence of the return to prominence of economic liberalism, the late 1980s witnessed the emergence of the so-called Washington Consensus (henceforth wc), which borrowed extensively from Hayek's and Friedman's seminal works. According to John Williamson (1990), who coined the term, the consensus represented the prevailing economic thinking at the U.S. Treasury, the imf, the World Bank, and many policy think tanks in Washington on how to tackle the Latin America economic crisis. Indeed, the relevance of the wc's agenda was that its thinking shaped much of the ifis' policy advice, chief among them the imf and the World Bank, as well as their conditionality clauses in disbursing financial aid (World Bank 2005; Woods 2006). Eventually, as more countries began to ask for the ifis' financial assistance, the wc's recommendations began to be applied, almost indiscriminately, to the former Soviet bloc, Asia, and Africa. As such, in line with Hayek's and Friedman's teachings, the wc advocated neoliberal policies along the following lines (Williamson 1994). First, the wc endorsed the establishment of macroeconomic stability through the efficient use of economic resources. This meant balancing government budgets while liberalizing the economy and opening up domestic markets to foreign competition. Reducing tariffs and quotas, ending price and exchange controls, eliminating agricultural/industrial subsidies, and lifting restrictions on financial inflows and services were all policies that the wc required for the disbursement of financial assistance. Second, private initiative had to replace government intervention in allocating resources. This implied reducing the size of government and its role in the economy only to fundamental tasks. Privatizing state-owned enterprises (SOEs), dismantling a web of business licenses and regulations, and breaking up monopolies were the most visible policy measures in this regard.

In justifying the inevitable hardship associated with the market reform agenda, the WC painted a rosy picture by promising to accomplish two interrelated goals in a relatively short period of time. Economically, its policies, after the initial social costs, would bring sustained growth. Politically, following Hayek and Friedman, it assumed that by freeing the market from government interference the individual's freedom would be enhanced and, consequently, democracy in emerging markets would be strengthened as well.

By the early 1990s, Przeworski (1991, viii) described the impact of the WC's policy advice to emerging markets in the following terms: "We are living in a highly ideological epoch. . . . They implement an intellectual blueprint, a blueprint developed within the walls of the North American academia and shaped by international financial institutions. They are radical: they are intended to turn upside down all the existing social relations. And they offer a single panacea, a magic wand, which, once waved, will cure all the ills. For the first time in history, capitalism is being adopted as an application of a doctrine, rather than evolving as a historical process of trial and error."

Neoliberalism and Accountability

To understand the WC's broad ramifications from a political economy perspective, it is worth remembering that, following Hayek and Friedman, its main proponents assumed two main conditions. First, economics drives politics, and once the right policies were designed, politicians would implement them. Second, and more important in our case, markets must operate within a polity where:

1. Executives are bound by constitutional checks and balances in the exercise of their authority.

2. The legislative branch is responsive to an appreciable degree to the electorate.

3. The judiciary is expected to render decisions that are predictable and fairly independent from political interference, which guarantees the upholding of property rights.

These three conditions are essentials for a thriving capitalist economy because they restrain politicians, legislators, and judges alike from making discretionary decisions that could otherwise spook the market and distort asset allocation (Kydland and Prescott 1997). By the same token, they are the essence of the principle, developed early on by James Madison, that government institutions must be accountable to their citizens and to one another.[7] Following this rationale, if accountability is a sine qua non for a modern capitalist economy, the same applies to market reforms because their goal is to create the same kind of economic regime in developing countries.

While theoretically sound in principle, the wc for the most part purposely neglected the importance of strengthening institutions of accountability. As Rodrik (2006) noted, the neoliberal proponents of the wc reform policies did not require major institutional changes. Indeed, even if the three assumptions mentioned above did not materialize, the wc hoped that the soundness of its policies would, in their own right, make up for possible institutional weaknesses (World Bank 2005). The rationale behind this line of thought rested on the belief that had market reform succeeded in promoting sustained economic growth, they would create the incentives for establishing effective institutions at a later stage. The strong bias against government institutions, which up until the 1980s had been instrumental in enacting interventionist policies, led the wc's advocates to emphasize instead the establishment of a few rule-based reforms with a narrow focus; namely, limiting policy discretion. This meant insulating central banks from political interference, joining international and regional trade agreements (General Agreement on Tariffs and Trade and its successor, the World Trade Organization), submitting government-foreign business disputes to international arbitration, and adopting currency boards or even dollarizing the economy to impose monetary discipline (World Bank 2005, 49).

7. See Alexander Hamilton, John Jay, and James Madison, *The Federalist*, ed. George W. Carey and James McClellan (Indianapolis, Ind.: Liberty Fund, 2001), 47–51.

Only in the mid-1990s as problems began to mount did the wc's policy recommendation list expand by adding the so called "second generation" reforms, some of which began to address institutional issues.[8] The policy approach just described explains why the neoliberals of the wc gave top priority only to one side of the equation (the economic one) despite abundant theoretical evidence (North 1994) suggesting that when a country adopts the formal rules (in our case, promarket reforms) of another, the results may turn out quite differently because the recipient country may have very different formal and informal institutions (in our case, political).

To make things worse, once the theory was put into practice, it was clear that the neoliberals leading the U.S. Treasury Department, ifis, and prominent think tanks were quite ambivalent about the democratic process and the feasibility of combining sweeping market reforms within the context of democratic principles and procedures (Orenstein 2001; Stiglitz 2002; Rodan 2004). Their fear was that democratic institutions and their processes could be manipulated by those parties and vested interests opposing market reforms.

It soon became evident that despite the official statements supporting democracy and the due process, the U.S. Treasury and the ifis' top priority was the quick implementation of trade liberalization, privatization, and anti-inflationary policies before the honeymoon period would evaporate. Likewise, the short-term costs of market reforms could prove too severe, thus resulting in a political backlash and reform-minded governments being voted out of office. Thus, the wc stressed a quick implementation of the reform package to take advantage of the window of opportunity opened by the demise of the previous economic regime before powerful interests could block it. The "shock therapy" approach (i.e., the adoption of the core neoliberal policies in very short order) was the main policy style to usher market-friendly reforms. This was an open rejection of the "gradualist approach," which had been tried unsuccessfully in Latin America and the Soviet bloc in the second half of the 1980s. Indeed at the time "a belief in gradualism had almost become tantamount to a confession of a lack of reforming virility" (World Bank 2005, 7).

Sachs (1993), one of the most influential supporters of shock therapy, having advised several key reformers including Bolivia, Argentina, Poland, and Russia in this direction, made the point quite clear on how such an

---

8. For a complete list, see Rodrik (2006).

economic approach should be managed politically. He stated that the executive should be (a) insulated from checks and balances and (b) entrusted upon with special decree powers bypassing the legislature to ensure a quick execution of the reform agenda. After all, this apparent contradiction between promoting free markets through not-so-democratic means could still be reconciled with Hayek's and Friedman's contention that market freedom drives democracy, not the other way around. Once you establish the first, the other will follow. Consequently, for the neoliberals the technocratic reforms imposing limits on democratic procedures were a short-term cost worth paying because if their policies were to be well executed they would strengthen democracy in the medium term (Orenstein 2001, 15). Thus, the neoliberals regarded the market reforms enshrined in the wc as the optimal technocratic solution to decades of economic mismanagement created either by ISI (Latin America, Asia, Africa) or Communism (Soviet Union, Eastern Europe). Such a belief was synthesized by Lawrence Summers: "Spread the truth—the laws of economics are like laws of engineering. One set of laws works everywhere."[9]

Unfortunately, from a political standpoint the problem was that all too often neoliberals were so eager to see market reforms take advantage of the window of opportunity presented by the demise of ISI and Communism that they trusted their execution on national leaders who had a troublesome track record. Their underlying hope was that former Communist and populist politicians would have a change of heart and become true believers in the power of the market. Regrettably, such leaders often manipulated foreign governments and IFIS rather than the other way around because, on many occasions, they pledged to enact some of the wc's policies but made sure that such policies would be crafted in a way that increased their power and favored economic groups close to them. Indeed, self-proclaimed economic reformers in Mexico, Argentina, Indonesia, Thailand, and Russia, to name a few, expressed willingness to embark on the reform process in exchange for substantial foreign aid but nonetheless continued to operate according to the shady formal and informal norms of the past through the emasculation of accountability institutions. The means may have changed (market capitalism replacing Communism or ISI), but the end game's ultimate goal, from a politician's perspective, remained the same: retaining

---

9. Quoted in Hedlund (1999, 112). Summers was World Bank chief economist (1991–93) and later served in the Clinton administration in various senior positions until he became U.S. Treasury secretary in 1999.

political power. Not surprising, when reforms were characterized by highly concentrated executive powers they often failed and ended, in some cases, in serious financial crises.

For instance, in order to "democratize" the market many countries in Latin America (Argentina, Brazil, Bolivia, Ecuador, and Venezuela) indiscriminately used executive orders/emergency decrees and in the case of Peru the closing of the Congress, which made a mockery of the democratic process. Government officials in these countries defended their unorthodox methods by arguing that time was pressing and that resorting to normal legislative procedures would give vested interests the opportunity to derail the reform effort. By 1992, however, there were already clear signs that some administrations, with the excuse of swiftly implementing government plans, were using loopholes, created by the emergency powers acquired by the executive, to pursue old-style corrupt and clientelistic ways. The impeachment of presidents Fernando Collor de Mello (Brazil) and Carlos Andrés Pérez (Venezuela) began to raise questions not only about the soundness of market reforms per se but also about the consequences for democratic governance of their controversial implementation. Brazil and Venezuela were able to get rid of corrupt leaders relatively quickly, but other countries were incapable of doing the same, which penalized them even further as time went on. In the end, it was not just individual countries that lost out but also the neoliberal argument to reshape the world economy.

The Meaning of Accountability

Since the late 1960s there has been a growing demand for the accountability of public officials in many countries around the world. In both developed and developing countries the gulf between citizens vis-à-vis the government institutions that are supposed to pursue the public interest has widened as a barrage of scandals has tarnished the reputation of politicians and civil servants. In fact, the past few decades have witnessed a marked decline in public trust and government effectiveness even in the strongest democracies (Pharr and Putnam 2000). People have become increasingly frustrated with the amount of government secrecy and lack of accountability in the industrialized world, much of which was tolerated during the cold war years but could not be justified after the demise of the Soviet bloc.[10] As research has shown, the less information is available to citizens, the more politicians are prone to pursue their own agendas and appropriate economic rents for their supporters (Barro 1973; Ferejohn 1986). However, the emergence of an aggressive investigative media, grassroots movements, and nongovernmental organizations (NGOs), among other factors, has placed greater and greater pressure on public institutions to become more accountable. The trend has not been confined to advanced industrial societies and in the last two decades has taken a global dimension (Kahler 2004; Held and Koenig-Archibugi 2005). Since the early 1980s in the developing world the demise of various types of autocratic and Communist governments has prompted citizens to question their politicians and the authoritarian manner in which they often use public institutions. In describing the phenomenon taking place in developing countries, Mulgan (2003, 3–4) noted: "[People] are looking to strong institutions of accountability, such effective political opposition, and independent judiciary and free media, as means of making their societies both [freer] and more prosperous. They see the lack of transparency and the potential for corruption as an affront to increasingly universal democratic values. Lack of accountability also detracts from the 'good governance' which is considered to be necessary for social and economic development." Indeed, political accountability is today regarded as being an indispensable component of good governance and economic growth because as political accountability increases, so do the costs that public officials incur when acting to their own personal benefit or that of their cronies. Thus, political accountability works as a powerful deterrent against illegal practices.[11]

What is accountability? In a democratic system, citizens delegate broad powers to their representatives (elected officials) and their agents (civil servants) to rule them. Restraining officeholders from abusing such powers is a defining feature of modern democracies that sets them apart from various types of authoritarian regimes where the exercise of authority is instead highly arbitrary and subjective (Schacter 2001). Ensuring that political power is exercised according to well-defined rules is therefore a pillar of democratic governance. In other words, in a democracy, both elected and nonelected officeholders must be accountable for their actions while exer-

---

10. For an extensive review of the literature on accountability, see Mulgan (2003).
11. World Bank, "Anticorruption," http://www1.worldbank.org/publicsector/anticorrupt.

cising the power granted to them by the citizenry. Thus, accountability works to promote fair, honest, and effective government. It implies the notion that elected and nonelected officials should answer and take responsibility for their actions (Keohane and Nye 2001). Equally important, "political accountability must be institutionalized if it is to work effectively" (Schmitter 2004, 48).

We can distinguish two broad types of accountability. The first is what scholars define as direct or "vertical" accountability, which is exercised by the citizenry on government officials. The most common forms of this type are "bottom up" in kind, such as elections through which voters have a chance to hold elected officials accountable for their past behavior. The assumption here is that citizens are capable through the ballot box to force the government to choose between addressing its wrongdoings and suffering declining support or potentially losing office.

However, this type of accountability suffers important limitations. As noted by Manin, Przeworski, and Stokes (1999), elections represent weak means in order to keep politicians accountable since they take place over relatively long periods of time, voters' preferences may be influenced by multiple issues that may not be linked to the intention of punishing incumbents for their past behavior, and voters often lack the necessary information to assess government performance. Other forms of direct accountability, however, can be even more effective. For instance, civil organizations and the media can play an important role as societal agents of control (Peruzzotti and Smulovitz 2006). As opposed to elections, they can do so continuously and their actions can be quite focused and clearly linked to specific issues of wrongdoing. As Wampler (2004) noted, "citizens now have access to a range of legal and political resources to pressure public officials, including lawsuits, public demonstrations, public hearings, and participatory institutions." Stark and Bruszt's (1998) "extended accountability" definition tries to incorporate both institutional and societal means to limit executive authority through networks of autonomous societal and political institutions.

The weakness of elections and other forms of vertical accountability is what first drove the United States, and many countries later, to devise an elaborate system of checks and balances. As democracies developed they embraced the idea of limited government, whose aim is to prevent the concentration of coercive power and its use in an arbitrary fashion. Limited government espouses the idea of respecting individual rights in the political and economic realm through a number of self-enforcing institutions and the upholding of the rule of law. Economically, limited government is fundamental because if elected and nonelected officials do not restrain themselves, investors will fear confiscation and sudden changes in the rules of the game that, as discussed earlier, is at the center of Hayek's and Friedman's theories. Politically, limited government in a democracy aims at safeguarding individual rights and is the fabric holding together the social contract between the citizens and their rulers (Shepsle 1991; Weingast 1997). Limited government institutions vary across democracies, but they tend to be multiple in nature, creating overlapping veto points in the decision-making structure. In this way, rulers can assure their citizens of their commitment to restrain their authority by creating institutional checks and balances. In fact, empirical evidence demonstrates that appropriate checks and balances create enough conflicts of interest between the executive and the legislature on public policy to force both institutions to compromise and thus discipline themselves to the voters' advantage (Persson, Roland, and Tabellini 1997).

This consideration brings us to the second type of accountability, which is exercised within the state through a variety of institutions to check and restrain itself (Schmitter 2004). It entails both monitoring and oversight functions. More recent works emphasize a broader, more encompassing definition, such as enforcement in addition to answerability (Schedler, Diamond, and Plattner 1999). The first element fits the standard definition. However, accountability does not necessarily imply punishment. One may account for his/her behavior but not be punished if the oversight institution in charge of controlling does not have the mandate to impose punishment.[12] This is not an unusual situation, and oversight institutions without the power to sanction are often perceived as weak and ineffective (Ostrom 1990). The second element, enforcement, explicitly adds the notion that power is subject to punishment if oversight institutions detect unlawful behavior on the part of officeholders. The effectiveness of oversight institutions is therefore not based solely on establishing the parameters of who answers to whom and on what matters; rather, it also depends on their having tools to prosecute those who violate the public trust (O'Donnell 1999). As Schedler, Diamond, and Plattner (1999, 17) pointed out, "unless

---

12. An example would be the ombudsman office in many European and Latin American countries. While it may expose government wrongdoing, it is not empowered to prosecute. The same applies to several fiscal tribunals in Europe and the U.S. Office of Government Ethics.

there is some punishment for demonstrated abuses of authority, there is no rule of law and no accountability."

Accountability also goes beyond the limits imposed by principal-agent relationships. Legislative scholars (McCubbins and Schwartz 1984; Laver and Shepsle 1999; Shugart, Moreno, and Crisp 2002) have usually stylized accountability as a way for the principal (voters/legislatures) to keep in check its agent (the legislator/prime minister/president). While this clear-cut application of the concept makes it suitable for statistical and game-theoretic analyses, it is restrictive (Ferejohn 1999). In fact, it limits the means of accountability to a few cases (voters and elected officials, parliaments and cabinets) while excluding a large number of other institutions that do not fall into the principal-agent relationship (Mainwaring and Welna 2003). These institutions are not elected (some administrative units of the bureaucracy) and in some cases are given autonomy in performing their tasks (special oversight agencies, the judiciary). Thus, principal-agent relationships can be better understood as a subset of a broader definition of accountability (Mainwaring and Welna 2003).

Who is accountable? Both elected and nonelected officials (civil servants) are. The latter fall primarily within the purview of the executive, but the legislative and judicial branches can also exercise considerable oversight over them. Which institutions are in charge of accountability? O'Donnell (1999, 38–39) labels the relationship interlocking different state institutions as "horizontal accountability," which in his view is "the exercise of state agencies that are legally enabled and empowered, and functionally willing and able to take actions that span from routine oversight to criminal sanctions, or impeachment in relation to actions, or omissions by other agents or agencies of the state that may be qualified as unlawful." Horizontal institutions of accountability include the executive, the judiciary, and the legislature, as well as an array of specialized institutions such as the auditors general, anticorruption agencies, ombudsmen, special prosecutors, electoral and human rights commissions, and public-complaints and privacy commissions. For O'Donnell, horizontal accountability can be violated in two ways—by "encroachment" of one institution on another (that is, the executive encroaches on the legislature and the judiciary) and by "corruption" (the use of public office for private gain).

O'Donnell's definition confines horizontal accountability to situations involving illegal behavior by individuals or institutions. Others, however, have espoused a broader understanding of accountability, which includes

holding elected and nonelected officials responsible for their political behavior (Schmitter 1999; Schedler, Diamond, and Plattner 1999; Mainwaring
and Welna 2003). According to this view, violations occur when political
actors behave in a way that undermines the institutional checks and balances even if that does not represent a violation of the law.[13]

So far we have examined accountability from the perspective of political
science, but interest has been growing in similar topics in economics as
well. Economists usually refer to some of the same issues under the mantle
of good governance.[14] What is the meaning of good governance? Governance, per se, describes the process of decision-making and the process by
which decisions are implemented. For economists good governance implies
a high degree of government effectiveness and efficiency in promoting economic policies that contribute to growth, stability, and the welfare of the
citizenry. Further characteristics are a high level of responsiveness (to societal demands), accountability, transparency, public participation, openness,
and a strong respect for the rule of law (Healey and Robinson 1992). According to the World Bank (1994, 2), good governance is "epitomized by
predictable, open and enlightened policy making, a bureaucracy imbued
with a professional ethos acting in furtherance of the public good, the rule
of law, transparent processes, and a strong civil society participating in
public affairs. Poor governance (on the other hand) is characterized by
arbitrary policy making, unaccountable bureaucracies, un-enforced or un-
just legal systems, the abuse of executive power, a civil society un-engaged
in public life, and widespread corruption."

Why did IFIs become so interested in good governance in the second
half of the 1990s? This is in part due to a change in perception of their
major shareholders, including the United States and to a lesser extent the
European Union and Japan. The collapse of the command economies in
the former Soviet bloc, combined with the abandonment of ISI in most

13. In the mid-1990s, for instance, once Peruvian president Alberto Fujimori obtained a
majority in Congress, he asked the legislature to approve bills restricting the prerogatives of the
judiciary and the legislature itself to the advantage of the executive. In 2008 Italian prime minister
Silvio Berlusconi had his parliament (where he enjoyed a large majority) pass new laws making
it impossible for state prosecutors to continue the trials involving (among others) him and his
closest aids for alleged corruption. In both instances the initiatives were perfectly legal, but most
observers saw them as severely reducing the accountability of the executive branch.

14. The indicators typically used to measure this concept are public sector performance;
judicial, legal, and regulatory systems; delivery of services to the poor, empowerment of civil
society; increase in transparency and accountability; support for decentralization, and promoting
results-oriented public sector management.

developing countries, created a historic opportunity for the promotion of trade liberalization and privatization around the globe. However, this required that capital and portfolio investments, coming primarily from the industrialized nations, be safeguarded from old-style-government corrupt and collusive practices. In other words, the changed geopolitical and economic conditions made it imperative that governance standards be substantially improved. Under the Clinton administration (1993–2001) the United States began to sponsor several efforts that resulted in the establishment of international anticorruption conventions through the Organization of the American States (1996), the Organization for Economic Cooperation and Development (1997), and the United Nations (2003).[15] Concomitantly, as a result of the United States' diplomatic effort, by the late 1990s the World Bank and the IMF began to include governance clauses in many of their loan agreements, placing strong emphasis on the fight against corruption and noncompetitive behavior.[16]

Moreover, although not publicly stated in the beginning, World Bank and IMF officials became increasingly worried that their aid funds aimed at combating inflation and promoting much-needed structural reforms were actually being wasted, and reforms were severely undermined by the lack of transparency in government accounts and in the regulatory environment for private sector activity (Broadman and Recanatini 2000). In the mid-1990s, World Bank and IMF cross-national studies invariably concluded that good governance in emerging markets was of fundamental importance for the success of structural reform programs, whereas poor governance was strongly associated with slow economic progress. More specific, some studies (Mauro 1995, 1997; Knack and Keefer 1995) showed that the quality of governance was important for growth and investment rates, foreign aid,

15. The United States' interest in this regard was not unselfish. As emerging markets were opening up, many U.S. corporations complained about losing important business opportunities to the advantage of European and Japanese competitors. Part of the problem, company representatives claimed, stemmed from the 1977 Foreign Corruption Act, which prohibited U.S. corporations from bribing to do business abroad. This restriction did not apply to European competitors, who in some cases well into the 1990s could discount bribes paid abroad from their corporate taxes (e.g., Germany). It must be also stressed that such an effort was unevenly applied. Good governance issues were ignored when they affected countries designated as strategic, as we shall see in the case of Russia.

16. For some, the IFI's turning point came with the appointment of James Wolfensohn as president of the World Bank in 1995. A year later, at the annual IMF–World Bank meeting, Wolfensohn identified corruption as one of the main causes of world poverty and began to redesign the World Bank's lending policies to diminish its impact.

and in preventing inefficient government spending. Subsequent studies found that reducing transparency had negative effects on finance and governance in both industrialized countries and emerging markets (Mehrez and Kaufmann 1999). Better governance was positively associated with substantial improvements in poverty reduction and standards of living. For instance, an improvement of one standard deviation in the rule-of-law indicators for Russia or the Czech Republic or a reduction in corruption in Indonesia or South Korea was correlated with a twofold improvement in income per capita, a similar decline in infant mortality, and an increase of fifteen to twenty-five points in literacy levels (Kaufmann, Kraay, and Zoido-Lobatón 1999). Researchers also found a strong causal relationship between civil liberties and the performance of World Bank projects (Ritzen, Easterly, and Woolcock 2000). Improved property rights protection and civil liberties could significantly reduce regulatory capture, while banking crises were more likely in those economies with poor transparency requirements (Hellman, Jones, and Kaufmann 2000; Hellman and Kaufmann 2001; Mehrez and Kaufmann 1999). Finally, state capture (to be discussed more in depth later) had very negative consequences for privatization and market deregulation in many Eastern European and former Soviet republics (Hellman and Kaufmann 2001).

Neoliberal Assumptions and Transaction Costs

Despite being closely related, political and economic research have often developed separately. While economists acknowledge the role of politics but do not incorporate it in their models, political scientists often neglect how macroeconomic policy can be manipulated to pursue collusion, political patronage, and corruption. In the late 1990s, however, some economists began to acknowledge the deficiencies of the neoliberal approach to reforms in emerging markets and the fundamental role politics and government institutions play in shaping the final outcome. Based on their experience as advisers to the Russian government in the 1990s, Shleifer and Vishny (1998) contended that theories that may be excellent in providing policy solutions in some markets may deliver the wrong answers with disastrous consequences in markets that do not share the same characteristics. In analyzing the contribution of the neoliberal school, for instance, Shleifer and Vishny found it inadequate when addressing the problems of emerging markets.

Hayek's and Friedman's theories work on the assumption that government institutions defining and enforcing property rights as well as promoting antitrust policies are in place. What if they are not? What if the political and legal institutional foundations promoting competition, individual freedom, and property rights are not there in the first place? What if the private sector itself does not operate according to well-defined corporate governance rules?

The neoliberal recommendation is to create such institutions and rules, but it is usually much less helpful in indicating how to craft them. Yet, more important, the greatest shortcoming of the neoliberal approach is that it ignores politics entirely. As Shleifer and Vishny (1998, 10) put it, neoliberal economists ignore "the fundamental fact that institutions supporting property rights are created not by fiat of a public-spirited government but, rather, in response to political pressure on the government exerted by the owners of private property." Indeed, as we shall see in this book, when market reforms are implemented in an institutional vacuum, it creates enormous opportunities for politicians to pursue their corrupt ends and for privileged sectors of the business community to protect their rents. The crucial question then is how to prevent government from politically manipulating market reforms, which, on paper, are supposed to promote competition, individual freedom, and better living standards. For Shleifer and Vishny, if one is to comprehend in which direction reform is going, one must first understand the interests of the political actors involved and how such interests translate into the type of institutions and policies that cater into their personal interests. Unfortunately, as Shleifer and Vishny acknowledge, neoliberal economists do not focus either on corruption or on other politically related factors. In turn, this leads them to prescribe policies that ignore politicians' priorities and institutional deficiencies, thus resulting in disastrous consequences.

Economics and political science research can actually be reconciled if we look at the problem of accountability vis-à-vis economic performance from the vantage point of transaction costs. As theorized by Williamson (1986), Olson (1982), and North (1990), when political institutions reward efforts to alter government decisions, rather than technical innovation, people will devote much of their effort in capturing the state in order to acquire rents. Politically, when accountability and transparency in government policy making are lax, corruption, collusion, and patronage abound. Economically, these three factors can be regarded as transaction costs of the worst kind, as they add tremendously to the costs associated with understanding the environment, protecting property rights, and enforcing contracts.

Thesis

The contribution of this book to the scholarly debate derives from focusing on the transaction costs arising from the lack of political accountability; this allows us to explain how economic mismanagement and politics function as two sides of the same coin in democratic polities. Moreover, it brings evidence to some of the political science works mentioned earlier that are rich in theoretical insights but short on empirical applications. The thesis of the book is that if market reforms are carried out within a *democratic polity* where accountability institutions are weak (or even deliberately emasculated to accelerate policy implementation), then corruption, collusion, and patronage will be strongly associated with severe economic crises in the medium term. Conversely, where vertical and horizontal accountability institutions are in place, we should expect less economic upheaval and greater success in achieving the market reforms' stated goals. If the thesis were to be found correct, it would bring evidence about how accountability institutions, far from being an impediment to market reforms, help produce more effective policies. This is because they are more likely to prevent executive abuses and allow for changes based on a more consensual approach between government and opposition that enhances policy coherence and sustainability over time.[17]

Although other scholars have made similar arguments (Stark and Bruszt 1998; Orenstein 2001; Gould 2003), their analyses have been limited to a few country studies based on the experiences of Eastern Europe and Russia. This book instead brings greater empirical evidence based on a broader, cross-national sample using a multistage level of analysis. This book also complements Stiglitz's thesis (2002) that the recent financial crises in emerging markets can be traced back to the misguided policy advice of the IMF and the World Bank. However, it challenges Stiglitz's contention that governments' lack of transparency and accountability does not cause crises

---

17. There is no claim here that corruption, crony capitalism, and political patronage take place only under market reforms. Rather, when institutional checks and balances cannot enforce accountability, these factors are particularly detrimental as the reform process is manipulated at different stages of its development, which in the end derails and tarnishes neoliberal policies.

and is a convenient way for the U.S. Treasury, the IMF, and neoliberal economists in general to shift the blame to borrowing countries.

Summing up, this work aims to show that accountability plays a major role in understanding whether market reforms succeed or fail and how corruption, crony capitalism, and patronage result when accountability is weak. These three elements turn into transaction costs, which end up undermining the reform process along the following channels:

- *Corruption.* The manipulation of reforms allows elected and non-elected officials to use the proceeds from privatization and deregulation for private gain instead of the intended public use.
- *Crony capitalism.* Instead of fostering market competition, elected and nonelected officials craft economic policies to reallocate rents from the state to the private sector, thus depriving reforms of their potential for sustaining long-term growth.
- *Political patronage.* Elected and nonelected officials circumvent fiscal austerity agreements contracted with international lending agencies by borrowing massively in the international bond market to secure support from political clienteles.

The research design in this book adopts the definition of accountability that includes the two dimensions of answerability and enforcement. It also uses the broader definition of accountability that incorporates both legal and nonlegal transgressions, as discussed earlier. At the same time, it focuses not only on the three branches of government but also on the oversight agencies within the public administration. Let us briefly examine the significance of these three factors based on a selected sample of the existing literature.

Corruption

Today there is substantial agreement in both the political and economic literature on the fact that corruption turns formal property rights into very expensive, personalized exchanges of a tenuous nature since a change in the political personnel guaranteeing them can undermine the exchange itself at any time (Jain 2001; Johnston 2005).

This, however, was not always the case. From the 1960s until the late 1980s, the so-called functionalist theory dominated much of the academic debate on political corruption. It viewed corruption as a necessary evil to cut bureaucratic red tape, redistribute resources (Heidenheimer 1970; Waterbury 1976), and sustain socioeconomic development in countries whose governments opposed Communism (Leff 1964; Nye 1967; Huntington 1968). However, the end of the cold war, which had provided much of its rationale, made the functionalist perspective obsolete, and it quickly fell out of favor.

Since the early 1990s there has been a resurgence of studies on corruption that have highlighted its pernicious consequences. Such studies invariably show that corruption has profound negative effects on growth and a host of socioeconomic issues. High levels of corruption in countries facing poor economic performance are not coincidental; rather, these conditions are causally related. To this end, World Bank and IMF economists have developed much-needed cross-national data sets to test a series of hypotheses that have often confirmed what previously had been described by country analyses or journalistic accounts. The underlying assumption of the World Bank and the IMF studies is that much corruption stems from poor government administration, particularly when it comes to the realm of economics. What follows is that a good deal of corruption could be curbed by promoting well-meaning administrative reforms.

In addition to having negative effects on both gross domestic product (GDP) and the ratio of investments to GDP (Mauro 1995, 1997; Mo 2001), some studies have found evidence that the more open an economy is, the lower the level of corruption (Ades and Di Tella 1999). Wei (2001a) also found that corruption increases the likelihood of currency crises and reduces the benefits of globalization. Corruption also thwarts foreign aid (IMF 1997a). Likewise, countries with high levels of corruption tend to have low levels of tax collection relative to GDP (Tanzi and Davoodi 1997). Furthermore, Mauro (1998) concluded that corruption has more negative effects than taxation. It significantly hampers development by reducing domestic investments, discouraging foreign investments, ballooning government spending, and diverting government resources from health, education, and infrastructure maintenance to benefit often useless public projects (Wei 1999). In similar vein, corruption severely affects the investment strategies of foreign companies (Smarzynska and Wei 2000) with negative consequences on joint ventures with domestic partners when the risk involved is perceived as being very high. Another study challenged the old functionalist argument that "grease money" facilitates commerce. Kaufmann and Wei

(1999) point out that firms willing to pay more bribes are likely to have higher operating costs. Other works have focused on financial liberalization, demonstrating that financial crises are more likely and more severe in countries with poor government transparency (Mehrez and Kaufmann 1999). Hellman, Jones, and Kaufmann (2000) also found evidence that the improvement of property rights and civil liberties can significantly reduce state capture by powerful lobbies. Likewise, corrupt governments seem responsible for low tax collection, as entrepreneurs prefer to go underground to avoid corrupt officials and red tape (Johnson, Kaufmann, and Zoido-Lobatón 1999). By contrast, reducing corruption improves economic growth and technological change (Rivera-Batiz 2007).

For their part, political scientists and sociologists usually focus on the causes and effects of corruption, typically regarded as dysfunctional in a democratic system. High levels of corruption undermine interpersonal and government trust (Morris 1991; Mishler and Rose 2001), preventing collective action and the development of civic behavior. This, in turn, may have deleterious consequences for the survival of a political system—an issue particularly troublesome for new democracies (Rose-Ackermann 1999; Doig and Theobald 2000; Tulchin and Espach 2000; Montinola and Jackman 2002). Some have also focused on the pernicious effects of neoliberal policies. Weyland (1998), for example, noted that corruption in many Latin American countries increased since the 1990s due to the reemergence of populism and misguided market reforms. Others have focused on the relationship between corruption and electoral rules. Persson, Tabellini, and Trebbi (2003), Kunicova and Rose-Ackerman (2005), and Chang and Golden (2007) found that closed-list proportional representation electoral rules in presidential systems are particularly associated with corruption.

Other studies have looked closely at the relationship between corruption and system support. In their study of central and Eastern Europe, Rose, Mishler, and Haerpfer (1998) found that high levels of corruption negatively affected support for the democratic system and conversely increased the acceptance for authoritarian alternatives. In his analysis of Bolivia, El Salvador, Nicaragua, and Paraguay, Seligson (2002) also produced even stronger statistical evidence that corruption undermines the political legitimacy of democracy and negatively affects interpersonal trust in particular and civil society relations more generally. In a subsequent study using a broader country sample, Anderson and Tverdova (2003) confirmed earlier hypotheses contending that in countries experiencing high levels of corruption people display more negative attitudes toward civil servants than in industrial nations. Yet more interesting, they found that in such countries, negative evaluations are unlikely to be shared by government supporters, which may explain the ability of tainted administrations to retain power in the face of scandals and poor performance.

Within the context of market reforms, corruption can alter the policy process in a number of ways, which I will try to stylize with a few examples. One case that has received much attention is linked to privatization, which in many countries was the most visible and controversial reform advocated by the WC. As Rose-Ackerman explains (1996, 2), "a firm may pay to be included in the list of qualified bidders or to restrict their number. It may pay to obtain a low assessment of the public property to be leased or sold off, or to be favored in the selection process." How does this happen in practice? Privatization occurs primarily through direct sales or international bids. Direct sales are particularly susceptible to corrupt behavior since they occur behind close doors without any third party monitoring the process; as a result, illicit agreements can be hammered quickly (World Bank 2005, 264).

Government officials can even extract bribes through competitive bids by selling confidential information to firms willing to pay for "bidding specifications, the actual condition of soon-to-be-privatized firms, and the location of future capital projects" (Rose-Ackerman 1996, 2). Once the government selects incoming bids, it may rig the process to award the ownership (or concession contracts) of former SOEs based on the willingness of private investors to pay hefty bribes. In return, as a way of compensation, governments may award to a private bidder an SOE under monopolistic or oligopolistic conditions. In so doing, the new private owner can charge high prices because it does not face competition and, in the process, can recoup the bribe paid. Of course, this arrangement is detrimental to consumers who pay prices higher than under competitive conditions, as well as firms using the same goods and services. In the latter case, corrupt competition penalizes the economy as a whole because it increases the cost of doing business. Moreover, by not facing competition, the new private owners have few incentives to improve their companies in terms of technology and customer service. Another drawback is that at times the private companies that are more willing to bribe are the ones that have the weakest qualifications to bid. In that case, bribing works as a way to beat better rivals. Thus, inefficient firms facing stiff competition may actually initiate a corrupt deal rather than be on the receiving end of it.

Another, more subtle way to pursue corruption through privatization is through concession contracts and their regulation after state divestiture. Such contracts usually affect the largest privatization transactions, which tend to be in public utilities, such as telecommunications, electricity, gas generation and distribution, water and sanitation services, and transportation. Many soes in these sectors often are not sold but transferred through concession contracts for a fixed term, which may be susceptible to renewal. Early literature on privatization underscored the need to create regulatory institutions prior to privatization since soes were left regulating themselves under state ownership. Regulatory agencies are important in ensuring that contracts are enforced, the rights of private operators and consumers are protected accordingly, and tariffs strike a sensible balance between affordability (for the consumer) and profitability (for the utility provider). Moreover, regulatory agencies should foster competition when technology and market size allow it. However, corrupt governments are likely to act in the opposite direction. In return for bribes, they may prevent regulatory agencies from doing their job by negotiating sensitive issues directly with private utility companies to their mutual satisfaction. In a scenario of this kind, government officials may renegotiate tariff rates to the benefit of the utility companies, fail to enforce penalties when private operators do not meet investment and service requirements, extend concession contracts, and provide subsidies and tax breaks in return for kickbacks. Even in those cases where infrastructure privatization leads to increased investments, studies show that they are still prone to open the door to corrupt deals (Martimort and Straub 2006). For some scholars this helps explain the widespread public dissatisfaction with state divestiture, particularly among middle-class consumers who believe that they end up paying the costs of corruption through high utility rates (Bonnet et al. 2006).

Crony Capitalism

Crony capitalism thrives on government-created rent conditions. An economic "rent" is the result of a financial income that is not matched by corresponding labor or investment. According to the seminal works of Tullock (1967) and Krueger (1974), rents occur through distortions to the competitive environment (i.e., monopolies, oligopolies, import and trading restrictions, subsidies), often by lobbying political authorities to create rules and regulations that prevent market competition. Economic rents are generally considered to be very harmful for economic activity because they create price distortions, prevent competition, and fuel corruption. For instance, Ades and Di Tella (1999) showed that corruption is much higher in countries where domestic firms enjoy monopoly conditions and protective trade barriers.

Rent seeking is a phenomenon that affects even the most advanced economies worldwide, where it artificially allows protected markets to co-exist with competitive ones. However, recent scholarship has suggested that in developing (particularly East Asia) and postcommunist countries, rent seeking becomes *the* system on which economies are organized.[18] Some analysts define such a system as "crony capitalism" (Pye 1997; Soros 1998; Bernstam and Rabushka 1998; Haggard 2000; MacIntyre 2001; Kang 2002; Putzel 2002). In other words, the difference between economic rents that exist in an advanced industrial country vis-à-vis the crony capitalism of a developing nation is one of degree. In advanced industrial societies noncompetitive behavior exists but affects only a relatively small amount of the most crucial markets, whereas in many developing nations the noncompetitive behavior established by crony capitalism is an arrangement affecting the most important economic activities (Hutchcroft 1998). By definition, crony capitalism takes place in an economy where, according to Haber (2002, xii), "those close to the political authorities who make and enforce policies, receive favors that have large economic value. These favors allow politically connected economic agents to earn returns above those that would prevail in an economy in which the factors of production were priced by the market." In a system of crony capitalism, business people approximate what can be described as "political entrepreneurs," that is, entrepreneurs who can be in business and profit from it only thanks to the

---

18. Michel Camdessus (1998, 1), former managing director of the IMF, underscored the seriousness of crony capitalism in East Asia and Russia by stating: "In this regard, one cannot help but observe the similarities between the relationships that existed among chaebols, banks, and government in Korea under the system of 'crony capitalism' and the system that is now taking shape in Russia under the elegant name of 'oligarchy.'" Oddly enough, then U.S. Treasury Secretary Lawrence Summers (1998, 1) expressed a more fatalistic, if not benign, view when he noted: "Many people invoke what might be called a 'stages of capitalism' theory in thinking about the development of a market system in Russia and other emerging economies. This notes that highly concentrated ownership and public-private collusion—what we might now call 'crony capitalism'—has historically been a more or less inevitable part of moving toward mature market institutions."

government's special protection. These people are quite a different breed from "market entrepreneurs," who, in a context of market competition, must produce quality goods at a low cost if they want to succeed.

Economically, crony capitalism is a dysfunctional type of capitalism for a number of reasons (Khan and Sundaram 2000; Haber 2002). First, it misallocates resources, as it channels funds into unproductive or obsolete activities and allows artificially high prices to sustain rents, which in turn fuels inflation and depresses growth (Krueger 2002). Second, it discourages long-term investing since crony arrangements are by nature subject to sudden changes in political leadership. This situation puts business people in a short time-horizon situation because it forces them to lobby for high rates of return in a relatively short period of time. Third, crony capitalism has negative consequences on income distribution because the general public is subject to paying artificially high prices that benefit only a small minority. Because of its pervasiveness, crony capitalism is more likely to generate corruption, unlike a country in which markets are competitive. Moreover, according to some scholars (Wei 2001b), crony capitalism is strongly associated with a higher external loan-to-foreign-direct-investments (FDIS) ratio and can increase the likelihood of a financial crisis.

Politically, because of its collusive and secretive nature, crony capitalism thrives in authoritarian systems and weak democracies. In fact, Haber (2002) concluded that the more authoritarian the government is, the more efficiently crony capitalism works. Such an economic system also thrives where economic inequality between rich and poor is severe and where voting rights for most of the population have been restricted during a long period of time. Moreover, and equally important, crony capitalism flourishes in democracies where accountability institutions are weak, resulting in a lack of transparency, which can lead to serious economic crises. Michel Camdessus (1999), the IMF managing director during the 1990s, described the nexus between crony capitalism and transparency as follows: "A lack of transparency has been found at the origins of the recurring crises in the emerging markets, and it has been a pernicious feature of the 'crony capitalism' that has plagued most of the crisis countries and more besides. More positively, the very first principles of the market economy tell us that open, competitive markets function only where transparency exists."

Crony capitalism has been associated with market reforms in a number of ways. The most typical one has been tailoring reforms to pursue the interest of individuals or firms close to the government in return for party financing and/or bribes. Again, privatization is a typical case in point. In a country where there is a sizable domestic business class, the government may favor politically close domestic firms by preventing (or restricting) foreigners or domestic groups out of favor to bid on the most lucrative SOEs. This, for instance, was the case in Mexican, Russian, and many Eastern European privatizations. In these countries the government handed over to domestic businessmen very lucrative companies, often under monopoly conditions, in return for generous campaign financing. In Mexico alone this type of privatization turned several entrepreneurs into billionaires in a few years.[19] A variation on this method is when a government requires foreign investors to form joint ventures with domestic firms, even if such firms have little capital and expertise to offer in return, under the pretext of averting a nationalist backlash, as it was the case in Argentina in the early 1990s.

An alternative strategy is when government officials in charge of designing the privatization of SOEs end up, shortly after the state divestiture is completed, on the board of directors of the new private company or, even worse, turn out to be major shareholders as happened in Chile in the late 1980s. Moreover, the government can restrict the awarding of new import/export licenses related to trade deregulation only to politically connected businesses.

Political Patronage

Patronage imposes an additional and unnecessary cost on society by channeling resources to unproductive activities and unnecessary employment. It also often hampers the development of human capital by rewarding the wrong people with the right jobs (Desai and Pradhan 2005). For the most part, social scientists tend to agree that patronage politics perpetuates elite rule and its control on economic resources, which ultimately results in economic rents benefiting the elites and in economic stagnation due to the lack of competition (Bates 1981; Easterly 2001).

Although patronage is often associated with corruption, it can actually take place legally as officeholders and lawmakers can issue decrees and legis-

---

19. In 1993 the Mexican president Raúl Salinas invited his country's wealthiest business people, who were the biggest winners of the privatization process during his presidency, to a "fundraising" dinner where each invitee "donated" $20 million to the campaign fund of Salinas's party (Oppenheimer 1996).

lation channeling resources to their own clienteles. In our own case this is particularly relevant, as governments in developing countries not only spend their scarce resources to appease the narrow interests of their political clienteles but also divert the use of foreign loans and other types of foreign economic aid for the same purpose with very negative consequences on the quality of governance (Knack 2001) and economic growth (World Bank 1998; Easterly, Levine, and Rodman 2003)

Patronage, according to much of the literature, takes place in polities where resources are scarce and controlled by entrenched political cliques, and people willingly exchange their votes for whatever favors they can muster (Brusco, Nazareno, and Stokes 2004). For instance, Acemoglu and Robinson (2001) argued that patronage spending is a function used to maintain the strength of a particular political group. They added that weak political institutions, which do not constrain political elites from pursuing poor macroeconomic policies, are responsible for, among other things, widespread corruption, ineffective property rights, and a high degree of economic and political instability (Acemoglu et al. 2003).

What is at the root of the problem? According to Geddes (1994), political patronage and voting for corrupt leaders is the result of a lack of collective action, while Samuels and Snyder (2001) emphasize the importance of electoral rules. Medina and Stokes (2007) stylize the relationship between voters and candidates as one where the latter retain a monopolistic control of economic resources and restrict preferences to their advantage.

Economists have been mainly concerned with the question of why patronage politics induce elected and nonelected officials to opt for inefficient policy choice. In her pioneering work on rent seeking, Krueger (1993) first demonstrated that seemingly incompetent policies were not the result of poor knowledge but rather the rational decision by political elites to appropriate rents for themselves and their clienteles. More recently, scholars have examined the economic consequences of patronage politics. Robinson and Verdier (2003) provided evidence showing that political patronage can be quite attractive in countries where income inequalities are high, money in politics matters more than ideology, and productivity is low. Using a rational choice model, Robinson and Verdier (2003) contended that inefficiencies in income distribution are the result of clientelistic exchanges during which politicians dispense jobs and favors in return for votes. As a result patronage prevents the provision of public goods that would enhance economic conditions for all. In another study, Mauro (2004) asked why so many countries experiencing poor growth patterns and entrenched patronage systems that fuel corruption do not try to reform their political systems. His explanation is that when patronage and corruption are widespread, people do not have incentives to organize against it.

In another cross-national analysis, Keefer (2003) argued that the association between corruption and weak democratic institutions is related to patronage politics. He claimed that the reason young democracies have poor economic performance rests on the number of continuous years when countries had competitive elections. Keefer's point is that in young democracies, corruption and political patronage are clear symptoms of weak government institutions. Consequently, weak government institutions are unable to provide public goods based on fair and rational criteria because they tend to be captured by power groups that use them to dispense pork and create rent seeking favoring their clienteles. Thus, in such a context political parties do not make credible pre-electoral promises based on a clear program and voters are all too aware that such promises will not be honored. Consequently, the only credible promises are those on which politicians build a reputation for dispensing tangible goods in exchange for votes.

How can political patronage be related to market reforms? In most cases democratically elected leaders embraced the WC agenda based on pragmatic motives as they desperately needed the IFIS' financial assistance to keep their countries afloat. However, they also needed the economic resources to stay in power and retain political support while funds were being drastically reduced by the very reforms they were enacting. In fact, the combination of privatization, government downsizing, and fiscal austerity measures deprived them of traditional war chests to funnel money to appease their followers. Compounding the problem was the fact that several reforming leaders ran for a second term and, in some cases, had to amend their constitutions to do so. This meant disbursing a substantial amount of funds to veto players in Congress whose vote was crucial to this end.

Part of the problem could be solved by diverting privatization funds to political schemes. Ironically, another means came from the IFIS' financial assistance, which at times provided additional resources making up for the end of traditional ones. Indeed, once leaders had satisfied the IFIS' initial demands for policy implementation, they could receive a larger amount of loans to improve and expand on their reform effort. Moreover, as their countries' credit ratings improved, reforming leaders could receive the IFIS' seal of approval to obtain commercial loans from international investment banks, an option that was not available prior to the launching of market reforms. The key point here is that once loans were disbursed, IFIS and commercial banks had a limited ability to oversee how their funds were actually spent. Thus, governments found it relatively easy to use international borrowing for clientelistic purposes.

Indeed, empirical studies have shown that political elites are quite capable of continuing clientele-driven spending even if, at the same time, they are in the process of implementing market reforms whose philosophy runs counter to patronage politics. For instance, Schady (2000) found evidence that President Fujimori spent the Peruvian Social Fund disproportionately to favor his clienteles using proceeds from privatization with the blessing of the IMF and the World Bank. Likewise, Mexican president Carlos Salinas de Gortari used the poverty alleviation program PRONOSOL (Programa Nacional de Solidaridad) in much the same way (Oppenheimer 1996; Diaz-Cayeros, Estevez, and Magaloni 2001). Patronage spending was also very high at the height of market reforms in Argentina and Brazil during the 1990s (Rodden and Arretche 2003; Calvo and Murillo 2004).

Methodology and Case Selection

The research adopts a two-tiered approach to test the thesis, combining statistical measurements with an intensive examination of a few case studies, similar in conception to Lieberman's (2005) nested analysis method. Chapter 2 starts with a comparative analysis of countries under *democratic* or *partially democratic* forms of government that attempted market reforms at both the cross-national and the regional levels in the 1990s. This will allow us to scrutinize whether the general thesis that I proposed earlier can be supported by the examination of a large number of cases. Accordingly, in the cross-national analysis I include countries that suffered major financial crises as well as others that either did not experience such crises or had less severe recessions while implementing similar reforms (World Bank 1995, 2003, 2005).

The second part of the analysis (chapters 3 and 5) shifts from the comparative to the case-study approach. This is because cross-national analyses, though most useful for theory building, often miss specific variables and information that can complement and strengthen a general thesis by showing the importance of a given socioeconomic phenomenon and its multi-faceted manifestations over time. In the case study chapters I will assess the impact of a common set of accountability institutions to make the comparison more rigorous.

To accomplish this goal I use what is usually referred to as a theory-guided process-tracing method (George and McKeown 1985). The reason is that through this method it is possible to identify the "intervening causal processes—the causal chain and causal mechanism—between the independent variable (or variables) and the outcome of the dependent variable" (George and Bennett 2005, 206). Thus, while the statistical method in cross-national analysis aims at identifying the causal effects of one or more independent variable on the dependent one, process-tracing analysis allows us to discover the causal mechanisms linking causes and effects.[20] The theoretically explicit narratives in the country chapters "trace and compare the sequences of events of the constituting process" that we want to examine (Aminzade 1993, 108).[21] Through the process-tracing method we can better understand (than we can in cross-national statistical analyses) the decision makers' goals, "preferences, their perceptions, their evaluation of alternatives, the information they posses, the expectations they form, the strategies they adopt, and the constraints that limit their actions" (Bates et al. 1988, 11). By using two different methodological approaches I hope to establish in a more precise fashion whether accountability standards help explain differences in economic performance depending on how reforms were pursued. Should both levels of analysis uncover the same policy pattern, we could be more confident about our findings.

The case study is based on the experiences in Chile, Russia, and Argentina for the following reasons. Hayek and Friedman always hailed Chile as a textbook case of how market-oriented policies can dramatically turn around a languished economy. Moreover, because of its success in promoting steady growth from 1985 on, Chile became a primary example that the

20. George and Bennett (2005, 137) define causal mechanisms as "ultimately unobservable physical, social, or psychological processes through which agents with causal capacities operate, but only in specific contexts and conditions, to transfer energy, information, or matters to other entities."

21. Aminzade (1993, 108) points out that narratives "allow us to capture the unfolding of social action over time in a manner sensitive to the order in which events occur. By making the theories that underpin our narratives more explicit, we avoid the danger of burying our explanatory principles in engaging stories. By comparing sequences, we can determine whether there are typical sequences across [cases] . . . and can explore the causes and consequences of different sequence patterns."

IMF and the World Bank used to persuade countries considering the adoption of market reforms worldwide. Chile also provides a unique example where policy *variance,* under different political regimes, can be observed within one case. This is because it pioneered market reforms between 1973 and 1990 under a dictatorship that allowed no accountability. However, such reforms were continued and expanded on under a democratic regime after 1990 with a much greater emphasis on transparency and competition. In the 1980s, under Pinochet's authoritarian government, Chile's GDP grew an average of 3.2 percent; a decade later under a democracy it averaged 6 percent annually (Beyer and Vergara 2002). By 2008 poverty had been more than halved as opposed to in 1989. Although the economy grew at a slower pace between 1998 and 2008, it weathered well the international crises affecting emerging markets in East Asia and in neighboring Argentina.

The other two cases presented here, Russia and Argentina, are those in which market reforms were associated with major economic collapses. Russia (under the Yeltsin administration, 1991–99) and Argentina (under President Menem, 1989–99) promoted radical market reforms in the 1990s in a context of weak political accountability, and both eventually succumbed to major financial crises in 1998 and 2001/2002, respectively. These two countries are particularly important because during the early 1990s, in their respective regions of the world, they represented crucial test cases for the success of the neoliberal economic policies sponsored by the U.S. Treasury, the IMF, and the World Bank.

The international financial community's support of market reforms in Russia under Yeltsin's tenure, despite early signs that their design and execution were seriously flawed, was justified as being critical to destroy the command economy of the Soviet era and prevent the Communists from returning to power. Moreover, had Russia succeeded it would have induced many former Soviet republics to follow its lead and abandon what still was a political culture entrenched in government intervention and hostile to free enterprise and democracy. In August 1998, despite privatizing most SOEs and liberalizing capital markets, Russia suffered a devastating financial crisis, forcing it to default on its domestic debt and putting a moratorium on its foreign debt. It was partially restructured a few years later through the London Club, which represented some of Russia's largest creditor nations. According to most indicators, the consequences of Russia's debacle were far worse than those resulting from the Wall Street crash of 1929.

Likewise, Argentina led the way in Latin America by enacting sweeping market reforms. Indeed, during the 1990s the IMF, the World Bank, the U.S. Treasury, and a score of financial analysts hailed Argentina as a model for the rest of Latin America. According to the World Bank (2005, 34), the significance of Argentina's case rests on the fact that its crisis put into question the neoliberal model since that country "had provided the clearest and, for the better part of the 1990s, most successful example of a trend to reinforce macroeconomic stability." In fact, at the end of December 2001, Argentina defaulted on its $132 billion debt, the largest such event in history, which triggered a socioeconomic meltdown of unprecedented proportions.[22] By August 2002 fears of financial contagion in the region forced a grudging IMF to increase lending to Brazil and Uruguay to avert those countries with very close economic ties to Argentina lest they fall under the same spell. Indeed, "economically, the decade known as the 1990s, could be said to end with the Argentine crisis of 2001" (World Bank 2005, 31). Just as important, Argentina's collapse virtually sanctioned the demise of the WC and its policies.

Thus, since Chile, Russia, and Argentina were commonly regarded as test cases for the success of market reforms, their analysis is quite significant and can bring insights with broad theoretical ramifications for similar cases. The way these countries confronted similar policy problems can shed light on the importance of accountability in explaining the success and failures of market reforms since such cases should display enough variance. In fact, many of the challenges that these countries confronted were often observed in other emerging markets that embarked on the same policies. Within this context, we want to ascertain to which degree the strengths (or weaknesses) of their accountability institution environments made the difference.

Chapter 6 sums up the conclusions of the book by first assessing the degree to which the accountability thesis held up under cross-national and country-specific tests and then discussing what its implications are for both academics and policy makers in view of the latest development in the global economy.

---

22. In 2001 Argentina was the issuer of the largest amount of bonds among emerging markets. See Paul Blustein, "Brazil Aid Prompts Mixed Reaction; Argentina Fears U.S. Will Let It Tumble," *Washington Post*, August 7, 2001, E01.

two

FINANCIAL CRISES IN COMPARATIVE PERSPECTIVE

Financial Crises That Were Not Supposed to Happen

Financial crises have historically plagued developed and developing countries alike. In the 1980s overvalued exchange rates, coupled with large fiscal deficits and debt service obligations, were recurrent factors behind many crises, particularly in Latin America and Turkey. In most instances, crises occurred where governments had promoted for decades economic protectionism inspired by Soviet Communism and import substitution industrialization. As we saw in chapter 1, market reforms, with their emphasis on fiscal discipline, deregulation, privatization, and financial liberalization, were supposed to turn crises into growth, regardless of the previous economic regime. The IMF, which was the chief broker in securing international financial assistance, also insisted on the removal of capital account restrictions to promote foreign investments and increase the emerging markets' ability to access international finance.

As expected, capital flows to emerging markets did reach record levels, increasing six times between 1990 and 1996, but so did the number of financial crises—something that ran counter to the multilateral lending agencies' expectations, particularly in East Asia. Of the ten largest recipients of capital inflows, seven suffered financial crises (Table 2.1). Indeed, the World Bank (2005, 243) later soberly concluded that "the 1990s will be remembered as a decade of macroeconomic crises and turbulence in emerging markets."

What was the root of the problem? First, there is substantial agreement among economists that one of the main culprits of the crisis was the adoption of various forms of fixed-exchange-rate policy in virtually all the countries that experienced a financial crisis (World Bank 2005), including Chile in 1981–82. Although both Hayek and Friedman opposed fixed exchange rates, the international financial community accepted them as a means for emerging markets to deflate inflationary expectations. Fixed exchange rates were also used as a proxy for institutional reliability. Because many countries had a long history of manipulating laws, as well as political and economic institutions to change the rules of the game, fixed exchange rates or currency boards (particularly if enshrined into law) could momentarily address the lack of institutional credibility.[1] A second factor commonly mentioned (Summers 2000, 8) was the high level of foreign debt incurred by the private sector (particularly banks), which, although unsustainable over time, led indebted domestic companies and banks to pressure their governments to postpone the inevitable devaluation. Third, the size and amount of short-term maturity of foreign loans undermined the financial stability of many crisis countries. Besides these three factors, commonalities across crises are less clear. The fiscal deficit played an important role in Russia, Brazil, Ecuador, and Argentina but was not as serious in East Asia and Mexico. Likewise, current account deficits were a serious problem in Brazil, Mexico, Thailand, and Argentina but not so much in East Asia, save for Thailand (Table 2.2).

Financial Crises and Their Consequences

Financial crises occur when countries suffer large currency devaluations, provoking major changes in relative prices, but their consequences are often devastating, as they result in severe deteriorations in output, credit, employment, and wages' purchasing power (Baldacci, Mello, and Inchauste 2002). Another perverse consequence of such crises is their negative impact on the reputation of democratic institutions, as they erode their legitimacy in the case of prolonged economic downturns. Consequently, they can jeopardize the foundations of a political system, particularly in many countries that still have very fragile democratic institutions. Moreover, they also

1. Hanke and Schuler (1994) were among the most ardent advocates of currency boards in the 1990s. A currency board is a monetary institution that requires a central bank to maintain a fixed exchange rate with a foreign currency. It prevents the central bank from financing government deficit, but in doing so a country relinquishes its ability to shape monetary policy according to domestic needs.

have a profound and often ignored social dimension that seriously under-mines the development of human capital. In fact, financial crises are usually associated with sharp increases in poverty in its many manifestations. They may stop, and often reverse, decades of improvement in health, nutrition, education, and per capita income.

The consequences of such meltdowns in the 1990s were, at times, of unprecedented magnitude. Even though most crisis countries were able to return to sustained (and at times impressive) economic growth in a rela-tively short period of time, according to the World Bank (2005, 243) their cost was "simply staggering" as their recovery took a long time to compen-sate those who had been hurt the most. Indeed, "the average cost of a crisis [was] about 8 percent of GDP, and that of a financial crisis accompanied by a banking crisis at 18 percent" (World Bank 2005, 243). The contraction of GDP was equally harsh in the crisis year (Table 2.3). Table 2.4 compares key macroeconomic indicators before and after the crisis in a selected group of countries and shows the dire cost that countries continued to pay even three years after the events occurred. From a macroeconomic perspective, devaluations led to steep increases in governments' debt. However, from a microeconomic point of view, the so-called socialization of the costs of crises hit taxpayers hard, particularly in Argentina and Turkey, who had to foot the bill for their banks' bailout (World Bank 2005, 243).

The social consequences of financial crises were equally painful. If we look at some statistics by country, the severity of the initial shock in most cases was traumatic. In Russia about 11.3 million people were jobless at the end of 1998, amounting to 7.7 percent of the nation's total population.[2] Those who kept their jobs lost two-thirds of their income. Several Russian banks folded within months and millions of depositors lost everything. By 1999 roughly 40 percent of the Russian population was estimated to subsist below the poverty line. If we then turn to the composition of the poor, we notice that 20 percent of the Russian population fell into poverty due to the 1998 events alone, and about 61 percent of those who became poor after the 1998 crisis had not been poor in 1996 (World Bank 2001). In 2003 the United Nations Development Program (UNDP) estimated that 33 percent of the population still lived below the subsistence level ($4.30 per person per day).[3] The UNDP also calculated Gini coefficients to measure inequality of

2. European Bank for Reconstruction and Development, Transition Report (1999, 75).
3. United Nations Development Program, Human Development Report, Russia, 2006/2007, http://europeandcis.undp.org/environment/show/9F94B43C-F203-1EE9-B3DE08E54EC33AC5.

wealth distribution and found that income concentration increased after the crisis and remained steady for several years. From its 0.38 level in 1997 (the precrisis year), Gini coefficients averaged about 0.40 through 2003.[4] Only by 2006 did official surveys report that the percentage of people living in poverty had declined to 20 percent.[5]

In East Asia the long-term consequences of the 1997 crisis meant that several accomplishments made during the early 1990s were reversed for a while. According to the World Bank, "in a matter of months, the number of people without a job in Indonesia had swelled by at least 800,000, in Thailand by 1.5 million and in Korea by around 1.3 million. . . . Real wages dropped 12.5 percent in Korea by the end of 1998 and in Thailand, by 6 percent."[6] By the early 2000s as economic growth resumed, East Asian countries were quicker to recover than Russia and Brazil. Nonetheless, not until 2001 did Indonesia's GDP per capita, which had fallen by 13 percent, return to its precrisis levels (World Bank 2005, 31). Thailand and Indonesia had to wait until 2003 to see the number of people living on $2.00-a-day income returning to their precrisis income level (World Bank 2007, 58–59). The same trend can be observed when Gini coefficients were employed to measure wealth concentration.[7]

In 1995 Mexican GDP fell 6.5 percent and inflation reached 52 percent. Yet the crisis that hit Mexico at the very end of 1994 was shorter and less severe than in most other crisis countries, and by 1997 the economy rebounded. Nonetheless, the impact on poverty was unmistakable. The number of people living on $2.00-a-day income rose from 10.6 percent in 1994 to 17 percent in 1996. According to Baldacci, Mello, and Inchauste (2002, 21), "the average monthly household income in constant 1994 prices fell by 31 percent between 1994 and 1996, while the household consumption experienced a decline of 25 percent during the same period of time." Despite the economic recovery, the Gini coefficient remained fairly constant at 0.50 until 2000 (Andalón and López-Calva 2002).

4. Ibid.
5. United Nations Research Institute for Social Development, http://www.unrisd.org/unrisd/website/events.nsf/b5d6feaaede3218d80256eb3003862c7/3012b4f00b5d36d0c125717f003c993a/$FILE/Solimano.pdf.
6. World Bank East Asia and Pacific poverty analysis, http://web.worldbank.org/WBSITE/EXTERNAL/TOPICS/EXTPOVERTY/EXTPA/0,,contentMDK:20204053~menuPK:443280~pagePK:148956~piPK:216618~theSitePK:430367,00.html.
7. Thailand Gini coefficient was 0.43 in 1996 and 0.42 in 2003, while Indonesia scored 0.50 and 0.49, respectively, in each of those years (World Bank 2007, 58–59).

The crisis hitting Brazil in late 1998 was the least severe in terms of GDP contraction. This was due in part to the fact the IMF and the World Bank, which had been heavily criticized for their lack of response during the East Asian and Russian crises only a few months earlier, quickly came to Brazil's rescue by providing a rescue package to bail out the country. However, recovery took much longer in Brazil than in most other crisis countries. GDP growth, which averaged 2.9 percent a year between 1990 and 1998, was only 2 percent between 2000 and 2004.[8] Whereas between 1994 and 1998 Brazil had made substantial strides in poverty reduction, primarily by reducing inflation, which hurt the poor the most, progress stalled between 1999 and 2003. The Gini coefficient, which was at 0.59 in 1998, dropped below that level only in 2003.[9]

In Argentina per capita income fell from $8,909 in 1998 to $2,500 in 2002 and GDP shrank by 15 percent.[10] Seven months after the December 2001 crisis, the number of Argentines who had fallen into poverty increased by 11.7 percent and the number of those who had fallen into extreme poverty rose by 10.8 percent. Concomitantly, government authorities reported steep increases in infant mortality, malnutrition, crime, and primary school dropouts.

Argentina is a typical example of what happens when crises repeat themselves over a few decades. In the 1970s the richest 10 percent of the Argentine population earned twelve times more than the poorest 10 percent. By 2001 the wealthiest 10 percent was making thirty-four times more than the poorest 10 percent.[11] Finally in 2008, helped by five years of strong international demand for Argentine commodities (and a 70 percent devaluation), the country was able to return to precrisis levels of economic activity, but the social damage lingered. In fact, the return to economic growth did not provide quality jobs to many people who became unemployed and had fallen into poverty in 2002. Unemployment and underemployment reached 21.5 percent and 18.6 percent, respectively, in May 2003, at the peak of the crisis. By the last quarter of 2006, percentages had dropped by more than

8. World Bank Development Indicators: The Economy, http://devdata.worldbank.org/wdi2006/contents/Section4.htm.

9. World Bank Development Indicators: People, http://devdata.worldbank.org/wdi2006/contents/Section2.htm.

10. Anthony Faiola, "Despair in Once-Proud Argentina; After Economic Collapse, Deep Poverty Makes Dignity a Casualty," *Washington Post*, August 6, 2002.

11. *La Nación*, October 8, 2002.

half but remained stubbornly high.[12] In 2001 the number of people living below the poverty line was 26 percent of the population. At the peak of the crisis in 2002 this number had jumped to 47 percent and in 2009 it was still about 30 percent. More troubling was the fact that according to labor specialists, a large part of the improvement was not due to new jobs but rather to antipoverty programs and government subsidies that failed to address the long-term employment problems ensuing from the crisis since businesses had learned to produce more with fewer workforces since 2001.[13]

As already noted, all the economies that suffered financial debacles experienced a return to steady growth within eighteen months to three years from the start of the crisis. Russia and Argentina recovered amazingly well, but this was due in large part to a very strong demand for these countries' traditional exports, whose prices climbed almost exponentially from 1999 and 2003, respectively. The East Asian countries also made up much of the losses suffered in 1997, but their GDP growth during the 2000–2006 period was on average 2.5 percent less than during the 1990–96 period (Asian Development Bank 2007). All in all, the lasting effects of financial crises on poverty, income distribution, and health suggest that in most cases their social damage may last much longer than the economic one. Economic growth may resume even at a sustained level, but it tends to favor the wealthy rather than the poor, women, and the young. Market reforms were ushered in emerging markets on the promise that they would diminish poverty and create the bases for the enlargement of the middle class, the social group that has been most identified with democratic development. The financial crises of the 1990s brought much disillusionment and skepticism in all the affected countries about the power of the market, particularly when its rules lacked the necessary accountability to create a level playing field and, often, were designed in a way that picked winners and losers, as I will try to demonstrate in the remainder of this book.

Cross-National Analysis and Data

In the previous section I briefly described what economists believe to be the main determinants of the financial crises. Some of them have also con-

---

12. Data from the Instituto Nacional de Estadística y Censos, http://www.indec.mecon .gov.ar/.

13. *La Nación*, May 26, 2007.

ceded that political issues were very important. In his analysis of six financial crises between 1994 and 1999, Summers (2000) acknowledged that "general governance" issues were very serious in Indonesia and Russia and serious in South Korea, Mexico, Brazil, and Thailand (Table 2.2) but did not elaborate on it. Subsequently, the World Bank (2005, 246) pointed out that "politically motivated lending weakened the balance sheets of commercial banks, whose quasi-fiscal cost ultimately increased the domestic public debt." Indeed, there is no doubt that fixed exchange rates, large amounts of short-term foreign debts, weak and highly leveraged banking systems, and current account deficits were crucial factors in triggering the crisis. However, economic studies for the most part do not investigate the actual contribution that "general governance" variables had in determining financial crises of the 1990s and early 2000s. This is in part because many economists find political/institutional factors too hard to gauge or simply beyond their disciplinary interest. However, in countless interviews that I had with policy makers, IFIS' staffers, diplomats, and pundits, regardless of the country, it was clear that politics and institutions mattered a great deal. To which degree then were "general governance" indicators associated with financial crises? If we want to have a better understanding of the complexity of financial crises, and market reforms in general, this question needs to be answered.

As I argued in chapter 1, by focusing on accountability issues we can find parts of the missing puzzle. Ideally, if we were to find out the independent effect of accountability indicators on financial crises, one could use cross-sectional or time-series analysis. The problem is that institutional variables, such as surveys on the enforcement of the rule of law and property rights, are plagued by endogeneity and reverse causality problems (Przeworski 2004). For instance, if we want to avoid reverse causality problems, it is necessary to show that higher levels of institutional quality are independent factors determining better economic performance rather than being a result of it. Unfortunately, the statistical measurements at our disposal for institutional variables turned out to be heavily correlated with one another, making it impossible to count on them as sources of exogenous variation for time series or cross-section analysis. Given this constraint, the level of generalization will be at the "associational" level. To reiterate, my thesis is that the financial crises experienced by many countries in the 1990s and early 2000s were closely *associated* with poor accountability, resulting in high levels of corruption, crony capitalism, and political patronage. Thus, if the thesis is correct, we should observe empirically a clear pattern differentiating crisis from noncrisis countries in terms of the three factors mentioned above. To the best of my knowledge no study has verified this conjecture in the past at the cross-national level. The importance of these factors rests on the fact that they are serious transaction costs for any economy, as they adversely affect growth and waste badly needed economic resources in countries that can ill afford to spare any. Equally important, these factors undermine the public confidence in democracy and capitalism.

To verify whether this relationship exists between crisis countries and governance, I used a sample of eighty countries that adopted market reforms in the 1980s and 1990s according to the World Bank's classification system (World Bank 2005). Moreover, because the basic premise of the study is to inquire about the relationship between market reforms and accountability, I selected countries that were either "free" or "partially free" using Freedom House definition. This led to the exclusion of countries that enforced market reforms under totalitarian (e.g., China, Vietnam) or authoritarian political systems (e.g., Algeria, Egypt) that lack accountability institutions. Again, following the World Bank's classification system, the ten crisis countries were Mexico, Argentina, Brazil, Ecuador, South Korea, Thailand, Malaysia, Indonesia, Russia, and Turkey. The remaining seventy countries were drawn from Africa, Latin America, Eastern Europe, and Asia.

To ascertain the level of association between financial crises and accountability, I used the World Bank Governance Research Indicators from 1996 to 2006 (Kaufmann, Kraay, and Mastruzzi 2008). In this way we can account for the long-term effects of the reforms well after they were implemented. The World Bank data set is based on 194 different measures drawn from 17 sources of subjective governance data developed by 15 different organizations such as multilateral agencies, think tanks, nongovernmental organizations, and political and business risk-rating agencies. Among them we find the *World Economic Forum's Global Competitiveness Report*, the *Latinobarometro Survey*, the *Freedom House Polls*, and the *Pricewaterhouse-Coopers' Opacity Index*. Polls surveying experts and general public opinion are also included. The World Bank most recent governance indicators developed by Kaufmann, Kraay, and Mastruzzi (2008) use an unobserved components model. It provides point estimates for each of the countries surveyed in their data set. The choice of units of governance ensures that the estimates of governance have a mean of 0, a standard deviation of 1, and a range of about -2.5 to about 2.5. The higher values correspond to better governance performance.

Although the World Bank governance data set has been criticized on a number of counts, its strength rests on several grounds. It is the largest data of its type, accounting for most of the countries in the world, and its indexes are aggregated in such a way as to allow for comparability across countries.[14] Consequently, they may be used to work out further quantitative measurements for broad cross-national comparisons. This helps in assessing differences across countries on the same governance indicator. The data set also provides a ranking order of countries' scores on so-called good governance indicators. It treats "accountability," "corruption," and the "quality of economic reform and regulatory policy" as separate indicators, whereas in the thesis I presented in chapter 1 the last two are a function of lack of accountability. Nonetheless, the World Bank governance indicators approximate well the variables that we will examine in the country analyses. As an indicator, "corruption" can tap into both corrupt and political patronage practices, whereas the "quality of economic reform and regulatory policy" represents a good proxy to gauge collusion as it encompasses issues of market competition.

Using a comparative approach, scores help us asses whether countries that suffered major economic crises also displayed a poor performance in terms of accountability-related issues, as discussed in chapter 1. Before proceeding, it is important to clarify once more that the World Bank scores do not imply causality. The way I use them in this study only suggests possible levels of *association* between major economic crises and the level of accountability of specific countries.

Figure 2.1 shows the score of each group based on the three variables (accountability, corruption, and regulatory quality). The measure of accountability includes indicators measuring different aspects of the political process, civil liberties, and political rights. Corruption measures the effects of this phenomenon on the functioning of the public administration, the business environment, and government decisions in key policy areas. Regulatory quality measures the relevance of market-unfriendly policies, such

---

14. Kurtz and Schrank (2007, 538) contend that governance indicators suffer from "conceptual biases, adverse selection in sampling, and conceptual conflation with economic policy choices . . . and there is far more reason to believe that growth and development spur improvements in government than vice versa." For a pointed rebuttal, see Kaufmann, Kraay, and Mastruzzi (2007).

as erratic macroeconomic policies and regulations affecting foreign trade, excessive regulation of business transactions, and inadequate bank supervision. As previously noted, the governance indicators displayed in Figure 2.1 mirror the statistical compilation of perception of governance of a large number of survey respondents in industrial and developing countries.

As can be seen in Figure 2.1, crisis countries, as a group, score consistently worse than the noncrisis countries in all three categories surveyed by the World Bank. In terms of accountability and corruption, the gap is fairly substantial. Crisis countries, on average, score -0.02 on accountability and -0.29 on corruption, whereas noncrisis countries score, respectively, 0.29 and 0.01. In the case of regulatory quality the difference is less pronounced but still clear, with crisis countries averaging a score of 0.10 while noncrisis countries post a 0.27 score.

Regional Analysis

Let us now shift the analysis from the general to the regional level to see whether greater insights can be gained from a more focused comparison of a restricted number of countries using more detailed measurements. To do so, I chose Russia, a crisis country, and eight Eastern European countries (the Czech Republic, Estonia, Hungary, Latvia, Lithuania, Poland, Slovakia, and Slovenia) of the former Soviet bloc that did not experience financial crises.[15] The reason behind the case selection was based on two criteria. First, Russia and all the eight Eastern European countries implemented market reforms at roughly the same time. Second, the economic reforms took place in a context where means of vertical and horizontal accountability differed appreciably, which allows us in principle to have enough variance in terms of accountability.[16] In fact, while in the 1990s the eight Eastern European countries combined market reforms with major institutional reforms linked to political accountability, Russia did not. This is a discrimina-

15. As opposed to Russia, most East European countries were parliamentary democracies.
16. Poland introduced shock therapy in 1989 but did so within a context of a strong legislature and frequent elections. The Czech Republic and Slovenia opted for a more gradual approach than Poland and tried to incorporate a variety of compensation mechanisms to soften the impact of market reforms to appease congressional opposition in Congress. Congressional oversight in Hungary was much weaker than in Poland and the Czech Republic, but the courts were more independent from political power and on occasion forced the executive to revise its plans (Stark and Bruszt 1998; Orenstein 2001; Appel 2004).

tory factor that can shed some light on whether policy outcomes differ depending on the pursuit of market reforms with or without enhancing accountability institutions. The reason behind the Eastern European countries' emphasis on improving their political institutions had much to do with their petition to join the European Union (EU) in the early 1990s— something Russia did not pursue.[17] In response, the European Council set a number of preconditions to be fulfilled first, which were formalized in the Copenhagen Summit of June 1993, and stipulated that "membership requires that candidate country has achieved stability of institutions guaranteeing democracy, the rule of law, human rights and respect for and, protection of minorities, the existence of a functioning market economy as well as the capacity to cope with competitive pressure and market forces within the Union. Membership presupposes the candidate's ability to take on the obligations of membership including adherence to the aims of political, economic and monetary union."[18]

According to East European analysts (Rupnik 2007), the EU requirement that political institutions be strengthened while promoting market reforms was a key difference from the standard approach that the United States and the WC followed in supporting reforms in other regions of the world.[19] On the contrary, Yeltsin's economic team in 1992, consistent with Hayek's and Friedman's theories and with the encouragement of the United States and IFIS, believed that fixing the economic problem was the precondition to create a functional democracy at a later stage.

Let us now turn to the statistical test for the regional analysis. Homogeneous data is available for Eastern Europe, Russia, and many of the former Soviet republics. For comparative purposes it provides us with an interesting snapshot of the relationship between market reforms and accountability. The data comes from the Business Environment and Enterprise Performance Survey (BEEPS) of 1999, a joint project of the European Bank of Reconstruction and Development (EBRD) and the World Bank. This survey was the result of in-depth interviews with managers and owners of some three thousand firms during the period of June–August 1999. Using

17. In May 2004, the Czech Republic, Estonia, Hungary, Latvia, Lithuania, Poland, Slovakia, and Slovenia acceded to the EU. Rumania and Bulgaria also requested to be considered, but the EU regarded them far behind in terms of democratic requirements and delayed their entry until 2007.

18. European Commission, "Enlargement: Accession Criteria," http://ec.europa.eu/enlargement/enlargement_process/accession_process/criteria/index_en.htm.

19. I owe this point to Professor Stefano Bianchini.

its results, researchers created an index surveying the direct experience of representatives of over three thousand firms with the issue of governance. The sample design was random in order to closely represent the range of companies in any given country, though Poland, Russia, and the Ukraine tended to have a larger number of interviewees (Hellman, Jones, and Kaufmann 2000; Hellman and Kaufmann 2001). Questions tapped into different types of corruption, collusion, and patronage.

The goal of the BEEPS was to create an index that measured the incidence of "state capture" in transition economies. The World Bank defines state capture as an effort of private interests to influence how laws, rules, and regulations are shaped to pursue their own advantage. In this way, state capture unbundled the concepts of corruption and crony capitalism, thereby treating them as multifaceted phenomena manifesting themselves in different ways. The novelty of the state-capture concept is that it also looks at corrupt and crony activities where the principal (or primary instigator) is the private sector and government officials and institutions are its agent.

In an economy characterized by state capture public officials shape policies and make legal decisions in ways that openly favor a captor firm at the expense of its competitors. Some of the micro-indicators used to create the state capture index specifically measure different aspects of corruption and collusion presented in chapter 1. Political patronage, for instance, is measured independently, thus making the comparative analysis even more straightforward. Table 2.5 reports the scores for Russia and the eight Eastern European countries mentioned earlier.[20] Besides the composite index of state capture, also included are some of its component units such as legislative (the sale of legislative votes or executive orders), central bank (mishandling of funds and bank regulations), and legal capture (sale of arbitration or criminal court rulings). The two additional scores measure nontransparent party finance (contributions by private interests to political parties and election campaigns) and, as just mentioned, political patronage.

Based on the thesis presented in chapter 1 we should expect Russia (the only crisis country of the sample) to score consistently worse than the other eight transition economies in all indicators. This is usually the case on all counts, both individually and at the average level. Not surprising, in their

---

20. Estonia, Latvia, and Lithuania are, strictly speaking, Baltic countries, but for reason of simplicity I refer to them here as Eastern European.

analysis of the same data set Hellman and Kaufmann (2001, 3) found that while "high state capture economies" made progress in economic liberalization and privatization, they had been "much slower to enact the complementary institutional reforms to support the emergence of markets." Conversely, noncrisis countries had made important strides in both economic and institutional reforms. As a result, captor firms in high-capture economies grew twice as fast as other companies. However, this growth did not translate into equal growth throughout the sector in which they operated. In fact, economic sectors in low-capture economies grew twice as much as economic sectors in high-capture economies. In other words, capturing firms grew at the expense of their competition in particular and the whole economy more generally.

Such a result would indicate that in the latter case capture firms behave in a rent-seeking fashion that hampers overall growth because they are in an institutional setting that provides incentives for such dysfunctional behavior. This, in turn, is a trend consistent with the theories by Olson (1982), Williamson (1986), and North (1990) discussed in chapter 1. Moreover, Hellman and Kaufmann (2001, 3) found (counter to the assumption justifying market reforms in the late 1980s) that in high-capture economies FDIS associated with local partners were almost twice as likely to engage in capture activities as were domestic firms, a phenomenon that also emerged in Argentina, as we shall see in chapter 4.

Other studies correlating economic reform to political indicators found empirical evidence confirming that the Eastern European countries that reformed in a more transparent fashion than Russia during the same period of time did better in the political realm as well. Hellman (1998), for instance, correlated democracy in transition economies vis-à-vis the level of economic reform. The scores on economic reforms were based on the 1994 EBRD cumulative indicators, while the democracy scores were from the Freedom House index on political rights over the same period of time. Indicators of political freedom and economic reforms showed a strong and positive correlation ($r = 0.78$) as a whole. As expected, this was much more pronounced in Slovenia, Hungary, Poland, and the Czech Republic than Russia, which fared much worse. In other words, countries with higher levels of political freedom and participation tended to perform better in terms of economic reform. Thus, Hellman's empirical evidence fits quite nicely the trend in Russia in the 1990s where Yeltsin during his decade in office progressively moved to strengthen his authoritarian grip on power at the expense of democratic procedures and opposition rights, as we shall see in more detail in chapter 3. In the other Eastern European countries, for the most part, the trend was just the opposite. Different leaders from different parties alternated at the executive level and citizens enjoyed greater levels of political participation and individual freedom than in Russia.

Within this context, Hellman (1998) found that governments in transition economies that faced frequent elections, had short executive tenures, and faced electoral challenges from the short-term losers of reforms were more likely to enact comprehensive reforms than governments that enjoyed longer terms in office and were able to insulate the policy process. In other words, governments that were exposed to greater degrees of vertical accountability (e.g., elections) were actually more likely to promote a comprehensive and effective reform program. Moreover, Hellman challenged the notion prevalent in the 1990s that the biggest threat to reform was going to come from the losers of the reform process. Instead he found that governments that insulated themselves from political pressure (and presumably accountability and transparency requirements) were prone, at the outset of the reform process, to give rent-seeking privileges to powerful economic groups, bankers, and local officials in return for political support. This created a situation in which a massive transfer of wealth occurred very rapidly, as the winners of market reforms were a small and highly organized group. Consistent with Olson's theory of interest group behavior, once they acquired their privileged positions, such groups turned into the most formidable obstacles against the creation of competitive markets, which would have spelled economic disaster for their recently acquired fortunes. Indeed, such business groups used their wealth and political clout as an effective veto power over policies fostering competition that would threaten their rents. This resulted in partial economic reforms and created a web of monopolies/oligopolies and economic distortions that stunted economic growth and penalized the bulk of the population that was left making the sacrifices imposed by half-hearted and often crooked policy choices. As we shall see later in the country study analyses, Hellman's "winners take all" thesis is consistent with the experiences of Russia, and to some degree even Argentina. What I will argue, though, is that this was possible precisely because accountability and transparency were systematically emasculated or co-opted.

Hellman's (1998) work provides further indirect evidence about the dichotomy existing between Eastern European countries on the one hand and

Russia on the other by using income inequality and GDP scores. Between 1989 and 1993 income inequality measured through the Gini coefficient rose on average by 0.41 percent in the eight Eastern European countries as opposed to a whopping 1.00 percent in Russia (Table 2.6). Conversely, Russia over the same period recorded the highest increase (20 percent) of income concentration for the top quintile of the population. Table 2.6 also reports the ratio of 1993–94 GDP to 1989 (the benchmark year before market reforms began to be adopted in these countries). By 1994 GDP had fallen by 16.5 percent in the Eastern European countries as opposed to twice as much (33 percent) in Russia.

To further verify the robustness of the findings presented so far I decided to see whether, as I argued in the thesis presented in chapter 1, a clear relationship existed between, on the one hand, the World Bank accountability index and, on the other, the EBRD economic indicators and indexes that were created to track the progress of market reforms in Eastern Europe and the former Soviet Union. If the thesis is correct, we should expect the noncrisis Eastern European countries to display a higher level of accountability associated with high scores in economic indicators (which are positively associated with progress toward market reforms) than is the case for Russia.

The following data analysis replicates some of Broadman and Recanatini's (2000) and Hellman's (1998) early tests and adds others that they did not attempt. However, while Broadman and Recanatini (2000) aimed at proving causality, my intent is to show the degree of association by running Pearson's correlation tests (two-tailed tests) since several variables may suffer from multicollinearity problems in a regression model.[21] Moreover, given the limited number of countries, the small N problem created serious difficulties for a reliable regression test. To recap, what I want to discover is whether statistically significant correlations exist between accountability and key market-reform-related variables, and if so, whether Russia performed distinctively worse than the other eight noncrisis countries according to my initial thesis. Granted that correlation analysis does not warrant definite conclusions, given the limitations discussed above, it nonetheless provides a useful tool to discover important policy trends. To start, I analyzed the relationship between accountability and various forms of govern-

---

21. Tables 2.8 through 2.18 report correlations scores using EBRD and World Bank data for 1998, by which time many reforms had been completed.

ment subsidies. The literature on economic and political reforms in the former Soviet bloc during the 1990s underscored the importance of eliminating soft budget constraints and arrears that government-owned companies enjoyed during the Communist era.[22] This is because the survival of such subsidies prevented the establishment of market discipline while strengthening the antireform alliance binding together company managers and antireform politicians. Russia was a typical example of these practices, as we shall see in greater detail in chapter 3. For instance, some observers contended that President Yeltsin's quest to retain political support among company managers and regional politicians led him to stop or water down many market reforms aimed at curtailing soft budget subsidies, with devastating consequences for the national coffers (Gustafson 1999; Hough 2001).

Figure 2.2 displays the correlation between accountability and the soft budget constraints index measured by percentage of firms receiving state subsidies. Figure 2.3 instead correlates accountability with arrears index measured through the percentage of firms with substantial arrears with federal and local government. The assumption here is that executives operating under little accountability are more likely to engage in soft budget constraint practices. While the correlation between soft budget constraints and accountability turns out with the expected sign but results statistically weak, the one measuring firms' arrears is highly significant (0.60**) and with the expected sign. In this latter case, high percentages of firms in arrears are associated with low levels of accountability in the case of Russia. Conversely, in different degrees, the East European countries show the opposite trend as predicted.

The next set of correlations reports the relationship between accountability and market competition. The rationale behind it, following Hayek's and Friedman's theories, is that market competition is the best antidote to rent-seeking behavior. Consequently, higher levels of market competition should be associated with higher levels of accountability since accountability is likely to produce a level playing field. Indeed, there is plentiful empirical evidence showing that when markets are contestable, keeping them

---

22. Soft budget constraints refer to a situation in which the government covers the deficit of a company by using several mechanisms such as soft loans, tax waivers, subsidies, arrears, and so forth. They were widespread in the Soviet bloc and comprehended a variety of measures used by the Communist regimes to bail out inefficient companies, regardless of their losses, in order to retain full employment and political support.

under monopoly status is harmful to economic growth and fuels a cozy relationship between political power and businesses seeking rents, often leading to corrupt practices. Accordingly, in the 1990s some countries of the former Soviet bloc attempted to address the problem by promoting competition policies that never existed under Communism. Figure 2.4 reports the bivariate correlation between the competition policy and accountability indexes, which appears to be quite strong and highly significant (r = 0.67**). Once again, the East European countries are the very best performers displaying higher levels of competition policy and lower levels of corruption, as opposed to Russia, which lags far behind in the middle of the diagram.

To more precisely establish the relationship between market competition and accountability I used additional and more detailed indexes developed by the EBRD. The first one, entry barriers, is a composite index measuring six different types of obstacles that new companies face when entering a market. The second, exit barriers, is a different type of index calculating subsidies and barter factors that keep companies competing in businesses even though they may be earning low or even negative returns on investment.[23] The tests' results in Figure 2.5 show a negative but weak relationship between accountability and entry barriers (r = -0.34), whereas exit barriers are highly significant (r = -0.65**) and with the expected sign (Figure 2.6). In both cases, Russia displays by far the strongest relationship between low accountability and indexes of noncompetitive behavior, while the Eastern European countries (Hungary and Estonia in particular) are the best performers and their scores are fairly clustered together.

Another way to ascertain the level of competitiveness in an economy is to examine the level of competition in the most important infrastructure industries (telecommunications, electricity, and transportation). In order to be admitted to the EU, the East European countries in our sample had to make a major effort to establish procompetition policies besides lowering tariffs and quotas. Instead, Russia and most of the former Soviet Republics kept their economies highly protected. Figure 2.7 correlates the index of infrastructure competition vis-à-vis accountability. The correlation coefficient is again very strong and statistically significant (r = 0.82**), indicating that high levels of infrastructure competition are positively associated

---

23. For the methodology behind the compilation of entry and exit barriers, see Dutz and Vagliasindi (2000).

with high levels of accountability. As expected, save for Slovakia, the Eastern European countries turn out to be among the best performers in this regard, while Russia, which made little progress toward infrastructure competition, is among the worst.

I will now turn to the relationship between accountability vis-à-vis the extensiveness of commercial and financial laws and regulation, as well as the effectiveness of the institutions in charge of upholding the rule of law in these matters. Scholarly work that analyzed transition economies in the former Soviet bloc, consistent with Hayek's and Friedman's theories on the subject, contends that progress toward successful market reforms are associated with the establishment of a strong rule of law and property rights. This is because promarket legal institutions reduce the uncertainty by investors, both domestic and foreign, regarding sudden changes in the rules of the game and expropriation. By the same token, legal reforms are considered to be powerful tools in deterring political opportunism. In this regard I used two indexes created by the EBRD. One is legal extensiveness (Figure 2.8), which refers to factors related to the breadth and scope of legal reform, while the other is legal effectiveness (Figure 2.9), which comprehends factors assessing the actual impact of legal reforms on economic transactions. The bivariate correlation tests show high levels of association, although legal extensiveness ($r = 0.54^{**}$) is slightly less statistically significant than legal effectiveness ($r = 0.66^{**}$). Nonetheless, the trend is fairly clear. For the most part, the Eastern European countries that had to significantly overhaul their legal systems to appease the EU entry requirements are closely clustered together in the upper right part of both figures where accountability is higher and legal performance is better. On the contrary, Russia did little to improve its legal standards and, not surprising, particularly when it comes to legal effectiveness, is among the worst-performing countries.

Poor banking regulations are widely regarded as a serious impediment to transparent and efficient capital markets. They also create dangerous incentives for the neglect of depositors' rights, money laundering, hazardous lending practices, and all kinds of corrupt activities. Prior to the collapse of Communism, money and credit mattered relatively little in the former Soviet bloc. However, in the early 1990s the design of up-to-date bankruptcy laws came to be regarded as being imperative to improving the business climate and curbing illegal practices. Russia adopted new bankruptcy legislation in 1998, but its implementation subsequently remained difficult due to the lack of political will, trained personnel, and adequate infrastructures. For their part the Eastern European countries, particularly Slovenia, Hungary, Poland, and the Czech Republic, made substantial strides forward in this regard, as the EU demanded. Accordingly, we should expect to find better banking regulation associated with higher levels of accountability in the Eastern European countries than in Russia. The correlation test supports this view, as the relationship is strong and statistically significant ($r = 0.59^*$). As shown in Figure 2.10, the Eastern European countries are clustered together in the upper right corner of the diagram, indicating a fairly high level of bankruptcy law and high accountability, whereas Russia is again considerably far behind.

Dismantling trade barriers is another policy often advocated to promote growth and lure FDIS while diminishing the opportunity for crony capitalism and corruption. Under Yeltsin, Russia remained a highly protected economy, which allowed well-connected entrepreneurs to build large business empires while keeping foreign competition at bay. In point of fact, the business environment was very hostile toward outsiders, either foreign or domestic, who could not count on strong political connections. Such discrimination was often sanctioned by law, as we shall see in chapter 3. As a result, few foreigners ventured to enter the Russian market, while Poland, the Czech Republic, Hungary, Slovenia, and Slovakia significantly lowered many of their trade barriers and actively pursued FDIS, particularly from the EU. Indeed, these Eastern European countries posted much higher levels of FDIS than Russia despite their smaller market size. More specific, between 1989 and 2000, when most market reforms were implemented in these countries, Russia received $9.9 billion in FDIS as opposed to Poland's $29 billion, the Czech Republic's $21.6 billion, Hungary's $18.9 billion, and Slovenia's $1.5 billion (Hellman et al. 2002, 9). The bivariate correlation test confirms that accountability is strongly associated with trade openness ($r = 0.72^{**}$). As expected, the Eastern European countries that opened up their economies to foreign trade also display the highest levels of accountability throughout the sample, whereas Russia is among the worst cases, beaten only by Belarus and Uzbekistan (Figure 2.11).

A further economic problem that is often mentioned in the academic literature as being a major obstacle toward the establishment of an efficient market economy is the pervasiveness of the so-called underground economy—that is, business activity that occurs without paying any taxes or licenses to operate in a given country. Both academics and practitioners point to the fact that the cause behind the flourishing of the underground economy is the lack of accountability of governments and their bureaucracies when it comes to setting up and implementing tax rates and business regulations. As a result, the underground economy deprives governments of badly needed tax revenues, producing very negative socioeconomic consequences (Schneider and Enste 2002). In addition, analysts usually argue that the lack of accountability of government officials allows them to engage in bribe taking, thus raising the cost of doing business. High levels of unreported economic transactions are therefore assumed to be associated with high levels of corruption. The evolution of the underground economy in some Eastern European countries and Russia also displays an interesting pattern. During the 1990s Russia's underground economy grew much larger than in the eight Eastern European countries in our sample. Once we correlate the level of the official economy with accountability, the association between the two is both strong and statistically significant as postulated (r = 0.57*). In this case I used an official economy index for 1995 developed by Johnson, Kaufmann, and Shleifer (1997). Save for Lithuania, the other countries (Estonia, Slovakia, Poland, Hungary, and the Czech Republic) display high levels of GDP accounted for by the official economy and high levels of accountability. Conversely, Russia is marred by high levels of unofficial economy and low accountability, which relegates it among the worst performers (Figure 2.12).

The next set of bivariate correlations move from policy-specific indicators to more encompassing measurements in order to verify the existence of a close relationship between accountability on the one hand and general measures of economic and political performance on the other. The first of such test looks at GDP per capita in U.S. dollars. Following Hayek and Friedman, greater accountability should allow greater levels of individual freedom vis-à-vis government encroachment, and therefore greater opportunities to pursue economic interests and accrue wealth. Thus, we should expect high degrees of accountability to be associated with high GDP per capita. Figure 2.13 confirms such a relationship, as the correlation coefficient is both statistically significant and strong (r = 0.66**). As in previous cases, the Eastern European cases do outperform Russia.

Privatization was single handedly the most critical and controversial of all reform efforts that many countries of the former Soviet bloc attempted in their quest to establish a market economy. Again, following Hayek's and Friedman's rationale, the more pervasive private property is in an economy, the more freedom individuals should enjoy. Likewise, a country that fosters free markets also promotes checks and balances (restraining government discretion) and accountability. Consequently, we should expect higher levels of accountability to be associated with higher degrees of private ownership in an economy. Figure 2.14 confirms this assumption, as the correlation score is very robust ($r = 0.80^{**}$) and with the expected sign. The bivariate correlation test also lends support to the thesis presented in chapter 1, as the Eastern European countries are yet again the best performers of the whole sample, while Russia lags behind.

Next, to assess the trajectory of market reforms over time I correlated accountability to an index measuring progress toward structural reforms. With this goal in mind, I used the EBRD structural reform index, which measures the level of structural reforms. The results reported in Figure 2.15 are consistent with the initial thesis. More accountable governments made greater strides toward structural reforms ($r = 0.86^{**}$). As expected, the Eastern European countries turn out to be the best cases in this regard as opposed to Russia.

Scholars and policy makers have also regarded macroeconomic stability as an indicator of successful reform. Figure 2.16 correlates the relationship between the EBRD index of macroeconomic stability in many countries of the former Soviet bloc during the 1990s. The result confirms such an assumption, as the correlation coefficient is strong and significant ($r = 0.63^{**}$). It also indicates that the Eastern European countries that we have analyzed so far are again among the best performers while Russia is among the very worst. If we then correlate the number of years of comprehensive liberalization with accountability, the results are equally clear cut ($r = 0.83^{**}$), as the Eastern European countries are the best performers while Russia is considerably behind (Figure 2.17).

Finally, the last test examines the relationship between executive power and comprehensive reforms. As noted in chapter 1, at the beginning of the 1990s advocates of the WC strongly argued in favor of insulating reform-committed executives from public contestation. However, a number of later studies on market reforms in Russia and Eastern Europe (Hellman 1998; Stark and Bruszt 1998; Orenstein 2001; and Gould 2003) came to the opposite conclusion, bringing evidence that strong and insulated executives did not perform as well as more accountable ones. Figure 2.18 lends support to the latter argument ($r = -0.64^{**}$), as it shows that the more powerful the executive was, the less comprehensive the reform. Once more, this test is consistent with the previous ones, as the more accountable executives of the eight Eastern European countries in our sample are again the best performers, while Russia, which had a strongly insulated executive through the 1990s, scores rather poorly.

Concluding Remarks

In this chapter I tried to establish whether countries that promoted market reforms and experienced financial crises displayed a distinctive different trend from noncrisis countries when testing for different measures of accountability. The cross-national analysis using World Bank governance scores for eighty emerging countries brings empirical evidence supporting the thesis presented in chapter 1, as (lack of) accountability, corruption, and collusion are *associated* with countries that experienced severe financial crises. Conversely, noncrisis countries report overall better scores on such governance indicators. When the analysis then shifts to the regional level, it compares eight Eastern European countries (which promoted institutional and economic reforms simultaneously to meet the EU's membership standards) and Russia (which prioritized mostly economic reforms). Using simple correlation tests, again the statistical evidence shows that accountability is positively associated with good economic performance. This is not to say that accountability is the factor that explains economic performance since I do not test for causality and alternative explanations with this particular group of countries. What the various tests at the regional level do is to suggest that, depending on the country, there is a positive *association* between high levels of accountability and key indicators of market reform success. When we correlate accountability with a wide array of economic variables that have been deemed in the economic literature as crucial for the success of market reforms, the results are fairly straightforward: accountability matters and in many cases quite a lot. While not perfect, in the 1990s the eight East European countries in our sample, under pressure from the EU, made positive and important strides forward in terms of both market reforms and accountability. Conversely, Russia's poor economic performance was strongly associated with poor accountability. These results about Russia and the eight Eastern European countries that attempted to reform their political and economic institutions bring additional evidence to earlier qualitative studies on economic transition in the former Soviet bloc, contending that more constrained executives were more likely to perform better (Hellman 1998; Greskovits 1998; Fish 1998; Stark and Bruszt 1998; Orenstein 2001; and Gould 2003) than unconstrained ones.

Summing up, different cross-national correlations at different levels of analysis lend support to the thesis put forward in chapter 1. To corroborate these findings in greater detail I will now examine the benchmark cases of Russia, Argentina, and Chile.

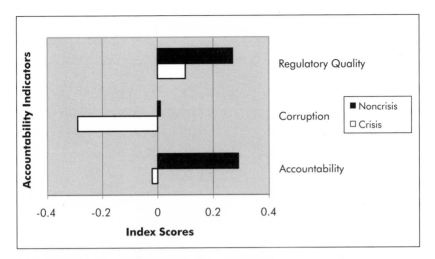

Figure 2.1 Accountability Indicators for Crisis and Noncrisis Countries, 1998
SOURCE: Kaufmann, Kraay, and Mastruzzi (2008).
NOTE: Sample size = 80 countries.

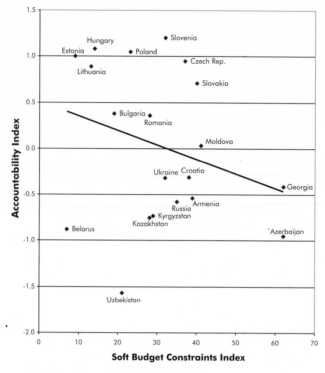

Figure 2.2 Soft Budget Constraints and Accountability, 1998
SOURCE: EBRD Transition Report (1999) and Kaufmann, Kraay, and Mastruzzi (2008).
NOTE: The Accountability Index is measured on a scale of −2.5 (low accountability) to 2.5 (high accountability). For the Soft Budget Constraints Index, higher values = worse performance. (Pearson's r = −0.28)

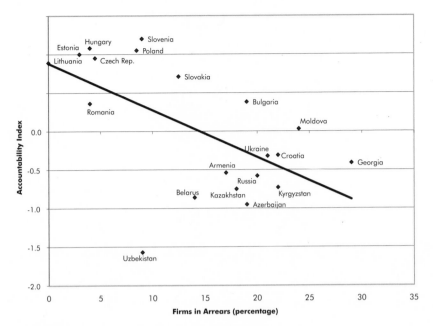

Figure 2.3 Firms in Arrears and Accountability, 1998
SOURCE: EBRD Transition Report (1999) and Kaufmann, Kraay, and Mastruzzi (2008).
NOTE: The Accountability Index is measured on a scale of −2.5 (low accountability) to 2.5 (high accountability). (Pearson's r = −0.60**)
**Significant at 1 percent

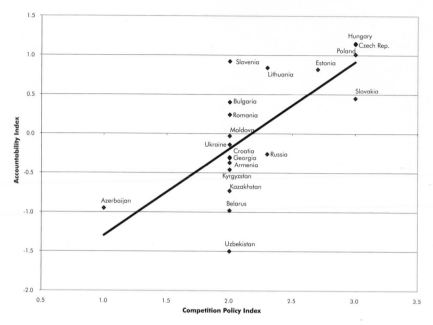

Figure 2.4 Competition Policy and Accountability, 1998
SOURCE: EBRD Transition Report (1999) and Kaufmann, Kraay, and Mastruzzi (2008).
NOTE: The Accountability Index is measured on a scale of −2.5 (low accountability) to 2.5 (high accountability). For the Competition Policy Index, higher values = greater competition. (Pearson's r = 0.67**)
**Significant at 1 percent

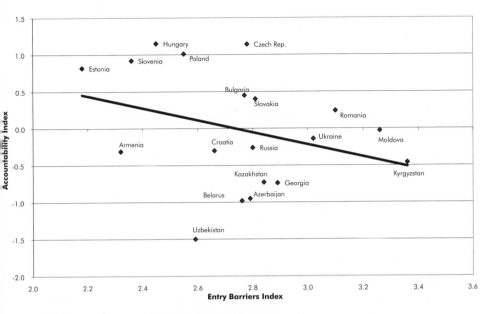

Figure 2.5 Entry Barriers and Accountability, 1998
SOURCE: EBRD Transition Report (1999) and Kaufmann, Kraay, and Mastruzzi (2008).
NOTE: The Accountability Index is measured on a scale of −2.5 (low accountability) to 2.5 (high accountability). For the Entry Barriers Index, higher values = higher entry barriers. (Pearson's r = −0.34)

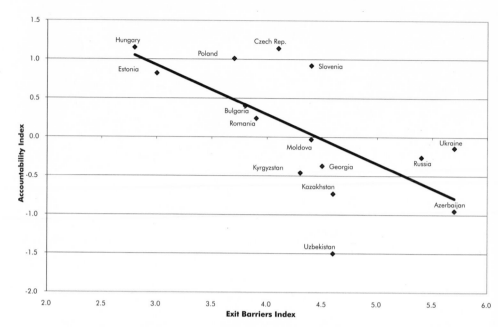

Figure 2.6 Exit Barriers and Accountability, 1998
SOURCE: EBRD Transition Report (1999) and Kaufmann, Kraay, and Mastruzzi (2008).
NOTE: The Accountability Index is measured on a scale of −2.5 (low accountability) to 2.5 (high accountability). For the Exit Barriers Index, higher values = higher exit barriers. (Pearson's r = −0.65**)
**Significant at 1 percent

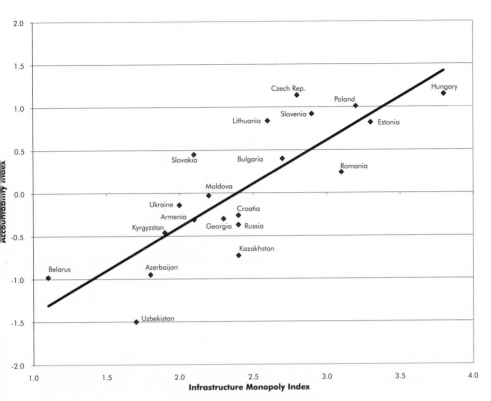

Figure 2.7 Infrastructure Monopoly and Accountability, 1998
SOURCE: EBRD Transition Report (1999) and Kaufmann, Kraay, and Mastruzzi (2008).
NOTE: The Accountability Index is measured on a scale of −2.5 (low accountability)
to 2.5 (high accountability). For the Infrastructure Monopoly Index, higher values =
higher competition. (Pearson's r = 0.82**)
**Significant at 1 percent

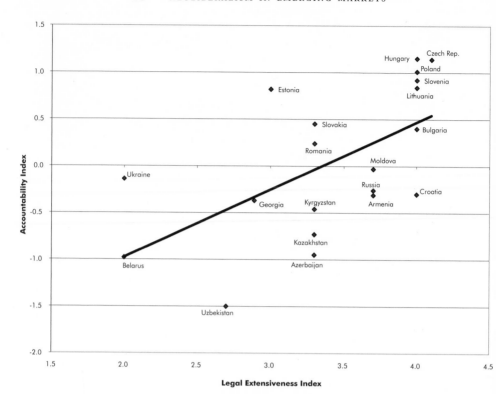

Figure 2.8 Legal Extensiveness and Accountability, 1998
SOURCE: EBRD Transition Report (1999) and Kaufmann, Kraay, and Mastruzzi (2008).
NOTE: The Accountability Index is measured on a scale of −2.5 (low accountability)
to 2.5 (high accountability). For the Legal Extensiveness Index, higher values = higher
legal extensiveness. (Pearson's r = 0.54**)
**Significant at 1 percent

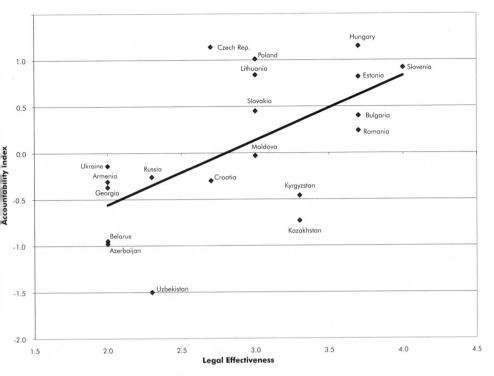

Figure 2.9 Legal Effectiveness and Accountability, 1998
SOURCE: EBRD Transition Report (1999) and Kaufmann, Kraay, and Mastruzzi (2008).
NOTE: The Accountability Index is measured on a scale of −2.5 (low accountability) to 2.5 (high accountability). For the Legal Effectiveness Index, higher values = higher legal effectiveness. (Pearson's r = 0.66**)
**Significant at 1 percent

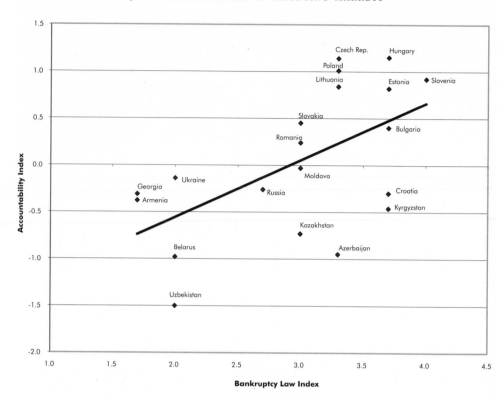

Figure 2.10 Bankruptcy Law and Accountability, 1998
SOURCE: EBRD Transition Report (1999) and Kaufmann, Kraay, and Mastruzzi (2008).
NOTE: The Accountability Index is measured on a scale of −2.5 (low accountability) to 2.5 (high accountability). For the Bankruptcy Law Index, higher values = better laws. (Pearson's r = 0.59*)
*Significant at 5 percent

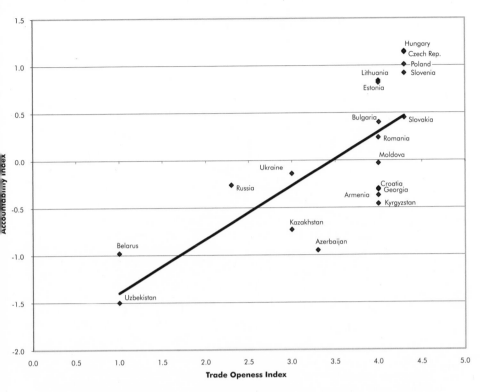

Figure 2.11 Trade Openness and Accountability, 1998
SOURCE: EBRD Transition Report (1999) and Kaufmann, Kraay, and Mastruzzi (2008).
NOTE: The Accountability Index is measured on a scale of −2.5 (low accountability) to 2.5 (high accountability). For the Trade Openness Index, higher values = greater openness. (Pearson's r = 0.72**)
**Significant at 1 percent

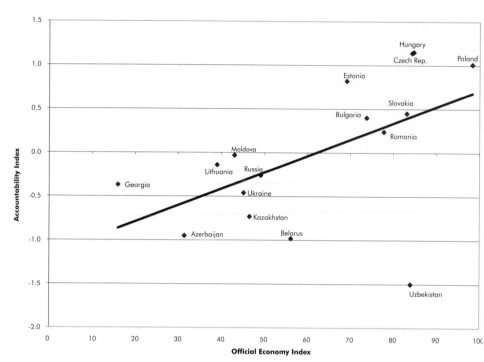

Figure 2.12 Official Economy and Accountability, 1998
SOURCE: EBRD Transition Report (1999) and Kaufmann, Kraay, and Mastruzzi (2008).
NOTE: The Accountability Index is measured on a scale of −2.5 (low accountability) to 2.5 (high accountability). For the Official Economy Index, higher values = higher levels of official economy. (Pearson's r = 0.57*)
*Significant at 5 percent

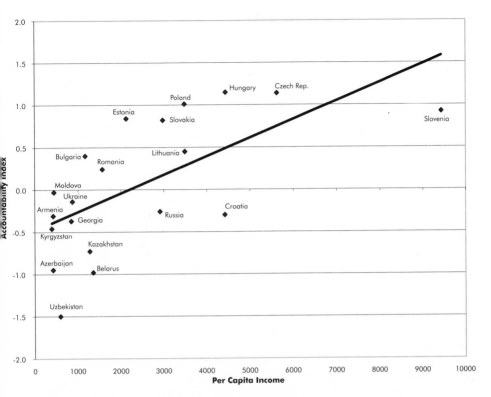

Figure 2.13 Per Capita Income and Accountability, 1998
SOURCE: Broadman and Recanatini (2000) and Kaufmann, Kraay, and Mastruzzi (2008).
NOTE: The Accountability Index is measured on a scale of −2.5 (low accountability) to 2.5 (high accountability). Per Capita Income in thousands of $US. (Pearson's r = 0.66**)
**Significant at 1 percent

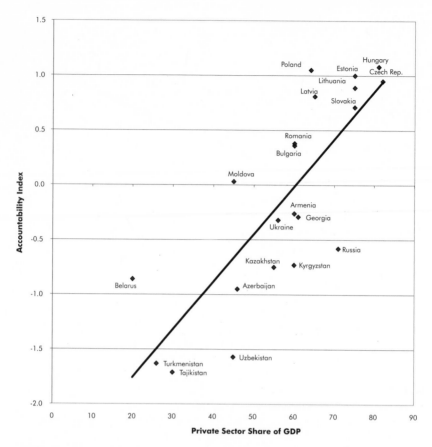

Figure 2.14 Privatization and Accountability, 1998
SOURCE: EBRD Transition Report (1999) and Kaufmann, Kraay, and Mastruzzi (2008).
NOTE: The Accountability Index is measured on a scale of − 2.5 (low accountability) to 2.5 (high accountability). For the Privatization Indicator, Private Sector Share of GDP in percentages. (Pearson's r = 0.80**)
**Significant at 1 percent

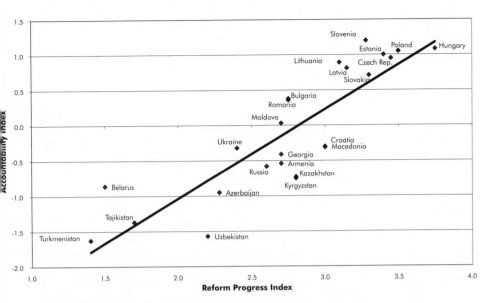

Figure 2.15 Progress Toward Reform and Accountability, 1998

SOURCE: EBRD Transition Report (1999) and Kaufmann, Kraay, and Mastruzzi (2008). NOTE: The Accountability Index is measured on a scale of −2.5 (low accountability) to 2.5 (high accountability). For the Reform Progress Index, 1 = low progress, 4 = substantial progress. (Pearson's r = 0.87**) **Significant at 1 percent

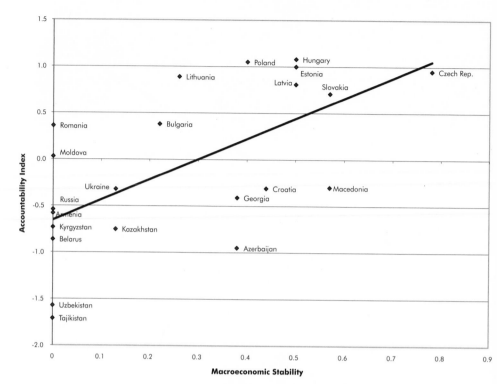

Figure 2.16 Macroeconomic Stability and Accountability, 1998
SOURCE: EBRD Transition Report (1999) and Kaufmann, Kraay, and Mastruzzi (2008).
NOTE: The Accountability Index is measured on a scale of − 2.5 (low accountability)
to 2.5 (high accountability). Macroeconomic Stability is measured in years. (Pearson's
r = 0.63**)
**Significant at 1 percent

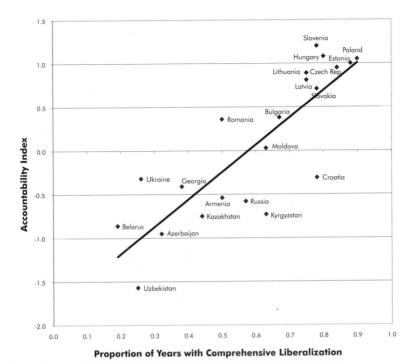

Figure 2.17 Comprehensive Liberalization and Accountability, 1998
SOURCE: EBRD Transition Report (1999) and Kaufmann, Kraay, and Mastruzzi (2008). For Proportion of Years with Comprehensive Liberalization, higher values = better performance over time. (Pearson's r = 0.83**)
**Significant at 1 percent

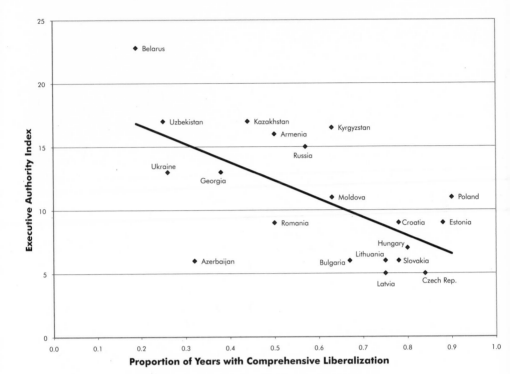

Figure 2.18 Comprehensive Liberalization and Executive Authority, 1998
SOURCE: EBRD Transition Report (1999).
NOTE: For Proportion of Years with Comprehensive Liberalization, higher values =
better performance. For the Executive Authority Index, higher values = greater
authority. (Pearson's r = − 0.64**)
**Significant at 1 percent

Table 2.1   Financial Inflows and Major Financial Crises

	Rank of Recipients, 1990–96 (by absolute volume of private flows)	Private Capital Flows, 1990–96 (% of GDP in 1996)	FDI Flows, 1990–96 (% private capital flows)
Crisis Countries/Year			
Mexico, 1994–95	2	33.0	42.8
Thailand, 1997	6	27.1	22.7
Indonesia, 1997	7	17.7	22.7
South Korea, 1997	na	na	na
Malaysia, 1997	5	62.7	47.2
Russia, 1998	11	4.8	18.7
Brazil, 1999	3	12.6	20.7
Turkey, 2000–2001	10	12.1	22.1
Argentina, 2001–2	4	23.9	33.4
Noncrisis Countries			
China	1	25.2	68.2
India	8	7.6	20.6
Chile	9	39.4	37.2

SOURCE: World Bank (2005, 247).

Table 2.2 Sources of Vulnerabilities in Financial Crises in the 1990s

Source of Problem	Country					
	Brazil	Indonesia	S. Korea	Mexico	Thailand	Russia
Pegged Exchange Rate	1.0	0.5*	0.5	1.0	1.0	1.0
Current Account Deficit	0.5	2.0	3.0	1.0	1.0	3.0
Fiscal Deficit	1.0	3.0	3.0	3.0	3.0	1.0
Banking and Financial Sector Weakness	3.0	1.0	1.0	1.0	1.0	1.0
Government Short-Term Debt	1.0	3.0	3.0	1.0	2.0	1.0
Total Short-Term Debt and Foreign Indebtedness	2.0	1.0	1.0	2.0	1.0	1.0
General Governance	2.0	1.0	2.0	2.0	2.0	1.0

SOURCE: Summers (2000, 8).

Key to table entries: 1, very serious; 2, serious; 3, not central.

*Indonesia let its exchange rate float in August 1998, and did exhibit strong signs of real exchange rate misalignment, and did not expend reserves defending the rate. However, the inflexible exchange rate regime does seem to have encouraged a large buildup of foreign currency debt in the private sector.

Table 2.3 Macroeconomic Indicators of Selected Countries a Year After the Crisis

Country	Argentina	Mexico	Ecuador	S. Korea	Indonesia	Thailand	Russia	Turkey
Crisis Started	Dec. 2001	Dec. 1994	Sep. 1998	Nov. 1997	Aug. 1997	Jul. 1997	Aug. 1998	Feb. 2001
Devaluation (%)	70.0	54.0	32.0	37.0	234.0	51.0	75.0	96.0
Inflation (%)	41.0	52.0	55.0	7.0	69.0	11.0	127.0	73.0
GDP Growth (%)	−15.0	−6.5	−8.0	−6.0	−13.0	−11.9	−4.9	−9.3

SOURCE: International Monetary Fund (http://www.imf.org/external/data.htm).

Table 2.4 Cumulative Change in Debt Dynamics in Crisis Economies

Three Years Before the Crisis	Mexico 1991–93	Indonesia 1994–96	S. Korea 1994–96	Malaysia 1994–96	Russia 1995–97	Brazil 1995–97	Turkey 1997–99	Argentina 1999–2001
Change in Public Deficit Sector	−22.8	−11.6	−2.6	−16.6	−8.8	6.3	14.5	21.5
Primary Deficit (−surplus)	−12.9	−7.5	−2.1	−22.1	9.3	0.7	1.8	1.7
Recognition of Contingent Liabilities (net of privatization)	0	0	0	−2.0	−9.3	4.0	−0.7	0.7
Contribution from Real GDP Growth	−3.9	−7.3	−3.1	−16.0	4.0	−3.0	−2.4	4.2
Contribution from Real Interest Rate	3.4	3.7	0	7.0	−7.4	3.6	20.7	10.7
Contribution from Real Exchange Rate	−5.9	−2.2	−0.6	−1.2	−29.7	−1.6	−0.4	2.4
Contribution from Debt Indexation	0.4	0	0	0	0	1.4	0	0
Residual*	−4.0	1.6	3.3	17.6	24.3	1.3	−4.5	1.9

Three Years After the Crisis	Mexico 1994–96	Indonesia 1996–99	S. Korea 1997–99	Malaysia 1997–99	Russia 1998–2000	Brazil 1998–2000	Turkey 2000–2003	Argentina 2002–3
Change in Public Deficit Sector	28.0	68.6	30.3	14.9	4.2	15.7	19.1	84.7
Primary Deficit (−surplus)	−16.8	−2.7	6.0	−19.6	−7.0	−6.7	−12.6	−3.9
Recognition of Contingent Liabilities (net of privatization)	0	0	−0.7	6.9	−5.9	5.0	15.4	0.3
Contribution from Real GDP Growth	−0.6	2.0	−2.9	−2.5	−9.4	−2.6	−6.4	−5.6
Contribution from Real Interest Rate	12.5	4.3	2.3	7.8	−4.8	17.1	21.7	1.3
Contribution from Real Exchange Rate	6.5	10.8	1.8	8.7	30.9	2.8	3.3	−4.6
Contribution from Debt Indexation	4.4	0	0	0	0	4.9	12.2	0
Residual*	22.1	54.3	23.8	13.6	0.4	−4.9	−14.5	51.0

SOURCE: World Bank (2005, 250).

*The residual captures the recognition of implicit liabilities such as banking sector bailouts, social security, and pensions debt, for which no hard data exist and are thus not included directly in the calculations. It also includes various cross products assumed away with the approximations made. For Argentina, data are available for 2000 and 2001.

Table 2.5 State Capture in Transition Economies in 1999

State Capture Indexes*	Czech Rep.	Hungary	Poland	Slovenia	Estonia	Lithuania	Latvia	Slovakia	Average	Russia
Composite Index of State Capture	11.0	7.0	12.0	7.0	10.0	11.0	30.0	24.0	14.0	32.0
Legislative Capture	18.0	12.0	15.0	8.0	14.0	15.0	40.0	20.0	18.0	38.0
Central Bank Capture	12.0	8.0	6.0	4.0	8.0	9.0	8.0	37.0	11.5	47.0
Legal Capture	14.0	6.0	18.0	7.0	10.0	15.0	na	34.0	15.0	28.0
Nontransparent Party Finance	6.0	4.0	10.0	11.0	17.0	13.0	35.0	20.0	14.5	28.0
Political Patronage	17.0	6.0	28.0	11.0	36.0	25.0	na	32.0	22.0	42.0

SOURCE: Hellman et al. (2000).

*Percentage of firms reporting each problem as an obstacle to business

Table 2.6 Partial Reform and Inequality

Country	Variance in EBRDC Scores	Gini Coefficient 1988–89	Gini Coefficient 1993–94	% Change Gini 1988–94	Income Share Top Quintile	GDP 1993–94 GDP 1988–89
Advanced						
Poland	0.25	26.0	31.0	0.19	3.43	88.0
Slovenia	0.36	24.0	28.0	0.17	3.76	84.0
Hungary	0.28	21.0	23.0	0.10	1.07	81.0
Czech Republic	0.28	19.0	27.0	0.42	5.77	81.0
Slovakia	0.19	20.0	20.0	0.00	−0.10	79.0
Average	0.27	22.0	25.8	0.18	2.79	82.6
High Intermediate						
Estonia	0.44	23.0	39.0	0.70	13.61	73.0
Bulgaria	0.53	23.0	34.0	0.48	7.78	69.0
Latvia	0.75	23.0	27.0	0.17	4.01	60.0
Lithuania	0.69	23.0	36.0	0.57	9.75	44.0
Albania	1.25	na	na	na	na	74.0
Romania	0.78	23.0	29.0	0.26	4.08	69.0
Average	0.74	23.0	33.0	0.43	7.85	64.8
Low Intermediate						
Kyrgyzstan	0.94	26.0	35.0	0.35	na	61.0
Russia	0.53	24.0	48.0	1.00	20.02	57.0
Moldova	0.53	24.0	36.0	0.50	8.89	53.0
Kazakhstan	0.36	26.0	33.0	0.27	na	57.0
Average	0.59	25.0	38.0	0.53	na	57.0
Slow						
Turkmenistan	0.11	26.0	36.0	0.38	na	69.0
Ukraine	0.19	23.0	33.0	0.43	na	56.0
Uzbekistan	0.25	28.0	33.0	0.18	na	89.0
Belarus	0.11	23.0	28.0	0.22	na	73.0
Average	0.17	25.0	32.5	0.30	na	71.7

SOURCE: Milanovic (1996, 58).

three

RUSSIA

Introduction

When Mikhail Gorbachev became the leader of the Soviet Union in 1985, he inherited an economy that was quickly moving toward the edge of collapse. Moreover, the Communist regime's failure to improve people's living standards as promised had created widespread apathy and cynicism. Gorbachev tried to reverse the tide by promoting economic restructuring (*perestroika*) and political openness (*glasnost*), believing that the regime could reform itself and win people's approval (Brown 2007). While it is beyond the scope of this chapter to analyze the Gorbachev period, it is important to outline some of his major policy changes, which would set the stage for the reforms that President Yeltsin ushered during the 1990s.

In a matter of a few years Gorbachev dismantled the essential control mechanisms of the command economy built during the Soviet era centered around Gosplan (the state committee in charge of central planning) and Gosnob (the ministry in charge of distribution). In May 1987 the Supreme Soviet approved the first law allowing small-scale privatization, granting cooperatives, students, and pensioners the right to engage in private trade activities. In 1988 he started with the Law of State Enterprises. This legislation allowed state-owned enterprises (SOEs) greater autonomy in decision-making from Gosplan in setting up production targets and managing their own finances. In the two years that followed, new legislation aimed at forcing SOEs to reorganize their production according to market needs further restricted Gosplan's and Gosnob's authority. Moreover, the government began to relinquish its control over foreign trade, banking, foreign exchange, and SOEs' revenues.

Politically, Gorbachev eased censorship and repression and loosened political controls over the Soviet republics and regions. In an effort to institutionalize the democratization process, Gorbachev stressed the need for the state to be bound to its own laws—in itself a philosophical watershed considering the arbitrary nature of power under both the czarist and Communist regimes. In 1988, to legitimize his power base away from the Communist Party of the Soviet Union (CPSU), he had the Supreme Soviet (the equivalent of parliament in the Soviet Union) elect him as its president as well as president of the Presidium.[1] In December 1988 the Supreme Soviet sanctioned the creation of the Congress of People's Deputies (CPD) as the country's new legislature and then dissolved itself. The 2,250 members of the CPD then proceeded to elect a smaller (542 members) legislative body, which again took up the name of Supreme Soviet.[2] The CPD that emerged after the 1989 elections still had 87 percent of its membership coming from CPSU, but for the first time open debates began to take place. In March 1990 the newly created CPD (1989) elected Gorbachev as its president. From that position, Gorbachev gave the final blow to the CPSU power by repealing article 6 of the Constitution, which granted to the Communist Party a political monopoly over all state institutions.

However, both political and economic reforms made Gorbachev's position progressively more untenable. Politically, Gorbachev, while successful in destroying the power of the CPSU, failed to create a mass following of his own. On the one hand, the Communists bitterly resisted his reforms as going too far, not so much because they contradicted Marxist-Leninist theory, since few true believers in Communism still existed among party affiliates by the 1990s, but because they threatened the special privileges that the regime granted them. On the other hand, for prodemocracy groups that had emerged as the result of *glasnost,* Gorbachev was not doing enough. The result was that Gorbachev failed to create a new political constituency supporting his reform agenda, which left him very vulnerable.

In the economic realm, Gorbachev commissioned an ambitious program to two reform-minded economists, Stanislav Shatalin and Grigory Yavlin-

---

1. The Presidium represented the office of the executive branch in a Western presidential system and ran day-to-day government operations when the Supreme Soviet was in recess. It had a membership of thirty-seven people, including fifteen representatives from each republic. Its chairman was regarded as the president of the Soviet Union.

2. In practice the CPD met for only brief periods of time, leaving the new Supreme Soviet with the task of performing legislative functions.

sky. Their recommendations were presented in the "500 Days Plan," which had the goal of ushering major market reforms while preserving the Soviet Union. The plan aimed at stopping the illegal privatization of government assets, which had been under way since the late 1980s. Consistent with the academic literature at the time, the 500 Days Plan called for a restructuring of state companies prior to privatization and the introduction of competition policy. Privatization was also to promote popular capitalism by distributing company shares to the public, thus creating the financial bases for a new middle class, which in turn would be supportive of democracy and capitalism. Other features of the 500 Days Plan called for the creation of antitrust legislation and the elimination of most subsidies, which benefited primarily company managers.

Despite its strong democratic features, the 500 Days Plan never got off the ground. A major blow came from the West, which refused to pay for its costs. German chancellor Helmut Kohl had already given the Soviets $30 billion in return for their permission to reunify his country, and U.S. president George H. Bush (1989–93) was in no mood to help as the United States was undergoing a painful recession. Instead, Bush proposed to the G-7 countries (France, Germany, Italy, Japan, United Kingdom, the United States, and Canada) that the Soviet crisis be handled by the IMF and the World Bank. This solution could save the G-7 significant amounts of money while preventing opposition in their respective legislatures. Moreover, the IMF and World Bank could be trusted to promote in the Soviet Union policies in line with the WC's tenets (Woods 2006).[3]

The West's decision played into the hands of the Soviet *nomenklatura*, the elite privileged class consisting of the people holding positions of authority in the Communist regime, as well as the emerging organized crime. As Reddaway and Glinski (2001, 177) pointed out, "immediate price liberalization in advance of legal privatization . . . essentially promised . . . uncontrolled price fixing by quasi state monopolies. Many members of the nomenklatura welcomed this project because they wanted to become the new capitalist owners of the nation's assets."

Rebuked by the West and facing a tough opposition at home, Gorbachev ended up producing the worst of both worlds. Some of his reforms made advances in creating embryonic forms capitalism, but they left intact price and wage controls and the special privileges of the industrial sector linked

---

3. Russia became a formal member of the IMF in June 1992.

to military production, which allowed state managers to continue their illegal appropriation of SOEs' financial assets (Åslund 2007). Gorbachev's reluctance to go ahead with the 500 Days Plan, in addition to opposition by the G-7, was his fear that going farther would have triggered a revolt of the conservative factions within the CPSU and the armed forces. The result was half-hearted policies that created economic paralysis. As a result, inflation, which was unheard of in previous decades, began to climb steadily. Concomitantly, the budget deficit and foreign debt soared to record levels and the distribution chain collapsed, provoking severe shortages of many essential goods by early 1991. Taking advantage of the unfolding socioeconomic crisis, the CPSU's hard-liners staged a coup in August 1991, hoping to remove Gorbachev and reverse the tide of reform. Ironically, the coup's ultimate failure marked the beginning of the end for both the Communists and Gorbachev.

Conversely, the coup represented a unique opportunity for Boris Yeltsin, who had led the prodemocracy forces, to replace Gorbachev as the country's new leader. Yeltsin was one of the CPSU high-ranking officials who had embraced the reform credo early on. This earned him Gorbachev's promotion to first secretary of the Moscow City Party Committee (the equivalent of a mayor's job) and a subsequent membership in the Politburo. Yeltsin's criticism of the slow pace of reform, though, prompted Gorbachev to dismiss him from all his official positions in 1988. Yet he was capable of an astonishing comeback by winning a fair election for Moscow's seat in the CPD in 1989. Shortly thereafter Yeltsin became a member of the Supreme Soviet. By 1990 his populist style built around a crusade against the corruption within the CPSU had earned him the support of many in the democratic reform movement. This, in turn, allowed him to quickly climb the ladder of power first by being elected chairman of the Russian Supreme Soviet in May, followed by a popular election to the presidency of the Russian Federation in June 1991. From that point on a dual power structure came into being that allowed Yeltsin to systematically corner Gorbachev into the defensive. Yeltsin, riding on popular dissatisfaction, pushed political and economic reforms that Gorbachev had feared to implement through the legislature, thus making Gorbachev appear as a reactionary in the eye of public opinion.

By the fall of 1991 the situation unraveled at a very fast pace. On October 28, addressing the Russian Congress of People's Deputies, Yeltsin outlined plans for radical market reforms. A week later, and without parliamentary approval, Yeltsin appointed himself prime minister and then appointed three deputy prime ministers in charge of different aspects of policy making. Of these three deputies a young academic, Yegor Gaidar, took control of economic policy (McFaul 2001, 147). In November Yeltsin issued ten decrees in which the Russian Federation took away most of the economic and political authority of the Soviet Union. On December 8 the presidents of Russia, the Ukraine, and Belarus signed behind close doors the so-called Minsk Accord, in which they disbanded the Soviet Union altogether, leaving Gorbachev no option but to resign as president of the Soviet Union on December 25.

In the two weeks that followed Yeltsin issued a number of decrees that would dramatically alter the Russian economy, combining at the same time price liberalization and privatization. On December 29 he approved the Basic Provisions of the State Program for Privatization. Then, on January 2, 1992, Gaidar adopted the shock-therapy approach as he eliminated price controls in many sectors of the economy and began to liberalize trade. In doing so, Gaidar aimed at simultaneously stopping runaway inflation and the "spontaneous privatization" perpetrated by SOE managers (often dubbed "red directors"), who, using Gorbachev's previous reforms, had been left with a substantial degree of discretionary power as most governmental controls had ceased to exist.

In late 1991 there was little support in Russia for shock therapy and most economists advocated more gradual strategies that targeted the solution to the structural problems of the post-Soviet economy (McFaul 2001, 164). Indeed, opinions were deeply divided. However, the significance of shock therapy rests also in the political realm. According to Reddaway and Glinski (2001), who wrote the most thorough analysis of the Yeltsin era, shock therapy served a deliberate political purpose. Yeltsin did not have a plan of his own, but Gaidar's program could provide the means to consolidate his power and destroy his opponents once and for all (Yeltsin 2000).[4] For Reddaway and Glinski (2001, 254), shock therapy amounted to a "politically conservative counter-reform designed by its principal strategists to weaken the potential for the continuation of the democratic revolution," which had emerged from the ashes of the Soviet regime.[5]

4. According to Gaidar's aid Pyotr Aven, "Yeltsin wanted to make sure that he totally destroyed Soviet Communism. . . . He was interested only in power. He wanted a team that would be very aggressive in throwing out all the old bureaucrats" (Hoffman 2002, 178).

5. There is disagreement among scholars on whether shock therapy truly took place in Russia. Stone (2002) contends that at best it was short lived. In point of fact, Gaidar did imple-

However, Yeltsin skillfully outmaneuvered his critics within the democratic movement who were crying foul. Indeed he adroitly portrayed himself as the true champion of democracy who was struggling to stop a Communist counterrevolution. The reality, as it turned out, was quite different. Realizing that the demands of the red directors, the former members of the *nomenklatura* turned capitalists, the regional political bosses, and the military-related industrial apparatus would be difficult to defeat, the president decided to strike a deal with these powerful groups and turned against the democratic movement, which up until that moment had been its main base of support. As Reddaway and Glinski (2001, 243), put it, "the real choice was about defining the place and role of the state power in relation to the 'Big Grab'—the furtive privatization of Soviet state assets. Yeltsin had to choose between fostering unbridled nomenklatura capitalism or using the non-privileged classes and the emerging civil society to create political, legal, institutional and moral counterweights to the new nomenklatura capitalists." In the end, he chose the former. Within the administration, the representative of Yeltsin's alliance with the red directors and the *nomenklatura* was Viktor Chernomyrdin, chairman of the oil and gas giant Gazprom (1989–92).[6] Thus, shock therapy resulted in what amounted to "a top-down expropriation and redistribution in disguise" to the benefit of a few powerful interests and at the expense of ordinary citizens through what Reddaway and Glinski (2001, 36) defined as "market bolshevism."

In late 1991 Yeltsin still enjoyed considerable voter support, and as the first popularly elected president of Russia his legitimacy was not in question. Moreover, the collapse of the Soviet system created ideal political conditions for the acceptance of market reforms as the lesser of two evils (Granville and Oppenheimer 2001, 21). Thus, the president gambled on his people's patience. He asked his fellow Russians to endure the sacrifices imposed by shock therapy but promised that within a year their living standards would improve appreciably. Persuaded by Gaidar and the IMF, the president ensured that price liberalization "will put everything in the right place."[7]

---

ment price liberalization and privatization but was unable to eliminate state subsidies, which was a key component of this policy approach.

6. Chernomyrdin guaranteed the interests of the *nomenklatura* within the Yeltsin administration. The president appointed him deputy prime minister for oil and gas in May 1992. He eventually replaced Gaidar as prime minister, a position that he held, on and off, longer than any other colleague (about five years) during Yeltsin tenure.

7. Quoted in Reddaway and Glinski (2001, 233).

However, Gaidar and his economic team, often referred to as the "young reformers," did not have the same legitimacy. They mainly came from academic centers and for the most part had not been involved in the democratic movement.[8] In fact, as time went on Gaidar and his closest associate, Anatoli Chubais, showed a strong inclination for confrontational and authoritarian solutions. Their main concern was that the political window of opportunity to promote a quick transition to a market economy could close suddenly. Thus, the Yeltsin economic team's highest priority was to enact their policy agenda as fast as possible. In drawing their plans, Gaidar and the young reformers borrowed heavily from the ideas of Hayek, Friedman, and another prominent academic from the University of Chicago, Donald Coase (Stavrakis 1993; Hough 2001). These scholars' advocacy for "economic freedom" as the best means to reduce government intervention—and, therefore, depoliticize economic decision—was particularly appealing to the young reformers who were looking for guidance on how to reverse eight decades of Communism.[9] The young reformers' preference for shock therapy was reinforced not only by the IMF and the World Bank, which in 1992 were beginning to provide technical assistance to Russia, but also by distinguished Western advisers, including Jeffrey Sachs, Andrei Shleifer, Maxim Boycko, Robert Vishny, and Anders Åslund (Wedel 2001; Goldman 2003). Although, in principle, Gaidar's plan aimed at creating the basis of a market economy by promoting price stability, economic deregulation, and private ownership, its true aim was political. That is, the destruction of the Soviet command economy before organized opposition could become too strong to overcome (Gaidar 1999). As Chubais (1993, 158), the mastermind of Yeltsin's privatization program, candidly stated, "This is not an economics program; it is a political program. It is 5 percent economics and 95 percent politics."

Equally important, the young reformers neglected the importance of institution building to facilitate their reforms. This, in part, stemmed from their economic approach to problem solving. In their view, as noted earlier, economic freedom needed to be promoted first. Consistent with the neoliberal view enshrined in the WC, Gaidar and his aides assumed that only after

---

8. Many of them were children of the Communist *nomenklatura*.

9. The young reformers were for the most part in their late twenties and early thirties and lacked any real government experience since they came primarily from academia. This made them particularly antagonistic toward a bureaucracy that was very entrenched in its privileges and often prone to corruption.

people had become property owners would they demand the creation of the institutions they deemed necessary. Such reasoning was based on Coase's theorem. Coase postulates that in the absence of transaction costs (i.e., property rights are well defined, bargaining costs are low, perfect competition and information exist), resources will be used efficiently and identically regardless of who owns them. In a situation of this kind, the theorem implies that government intervention should be minimal since interested parties will bargain privately to correct any externality. In adopting this view, Gaidar and Chubais assumed that even if some initial distortions would emerge, the market would eventually correct itself and eliminate the less efficient property owners, thus making government intervention useless and possibly dangerous. After all, their aim was not to build a strong state but just the opposite; that is, making sure that the old Soviet system would be destroyed and the new one be limited by the forces unleashed through market mechanisms. In short, institutional building was alien to Gaidar and Chubais's priorities.

The problem with this simplistic approach is that none of the preconditions spelled out in Coase's theorem existed in Russia at the time. In other words, transaction costs were plentiful. The rule of law, for instance, was absent. Moreover, as described by Hough (2001, 70), "property rights were not well defined, bargaining agents had little information and accountability, and the enforcement of agreements was scarcely without cost or even reliable."[10] The result was that economic reforms took place in an institutional vacuum that allowed all types of abuses within which organized crime and the politically well connected amassed large fortunes at the expense of the average citizen (Hellman 1998; Gaddy and Ickes 1998). The state, instead of creating a level playing field so that competitive markets could thrive, was conquered by vested interests, which established widespread rent seeking and the kind of crony capitalism that would have appalled Hayek and Friedman, whom Gaidar and Chubais so much admired (Wedel 2001). Sadly, this state of affairs contributed to the popular perception that markets were "essentially the freedom to do whatever one pleased, without restraint or limit" (Gustafson 1999, 21). Politically, the reforms

---

10. A corollary of Coase's theorem implies that in the presence of transaction costs, government may minimize inefficiency by allocating property initially to the party assigning it the greatest utility. This, of course, did not happen in Russia. Moreover, even for a minimalist like Friedman legal and economic institutions protecting property rights should already be in place for a market economy to function properly.

were implemented in an autocratic fashion that escaped transparency and undermined the democratic process. In the following paragraphs we will see how the lack of transparency was instrumental in derailing the reform effort.

Accountability in Yeltsin's Russia

Congress

Russia did not have a tradition of democracy nor a culture of political tolerance prior to the 1990s. Despite self-styling as the champion of democracy, Yeltsin was fundamentally a populist, frequently a demagogue, and often an authoritarian. His economic advisers saw themselves as the zealots of free markets and economic freedom, but when it came to dealing with democratic procedures to enact their policies they showed strongly entrenched authoritarian attitudes, arguing that the end justified the means. Throughout the 1990s Gaidar and the young reformers were generally regarded as arrogant (Hoffman 2002) and never earned popular support.[11] In fact, they hardly disguised their belief to be the only ones possessing the solution to what they perceived as Russia's imminent economic implosion. By the same token, they displayed contempt for politics and politicians in particular.

The legislative institutions inherited from the Soviet era were, in principle, quite strong. Article 104 of the 1978 Constitution ascribed to the Supreme Soviet and the parent CPD the power to decide on any matter of the Russian federation. This included the power to change the prerogatives of the president and amend the constitution itself by a vote of two-thirds. The legislative branch was also solely responsible for the appointment of the justices in the newly created Constitutional Court, as well as federal judges.[12] However, the constitution did not establish a clear separation of powers and spheres of authority. This created an unclear dual power struc-

---

11. In the 1993 elections Gaidar and Chubais's party, Russia's Choice, was expected to obtain between 30 to 40 percent of the seats but actually received only 15 percent, which was regarded by political observers as a clear defeat (Reddaway and Glinski 2001, 434).

12. The presidency was patterned after that of the French Fifth Republic. The president was the head of state and chief executive but acted on a prime minister who had to be approved by the legislature. The president had substantial latitude in issuing decrees, which, however, could be defeated by a simple congressional majority. In 1991 Yeltsin received congressional approval to name provincial and regional governors until elections were to be held.

ture, which fueled jurisdictional squabbles (McFaul 2001). Such a situation enabled the legislative branch to exercise checks on the executive branch until 1993. Indeed, in October 1991 Yeltsin had to ask the CPD for special decree powers to begin his reforms, which were granted for a year on the condition that the executive coordinated such reforms with the legislature. Nonetheless, from that point on Yeltsin proceeded in weakening legislative powers.

As noted, Yeltsin's goal was to strengthen his own power, which could only happen if the executive established its dominance over the legislature, a condition that did not exist in the fall of 1991 (McFaul 2001, 147). The president also concluded that shock therapy was incompatible with the democratic process (Reddaway and Glinski 2001). Accordingly, he moved quickly to insulate the policy-making process before the political opposition became too strong. Moreover, Yeltsin was not satisfied to obtain broad powers from Congress to enact economic reforms. In a matter of months he built up an administrative apparatus shielded from parliamentary oversight. According to McFaul (2001, 147), "Yeltsin also established several new positions and bodies within the presidential administration that effectively served as a parallel government." For instance, Yeltsin picked a handful of advisers, later named state councilors, who reported directly to the president. Not belonging to the government, these advisers could not be removed by the Congress of People's Deputies.

Much of the same power-concentration strategy applied at the local level. Yeltsin created the new post of "head of administration" to run the *oblasts* (regions). These people, who reported only to the executive, effectively worked as governors and de facto replaced the chairmen of the old Soviet Executive Committee at the *oblast* level. In turn, these new governors handpicked the mayors and other regional administrators within the *oblasts*, thus creating a vertical and homogeneous command structure accountable to the presidency. To make sure that these new administrators would remain personally loyal to him, Yeltsin created yet another institution at the subnational level, the "president representative," which shadowed the heads of the local administration. In practice, these bureaucrats served the purpose of making sure that local administrators would comply with executive decrees (McFaul 2001, 147–49).

Yeltsin justified his aggressive strategy of encroaching on legislative authority by arguing that the Supreme Soviet had been elected in 1990 and its deputies were Communists who opposed any meaningful reform. However, this was a deceiving argument. Congressmen were no more a relic of the Soviet past than Yeltsin and his cabinet. According to Reddaway and Glinski (2001, 374), although "more than 80 percent of the 1,041 members of the Congress of People's Deputies elected in March 1990 were members of the CPSU," Yeltsin's own cabinet had a ratio close to 100 percent. The point of the matter is that by the late 1980s very few members of the CPSU, let alone its top echelon, remained loyal to Marxist-Leninist principles (Solnik 1998). This is evidenced by the fact that the number of Communist deputies in October 1991 was about 6 percent (Reddaway and Glinski 2001, 374). The truth of the matter is that Yeltsin did not want any institutional restraints to the exercise of his power, regardless of the policy in question, and Congress was the most powerful obstacle remaining in his way. Leslie Gelb, a former U.S. State Department officer, described the situation: "The Russian parliament . . . has not been a reformer's delight, but it's not dominated by a bunch of right-wing crazies. . . . About one fifth of the deputies are hard-line nationalists. A roughly equal number are Yeltsin' loyalists. The diverse center group stretches from conservatives to industrial managers to former Yeltsin backers. . . . A solid majority of this parliament would pursue reforms more slowly than Mr. Yeltsin, but would not dream of reverting to Communism" ("How to Help Russia," New York Times, March 14, 1993).

Upon returning from Russia, Henry Kissinger made similar comments: "On economic policy, the major controversy concerns the pace, not the direction of reform. No significant group wants to return to the centrally planned system."[13] Even analysts supportive of the reforms found the depiction of the legislative branch as a nest of reactionaries an oversimplification (Yergin and Gustafson 1993, 76). In point of fact, in April 1992 Congress amended the constitution in order to strengthen presidential authority. For Hough (2001, 78), in several instances many deputies actually had no qualms with the reforms' final results as they actually "had a personal interest in the [privatization] and the concentration of the financial power in Moscow." By using presidential decrees Yeltsin actually relieved the legislature of its political responsibilities had things gone wrong. Indeed, the administration was able to have Congress approve much of its economic measures (Hough 2001, 78). The issue is that Yeltsin's autocratic style went too far too fast. By mid-1992 many members of the democratic

13. Washington Post, March 23, 1993. Kissinger also warned about the use of a referendum to overcome the executive-legislative gridlock as such a means "historically . . . has smoothed the way to dictatorship more frequently than democracy." The events proved him right.

movement in and out of Congress who had been some of Yeltsin's earliest supporters in 1990, including the vice president Alexander Rutskoi, eventually became so angered by the president's authoritarian style that they turned into some of his fiercest enemies. Contrary to the government-sympathetic media at the time, the hard core of the congressional opposition did not come from the *nomenklatura* (since Gaidar's policies were already ensuring the preservation of its privileges) or the Communists (who remained on the sideline) but rather "from the ranks of the democratic intelligentsia" (Reddaway and Glinski 2001, 376).

On those occasions when the CPD refused to cooperate with his plans, Yeltsin resorted to decrees and used a series of deceiving tactics, which escalated the confrontation with the legislature. Meanwhile, Gaidar and Chubais tried to shield their policies from public scrutiny by arguing that legislative oversight was going to be used by opponents of reforms to derail the process. A typical case in point was the privatization program that Chubais managed as head of the State Property Committee (GKI). On June 11, 1992, the Supreme Soviet approved a GKI proposal aimed at distributing property to the general population, which took the label of voucher privatization. A key feature of the legislation was that individuals could buy state property using nonnegotiable government-issued privatization checks bearing their name. On the same date, Chubais presented a substantially different privatization plan to the Council of Ministers that eliminated the bearer's name from the privatization checks, made them negotiable, and set a deadline for their use. The Council of Ministers approved the new privatization scheme and since the Supreme Soviet was going into its summer recess, Yeltsin decided to implement it through a decree in August, which infuriated most legislators (Nelson and Kuzes 1995, 48). This deception was in fact in open violation of Yeltsin's pledge to involve the CPD in drafting major legislation when he received emergency powers the previous October. Adding to the sense of betrayal were subsequent statements by government officials. When he first disclosed the original legislation, Chubais tried to win support for voucher privatization by arguing that the administration's aim was to turn citizens into property owners, but in addressing a congressional hearing in March 1994 he flatly denied that that was indeed the case (Nelson and Kuzes 1995, 48). The voucher privatization decree was also legally flawed. A report of the Supreme Council of the Supreme Soviet found that the divestiture program was in violation of the Russian Soviet Federal Socialist Republic law on registered privatization accounts and deposits. The report also warned that voucher privatization had little chance of improving economic conditions and could open the door to criminal activities (Nelson and Kuzes 1995, 51). Unfortunately, such misgivings turned out to be true.

To further emasculate the role of the legislative branch from mid-1992 on, Yeltsin resorted to the doctrine stating that a decree would automatically be approved if the legislature did not reject it within fourteen days from its adoption (Hough 2001, 78). According to the German weekly *Die Zeit*, "between 1991 and 1992, Yeltsin issued about 1,200 decrees and orders, of which strictly speaking 50 percent were illegal."[14] Executive-legislative relations deteriorated steadily with each side trying to subjugate the other. However, in December 1992 Congress showed its willingness to meet many of the president's demands in exchange for greater control on economic policy and the right to ratify presidential nominations for prime minister and the ministers of defense, interior, security, and foreign affairs. In return, legislators granted Yeltsin's request to hold a referendum on economic and social issues the following spring that could have seriously hampered their legitimacy. The armistice did not last long, though. On March 20, 1993, Yeltsin issued a decree that granted the executive extraordinary powers and suspended the Supreme Soviet's authority to nullify presidential decrees. This time, however, Yeltsin had to momentarily back off once the Constitutional Court ruled that such a decree was unconstitutional. This setback prompted Yeltsin's opposition in the CPD to file an impeachment motion, which narrowly failed. The legislature suffered another serious defeat when the April 1993 referendum showed that a majority of voters approved of his personal leadership as well as his economic policies.[15] This gave the administration the necessary ammunition to put the legislature on the defensive and insulate privatization from congressional oversight. In this regard, Chubais was quite outspoken when he declared that there would no longer be any congressional influence in the way the GKI was going to handle its job (Nelson and Kuzes 1995, 55).

As the fall of 1993 approached, Yeltsin proceeded to destroy the independence of the legislature once and for all. On September 21 the president

---

14. Quoted in Reddaway and Glinski (2001, 377).

15. The referendum asked if citizens (1) had confidence in the president, (2) approved of his reforms, (3) agreed on early presidential elections in 1993, and (4) approved of early elections of deputies in 1993.

issued decree 1,400.[16] It suspended several articles of the constitution and imposed presidential rule until December when Russians would go to the polls to vote in a referendum for a new constitution (that his advisers had drafted the previous spring) and to elect a new Congress. The decree also dissolved the CPD and the Supreme Soviet. Even scholars sympathetic to Yeltsin found this move to be highly controversial: "Yeltsin's decision to hold a referendum and parliamentary elections simultaneously was awkward, because he was asking people to vote for representatives to parliamentary elections bodies that did not exist. Had the referendum failed, the parliamentary elections would have been invalid. The simultaneity of these elections strongly suggest that Yeltsin and his associates were determined to make sure that the new constitution passed" (McFaul 2001, 215).

Since decree 1,400 amounted to a de facto coup, Rutskoi and the speaker of the house Ruslan Khasbulatov appealed its validity to the Constitutional Court, which found Yeltsin's measures in violation of the constitution. Shortly thereafter the Congress impeached the president and stripped him of his powers, precipitating the events. In the armed conflict that ensued in early October, Yeltsin prevailed by militarily crushing the legislature's resistance, resulting in a bloodbath.[17] Following these events the administration disbanded the CPD and Supreme Soviet, arrested Rutskoi, Khasbulatov, and many legislators, suspended the Constitutional Court, forced scores of independent union leaders and provincial administrators to resign, and closed several opposition newspapers (Reddaway and Glinski 2001, 429–30).

Despite this blatant repression and suppression of the rule of law (Yeltsin continued to rule autocratically until January 1994), the United States and the rest of the G-7 countries threw their support to Yeltsin as the "best hope" if market reforms were to prevail.[18] For the United States in particular, the geopolitical importance of Russia (its large nuclear capability) and the potential threat posed by Communists and nationalists in the Duma

16. In announcing the decree, Yeltsin admitted that he was in violation of the constitution but justified his action to rid the legislature of its "Communist" hardliners who were obstacles to reform.

17. It must be noted that contrary to Yeltsin's claim that the legislature had become the center of the old guard's resistance to his market reforms, the Communist Party leadership did not play any meaningful role during the bloody events of October 1993.

18. Secretary of State Warren Christopher summed up the West support: "The United States does not easily support the suspension of parliaments. But these are extraordinary times. The steps taken by President Yeltsin responded to exceptional circumstances." Quoted in Reddaway and Glinski (2001, 431).

created a special case. Yeltsin fully exploited this perception and time and again successfully lobbied the Clinton administration, demanding special treatment and a softening of the IMF and World Bank conditionality clauses. In turn, Clinton was instrumental in convincing the IMF and the World Bank to disburse large amounts of loans in 1993, 1996, and 1998, despite the repeated violations of the Russian government in meeting performance targets (Stone 2002). As Woods (2006, 114) noted, from 1992 onward Yeltsin "would alternately play to Russia's most powerful vested interests on the one hand and to more or less reformist governments, international financial institutions, and bilateral allies such as the United States on the other. In each case Yeltsin sought to maximize his own power and authority."

Having secured international support, Yeltsin took no chances to ensure a referendum victory. He issued a decree on October 15 that changed the rules regulating the referendum in his favor.[19] After the votes were cast in December, the president claimed victory. Official results showed that 54.4 percent of the electorate voted and 58.8 percent did so in favor of Yeltsin's constitution, but subsequent research suggested that the minimum threshold was never reached and the government probably engaged in widespread fraud (Reddaway and Glinski 2001, 432).

The 1993 constitution established an extremely powerful executive presiding over a subordinated bicameral system (Remington 2001), as Yeltsin had wished all along.[20] The president's advisers made sure that checks and balances were heavily skewed in favor of the president (McFaul 2001, 213). The new legislature consisted of the Duma (lower house, representing the population) and a weaker Federal Council (upper house, representing the country's eighty nine regions). The Duma no longer had any veto power over the appointment of ministers. While under the 1991 constitution the Duma appointed the prime minister, the 1993 version limited the lower house to a confirmation role, but after three consecutive rejections the executive could call for new legislative elections. Moreover, the 1993 constitution made it very difficult to impeach the president by limiting it to offenses

19. Under the existing statute a referendum was approved if 50 percent of those registered to vote decided in its favor. After the change, it took only 50 percent of those who actually voted to approve it.

20. Indeed, according to Shugart and Carey (1992), by the early 1990s Yeltsin had accrued the largest amount of power of any elected president examined in their cross-national analysis at the time.

such as treason or "high crimes" whose relevance had to be first determined by the Supreme Court. Under the new rules a two-third majority was necessary in both houses of Congress and the Supreme Court and Constitutional Court had to subsequently ratify the decision.

Executive veto powers over the legislature were substantially strengthened, and overriding them became very difficult as well. The same applied to presidential decrees that would now require a majority of both houses of parliament to be repealed. The new system assured Yeltsin that the legislature would not unite to challenge him due to the fact that the Federal Council representatives were elected by their regional legislatures, which, in turn, were heavily dependent for funds from federal transfers controlled by the executive (Reddaway and Glinski 2001, 568). In practice, this meant that Yeltsin had co-opted the Federal Council.

A further factor that helped the president in keeping the Duma at bay was that the large number of parties represented in the legislature made opposition building difficult. On paper, progovernment parties could master roughly 40 percent of the votes. However, Vladimir Zhirinovsky's far right Liberal Democrats, which claimed to be in the opposition, in reality supported Yeltsin on most issues, thus providing the president with a working majority (Hough 2001, 177). The same applies for other "opposition" parties such as the Women for Russia and the Agrarian Party.

The 1993 constitution also severely weakened legislative oversight of the executive branch thereafter.[21] The legislature's most powerful prerogative remained over fiscal policy, which required its approval. Nonetheless, on other policy areas there was little it could do. The Duma could still use its committees to pursue inquiries, but it had no means to sanction the executive or at least to force a compromise. It had been reduced to a mere advisory role at best.

Although some scholars argued that Yeltsin actually worked with Congress to enforce his legislative agenda more than he is credited for (Remington, Smith, and Haspel 1998), the reality was that the rules disproportionately favored the president and any attempt to defy his authority would have come at high cost. Opposition forces simply did not believe that they had the power to challenge Yeltsin. As McFaul (2001, 263) aptly put it, the president's parliamentary opponents "calculated that they were better off abiding by Yeltsin's new political institutional order, however

---

21. For a contrary opinion, see Granville and Oppenheimer (2001, 53).

flawed, than remobilizing for revolutionary confrontation." After all, the 1993 repression was a painful reminder of what Yeltsin was capable of and served as a powerful deterrent. Moreover, the new decree powers entrusted on the presidency allowed Yeltsin to easily bypass the legislature on most policy issues; when necessary, he showed no hesitation to use them. A typical example of this trend occurred in mid-1994 when the administration introduced a postvoucher privatization bill in the Duma. In announcing the bill, a defiant Chubais told the legislators that they had two weeks to ratify it as it was, otherwise he would implement it by decree. In July 1994 the Duma narrowly defeated the bill, but the next day Yeltsin issued a decree containing the same features that had been rejected (Nelson and Kuzes 1995, 160). The signal was clear. Either the Duma cooperated or would be ignored. A further indication of the Duma's weakness came in May 1994. In analyzing the privatization process, the Duma's Security Committee concluded that "55 percent of capital and 80 percent of voting shares [of enterprises] are in criminal hands, Russian and foreign" (Nelson and Kuzes 1995, 74). These were serious revelations with which most pundits seemed to agree. However, the legislature failed to act on them.

Summing up, Yeltsin succeeded in reversing the positive strides forward that Russia had made in the early 1990s in attempting to establish a Western-style democracy. The presidential system that ensued from the 1993 constitution was authoritarian in nature and operated with virtual impunity. It resembled more the defunct Soviet regime than the democratic system Yeltsin had promised only a few years earlier (Roeder 1994). Whatever accountability previously existed to a large degree disappeared because the legislature was either too weak or too inept to do anything about it. Gaidar, Chubais, and the young reformers chose political expediency over principle. They came to the conclusion that democratic ideals and institutions in Russia, oddly enough, were at odds with their quest for economic freedom. Thus, for them, steamrolling reforms through autocratic executive orders was the only way out, even if that meant sanctioning into law all kinds of abuses.

The Courts

As noted in chapter 1, strong legal institutions upholding the rule of law and property rights are fundamental prerequisites in the economic theories of Hayek and Friedman, whose ideas inspired Gaidar and Chubais in crafting their economic policies. However, such institutions did not exist in Russia when market reforms were introduced. Worse yet, the country's legal system was still the one of the Soviet era and in many ways was incompatible with the very tenets of the reform agenda (Hendley 1997). These problems notwithstanding, the Yeltsin administration showed little interest in legal reform, leading worried foreign observers to note from the start that economic policies were being pursued in a judicial vacuum.

Compounding the problem was the fact that both czarist and Communist regimes had used the legal system as a means to promote autocratic rule and, historically, the judiciary had been completely subordinate to the government. Thus, as far as the individual citizens were concerned, the law and its institutions were viewed with distrust and not as the ultimate source of authority (Solomon 1992). In economic transactions the popular approach was no different, as the law was "viewed as an obstacle to be manipulated, bypassed, and respected only when it fits one's interest" (Granville and Oppenheimer 2001, 10). Unfortunately, the Yeltsin administration often behaved in ways that reinforced such an ingrained cynicism and opportunistic behavior.

Despite this background, as McFaul (2001, 327) noted, in the early 1990s the democratic movement pushed for the establishment of an independent judiciary. In 1991 this resulted in the creation of the Constitutional Court, which quickly tried to assert its independence from political power and develop a jurisprudence in tune with Western standards. Indeed, it was one of the very few institutions that gained a certain degree of respectability abroad, particularly on human rights issues. However, the Constitutional Court lacked the power and resources to enforce its decisions. More troubling, though, was the fact that Yeltsin saw in the court's activism, particularly in trying to establish a doctrine of separation of powers, a menace to his own prerogatives. The president interpreted the court's decisions to side with the legislature on crucial moments during the 1992–93 period as a clear sign of court politicization at his expense. When the 1993 constitution came into effect, the Constitutional Court's powers were, therefore, substantially curtailed. Unlike in the past, the court could no longer take up what were considered "political issues," nor could it start a case on its own initiative. Moreover, it could no longer rule on the constitutionality of individual decisions by government officials such as the president. Likewise, the court could no longer examine pleadings by individual citizens challenging the validity of presidential decrees and other governmental regulations. Not surprising, these changes resulted in the Constitutional Court siding with the executive branch on most cases after 1993 (Nystèn-Haarala 2001). By the time it reconvened again in March 1995 the Constitutional Court had been purged of its most independent members. Adding to the problem was a series of clashes with the Supreme Court over issues of jurisdiction, which allowed lower courts to ignore rulings by both institutions (McFaul 2001, 327).

As for lower courts, although the 1992 Law of Judges granted life tenure to the judges, the 1993 constitution granted the presidency the right to nominate them. This meant that Yeltsin could exercise a substantial influence over the new judges and politicize them. Moreover, the executive could assert pressure on the judiciary since the Ministry of Justice controlled the courts' budgets, salaries, housing, and other perks (Solomon 1995). Thus, Yeltsin's initial efforts aimed to neutralize the courts from posing a problem rather than make them more efficient. In the short term, this strategy paid off as it assured the executive that the courts could not be used to challenge controversial privatizations and other market deregulation policies. However, such policies were based on shaky legal grounds, which could cause a flood of recourses once a new administration with different priorities would take over (Gustafson 1999). Indeed, after 1999 this is exactly what happened under president Vladimir Putin, who forced several companies out of business, claiming that the privatization contracts were legally flawed and had allowed companies to engage in tax evasion and other illegal practices during the Yeltsin years.[22]

Compounding these problems, ministries and agencies continued the old Soviet practice of issuing secret rules and directives in violation of the 1993 constitution, which had made them illegal. Yet such directives, which often ran counter to the tenets of the law they aimed to regulate, were widely used depending on the government's priorities. In the meantime, the Yeltsin administration seemed oblivious to reports of corruption within the judiciary supposedly growing out of control. Judicial rulings affecting most economic transactions could easily be sold and bought. In this regard there were "thousands of examples of the weakness of the Russian justice system—murders covered up, multi-million dollar court cases won by the party with the best connections or the fattest check-book" (Freeland 2000,

---

22. The most notorious case was Yukos, which the government repossessed in 2004 and whose chairman, Mikhail Kodorkovsky, was convicted on charges of tax fraud (*The Economist,* March 28, 2008).

20). This happened because many judges could operate with relative impunity and continue to sell their decisions or cooperate as long as they did not run afoul with their political sponsors.[23]

Oversight Institutions

Under Communism Russia did not have independent oversight institutions. The Procuracy of the Soviet system was a powerful means to support the Communist regime. It was in charge of judicial oversight (including the execution of law by ministries, departments, and special agencies) and criminal investigations. In 1992 the Supreme Soviet passed the Law of Procuracy, which reaffirmed the Procuracy's prerogatives. From an organizational standpoint, things remained the same.[24] Save for a few republics, the Procuracy remained highly centralized, with field offices across Russia. Under the new democratic system, the president appointed the general prosecutor, pending the Duma's approval. The general prosecutor worked under the supervision of the legislative branch and supervised the execution of the law by the federal administration and the legality of its own rules and regulations. The Procuracy could submit recommendations to address wrongdoings and appeal to the courts to nullify illegal government acts. Despite such powers and an avalanche of scandals, the procurator general, Yuri Skuratov, remained quiet through most of Yeltsin's tenure. For example, Hoffman (2002, 235) alleged that Skuratov's office dropped a major investigation on a massive fraud that led to the collapse of the MMM investment fund due to government pressure. Only in 1999, when Yeltsin had become a lame duck president, did Skuratov suddenly announce major inquiries on a variety of corruption and economic crimes affecting the president's daughters and 780 administration officials, including Chubais and Boris Berezovsky. Although Skuratov's charges were never proved, Yeltsin took no chances and tried, albeit unsuccessfully, to dismiss him.[25]

Oversight by government agencies and ministries was just as ineffective. In the Soviet Union individual ministries exercised great controls in terms

23. Until 1994 only one judge was removed from the bench due to corruption charges. Not until 1995 did the Duma approve new legislation making it easier to prosecute judges for misconduct.

24. The Law of Procuracy was amended on October 1995 to conform to the constitution of 1993.

25. The Federation Council, whose approval was necessary for the dismissal, voted against Yeltsin's request (*New York Times*, April 22, 1999).

of ownership and planning over their own enterprises. This, of course, came to be a problem for Chubais and his GKI since their priority was to expedite the state divestiture process as quickly as possible. The ministries constituted a serious stumbling block because they could modify the list of the companies being slated for privatization and their terms of sale. The 1992 privatization program assigned the ministries the right to approve the GKI's transfer plans affecting their own companies. On the one hand, ministries feared that the GKI's plans to break their companies and sell some of their units separately would hurt production cycles. On the other hand, Chubais believed that ministerial bureaucrats could use this prerogative to preserve the command economy and convinced Yeltsin to sign a decree in May 1993 that allowed the GKI to bypass the ministerial approval in many instances (Nelson and Kuzes 1995, 145). This is one of the factors that contributed to the escalation of the confrontation between the president and the legislature in the summer of 1993, which was discussed earlier. The CPD, in fact, sided with the ministries, claiming that the use of decree powers was illegal since it had not authorized their renewal. In the end, though, Chubais prevailed.

The Central Bank was equally ineffective. Although theoretically independent and accountable to the legislature, it was in practice dependent on Yeltsin on all major decisions (Hough 2001). The president retained the support of regional leaders, political cronies, SOE managers, and private businessmen by having the Central Bank subsidizing their operations through loans at very negative interest rates (Stone 2002). According to Sachs and Pistor (1997), this amounted, in GDP terms, to as much as 40 percent in 1992 and 20 percent in 1993. The Central Bank also stood idle in the face of illegal capital flight, although it had some power to curb it, primarily because it would have hurt too many people with powerful political connections (Hoffman 2002, 447). More to it, an audit by Pricewaterhouse Coopers found that the Russian Central Bank had funneled $1.2 billion of an IMF loan into offshore accounts in 1996.[26]

The other prominent institution was the General Accounting Office, which had investigative prerogatives but no means to prosecute offenses. It gained a good reputation for some of its high-profile investigations exposing government corruption. In response, the government usually accused it

---

26. "Foreign Loans Diverted in Monster Money Laundering? The Mafia, Oligarchs, and Russia's Torment," http://www.worldbank.org/html/prddr/trans/julaug99/pgs11–13.htm.

of being a tool in the hands of the Communists and antireform groups in the legislature. In 1995 its report on the "loans for shares" (henceforth LFS; see details later in this chapter) scandal described the collusion between the executive and the companies engaged in that transaction. In another instance, it denounced the mismanagement of a $30-million loan that the World Bank gave to the Yeltsin administration for partial compensation of those people who lost their investments in the voucher-privatization schemes. However, such funds never reached their intended recipients (Reddaway and Glinski 2001, 598). Unfortunately, neither Congress nor the judiciary used these findings to launch a major inquiry or criminal investigations since Yeltsin had pretty much neutralized both institutions.

The fight against corruption is another example of how Yeltsin prevented the executive-controlled oversight institutions from performing their functions. The president launched six different initiatives to crack down on state property theft, money laundering, inside trading, and other economic crimes as a way to appease public outcry. Yet whenever government-controlled agencies and special commissions started to uncover damaging evidence leading to top officials of the administration, Yeltsin systematically stopped the investigations and sacked those who conducted them. For instance, Yuri Boldyrev, whom the president had appointed as director of the anticorruption campaign in March 1992, was summarily dismissed after a year for allegedly having found serious wrongdoings implicating Yeltsin's entourage. The same fate affected the chief of internal security Viktor Ivanenko, a KGB (Committee for State Security) general who was fired in early 1992 after informing the president of criminal activity within his inner circle. Yeltsin also dismissed Vice President Rutskoi, who headed a special task force investigating government corruption in early 1993, fearing that some of the evidence the committee was gathering could be used against his administration (Klebnikov 2000, 121). Andrei Makarov, who headed another committee investigating corruption crimes, was forced out in November of the same year.[27]

Corruption

By the end of 1993 Yeltsin had concentrated a tremendous amount of authority in the presidency that allowed him to avoid congressional, judicial,

27. A detailed analysis of these events can be found in Waller and Yasmann (1995).

and administrative oversight to a large degree. The lack of control over executive authority opened plenty of opportunities for the abuse of power by government officials to an extent that shocked even the most seasoned foreign observers. However, as I just described, there was no institutional mechanism left in place to prevent illicit behavior from government officials. Both the domestic and foreign press kept disclosing scandal after scandal, but it fell on deaf ears since those in charge of enforcing the law were at the heart of the problem. During the Yeltsin tenure (1991–99) corruption was rampant and visible at any level, and market reforms became the prime target of illicit activities (Freeland 2000; Klebnikov 2000; Hoffman 2002; Goldman 2003). Privatization, for instance, was so overtly manipulated that disgusted citizens dubbed it "grabization" (*prikvatizatsiya*). A small minority of Russians, mostly coming from the ranks of the Soviet *nomenklatura*, was the main beneficiary of the reforms at the expense of ordinary citizens. Within this group an even smaller number of people referred to as the "oligarchs" came to dominate the new Russian entrepreneurial class. In a few years the oligarchs accrued large fortunes by cutting sweet deals for themselves using government resources thanks to the complicity of high-ranking administration officials. The cozy relationship between the Yeltsin administration and the oligarchs resulted in government decisions tailored to the oligarchs' enrichment. It amounted to the "privatization" of policy making. As Berezovsky, the most controversial of the oligarchs, candidly put it at the apex of the oligarchs' alliance with Yeltsin shortly after the 1996 elections, "government should represent the interest of business."[28]

Most reform policies were exploited for corrupt ends in one way or another. In addition to privatization, which received the greatest attention from both domestic and foreign analysts, market deregulation, trade liberalization, and the reform of government subsidies were all marred by irregularities. In defending their record, Gaidar, Chubais, and their foreign advisers argued that their original intention was to sell SOEs for cash to outside bidders (as opposed to company managers) in order to bring fresh capital and new management skills, but this proved politically unfeasible (Gustafson 1999, 39). Their argument was that to succeed privatization needed the support from the industrial managers, had to be kept simple, and needed to be executed quickly before opposition could derail it. Attaining these goals implied making undesirable compromises that ran counter

28. *Komerzant*, November 16, 1995.

to transparency and best business practices. Yet according to this view, the choice was between privatizing in a quick and dirty fashion or not privatizing at all. Åslund (2002, 279–80), who advised Chubais in crafting the state divestiture program, summed up the young reformers' defense: "Privatization became the art of the possible. . . . As a consequence, the strategies involving little corruption were downgraded to the benefit of strategies that offered privileges. . . . Hence, the problem was not that privatization by itself caused corruption, but that only reasonably corrupt forms of privatization were politically acceptable."[29]

However, this ex-post justification has been challenged by many Russian and foreign scholars who believe that more democratic and transparent forms of state divestitures were possible. Instead, Yeltsin preferred to go the corrupt way because it was politically expedient, as it would lure the support of oligarchs and red directors into his camp.[30]

Yeltsin's defenders also point out that the Law on Property of 1990 had already opened a Pandora's box to all kinds of illegal activities as it dismantled most controls over management. However, Yeltsin made things worse when he issued a decree in November 1991 that freed SOE managers in supply and distribution companies from the commercial obligations they had had up until then. By default, the red directors could take management control and manipulate their own enterprises for personal use without fearing control of the Soviet bureaucratic apparatus. For some analysts this amounted to the right to steal.[31] These reforms also permitted managers to create cooperatives that took control over the company cash flow, which eventually found its way in safe accounts abroad. By de facto controlling their companies (and in many cases looting them too), the red directors made up a lobbying group with considerable influence. By promoting price liberalization prior to privatization, Gaidar effectively destroyed the possibility of spreading ownership among the population, as it had been proposed in the 500 Days Plan. The hyperinflation ensuing from the price liberalization of early 1992 wiped out people's savings. This allowed only a handful of individuals who had grown rich by taking advantage of Gorba-

29. It is important to add that in the early 1990s Åslund was one of the most influential foreign experts who embraced the idea that shock therapy had to come first on the assumption that it would eventually pave the way for political reforms.

30. For an analysis of this debate, see Reddaway and Glinski (2001, 252–55).

31. The comment was made by economist Larisa Piiasheva, quoted in Nelson and Kuzes (1995, 44).

chev's reforms to acquire most SOEs. Under pressure from Yeltsin to make concessions to the red directors, and fearing that the quick deterioration of the economic situation could stop the privatization process from moving forward, Gaidar and Chubais decided to make the red directors the new capitalist class of Russia (Shleifer and Boycko 1993). In so doing, Chubais and Gaidar claimed that they had achieved two important goals. They stopped the "spontaneous" privatization already under way and turned the red directors into their allies, which helped them thwart the opposition of the Communists, the ministerial bureaucracy, and regional leaders who wanted to retain government ownership. In June 1992 the Supreme Soviet approved the new privatization law that came to be known as "variant two."[32] This legislation granted workers and management the right to buy 51 percent of controlling shares at very discounted prices and prevented outsiders from gaining control of the company. As Freeland (2000, 57) noted, "it was the most generous provision for company insiders any privatization in the world had ever offered." Not surprising, about 75 percent of Russian SOEs were divested using this mechanism (Goldman 2003, 80). In the end, the red directors easily outmaneuvered the workers and took managing control of their companies. They did so by buying workers' shares at a minimal cost to themselves and preventing their employees from selling to outsiders through technicalities and intimidation tactics (Gustafson 1999, 47). Of course, this ran counter to the spirit of the reform, but, as I argued earlier, the Yeltsin administration had political rather than economic objectives in mind. In fact, if the red directors tried to acquire more of their companies than variant two allowed, Chubais and the GKI looked the other way (Freeland 2000, 70). Theft had been sanctioned by law.[33]

Retrospectively, Gaidar admitted that variant two was a mistake (Goldman 2003, 81), but given the circumstances some argue that the young reformers had very little room to maneuver.[34] This is probably true, but the young reformers bear serious responsibilities for leaving minority shareholders, who later bought into the privatized companies, legally defenseless against the abuses of majority stakeholders. The legal vacuum discussed

32. For a detailed description, see Goldman (2003, 80–81).
33. Allegedly, Chubais was thoroughly disgusted by the corruption practices of the red directors turned businessmen, but he hoped that in the end the market would turn them into efficient property owners. The pragmatic explanation of the reformers was "corruption for the sake of democracy" (Freeland 2002, 70).
34. For a sympathetic view of Gaidar and Chubais's decision, see Shleifer and Treisman (2000).

earlier allowed fraudulent practices that kept a corrupt and often incompetent management on top. The most emblematic case of this trend was the giant gas monopoly Gazprom, whose chairman, Viktor Chernomyrdin, replaced Gaidar as deputy prime minister in December 1992. Gazprom not only controlled the world's largest gas reserves but was also the country's most important exporter. Chernomyrdin first secured 15 percent of the company shares for management and workers and then made sure that another 35 percent would be sold at closed auctions in remote Siberian locations, which allowed management to keep out outsiders.[35] Furthermore, Prime Minister Chernomyrdin granted his successor at Gazpromr, Rem Vyakhirev, the right to vote at shareholder meetings in representation of the Russian state, which had kept 40 percent of voting shares.[36] Jeffrey Sachs, who had advised Gaidar early in the reform effort, contended that Gazprom had been literally "stolen" and suggested that the company be nationalized again and then privatized in a more transparent manner (Freeland 2000, 74–75).

Gazprom, unfortunately, was not an isolated case. As Åslund (2002, 275) acknowledged, "embezzlement hardly diminished after . . . privatization, as the new majority owners defrauded shareholders through transfer pricing." By 1996 the Russian Federal Securities Committee estimated that 65 percent of the privatized SOEs were controlled by insiders whereas the outsiders' share was no more than 17 percent.[37]

The reformers' responsibilities were just as serious in subsequent scandals affecting privatization. One affected the so-called voucher privatization program, which was mentioned earlier. Vouchers complemented the variant two strategy as they allowed people to buy the remaining shares that had been set aside for the public once red directors and workers had exercised their option rights.[38] Chubais's aim was to spur some semblance of popular capitalism, which could shore up the government popularity and, at the same time, create the basis for a security market by increasing stock

---

35. According to former finance minister Boris Fyodorov, upon the privatization of Gazprom in November 1992, Chernomyrdin received 1 percent of the company's stock, which by 1995 was worth $1 billion. Details on Chernomyrdin's alleged corruption deals through Gazprom were reported in the *New York Times* (Reddaway and Glinski 2001, 444, 487).

36. According to the Central Intelligence Agency (CIA), Chernomyrdin through Gazprom and other shady deals had accumulated a fortune estimated at $5 billion (Klebnikov 2000, 114).

37. *Financial Times*, September 6, 1996, p. 10.

38. Each citizen was granted 10,000 rubles' worth of vouchers, which could be redeemed by paying 25 rubles, equivalent to US$0.10.

ownership. At the beginning, the program was hailed as a success since 146 million Russians, or about 98 percent of the eligible population, chose to use vouchers.[39] Vouchers could be traded at auction for shares or for shares in what became known as "voucher funds." Such funds sprung up so quickly that by February 1994 some 620 of them were in business (Goldman 2003, 88).

Technically, managers of voucher funds, once they obtained vouchers from individuals in return for their shares, would then cash in customers' vouchers for privatized companies' stock. The assumption was that the new privatized firms would pay high dividends, which in turn would be used to pay off the funds' investors. In the early days of the voucher frenzy, many funds promised yields often double the inflation rate, which in 1994 alone increased by 215 percent.[40] Considering that bank deposits during the same year paid interests at around 50 percent, approximately twenty-five million people found the temptation of voucher funds too strong to resist and some put their life savings into them (Goldman 2003, 88). There were two major problems with this type of investment. First, only a handful of privatized firms ever paid any dividends as the red directors, freed from any government control, kept the profits for themselves. Second, the security markets operated without any regulation that could protect investors' rights from unscrupulous fund managers. Gaidar and Chubais had omitted to support the infant capital markets with institutions and laws that could make them run in a transparent manner.[41] The newly constituted Department of Securities and Financial Markets in the finance ministry was just trying to catch up with the fast pace of events and had no real power to timely intervene if things went wrong, which they did (Åslund 2002, 281; Hoffman 2002, 225).[42] In fact, many voucher funds turned out to be financial pyramids, which paid high interests by using money deposited by new customers to earlier investors. However, most funds either squandered the money in bad financial ventures or, quite often, were scams in which the fund managers

---

39. *Ekonomika I Zhizn'* 7 (February 1999): 3. Vouchers were distributed in the fall of 1992.

40. A typical example was the Tekhnichesky Progress fund, which lured 300,000 small investors in 1993 by promising interests of 500 percent only to disappear shortly afterward (Klebnikov 2000, 138).

41. In early 1992 the Yeltsin economic team had debated whether to create a security commission, but the project never took off for lack of interest (Hoffman 2002, 225).

42. Legislation protecting minority shareholders' rights was finally approved in 1998 but was not enforced (Granville and Oppenheimer 2001, 10).

ran away with the money never to be seen again (Pistor and Spicer 1996).[43]
As the trick began to be uncovered and people tried to recover their money
in the summer of 1994, most funds went bankrupt in rapid fashion. In the
wake of the collapse of the MMM fund, the largest one, the Yeltsin administration not only denied any government responsibility but also stopped a
judicial inquiry about it as it was mentioned earlier.

The privatization process also provided Russian organized crime, which
had mushroomed to alarming proportions during the Gorbachev era, a
golden opportunity to invest its profits in legitimate business. In early 1993
Yeltsin himself acknowledged that as much as two-thirds of Russian commercial businesses were linked to the mob (Klebnikov 2000, 29). Nonetheless, the Yeltsin administration's privatization policies actually helped
organized crime diversify its portfolio.[44] In fact, at the beginning of the
voucher program the government eliminated the requirement that forced
people to disclose the source of their income if they wanted to invest large
amounts of money in privatized companies (Nelson and Kuzes 1995, 53).
As expected, the mob took full advantage of this situation. According to
the Ministry of Internal Affairs, about 60 percent of SOEs had been infil-
trated by organized crime, along with 85 percent of the banks and 40 percent of the private businesses (Klebnikov 2000, 29). This situation
prompted Petr Fillipov, a Yeltsin adviser, to admit that privatization had
earned an indisputable criminal character (Fillipov 1994). Polls showed that
the public had come to the same conclusion, as 82 percent of respondents
in one survey believed that mobsters were among the greatest beneficiaries
of the divestiture program (Nelson and Kuzes 1995, 203).

Privatizations managed at the local level often did not fare any better.
The city of Moscow was the most visible case. The city mayor, Yuri Luzkov,
pledged his political support for Yeltsin during his confrontation with the
legislature in 1992. In return, Luzkov received the president's permission to
have sole jurisdiction over the SOEs of his city, thus sheltering him from
Chubais's GKI, with whom he had clashed repeatedly (Boycko, Shleifer, and

43. According to Hoffman (2002, 197), ninety-nine voucher funds disappeared without a
trace.
44. According to the U.S. Federal Bureau of Investigation (FBI), government corruption was
the single most important factor that helped the financial success of the Russian mobsters. In
1996 John Deutsch, then CIA director, informed Congress that crime organizations had close
links with Duma representatives (Klebnikov 2000, 37).

Vishny, 1995). Then he proceeded to create a financial empire built around a company named Systema, which by 1996 had assets worth $1 billion (Hoffman 2002, 266). A good deal of Systema's profits came from lucrative city contracts and privatization of municipal companies. It was not unusual for representatives of Systema and other businesses friendly with Luzkov to serve on the city property committee in charge of awarding companies in which they were interested (Handelman 1995). The most lucrative state divestiture was the concession rights for the Moscow telephone monopoly, which was awarded to a front company controlled by Systema without any clear terms or conditions.[45] Regional governments that handled privatization were just as effective in awarding companies to well-connected cartels or even front companies owned by politicians in office (Gustafson 1999, 30).

Another strategy used by members of the *nomenklatura* was the so-called virtual privatization. This consisted in gaining control over the cash flow of an SOE still in government hands. SOE managers could do so often due to Gorbachev and Yeltsin's reforms, mentioned earlier, which made companies independent from most controls. Company outsiders could achieve the same goal by co-opting the SOE management or obtaining presidential authority if management opposed them. Organized crime could simply use intimidation and be just as effective. Many oligarchs built part of their fortunes using this stratagem. Berezovsky was the oligarch who pioneered this modus operandi. He started out by purchasing cars from the Avtovaz automobile company, which generated a loss for the SOE and a hefty profit for himself. He then moved to controlling the advertising cash flow of the Russian Public Television (ORT). On both occasions, this resulted in huge losses for the SOEs, which were left with paying salaries and debt but without their earnings. Once both companies were slated for privatization, Berezovsky used his political influence with President Yeltsin to acquire their controlling equity stake. On November 29, 1994, the president signed a decree that, in violation of the existing privatization law, awarded 49 percent of ORT shares to Berezovsky for only $2.2 million (Hoffman 2002, 281; Klebnikov 2000, 159). In return, Berezovsky turned the country's largest television network into a strong supporter of the Yeltsin administration. In yet another case, Berezovsky tried the same approach with the national airline Aeroflot in 1995. Through a number of shell companies, the oligarch

---

45. Gaidar publicly denounced Luzkov's corrupt practices, which ended up in court where eventually a judge dropped the case without explaining his decision (*Moskovska Pravda*, October 29, 1998).

obtained from Yeltsin the right to manage the airline's funds and publicity relations for extremely high fees despite the fact that the company had no need for those services to be outsourced (Klebnikov 2000, 186). Aeroflot's management questioned why private companies were hired to manage the airline's hard currency revenues, but the standard reply was that they were needed to fund Yeltsin's reelection campaign in 1996. When Aeroflot chairman Yevgeny Shapashnikov joined his subordinates in questioning Berezovsky's management when the airline profits had turned into severe losses, he was replaced with Valery Okulov in 1997. Okulov's main qualification for the job was being one of Yeltsin's sons-in-law and a friend of Berezovsky. The scheme collapsed only when in 1999 Berezovsky fell out of political favor and a suddenly energized prosecutor general office started a criminal investigation against the oligarch for having "diverted" $973 million of Aeroflot money (Goldman 2003, 141).

Trade deregulation was another example of well-meaning reforms that went terribly wrong. Yeltsin's decree liberalizing trade in early 1992 gave a golden opportunity to organized crime and members of the *nomenklatura* placed in strategic positions to make fortunes at the expense of the national treasury. The decree allowed select private companies to buy Russia's most profitable export commodities (oil, gas, nickel, timber, etc.) at controlled prices and then to sell them abroad at many times over the original price. The special export licenses that the government awarded to well-connected businesses and cooperatives often included clauses that granted them tax-exempt status.[46] This meant that such export companies could get an additional windfall because they could import Western goods in high demand and sell them at inflated prices without paying taxes. As Mikhail Khodorkovsky, one of the most successful oligarchs at the time, explained, what mattered in such a business was to have good political connections in high places (Hoffman 2002, 101), which usually implied corrupting government officials. By 1993 there were plenty of press reports detailing how high-ranking government officials were receiving kickbacks deposited in Swiss accounts for granting special import-export licenses (Klebnikov 2000, 122). Much of the wealth of the Russian oligarchs was initially accumulated in this way. Compounding the problem was the fact that a large amount of the money made by private export companies in this fashion was deposited

---

46. The National Sports Fund, for instance, accrued through export-import licenses an estimated $1.8 billion in a couple of years alone during the early 1990s (Klebnikov 2000, 231).

through shell companies all over the world.[47] By the end of 1994 the bulk of commodity exports was handled by private companies (Klebnikov 2000, 97). This translated in a massive illegal capital flight estimated between $127 billion and $350 billion from 1992 to 1998 (Table 3.1).[48] The finance ministry also estimated that tax exemptions and other loopholes deprived the government of an additional $5 billion yearly (Freeland 2000, 104). In early 1995 this state of affairs prompted the IMF to require Russia to eliminate such sweet deals. The Russian government reluctantly agreed, but despite its pledge the Yeltsin administration crackdown was lax and many schemes continued to survive for a few more years (Fischer 1998).

The privatization of government resources came at a time when Russia could least afford it and had major consequences for the crumbling state finances. In fact, in 1995 alone the budget deficit was $10 billion, which forced government to cut essential services. From 1993 onward one of Yeltsin's stratagems to reduce the fiscal deficit was the delaying of wage and pension payments (Woods 2006, 114). This resulted in 26 percent of the population falling below the poverty line, as opposed to no more than 5 percent in Soviet times. By 1996 wage and salary arrears climbed to $4.5 billion (Tikhomirov 2000, 154). However, such tactics could only go so far given the mounting fiscal deficit. Thus, the Yeltsin administration found the easy way out by borrowing more and more from abroad since the IMF and the World Bank, under pressure from the United States and other Western governments, were willing to wave or relax important loan clauses. Russia's own foreign debt (as opposed to the one inherited from the Soviet Union) rose from $8.8 billion in 1993 to $55.2 billion in 1998 (Table 3.2). This implied a yearly average of $18.1 billion worth of interest payments falling due during the same period, once the debts of the old Soviet Union were added.

Oligarchs, red directors, *nomenklatura* members, and mobsters were the primary beneficiaries of the market reforms. As mentioned earlier, government officials also found a way to enrich themselves by using their discre-

---

47. Capital flight was facilitated through tax treaties with other countries. Companies registered in Cyprus, for instance, could send their profits back to the Mediterranean isle without paying a 20 percent surcharge. Despite being cash starved, neither Yeltsin nor the Duma showed any interest in closing this loophole (Klebnikov 2000, 100). For the higher estimate, see "Foreign Loans Diverted in Monster Money Laundering? The Mafia, Oligarchs, and Russia's Torment," http://www.worldbank.org/html/prddr/trans/julaug99/pgs11–13.htm.

48. Other estimates on capital flight put the total at $97 billion between 1992 and 1997 (Tikhomirov 2000, 155).

tionary powers to pick the reforms' winners and losers. In 1995 Chubais, now deputy prime minister, received (along with four of his aides) a $450,000 cash advance for a book contract on privatization from a publishing house controlled by oligarch Vladimir Potanin, who had just won the privatization bid for the giant telecommunication SOE Sviazinvest. Alfred Kokh, who had replaced Chubais as GKI chief in 1995 and directly managed the Sviazinvest privatization, was found to have accepted a $100,000 honorarium for another book by a company allegedly linked to Potanin's Onexim Bank. While the amounts were small and evidence of bribe taking was never found, the book contracts destroyed the credibility of the young reformers as civil servants of superior moral standards (Freeland 2000, 289–96). In February 1996 Chubais was temporarily dismissed from his government post, but shortly thereafter he received an interest-free $3-million loan from oligarch Alexander Smolensky, which by 2002 had yet to be repaid (Goldman 2003, 142).[49]

Foreign consultants were not immune from scandals either. Between 1992 and 1997 the U.S. Agency for International Development (USAID) gave Harvard's Institute for International Development (HIID) more than $60 million to help Russia first with its privatization effort and, later, to reform its legal system and design capital market regulations. Ironically, the noted Harvard economist Andrei Shleifer, whose works were regarded as some of the best analyses of the Yeltsin administration, came under fire. In 2000 the U.S. government sued Shleifer (the head of the HIID program in Russia) and his associate Jonathan Hay for defrauding the USAID of $30 million by using inside information to invest in Russian securities through family members. According to the civil suit, this constituted a violation of conflict-of-interest clauses of the USAID grant. The suit stated that Shleifer and Hay, instead of promoting "transparency [and] the rule of law," had taught the Russians the "opposite lesson: that good connections were more important than fair play."[50] In August 2005 Harvard and Shleifer reached a settlement with the U.S. Justice Department.[51]

Another major source of corruption came from government regulation.

49. The money went into a foundation that Chubais had just created called Center for the Defense of Private Property.

50. *Wall Street Journal*, October 12, 2004, A1 and A10.

51. Harvard University and Shleifer agreed to pay $26.5 million and $2 million in damages, respectively. Shleifer's wife had previously settled out of court for $1.5 million (*Boston Globe*, March 25, 2006).

Contrary to the spirit of market reforms, under Yeltsin not only did the government bureaucracy increase in size, as we shall see later, but so did its regulatory intrusion in business transactions. This was possible because the federal and local governments in many cases actually expanded their regulatory powers, which allowed government officials to extort bribes. As an illustrative example, a deputy governor admitted that in order to open a new business in his Siberian region a company had to bribe around forty bureaucrats (Freeland 2000, 268). As described by Shleifer and Vishny (1998, 231), politicians "use regulatory powers to create rents for their allies, who presumably share with them, as well as to collect bribes." Upon assuming the office of acting president in December 1999, Putin acknowledged that there were fifty-one different agencies overseeing business operations (Goldman 2003, 212). In short, as regulation remained pervasive and highly discretionary, it created plenty of opportunities for corruption, which in turn undermined market reforms. Regulatory-driven corruption was particularly hard on small businesses, which after a fast start in the early 1990s failed to grow beyond 10 percent of GDP. In explaining why small businesses thrived in Poland but not in Russia, Frye and Shleifer put the blame squarely on the Russian bureaucracy. They found that it took four times as long for Russian entrepreneurs to get all the necessary permits compared to their Polish counterparts.[52] Some businessmen also blamed Gaidar, whose reforms at times made things worse (Nelson and Kuzes 1995, 108). For his part, Yeltsin not only condoned this phenomenon but was an active participant since he issued a barrage of new federal regulations and allowed regional governors to do the same if they supported him. In fact, politicians at the local level retained extensive power over economic life, which allowed them to play a predatory role at the expense of economic growth (Shleifer and Vishny 1998, 233). Indeed, for Shleifer and Vishny the reason why shock therapy was capable of promoting growth in Poland, but not in Russia, is that under Yeltsin regulatory policy was extremely extensive, politicized, and inherently corrupt.

Yeltsin himself seemed to have personally benefited from dispensing favors. In 1997 the Swiss prosecutor general Carla del Ponte alerted Skuratov that a company by the name of Mabetex, based in Switzerland, had been paying about $10 million to Yeltsin and his daughters through a variety of

52. Cited in Goldman (2003, 213).

accounts in return for government contracts (Reddaway and Glinksi 2001 604–6).[53]

Collusion and Crony Capitalism

Unfortunately, the Yeltsin administration actively promoted collusion and uncompetitive behavior, which in turn became a formidable obstacle to economic growth. The most notorious and best-documented case of collusion is the LFS deal (Hedlund 1999). By early 1995 the young reformers had failed to bring inflation under control and privatization had been disappointing since it raised revenues well below the GKI's initial forecasts.[54] At the same time, with the tax base shrinking and federal expenditures still out of control, the government faced a severe revenue shortfall.[55] This was even more troublesome because in 1996 Yeltsin planned to run for reelection and needed economic stability and the necessary financial resources to appease his clientelistic networks if he were to win a second term. Under the leadership of Potanin, the most prominent oligarchs proposed to loan to the government $2 billion to meet its obligations. As collateral Yeltsin would allow the oligarchs' banks to auction off the right to manage the government's shares in some of the country's most profitable SOEs in oil and raw materials until the loan would come due in September 1996. In the event the government could not honor its debt, it would pay the oligarchs' banks a hefty commission and allow them to sell the shares of the same SOEs in 1997. The first auction phase would take place in late 1995 and the second in late 1996 (Moser and Oppenheimer 2001). In practice this meant that the first auction process would be rigged to allow the participating oligarchs to receive the managing rights while in the second auction they would buy themselves what they were supposed to sell to private tenders.

The quid pro quo between the Yeltsin administration and the oligarchs was not just financial but political. The oligarchs and the president shared the same enemy: the Communists. The failure of shock therapy, and the

---

53. Skuratov launched an investigation, which was bitterly opposed by Yeltsin. In the end, Yeltsin's sudden resignation in December 1999 put an end to Skuratov's quest.

54. In 1995 privatization revenues raised only 143 billion rubles instead of the expected 8.7 trillion rubles (Hoffman 2002, 309).

55. Between 1992 and in 1996 federal tax revenues in terms of GDP declined by 40 percent (from 17.8 percent in 1992 to 10.7 percent). Conversely, federal government expenditures dropped only by 15 percent (from 26 percent to 22.1 percent) during the same period (Woods 2006, 124).

corrupt nature of privatization and economic deregulation, had destroyed the president's popularity. Conversely, the Communists had regained substantial popular support and scored an impressive victory in the Duma elections of December 1995. By agreeing to LFS, Yeltsin assured himself the support of the oligarchs for the 1996 presidential contest. This was deemed vital because many of the oligarchs participating in LFS not only could finance the president's campaign but had the potential to swing public opinion through the use of the television and printed media, much of which had come under their control since 1991. For their part, the oligarchs needed Yeltsin to consolidate their fortunes, which were likely to be expropriated under a Communist administration. Decree 889 authorizing LFS in August 1995 was a marriage of convenience. It would inexorably tie the oligarchs' fortunes to those of the president at the expense of the Russian people.[56]

Eventually, thanks also to the oligarchs' media campaign in his favor, Yeltsin won a second term in June 1996. The following September, to no one's surprise, the administration declared that it did not have the money to repay its loan and allowed the oligarchs of the LFS deal to manage the privatization process of selected SOEs, as agreed upon in 1995. To avoid competition, the oligarchs decided in advance who would get what and occasionally would help one another prevent unwanted competition (Freeland 2000, 174). The 1995 auctions were, as agreed upon, completely rigged because the oligarchs' banks were often, at the same time, auction managers and bidders (Hoffman 2002, 315). Foreigners were not allowed and competing Russian groups never had a chance. A few cases illustrate the point. A consortium of Potanin's Onexim Bank won the bid for Norilsk, the world's largest producer of nickel, by offering $170.1 million ($100,000 more than the floor price) even though a company controlled by the Rossiisky Kredit Bank had offered $335 million (Klebnikov 2000, 205). Because it controlled the bidding process Onexim Bank disqualified the higher bid, claiming that it lacked the necessary financial guarantees. Interestingly enough, one of the companies in Potanin's consortium itself lacked the necessary financial credentials. The same story repeated itself in the auction of the oil company Sidanco, again controlled by Onexim Bank. Rossiisky Kredit Bank's competing bid was rejected, but this time for lacking the necessary deposit. The

---

56. The September 1996 deadline for the loan repayment and the 1997 privatization plan were scheduled on purpose after the June 1996 presidential elections so that the oligarchs could not defect Yeltsin.

winner was another company controlled by Potanin, which bid $5 million more than the minimum price. Rossiisky Kredit Bank appealed to GKI's president, Alfred Kokh, who supervised the auction, but was rebuffed. Potanin's efforts paid off handsomely. In 2000 Norilsk alone posted $1.5 billion in profits (Goldman 2003, 120).

Khodorkovsky's Menatep Bank was in charge of the Yukos oil company auction.[57] During the LFS negotiations Khodorkovsky had been instrumental in inserting a clause that would keep foreign bidders out because he feared that oil companies would have been attractive to large multinationals with plenty of cash to spare.[58] Laguna, a front company controlled by Menatep Bank, won the auction by bidding $159 million, or just $9 million over the starting price. Despite the fact that Khodorkovsky used hardball tactics to stop potentially competitive bids, a consortium of rival Russian banks offered $350 million but was disqualified over a technicality (Hoffman 2002, 317–18).[59]

Another major oil company on the auction block was Sibneft. Berezovsky managed to win its bidding process by putting pressure on the only other competing group, Inkom Bank, to quit. Because the bidding procedures required a minimum of two bidders, a front for Menatep Bank participated with no intention of making any serious attempt. In fact, Menatep Bank was part of the consortium headed by Berezovsky, who gained control of Sibneft by paying a meager $100.3 million, which was just $300,000 over the floor price. When the chairman of Inkom Bank later denounced to the press how the auctions of the LFS deal had been fixed, the Russian Central Bank, rather than launching an investigation over the nature of the transaction, began to harass Inkom Bank (Klebnikov 2000, 207).

The sham just described was carried out with the complicity of Chubais and Kokh, who had assured the press, before the whole process started, that the auctions would be "free and competitive" (Hoffman 2002, 314).[60] Had they been true to their words, the Russian government could have earned a sizable amount of money to pay for back wages and pensions and rescue

57. Khodorkovsy was appointed special adviser to the minister of fuel and energy in 1991 and from this insider position began to co-opt Yukos's management.

58. Foreigners were barred from seven companies that happened to be the most lucrative, including Yukos, Norilsk, Lukoil, and Sidanko.

59. In the case of Surgut, the auction was held at a remote company site in Siberia. Oligarch Vladimir Bogdanov, who already managed the company, prevented truly competing bids from being filed by closing the local airport on auction day.

60. For a defense of Chubais in the LFS affair, see Åslund (2002, 298–99).

a public health system that was falling apart for lack of funds. Instead the Yeltsin administration sold its shares in SOEs, whose exports up until then had generated a substantial portion of its revenues, for a fraction of their value in order to forge a political alliance. Systematically, at each auction the winning bid offered just over the minimum price, which is a clear sign of collusion. The LFS turned out to be a bonanza for the participating oligarchs. As can be seen in Table 3.3, the sale of the management rights in 1995 generated around $682 million. The winners of the second auction phase (1996–97) were exactly the same as in the first one.[61] In August 1997 the market value of the same companies was $39.7 billion. Yukos alone was worth an estimated $30 billion in 2004.[62]

Adding insult to injury were subsequent press reports that much of the money used by the oligarchs' banks in the LFS deal was coming from the government's own funds either in the form of loans or deposits to pay state employees or bills. The oligarchs' banks would receive Central Bank loans at interest rates well below the inflation rate and then use such funds not for making loans themselves but for lucrative financial speculations such as short-term GKOs (Gosudarstvennye Kratosrochnye Obyazatyelstva). GKOs were government bonds yielding up to an average of 100 percent or more in dollar terms.[63] The same banks were also notorious for delaying for months the payment of government wages so that they could use those funds for their own speculative activities without incurring in any sanction by the Central Bank (Klebnikov 2000, 210). Some of the oligarchs even supplemented government funds under their control with cash coming from the very companies they were trying to acquire. Kokh, for instance, hinted that the president of Yukos, Sergei Muravlenko, gave Khodorkovsky some of his company's money to finance Menatep Bank's bid on Yukos's stake (Hoffman 2002, 317–18). These events created such a scandal that in January 1996 Yeltsin, claiming that he had been kept in the dark, fired

---

61. Kokh explained the oligarchs' rationale in the second auction phase of the LFS deal: "For two years we have been investing our brains, time, and money into this enterprise. Now what am I supposed to do—sell it to someone else? Of course . . . I will sell it to myself" (Klebnikov 2000, 267).

62. Klebnikov 2000.

63. It was customary for banks to pay back their loans long past the deadline and it was not unusual for them not to pay at all. Government officials supervising these loans usually looked the other way either because they were corrupt or physically intimidated. Oligarchs such as Smolensky, Gusinsky, Khodorkovsky, and Berezovsky, thanks to their political connections, enjoyed special authorizations for handling government accounts and receiving credit from the Central Bank (Hoffman 2002, 316–32, 412).

Chubais, stating that his deputy prime minister had "sold off big industry for next to nothing. We cannot forgive this" (Hoffman 2002, 324). However, Yeltsin's ire did not last long. Two months later a grateful Berezovsky, the most powerful Russian oligarch, asked Chuabis (with Yeltsin's blessing) to orchestrate the president's reelection campaign (Weir 2004).

The international community had serious responsibilities in the LFS affair. In spite of the serious misgivings coming from their field officers stationed in Moscow, the IMF and the World Bank remained silent about the crooked nature of the LFS arrangement and continued to publicly regard the Russian privatization policy as a success.[64] At the time, the Clinton administration was exercising strong pressure on both institutions to support Yeltsin in his reelection bid to prevent a Communist comeback. However, it is also important to note that the upper echelon of those IFIS at the time believed that bad privatization was still better than no privatization at all (Woods 2006).

Let us now turn to competition policy, which the young reformers had listed as one of their top priorities in 1991. In practice, it was purposely ignored (Granville and Oppenheimer 2001, 8). Contrary to Gaidar and Chubais's initial statements in 1992, market reforms failed to bring economic efficiency. Instead, the Yeltsin administration deliberately pursued policies that created one of the worst forms of crony capitalism in which the state allowed private citizens to accrue capital based mostly on an individual's privileged access to government officials. Privatization and deregulation policies transferred Russia's wealth to a concentrated group of *nomenklatura*, mobsters, and oligarchs under the crudest monopolistic/oligopolistic conditions. A typical example was the gas and oil industry. In November 1992 Yeltsin, through a decree, had reorganized most of the sector's companies into four major vertically integrated groups.[65] The gas monopoly Gazprom was left intact and as inefficient as ever. This situation, in varying degrees, affected most economic sectors not facing foreign competition (Granville and Oppenheimer 2001, 8). According to a 1996 estimate, "75 percent of Russia's most basic goods were supplied by a single producer" (Goldman 2003, 75).

64. At the end of 1995 the IMF expressed its approval for the Russian progress in meeting the agreed macroeconomic targets when, in fact, that was not true (Woods 2006, 121).

65. The largest company of the SFL was Lukoil, but its privatization had started much earlier when its manager, Vagit Alekperov, had built a de facto vertically integrated oil giant. Yeltsin's decree sanctioned into law Alekperov's efforts and paved the way for the oligarchs' takeover of Lukoil.

In the absence of any competition policy, former SOEs became predatory monopolies thanks to the rent-seeking conditions that the Yeltsin administration put in place (Havrylyshyn and Wolf 1999; Nellis 1999). The EBRD (1999), which was one of the main IFIS supporting the reform process, made a similar point when it concluded that state divestiture through collusive practices was counterproductive. Basically, the incentives that the Yeltsin administration created in the 1990s fostered collusion and corruption. The change from government to private ownership produced goods still under monopolistic production but sold at much higher prices. As Gustafson (1999, 50) pointed out, if the government had promoted competition and accountability, things would have turned out quite differently. Examples of what could have been are Lukoil and Gazprom. When faced with tough competition abroad both companies were quite successful in making the necessary management and investment changes to gain new markets (Gustafson 1999, 55).

Summing up, the government's incentive structure encouraged spending resources not on productive investments but toward affecting government decisions. Thus, consistent with the theories of Olson (1982) and North (1990), under these conditions it was quite rational for insiders to neglect the restructuring of their companies and spend their money and energy to keep outsiders away by having the government erect entry barriers (Gustafson 1999). Thus, most companies kept being run poorly and received little or no investments at all after privatization (Freeland 2000, 70). This in part explains why in the Russian Federation gross domestic investments were only 19.4 percent of GDP in 1997 as opposed to 31.8 percent in 1989 (Åslund 2002, 148). Such a large decline in investments contributed to the collapse of Russia's GDP. Depending on the estimate, GDP shrank by 40–50 percent during Yeltsin's tenure (Åslund 2002, 118; Goldman 2003, 14), which is twice as severe as the Great Depression contraction in the United States during the 1930s.

The Yeltsin administration not only promoted crony capitalism but went a step farther by allowing private interests to shape economic policy. This phenomenon, already described in chapter 1, is defined as state capture. According to an EBRD survey in 1999, the degree of state capture in Russia, regardless of the institution, was perceived as being far greater than in any of the former Communist countries of Eastern Europe that adopted market reforms during the same period of time.

The oligarchs who emerged in the 1990s personified state capture more than anyone else (Shleifer and Treisman 2000, 102). In late 1996 Berezovsky claimed that the seven wealthiest oligarchs controlled half of the Russian economy.[66] In the political sphere, their direct influence reached its apex during Yeltsin's second term (1996–99). Shortly after his reelection in June 1996 Yeltsin rewarded Potanin with the post of first deputy prime minister, while Berezovsky became deputy secretary of the National Security Council and later executive secretary of the Organization for Coordinating the Commonwealth of Independent States.[67] Berezovsky justified his appointment because "[we the oligarchs] hired Chubais and invested huge sums of money to ensure Yeltsin's election. Now, we have the right to occupy government posts and enjoy the fruits of our victory" ("Same Old Story for Russian Market Reform," *Russian Journal*, December 14–20, 2001).

Berezovsky also played an important role in convincing Yeltsin to pick Vladimir Putin as the new prime minister in August 1999 and, eventually, as his successor for the 2000 elections (Klebnikov 2000, 293–99). The Russian oligarchs often liked to compare themselves to the U.S. robber barons of the late nineteenth century. They saw their roles as the builders of the new capitalist Russia. However, the U.S. robber barons built economic empires through their own ingenuity and capital. The Russian oligarchs instead, for the most part, accumulated wealth through political sponsorship, but once their sponsors disappeared, many of them proved to be incapable of managing the fortunes that they had accrued (Freeland 2000, 312).

Indeed, by April 1997 things had become so bad that Michel Camdessus, the managing director of the IMF, admitted what many analysts and scholars had detailed since Yeltsin had taken office. Crony capitalism was rampant and it was derailing market reforms (Woods 2006). Lawrence Summers, who had been one of Yeltsin's and Chubais's staunchest supporters through the previous years, suddenly echoed the same misgivings. Gone were the early statements that unleashing the market forces would fix all problems by themselves. Government was no longer the obstacle but the possible solution. In Summers's opinion the real challenge in Russia had become one of institution building, which he now regarded as a sine qua

---

66. *Financial Times,* November 1, 1996, p. 5.

67. The postelection rewards included other financial concessions. Potanin's Onexim Bank received new government accounts as well as permission to restructure $1 billion worth of overdue taxes on favorable terms, while Berezovsky's Stolichny Bank was allowed to take over the state-owned Agroprom Bank, one of Russia's largest, which gave birth to SBS-Agro (Klebnikov 2000, 253).

non condition for the creation of a competitive economy (Reddaway and Glinski 2001, 597). These statements notwithstanding, the Clinton adminis-tration urged the IMF to disburse $17 billion to Russia on July 20, 1998, as Chubais successfully argued that it would prevent a major financial crisis. The crisis instead was only postponed by a month. Nonetheless, in a last stroke of vintage crony capitalism, government officials informed some of the oligarchs about the approaching meltdown, which allowed them to transfer their money abroad before the ruble devalued (Reddaway and Glinski 2001, 597).[68]

Patronage Politics

During his two terms in office Yeltsin failed to deliver on every promise he had made in 1991. Notwithstanding these dreadful results, the president was quite successful in retaining the political support necessary to run the coun-try until his sudden resignation in 1999. Equally interesting is that Yeltsin managed to rule Russia without creating a political party of his own. Ex-tremely suspicious of politicians and institutions that could curb his pow-ers, he built an autocratic, personalistic system. Indeed, as some of his foreign advisers later recounted, Yeltsin's appointees were selected for their loyalty to the president, rather than to market reforms (Shleifer and Vishny 1998, 248).

The key to Yeltsin's success in retaining power rested in his skillful use of patronage (Thames 2000). While claiming to promote capitalism, Yeltsin quickly created an extensive clientelistic network that undermined market reforms from within as it established all kinds of expensive privileges and additional government regulations that strangled economic activity. During the 1990s Russia operated on a two-budget system. One was the official budget submitted to the IMF and the World Bank, and the other was made up by extrabudget expenditures, which were mostly controlled by the exec-utive branch and escaped any supervision let alone accountability from the legislature. Thus, while on the one hand the Yeltsin administration claimed to promote fiscal austerity coupled with privatization and deregulation pol-icies to appease foreign lenders, on the other it kept spending lavishly, fuel-

---

68. "Foreign Loans Diverted in Monster Money Laundering? The Mafia, Oligarchs, and Russia's Torment," http://www.worldbank.org/html/prddr/trans/julaug99/pgs11–13.htm.

ing inflation. In so doing, Yeltsin perpetuated the soft-budget-constraint practices of the Soviet period. The soft-budget-constraint concept, first developed by Kornai (1992), showed how in command economies inefficient enterprises were kept in business through extrabudget financing that eluded official statistics. It is estimated that in the 1993–97 period extrabudgetary funds accounted for 20 percent of GDP (Sachs and Pistor 1997; Grafe and Richter 2001). These funds took a variety of forms such as subsidies, barter, loans, ad hoc transfers, tax and tariff exemptions, and special permits and licenses. According to Åslund (2002, 289), neither Gaidar nor his successors were able to control these extrabudget expenditures, which in turn torpedoed their stabilization attempts and worsened a fiscal deficit already in a very bad shape (Table 3.4).

This, of course, was part of Yeltsin's strategy to retain a populist appeal with the electorate. It took the form of hidden subsidies for food and utility costs. Likewise, the president used subsidies to keep large, inefficient sectors of the economy afloat, including the defense industry and the farm sector. A typical example of hidden subsidies was energy costs. Yeltsin struck a political bargain with the oil, gas, and electricity companies. The government would tolerate tax evasion if strategic firms would continue to provide services even to delinquent customers. The top fifty companies in these sectors, in large part controlled by the oligarchs, included Gazprom, Lukoil, and Nizhnevartovskneftegaz and were, ironically, some of Russia's most profitable. These political deals meant that those firms that could actually afford to pay corporate taxes did not (Table 3.5), resulting in almost half the debt of the federal budget (Shleifer and Treisman 2000, 75–76).

Yeltsin also used off-budget funds in a covert manner for clientelistic purposes in order to keep regional governors, the red directors, the oligarchs, and other important power groups on his side (Hough 2001). For instance, Treisman (1999) found that often the federal government used fiscal transfers to the regions responding to Yeltsin's political exigencies. Regional leaders were particularly important to Yeltsin's power for two reasons. First, as discussed earlier, they effectively controlled the selection process of their delegations to the Federation Council. To bring local government under his control, in 1991 Yeltsin appointed the great majority of the chief executives of territories, *oblasts,* and autonomous regions. In 1994 the president strengthened his grip on local government by having new elections for the legislatures of all federal subunits, except independent republics, which elected predominantly Yeltsin's loyalists. In turn, local legislatures elected representatives to the Federal Council who were supportive of the president, thus preventing a possible alliance of the upper house with the Duma to oppose the government agenda. Second, regional leaders could turn out the vote at election time. In fact, they controlled grassroots organizations that could mobilize voters much more effectively than most national parties, save for the Communists. Thus, in personalized contests such as presidential elections, regional leaders and their voting machines were the key to success, something that Yeltsin appreciated from the start. According to most observers, these regional political machines were crucial in Yeltsin's reelection in 1996 (Hough 2001).

Within this context, for Yeltsin off-budget funds played an important role in enlisting the cooperation of regional leaders because the president dispensed them at his discretion. Moreover, Yeltsin had ample authority in disbursing the share of federal taxes regularly earmarked for local government expenditures. Although the tax-sharing agreement between the federal and regional government stipulated precise mechanisms for the disbursement of revenues, in practice Yeltsin negotiated such funds behind closed doors (Shleifer and Vishny 1998, 248). Thus, it is no coincidence that regional leaders failed to join major parties. According to Hough (2001, 197), during the 1996 presidential elections Oleg Soskovets (at the time deputy prime minister, chairman of the Inter-Enterprise and Inter-Regional Debt, and Yeltsin's campaign manager) warned regional leaders that sponsoring anti-Yeltsin candidates was tantamount to immediate cuts in federal transfers. In return for their loyalty, regional leaders were allowed a substantial amount of power in handling local affairs, as long as they did not clash with presidential interests. Because such leaders were former members of the Soviet *nomenklatura*, they had no interest in pursuing market reforms locally, unless such reforms benefited them. Thus, regional leaders, once they appeased Yeltsin's wishes, proceeded to act like bosses by manipulating local privatizations to their personal advantage (Hough 2001, 43) and by strengthening bureaucratic controls to extract rents (Gustafson 1999, 31).

The squandering of government resources for political patronage was also evident during crucial electoral contests in which the president's future was at stake. While campaigning for the 1996 presidential election Yeltsin promised "greater benefits for nearly every conceivable group—higher scholarships for students, payment of back wages for everyone, a rise in the minimum wage, [and] higher pensions" (Hough 2001, 192). Although the electoral laws limited campaign expenditures to $2.9 million, Yeltsin surpassed that limit by far and large. When polls showed him far behind the leading candidates with only a few weeks left, Yeltsin decided to use the "coffers of the state budget for an aggressive clearance sale of government favors and services (Reddaway and Glinski 2001, 514). Yeltsin created a "President Fund" to pay back wages and pensions. He also used his decree powers to replenish pension funds so that they could pay arrears by the end of April and make up for the savings that people had lost during the hyperinflation of the 1992–93 period.[69]

According to Hough (2001, 192), Yeltsin issued "a decree which established twenty-five-year interest-free mortgages for private houses . . . [and] promised to restore a tax break for failing companies and give agriculture a special subsidy. . . . Commercial electrical rates in the countryside were lowered by 50 percent." To appear as the man of the people, he even gave gifts or cash to individuals during the campaign trail for cars, telephone installations, cultural centers, and churches.[70]

Yeltsin ran a very expensive campaign, spending large amounts on foreign consultants, pollsters, advertisement, sympathetic journalists, and television coverage, which he totally dominated. Moreover, according to Hough (2001, 198), Yeltsin provided funds under the table to candidates who could lure away votes from his main competitor, the candidate of the Communist Party, Gennady Zyuganov. Where did Yeltsin find so much money? The independent press that followed the 1996 campaign identified three main sources. One was coming from businesses with operations that depended on government licenses, permits, and loans. In this case, businessmen made "voluntary" contributions (Klebnikov 2000, 223), fearing certain retaliation otherwise. A second source came from government funds that were diverted to powerful oligarchs. The scheme worked along these lines. The government would sell high-yielding government bonds to selected oligarch-owned banks at a heavy discount. Then the banks would sell the bonds at a much higher price on the market and pay the difference to Yeltsin's campaign fund. However, many observers believed that the banks kept much of the profit for themselves (Hoffman 2002, 348–49).

The third source of the "President's Fund" allegedly came from the IMF, which in March, a month before the elections, coincidentally disbursed

69. The president also allowed $6.7 billion for rescheduling business taxes and allocated $2.2 billion to end a coal miners' strike demanding back wages (Stone 2002, 139).

70. *New York Times*, May 4, 1996, p. 1.

$10.2 billion of a three-year loan. According to Klebnikov (2000, 229): "Despite the cash infusion, the Russian treasury's foreign currency reserves declined from $20 billion to $12.5 billion in the first half of 1996. The Russian government, in other words, spent at least $9 billion in foreign currency during the first half of 1996. Some of the money went to Yeltsin campaign, some to well-connected businessmen and government officials, some to pay ordinary Russians their long-overdue paychecks." Patronage came also in the form of greater government payroll. As noted earlier, because Yeltsin did not trust the bureaucratic apparatus he inherited from the Soviet system, he established a parallel bureaucracy through the presidential administration. Yeltsin also created his own secret service and reshuffled ministries and special agencies and staffed them with newly hired people who were loyal to him. In the 1992–93 period alone the payroll of the Russian Federation increased by 2.4 times (Khakamada 1993). Between 1992 and 1997, based on data that the prime minister Sergei Kirienko provided to the Duma, the number of government employees increased by 1.2 million. According to Reddaway and Glinski (2001, 442), the cost involved in financing this new bureaucratic apparatus in 1997 rose by 62 percent compared to the previous year. Thus, market reforms did not make the government leaner and more efficient. If anything, Yeltsin's presidential administration created an unnecessary fiscal burden, more red tape, and jurisdictional battles from duplicating the functions of existing ministries and agencies. However, efficiency was not what mattered to Yeltsin; power and patronage were. This new army of federal employees and their families not only provided the president with a large mass of personal supporters but allowed him strengthen his patronage networks by using government resources to dispense favors to friends and co-opt potential enemies.

Concluding Remarks

In chapter 1 I theorized that if market reforms are carried out within a polity where accountability institutions are weak (or even deliberately emasculated to accelerate policy implementation), corruption, collusion, and patronage will ensue and promote disastrous economic crises in the medium term. On the contrary, where vertical and horizontal accountability institutions are in place we should expect less economic upheaval and greater success in achieving the market reforms' stated goals. This of course is not to say that the lack of accountability is the paramount factor in explaining financial crises, but rather that it would contribute to making a possibly difficult macroeconomic situation much worse as needed economic resources are squandered away and the potential benefits from market competition fail to materialize. When market reforms are plagued by the lack of accountability, chances are that economic rents are simply reassigned to those close to the levers of power. This situation thus fuels rent-seeking activities that prevent growth from happening.

The experience of Russia in the 1990s supports the thesis that the financial crisis of 1998 was closely associated with the lack of accountability. While the country made important strides in the late 1980s and early 1990s toward the creation of democratic institutions and an embryonic market, from 1992 onward this process, particularly in the political realm, was reversed. During his two terms in office Yeltsin systematically destroyed those institutions of horizontal accountability that could have restrained his power. By allowing the rigging of many privatizations, the manipulation of trade liberalization policies, and the transferring of government funds to banks owned by friendly oligarchs, Yeltsin gave away tens of billions of dollars to a close group of political allies in return for their support. While it is impossible to quantify with any degree of certainty how much the Russian government lost due to the lack of accountability, at least in one case we have a fairly good clue, which gives us a glimpse of the problem's magnitude. In the loan-for-share deal alone the government lost an estimated $39 billion, if we take as a parameter the price paid to the government ($680 million by early 1997) as opposed to the stock market value of the same companies once in private hands a few months later (Table 3.3). Considering that in 1998 Russia's foreign debt was $158 billion (Table 3.2), $39 billion could have decreased the country's foreign obligations by almost 25 percent that year. This estimate, of course, is very limited and does not take into consideration losses (for lack of reliable data) in other privatizations as well as subsidies and special privileges granted to the oligarchs. However, it is reasonable to think that the total losses must have been very high.[71]

Indeed, during the Yeltsin presidency Russia became a textbook case of how corruption, political patronage, and crony capitalism can derail a

71. Some scholars and pundits speculate that much of Russia's capital flight already discussed is the result of the fraudulent nature of many market reforms, but there is no way to prove it independently.

country's economy and reduce appreciably its citizens' access to pensions, government wages, health care, and education. By the time he retired from office in December 1999 Yeltsin claimed that he had succeeded in destroying Communism. Roughly 70 percent of the largest soes had been transferred to the private sector. The command economy of Soviet times was finished, and most assets were in private hands. In itself this was a major accomplishment. However, the way it was achieved was all the more troublesome. As Hellman (1998) postulated, the early winners of the reforms (oligarchs, the red directors, the *nomenklatura*, and mafia-mobsters-turned-businessmen) effectively blocked many market-friendly economic and legal initiatives because they would have jeopardized their rent-seeking privileges. Their veto power created many political and economic distortions that left many observers wondering whether Russia could become a true democracy based on competitive capitalism. In short, Yeltsin had defeated Communism, but in the process created many vested interests conspiring against competition and many new regulations thwarting private initiative.

In April 1992 Yeltsin had declared that what Russia needed were millions of owners, not hundreds of millionaires, but his policies produced just the opposite results. By 1999 a select few amassed fabulous fortunes, whereas most of the population was much worse off than in 1991, particularly in the countryside. Between 1991 and 1999 savings were wiped out as inflation rose twenty-six-fold. With the exception of 1997 and 1999 the economy shrank every year (Table 3.6) and in 2003 GDP was still 20 percent less than in 1990 (Dabrowski, Rohozynsky, and Sinitsina 2004). Privatization never materialized into the major source of cash flow that the young reformers had envisioned. According to Goldman, privatization netted only $6 billion, and the state received very little in dividends for its remaining shares in former soes because the red directors refused to pay them (Table 3.6).[72] As Russia's tax base shrank precipitously in the 1990s, the government was no longer able to pay wages and pensions on time. In 1998, 64 percent of government workers and retirees suffered wage and pension arrears (Dabrowski, Rohozynsky, and Sinitsina 2004). Pensioners were among the hardest hit, as their purchasing power declined by 57.2 percent between 1991 and 1995 alone (Klugman and Marnie 2001, 469). By 2002 about 40 percent of the total population still lived below the poverty line (Dabrowski, Rohozynsky, and

72. Another analysis by Tikhomirov estimated privatization revenues to be $8,756 million (2000, 250).

Sinitsina 2004). In the process, the federal government lost its capacity to perform basic functions in health and education. Between 1990 and 1994 mortality rates among men and women rose by 53 percent and 24 percent, respectively. Life expectancy dropped from sixty-four years to fifty-eight years (Klebnikov 2000, 107). Tuberculosis and HIV epidemics began to spread at alarming rates while state hospitals lacked basic drugs to treat patients. As poverty mushroomed, many young couples and single mothers found it impossible to keep their children. As a result, the number of abandoned newborns rose from 4 percent in 1992 to 9 percent in 1999.

Likewise, state divestiture failed to trigger the promised efficiency since many red-directors-turned-entrepreneurs retained government subsidies and protection from competition. Entry barriers and the lack of property rights discouraged foreign investments, which were far below the level that Poland and Hungry achieved during the same period. After nearly a decade of attempts at economic stabilization, Russia suffered yet another devastating financial crisis in 1998 as misled government policies led to too much debt, bankrupting the country. Between October 1997 and August 1998 market capitalization dropped by an astonishing 84 percent (Åslund 2002, 281). Although eventually the economy rebounded after 1999, by 2009 its wealth remained concentrated in commodities, which accounted for 80 percent of Russian exports, whereas new industries failed to emerge for lack of investments.

Indeed, the market reforms of the 1990s produced a new class of entrepreneurs dedicated to rent seeking rather than new business activities. In fact, for many observers the emergence of the oligarchs was heavily responsible for the reforms' fiasco. Yeltsin's reforms created a corrupt capitalist system without rights, rules, and accountability. Eventually, some of the early oligarchs were badly hurt by the 1998 crisis and quickly faded away. This, on paper, could vindicate Chubais, who had predicted that the market eventually was going to purge the bad entrepreneurs and reward the good ones. However, the demise of many oligarchs had much to do with the fact that political connections with the Yeltsin administration could not be successfully renewed under Putin and in some cases turned sour.

The fact that many reforms were tainted by corruption and pressed through within a shaky legal ground turned against many oligarchs after Yeltsin's retirement. Once elected President Putin came into a collision course with some oligarchs who thought they could impose on him their political agenda as during the old days, thus precipitating the situation.

Using the tremendous powers that Yeltsin had created, Putin moved swiftly to destroy those businessmen he believed to be a menace to his consolidation of power (Goldman 2008). He first forced Berezovsky and Gusinky into exile and then had Khodorkovsky jailed for tax evasion. He also used the corruption scandals that had plagued Yeltsin's divestiture program to reverse privatization and regain effective control of key companies in commodities, telecommunications, transportation, and manufacturing, including Gazprom, Sibneft Oil, Yugansneftegaz, Transneft Pipeline, United Energy Systems Electricity, Svyazinvest Telecom, Avtovaz Automobile, Aeroflot, and Tupolev (Goldman 2008, 135). By 2008 a new generation of oligarchs tied to President Putin controlled large shares of the production of profitable commodities in aluminum, copper, oil, gas, and telecommunications.[73] According to some estimates, they accounted for $715 billion (more than half of Russia's GDP) in a country where retirees lived on less than $60 a month ("Billionaires Boom as Putin Puts Oligarchs at No. 2 in Global Rich List," *The Guardian*, February 19, 2008). The cozy relationship between business and political power remained as pernicious under Putin as it had been under Yeltsin.[74] As a businessman acknowledged, "the system rewards those who are closer to the center of power, not those who work better. It is easier to get a competitor into a jail than to compete with him" ("The Mysteries of the Russian Economy," *The Economist*, February 28, 2008). The difference is that Putin, as opposed to Yeltsin, now had the upper hand. The shady way in which he eventually auctioned Yukos in 2004 showed that the arbitrary use of power and insider trading was alive and well. As a *New York Times* editorial noted, "reversing a piratical privatization through a piratical nationalization only confirms that doing business in Russia remains highly risky."[75]

The Russian bureaucratic apparatus under Yeltsin remained as corrupt as ever and a serious impediment to development. The federal and regional

73. Oil, one of Russia's main exports, played a key role in the country's turnaround under Putin. The Brent crude oil price went from $10.11 a barrel in December 1998 to more than $100 at the end of December 2008.

74. In June 2008 Peter Sutherland, the British Petroleum (BP) chairman, stated that Putin was supporting the strong-arm tactics of some Russian oligarchs in order to take control of the oil company TNK-BP away from BP.

75. "The Strange Yukos Sale," *New York Times*, December 25, 2004. A previously unknown company named Baikal won the Yugansneftegaz (Yukos's main production unit) auction for only $500 million more than the starting price of $8.87 billion. Most analysts regarded it as an awfully low price for a company so profitable. Shortly thereafter, it came to be known that Baikal had been bought by the oil SOE Rosneft.

government bureaucratic control over the economy allowed what Shleifer and Vishny (1998, 230) defined as "predatory policies." Red tape trapped the economy into a web of regulations, permits, and registrations, which continue to force business to circumvent the law and pay bribes to survive. By 1991 Russia had some 30 separate federal taxes and more than 170 local and regional taxes (Himes and Millet-Einbinder 1999). Coincidentally, business surveys showed that it was impossible to run private companies without violating the law (Goldman 2003). As a result, small corporations that had thrived in the early 1990s began to shrink in 1994 (Gustafson 1999, 110). Conversely in Poland, where reforms were supportive of business and dismantled many regulations of the Communist era, the economy thrived over time. In Russia the winners were the politicians and bureaucrats who created a vast regulatory framework to extort bribes and get rich in the process (Shleifer and Vishny 1998, 251). Gaidar himself admitted in 1994 that the bureaucracy was expanding and its goal was to get rich quickly at the state's expense (Nelson and Kuzes 1995). Of course, the mushrooming of bureaucrats and regulations was part of Yeltsin's effort to dispense patronage and favors to his clienteles. In the process, the young reformers turned a blind eye to it. The end result was that reforms did not facilitate entrepreneurs and in many cases worsened the regulatory burden on business and the corruption associated with it.

Some of Yeltsin's former foreign economic advisers, such as Sachs, claimed that the reforms failed because they did not go far enough and were not implemented fast enough. Their criticisms focused particularly on price liberalization, which they argued was only partial. Sachs, more specifically, attacked the IMF and the international community in general for not providing enough financial assistance in the early 1990s. Price liberalization was in effect inconsistent and, as many things, done half-heartedly, resulting in the worst of both worlds. Similarly, due to the soft-budget-constraint tactics that Yeltsin used to cultivate patronage, the Central Bank issued large amounts of funds to SOEs and regional governments that ran counter the anti-inflationary policies of Gaidar and the prime ministers who followed him. Åslund (2007) instead concluded that capitalism succeeded in the end. For him shock therapy was the best way to proceed. It did not bring the expected results only because Gaidar, his mastermind, was sacked too quickly and afterward his successors opted for gradualism, which left in place the economic distortions inherited from Soviet times. However, for Åslund the 1998 crisis was actually a blessing in disguise. It forced the government to finally eliminate the barter economy and attack the budget deficit. Unfortunately, Åslund added, democracy failed to materialize because Yeltsin paid little attention to its consolidation and left in place or created (e.g., the 1993 constitution) too many institutional weaknesses, which Putin eventually exploited to reestablish an autocratic state.

Although some of these contentions may have merit, they often miss an important point. Market reforms failed in Russia in part because they ignored good governance criteria and did not create the political and economic institutions that make markets flourish. As Shleifer and Vishny (1998, 251) pointed out, Russia needed a radical reform of its political institutions that would have made markets thrive. State institutions were not reformed to promote democratic behavior and promarket policies. Yeltsin and his allies joined the market reform bandwagon as a way to defeat the Communists, but from a political standpoint they were men rooted in an authoritarian culture as much as their Communist foes. Thus Yeltsin, in his quest for power, moved progressively in the opposite (authoritarian) direction, undermining the reform process from within and destroying the embryonic democratic forces that had emerged from the collapse of the Soviet Union.

Åslund and other analysts have defended Yeltsin, arguing that in late 1991 he and Gaidar had no real option. They also contend that the possibility of a Communist comeback was real and that little authority was left in the hands of the executive after the crumbling of the Soviet empire. Reddaway and Glinski (2001) in their meticulous analysis of the Yeltsin years challenged these arguments one by one, pointing out that the 500 Days Plan was a plausible alternative, among others, that could have been tried at the time. Moreover, the Communist threat was essentially Yeltsin's creation rather than a real possibility since the new Communist Party under Zyuganov was primarily a nationalist-populist party that had abandoned most of the Marxist-Leninist principles.[76] The quick buildup of the presidential administration that Yeltsin orchestrated soon after assuming power, and his ability to bring the old Soviet *nomenklatura* in to his camp, also cast doubts about the argument that the president was impotent in exercising his power.

If we look at the most controversial policy of all, privatization, Åslund

---

76. Konstantin Kegalovsky, who as a young reformer represented Russia at the IMF during the 1992–95 period, admitted in 1999 that "if the Communists had won in 1996, I am not sure we would be in a worse situation than now." *The New York Times Magazine*, August 15, 1999, p. 52.

(2002, 2007) defended its implementation by contending that the problem was not the policy per se, but a weak state, rudimentary democratic institutions, and lack of accountability. The truth of the matter is that the whole reform process, not just privatization, suffered from the same problems. Ironically, the same Western advisers, including Sachs and Åslund, applauded the autocratic nature of the 1993 constitutional reform, hoping that it would expedite reform. Instead it granted Yeltsin more ammunition to destroy those checks and balances that could have avoided the disasters that followed. The international community did have very serious responsibilities in all this. Western countries and IFIS were just as guilty because they continued to support an administration whose mismanagement and collusive practices were well known. In being associated with a discredited administration, the West betrayed the hope of many Russians that democracy and capitalism were the solution to their misery.

The Clinton administration called for the respect of property rights but allowed their de facto violation by condoning insider privatization and the gross manipulation of other reforms. Moreover, because of strategic exigencies it put very strong pressure on the IMF and the World Bank to finance programs that were doomed to fail and insisted on watering down conditions that undermined the bargaining credibility of both institutions (Stone 2002; Woods 2006). Neither the Clinton administration nor the IMF and the World Bank confronted government corruption (which ended up squandering a lot of foreign loans), off-budget subsidies, or authoritarian political initiatives. For some (Hough 2001, 8), the Clinton administration and the IMF not only tolerated Yeltsin's unwillingness to comply with important aspects of the stand-by loans but by condoning such a behavior they "often contributed to the effort to reduce transparency."

In the end, it was Yeltsin's mismanagement of market reforms that turned people against them, not the reforms themselves. Several public opinion surveys showed that respondents objected neither to privatization nor market reforms in general but to the way Yeltsin and his cronies manipulated them for personal advantage. Privatization not only became synonymous with stealing, but democracy, due Yeltsin's manipulations, came to be commonly referred to as "shitocracy" (Klebnikov 2000, 320).

Indeed, Yeltsin departed with his reputation destroyed and tainted by a score of scandals involving him and his family (Goldman 2003, 218). Nonetheless, he went into early retirement, allegedly a wealthy man, and escaped any legal repercussion. Upon assuming office as a provisional president,

Putin issued a presidential pardon that made Yeltsin and his family immune from any prosecution. After all, Yeltsin and his inner circle had picked Putin precisely because of his loyalty and his willingness to carry out the aging president's last wishes. As the twenty-first century began, Russia had become a capitalist country, but one where crony capitalism and authoritarianism were the dominant traits.[77] In point of fact, the strengthening of presidential authority at the expense of democratic checks and balances continued unabated under Putin (McFaul and Stoner-Weiss 2008).

Moreover, Putin presided over an escalation of human rights violations, harassment of the free press and civil society organizations, and allegations of fraudulent elections. The main difference was the economy, which between 2000 and 2008 grew at an average of 6.5 percent. However, this positive trend did not emerge because of new competitive businesses, as the advocates of market reforms had hoped in the early 1990s. In reality, much of the domestic industry remained backward by international standards and in many cases protected from foreign competition. The unexpected change in the overall economic picture was circumstantial and resulted from the high international prices for Russian commodities, particularly oil and gas.[78] The windfalls from commodity prices, however, did have a positive impact on incomes, as wages and salary increased eightfold by the end of Putin's second term and poverty declined to 14 percent of the total population.[79] These positive trends, coupled with his tough stands against U.S. foreign policy in Chechnya and Georgia, made Putin very popular at home. Despite his autocratic style, he enjoyed approval ratings of 80 percent by the time he retired from the presidency in August 2008. Russians seemed to like the return to strong leadership and government control of key economic activities that could produce good economic results. An indication

77. In October 2007, U.S. secretary of state Condoleezza Rice clearly stated that Putin's authoritarian measures raised serious concerns about Moscow's commitment to democracy: "In any country, if you don't have countervailing institutions, the power of any one president is problematic for democratic development." Rice also added, "I think there is too much concentration of power in the Kremlin. I have told the Russians that. Everybody has doubts about the full independence of the judiciary. There are clearly questions about the independence of the electronic media and there are, I think, questions about the strength of the Duma" (Associated Press, October 14, 2007).

78. As a result of the boom in commodity prices, Russia's reserves climbed from $12 billion in 1999 to $446 billion in 2008 (Central Bank of Russia Official Statistics, August 2008, http://www.cbr.ru/eng/statistics/).

79. During Putin's presidency average wages grew from $80 a month to $640. ("Russians Weigh an Enigma with Putin's Protégé. Can the Forty-two-year-old President Move out of His Mentor's Shadow?" *MSNBC*, May 3, 2008).

of how profound citizens' resentment was toward Yeltsin's version of market reforms came from an independent public opinion survey in 2006, which showed that 85 percent of people polled endorsed the renationalization of the oil and gas companies, and 65 percent were favorable to the "nationalization of other industries that are presently in private hands." Moreover, not only did 56 percent of respondents support greater government control over the media but 44 percent preferred "a centrally controlled government such as China's," as opposed to 30 percent in favor of "a liberal democracy as in the United States."[80] In brief, if in 1990 the intention of the United States and the IFIS was to consolidate the democratic process through the adoption of market reforms, by 2008 the results were pretty poor and did not bode well for the future of Russian democracy, let alone a free, competitive capitalist economy.

80. "Russians Support Putin's Re-Nationalization of Oil, Control of Media, But See Democratic Future," http://www.worldpublicopinion.org/pipa/articles/breuropera/224.ph p?nid = & id = &pnt = 224&lb = breu.

Table 3.1 Russian Capital Flight and External Assets, 1992–98 (in US$ billions)

	1992	1993	1994	1995	1996	1997	1998	Total
Legal Capital Flows	4.03	3.27	5.58	4.46	9.67	12.47	1.92	41.40
Illegal Capital Flows	19.71	15.29	10.88	15.96	21.85	22.98	20.46	127.13
Legal External Assets*	14.03	17.03	22.88	18.42	28.09	40.56	38.46	38.46
Illegal External Assets**	14.50	23.62	30.23	42.16	60.21	80.31	98.40	98.40

SOURCE: Lushin and Oppenheimer (2001, 286–87).

*Accounts and deposits in 1991 were $5 billion.

**Stock in 1991 was $3 billion.

Note that legal and illegal assets are cumulative figures.

Table 3.2 Russian Foreign Debt, 1993–98 (in US$ billions)

	1993	1994	1995	1996	1997	1998
Inherited from the Soviet Union	103.9	116.2	110.6	108.4	99.0	102.4
Borrowing by Russia	8.8	11.3	17.4	27.7	35.6	55.4
Total Russian Debt	112.7	127.5	128.0	136.1	134.6	158.2
Payments Falling Due	20.7	20.2	20.2	18.7	14.2	14.6
Payments Made	3.6	4.6	7.1	7.7	7.7	9.1

SOURCE: Lushin and Oppenheimer (2001, 289–90).

Table 3.3 Russian Loans for Shares Auctions, 1995–97

Company	% Auctioned	Bank Managing Auction	Auction Price, 1995*	Auction Winner	Minimum Sale, 1996–97*	Price Paid*	Auction Winner (by oligarch)	Stock Market Value (8/1/97)*
Lukoil	5	Imperial Bank	35	Lukoil, Imperial Bank	43	43.6	Alekperov	15,839
Yukos	45	Menatep Bank	159	Laguna (Menatep)	160	160.1	Khodorkovsky	6,214
Surgut	40	Uneximbank	88	Surgutneftegaz	74	74.0	Bogdanov	5,689
Sidanco	51	Uneximbank	130	MFK (Uneximbank)	129	129.8	Potanin	5,113
Sibneft	51	Menatep Bank	100	NFK, Stolichny Bank	100	100.3	Berezovsky	4,968
Norilsk	51	Uneximbank	170	Uneximbank	170	170.1	Potanin	1,890

SOURCE: Klebnikov (2000, 209) and Moser and Oppenheimer (2001, 310).

*In US$ millions

Table 3.4 Russian Public Finances, 1992–98 (in billions of 1990 rubles)

Year	1992	1993	1994	1995	1996	1997	1998
I. Gross Revenues	146.7	138.5	121.2	131.4	100.8	110.1	93.4
Corporate Tax	43.1	46.8	33.4	30.6	17.5	16.3	13.7
Value Added Tax	55.0	31.2	25.5	25.0	26.1	28.5	22.4
Income Tax	11.9	12.2	12.0	9.5	10.2	11.6	10.1
Taxes on International Trade	12.9	6.5	13.1	5.2	2.6	1.5	1.9
Excise Duties	5.8	5.0	5.1	6.3	9.7	10.6	9.7
Natural Resources Use Tax	4.1	3.2	3.2	3.5	4.2	6.3	2.1
Privatization Revenues	1.7	0.9	0.5	1.2	0.5	3.6	2.5
Other	11.4	31.8	28.5	32.3	30.5	32.6	31.4
II. Gross Expenditures	164.3	160.6	160.5	127.4	118.9	131.2	108.1
National Economy	56.7	45.1	43.3	36.2	31.5	12.7	9.1
Social Services and Culture	38.1	39.9	37.8	33.8	34.3	42.2	34.3
Government Management and Law Enforcement	9.7	11.7	12.7	9.8	10.2	13.7	10.4
Government Management Only	2.9	4.1	4.9	3.1	3.1	4.5	4.3
Defense	23.5	20.1	19.1	13.0	11.6	12.7	8.1
Foreign Economic Activities	11.5	7.7	3.4	5.6	4.8	0.4	15.2
Other	24.9	74.8	44.2	28.9	38.4	44.9	26.6
III. Surplus/Deficit (−)	−17.7	−22.1	−39.2	−12.9	−17.2	−20.0	− 13.8

Source: Tikhomirov (2000, 51).

Table 3.5   Largest Russian Tax Debtors on August 1, 1995

Company	Sector	Debt in Billions of Rubles
Nizhnevartovskneftegaz	oil, gas	1,138
Yuganskneftegaz	oil, gas	842
Lukoil-Langepasneftegaz	oil, gas	814
Noyabrskneftegaz	oil, gas	753
Lukoil-Kogalymneftegaz	oil, gas	749
Autovaz	automobile	684
Gaz	automobile	530
Uraltransgaz	gas	404
Kondpetroleum	oil	397
Orenburgneft	oil	342
Megionneftegaz	oil, gas	329
Samaraneftegaz	oil, gas	245
Yamburggazdobycha	gas	240
Irkutzkoe	railway	222
Gorkovskaya	railway	222
Tyumentransgaz	gas	217
Moskovskaya	railway	209
Purneftegaz	oil, gas	195
Komineft	oil	192
Oktyabrskaya	railway	191
Yaroslavskoe	railway	191
Yakutnefteproduct	oil	184
U. Sverdlosvskoi	railway	182
Moskvich	automobile	163
Lukoil-Permnefteorgsintez	oil	160
Irkutskenergo	electricity	158
Moskovsky Neftepererab	oil	149
NLMK	metals	144
Krasnoyarskaya	railway	140
Tomskneft	oil	116

SOURCE: Shleifer and Treisman (2000, 74).

Table 3.6 Russian Economic Statistics, 1992–99

	1992	1993	1994	1995	1996	1997	1998	1999
GDP Growth	−14.5	−8.7	−12.7	−4.1	−3.4	0.8	−4.9	5.4
GNP Per Capita (% of annual growth)	−15.3	−8.4	−12.5	−4.4	−3.5	0.7	−6.4	3.3
Consumer Prices	1,345.0	895.0	303.0	197.4	47.8	14.7	27.7	85.7
Unemployment	4.8	5.6	7.8	9.2	9.6	11.9	12.2	12.0
Privatization Revenues (US$ millions)	80.0	26.0	52.0	1,253.0	198.0	3,172.0	813.0	85.0
Dividends from Privatized Companies				25.0	21.0	48.0	113.0	255.0

SOURCE: Goldman (2003) and IMF.

four

ARGENTINA

Introduction

For many years Argentina's growth was a textbook case of what sociologists termed a "reversal of development." Endowed with some of the most fertile lands in the world, rich in oil and minerals, and with a population whose literacy and cultural heritage resemble more those of southern Europe (from whence most of its settlers came) than Latin America, Argentina was considered ready to emulate the socioeconomic success of the United States at the beginning of the twentieth century. Although the golden years of Argentina were from the 1890s until World War I, the country continued to grow at a moderate pace into the 1920s. Beginning in the 1930s, however, it entered a steady period of economic decline punctuated by brief periods of recovery. Politically, authoritarian governments became more the norm than the exception, reversing the democratic progress that Argentina had experienced up until 1929.

In the mid-1940s president Juan Perón tried to reverse the trend through a new brand of conservative populism. During his first presidency (1946–51) Perón, through his labor-based populist movement, made an explicit effort to redistribute wealth to the urban working and middle classes by establishing a very generous welfare state. Simultaneously, he promoted domestic industry and sheltered it from foreign imports. Although the military deposed Perón in 1955, halfway into his second term, the thrust of his policies had created strong, vested interests among labor, industrialists, and the military, making drastic policy changes impossible. However, as a result, the Argentine economy became increasingly stagnant and plagued by one of the world's highest inflation rates.

In 1976 the last military regime promised to bring economic stability once and for all. In the meantime, using indiscriminate violence it crushed left-wing terrorist organizations, which had developed during the late 1960s. By the time the military withdrew from power at the end of 1983, thirty thousand people were reported to be either dead or missing. Economically, the armed forces' experiment left Argentina in ruins with a foreign debt three times greater than in 1976.

Raúl Alfonsín (1983–89), leader of the Unión Cívica Radical (UCR), won the elections in 1983.[1] Although widely credited for his effort to promote a democratic environment, Alfonsín failed to bring economic stability. Due to relentless labor and business opposition to his reform policies, as well as his administration's policy mistakes, Argentina was near economic collapse by the time Alfonsín left office, with prices rising by nearly 5,000 percent in 1989 alone.

Within this context, Carlos Menem won the nomination of what was once Perón's party, the Partido Justicialista (PJ), for the 1989 presidential contest. Prior to the election he promised more government spending, full employment, and a rejection of the IMF/World Bank structural reforms, whereas his contenders preached fiscal restraint, privatization, and the opening of the Argentine economy to foreign competition. Portraying himself as a charismatic, almost messianic figure, Menem gave no specifics about his policies, preferring to use catchy slogans such as "productive revolution" or "follow me, I am not going to betray you."[2]

Once elected, Menem reneged on his promises and adopted a draconian stabilization plan that went against everything the PJ had stood for until then. His reforms also went well beyond the harsh solutions proposed by the UCR and conservative parties. To thwart opposition from his own party, and particularly the unions, which traditionally had been the backbone of Peronism, Menem forged strategic alliances with historical enemies of the PJ: large domestic corporations and conservative parties. Having inherited

---

1. Despite their name, "the Radicals," as they are known in Argentina, have been traditionally a moderate party, drawing their electoral support primarily from middle- and upper-middle-class voters.

2. Juan Perón founded the PJ in the mid-1940s as an electoral machine to serve his political ambitions. During his first two terms in office (1946–55) Perón was one of the most typical Latin American populists. He used import substitution industrialization and government programs to expand his electoral base of core voters from the working class and lower-middle classes. Economic protectionism, nationalism, and redistributive income policies remained the hallmark of the PJ even after the death of its founder in 1974.

a bankrupt state, Menem believed that the only way out was to give an even greater share of the national income, via privatization and business deregulation, to agricultural exporters and industrial and commercial conglomerates in return for political and financial support. At the same time, Menem systematically attacked the prerogatives of the legislative and judicial branches of government, which had started to assert themselves vigorously under Alfonsín. Consequently, Menem's market reforms, as in a natural selection process, allowed Argentina's largest business groups to fill the power vacuum produced by the retreat of the state to more basic functions. Small industrialists, now exposed to foreign competition through trade liberalization, and unionized workers were forced to bear the cost of economic restructuring.

By the same token, the president understood that no financial assistance would be forthcoming without the support of the United States, which had a large say in approving the IMF's and the World Bank's structural adjustment loans. Therefore, Menem made a deliberate effort to court the George H. Bush administration. While Perón had often antagonized the United States in the 1940s, Menem, his self-proclaimed heir, wanted to have what Guido Di Tella, the Argentine foreign minister at the time, described as "carnal relations" with Washington. Bush responded to Menem's unexpected overtures in the most positive fashion. In August 1989 U.S. secretary James Baker "ordered the U.S. ambassador in Buenos Aires to support the Menem administration in every possible way" (Veigel 2009, 174) and put pressure on the IMF to resume lending to Argentina, which had been stopped in 1988. The following November, Argentina signed a stand-by agreement with the IMF for $1.5 billion, with additional assistance coming from the World Bank to support privatization and other major market reforms.[3]

As a result, during the 1990s Argentina became the United States' closest ally in Latin America. It was a controversial move, but it paid off handsomely as Argentina became one of the world's largest recipients of multilateral banks' foreign assistance and a poster child of the WC. Although hailed at home and abroad as the beginning of sound economic management, Menem's market reforms did not end monopolistic or oligopolistic practices. Disguised as free-market initiatives, Menem's reforms, far from impeding the pursuit of special interests and collusion, simply raised the

3. The IMF had withdrawn its assistance to Argentina in 1988.

stakes of the redistributive struggle by picking the new winners (Schamis 2002). Accordingly, during his first term in office (1989–95) Menem implemented the most radical privatization program in Latin America, slashed public employment and government spending, and opened many economic sectors to foreign competition.

In the beginning structural reforms met with scarce results, as inflation remained very high and Argentina missed important targets of its stand-by loan with the IMF.[4] Nonetheless, Washington's efforts only intensified and put pressure on Menem to show greater commitment in the face of mounting domestic opposition. In fact, inflation remained very high, forcing the Argentine authorities to adopt a measure of the last resort to ensure policy credibility: a fixed exchange rate. Despite the IMF skepticism (previous fixed exchange rate regimes had repeatedly failed in the past) in April 1991 new economy minister Domingo Cavallo launched what became known as the Convertibility Plan. However, unlike previous experiences, Congress approved the exchange rate reform to legitimize its most important features and no changes were allowed unless Congress decided on it. Once turned into law, the Convertibility Plan established a de facto gold standard system as the Argentine currency was made fully convertible with the U.S. dollar at a fixed parity of one to one. Moreover, the Central Bank could no longer finance government debt or issue new currency unless it had an equal amount in foreign currency reserves or gold. In comparing the World Bank's influence on policy reform in Argentina and Mexico during the 1990s Teichman (2004, 41) wrote that "the bank was much more intimately involved in the reform process in Argentina and was able to exercise considerably greater direct influence, especially during the initial years of reform. In both cases, domestic and multilateral deliberations took place in highly personalistic policy networks, which excluded democratic deliberative institutions (congresses) and precluded public accountability."

The initial results of the Convertibility Plan were dramatic. Inflation dropped to 3.7 percent by August 1995. The government's fiscal accounts, chronically in the red, turned into a surplus in 1993. Privatization receipts, either in cash or debt-equity swaps, raised $20 billion. With the elimination of most legislation limiting ownership and capital repatriation, foreign investments poured into the country, totaling about $24.5 billion between

---

4. Between 1989 and 1998, Argentina and the IMF agreed on four different stand-by agreements (November 1989, July 1991, March 1992, April 1996) totaling $6.2 billion, of which $4.9 billion was disbursed (Hornbeck 2003, 5).

1990 and 1993. Large amounts of the estimated $50 billion that Argentine citizens had taken abroad also came back home. Low inflation and a favorable investment environment made Argentina the third largest recipient of foreign investments among emerging markets, after Mexico and China. The economy, which had grown at an average of 1 percent a year between 1976 and 1989, posted a 30 percent cumulative growth rate between 1990 and 1994. During the same period of time the country's GDP tripled, reaching $270 billion.

By 1994 most analysts agreed that the Argentine "riddle" had turned into a "miracle," with Menem claiming full credit for it. His bold policies won him high praise from the IMF, the World Bank, the U.S. Treasury, and foreign investors, which pointed to Argentina as a role model for the rest of Latin America to emulate. As late as October 1998 the managing director of the IMF, Michel Camdessus, had only words of praise for Argentina: "In many respects the experience of Argentina in recent years has been exemplary, including in particular the adoption of the proper strategy at the beginning of the 1990s and the very courageous adaptation of it when the tequila crisis put the overall sub-continent as risk of major turmoil . . . Notable, too, are the efforts of Argentina since that time to continue its excellent compliance with the performance criteria under our arrangements and much progress in implementation of the structural reforms. So clearly, Argentina has a story to tell the world: a story which is about the importance of fiscal discipline, of structural change, and of monetary policy rigorously maintained."[5]

Consistent with the assumptions of the WC, IFIS, foreign governments, and international and domestic investors seemed to be convinced that the country was on the right track.[6] They dismissed mounting evidence pointing to corruption, administrative irregularities, and authoritarian means simply as temporary problems that would be quickly overcome on the assumption that once market reforms had been firmly established people would eventually demand better institutions and vote into office more responsible politicians. Indeed, despite the fact that Argentina kept missing its fiscal deficit targets every year from 1994 until 2001, the IMF kept granting waivers (IMF 2004).

---

5. Quoted from Blustein (2005, 58).
6. As late as June 1997 the IMF (1997b, 175) stated that "Argentina has been successful largely because sound macroeconomic policies have remained firmly in place for a number of years, and considerable progress has been made on what might be described as the 'first generation' of structural reform."

In the meantime, Menem acted swiftly. Backed by strong approval ratings he convinced Alfonsín, now leader of a badly divided UCR, to approve a series of constitutional reforms. The Olivos Pact, as the backdoor agreement was dubbed, was eventually ratified by a constitutional assembly a year later. It allowed Menem's reelection (the 1853 constitution barred a second consecutive term) in return for (a) a restriction on presidential authority in issuing emergency decrees; (b) an increase in opposition candidates (primarily favoring the UCR) in the Senate; (c) a pledge to reform the judicial system making it less dependent of the executive branch; and (d) a reduction of the presidential term from six to four years. In May 1995, as expected, Menem won a second term by a landslide, polling 49.5 percent as opposed to 47 percent in 1989.

However, during Menem's second term (1995–99), the shaky basis on which he had built the "Argentine miracle" became apparent and, as a result, the socioeconomic picture began to slowly deteriorate. By mid-1998 Argentina fell into a recession that grew progressively worse. With most privatization transactions completed by 1997, foreign investments dropped significantly, and so did tax receipts at a time when government spending accelerated. Market reforms failed to spur competition and economic growth in the long run because important markets, as in Russia, remained heavily protected even after privatization as the beneficiaries of state divestitures successfully lobbied government to create entry barriers to protect their rents.

However, instead of confronting the problems he had created, Menem chose the easy way out. He breached the fiscal gap by borrowing more and more from abroad, with the blessing of the IMF and the World Bank, which only postponed the magnitude of the looming crisis. As the recession deepened, the popular support that the reforms enjoyed in the early 1990s turned into open discontent just as rapidly. Opinion surveys increasingly reported public dissatisfaction with market reforms due to the perception that they were highly corrupt and the upper classes and big domestic and foreign investors were the only beneficiaries. The middle class felt it had been left behind and so did many marginal popular sectors that initially had benefited from low inflation but then suffered from rising unemployment. These perceptions were well founded. According to the Inter-American Development Bank (2000), between 1990 and 1999 income concentration increased twice as fast as in 1975–90. While in 1990 the poorest 10 percent of the population accounted for 2.15 percent of the national income, by 1999 it received only 1.5 percent. During the same period of time, in Buenos Aires alone income disparities between rich and poor increased an astounding 127 percent. Adding to the popular frustration was the mounting number of corruption scandals involving members of the Menem administration.

Opposition parties capitalized on this popular malaise and in October 1999 their leader, the UCR's Fernando de la Rúa, won the presidential election with nearly 50 percent of the popular vote.[7] De la Rúa promised to crack down on corruption but decided to stay the course on economic policy by keeping the Convertibility Plan in place as the only means to fight inflation since polls showed strong support for it.[8] Unfortunately, De la Rúa proved an indecisive president whose leadership flaws were quickly exposed as the economic crisis accelerated during 2000–2001. Under pressure from the IMF to cut the country's fiscal deficit, De la Rúa increased taxes and cut expenditures. This move backfired. It exacerbated the recession and turned the public and many members of his governing coalition against him. A major corruption scandal in 2000, allegedly involving one of the president's closest aides, destroyed much of whatever credibility the administration still had.[9]

In March 2001, as the situation kept deteriorating, De la Rúa asked Cavallo to return to the helm of the Ministry of the Economy. In the end, however, not even Cavallo could save the Convertibility Plan from its demise. The following November, facing default on several loans coming to maturity at the year's end, Cavallo went again to the IMF for an advance of $1.2 billion in approved credit. When the IMF refused, citing its doubt in the government's ability to meet its fiscal targets, a run on the banks occurred, fueling a massive capital flight.[10] When the economy minister asked Congress in mid-December to approve a balance budget bill for 2002, contemplating cuts for $9.2 billion, the Peronists refused to go along with it and social order fell apart. Often instigated by Peronist union leaders and politicians, violent riots exploded in different parts of the country, leading

7. By 1999 the UCR had forged an electoral alliance with the center-left Frente Pais Solidario (FREPASO).

8. Most polls showed between 70 and 80 percent support for the Convertibility Plan.

9. Allegedly, Fernando de Santibañes, the head of the security services, had paid four Peronist senators to secure their support for the approval of a new labor law. De la Rúa's unwillingness to sack Santibañes prompted the resignation of Vice President Carlos Álvarez, thus creating a major institutional crisis.

10. Between 2001 and 2002 capital flight reached $33 billion (*La Nación*, June 16, 2004).

to the death of twenty-seven demonstrators. On December 19 Cavallo resigned, and a day later it was De la Rúa's turn, leaving the country economically and politically bankrupt. Later that month Argentina recorded the world's largest debt default ever, as it failed to honor payments on $132 billion in foreign loans.

After a series of provisional presidents, on January 1, 2002, Congress appointed Senator Eduardo Duhalde (Peronist) as interim president to pick up the pieces and pave the way for negotiations with the IMF and new elections. Having been an open critic of the fixed exchange rate, Duhalde immediately abandoned the Convertibility Plan, which soon turned into a 70 percent devaluation of the peso. At the same time, the Duhalde administration (January 2002 to May 2003), in open defiance of constitutional guarantees on property rights, converted all dollar-dominated bank deposits into pesos. This further angered an already exasperated citizenry whose assets were further pulverized by such an arbitrary decision. Lacking a clear mandate, and with the country struggling to survive a crisis of monumental proportions, Duhalde called for new elections in April 2003. When they took place, the contest was a Peronist affair, pitting former president Menem against a little known governor from Southern Argentina, Nestor Kirchner. While Menem represented the traditional conservative core of Peronism, Kirchner was a member of the much smaller left-wing faction of the PJ. Kirchner eventually prevailed primarily because most voters rejected the former president, whose policies and corruption had in their eyes drawn the country into financial ruin and unprecedented poverty.

Once in office, Kirchner's left-wing populism quickly materialized in the rejection of the free-market model of the Menem era. The new president took a tough stance vis-à-vis foreign capital. In particular, he assailed foreign operators of public utilities by charging that they had taken advantage of the country through high rates while not living up to their contractual commitments in terms of investments and service provision. Thus, Kirchner prevented utility rates from being updated (Duhalde had frozen them in early 2002) and pursued a clear strategy to replace foreign utility companies with domestic investors. Moreover, thanks to unusually high prices for Argentine commodities from 2003 onward, the country's economy grew at a spectacular level fueling an unexpected recovery, which allowed the government to increase tax receipts and accrue large foreign reserves. This enabled Kirchner to take a tough stand against the IMF and foreign creditors on the debt moratorium, which made him extremely popular at home. The president attacked the neoliberal policies of the WC that guided Menem's reforms. More specifically, he blamed the IMF for the economic debacle of 2001–2002 and for plummeting half the country's population into poverty. In the spring of 2005 Argentina created another precedent by forcing many of its private creditors to accept a two-thirds reduction on the principal of external debt (about $81 billion) that had defaulted in 2002. From 2005 on it would be paid at lower interests and longer maturities. This was the largest debt discount that a developing country had ever been able to obtain from foreign creditors.

Domestically, Kirchner also won public approval when he forced out five members of the Supreme Court who had steadfastly supported Menem's market reforms. While this constituted yet another blow to the independence of the judiciary, public opinion surveys showed that 80 percent of respondents sided with the presidential initiative, as they were disgusted with the way the Supreme Court had conducted itself in the 1990s. Kirchner also gained a lot of popularity among the working class by dispensing food and financial aid in a very clientelistic way to poor families and by harassing companies that in his opinion were marking up prices. Moreover, he launched an anticorruption campaign targeting primarily former high-ranking officers of the Menem administration. In brief, Kirchner in only four years in office completely turned around the socioeconomic equation. The failure of market reforms and the crooked manner in which Menem implemented them gave Kirchner's brand of left-wing populism plenty of support to revive the idea of economic nationalism and state intervention, putting both domestic and foreign private capital at the mercy of an all-powerful and rather authoritarian presidency. Thus, if in the 1990s Argentina was hailed in Washington as a poster child of market reforms, by 2008 it had become one of the leaders of the developing countries' opposition to globalization and neoliberal economics. In the following paragraphs I will examine how Menem's version of market reforms turned high hopes into widespread hostility and how accountability issues had much to do with Argentina's market experiment fiasco.

Accountability in Menem's Argentina

Before assessing the role of the Argentine accountability institutions during the 1990s, it is necessary to briefly survey the main features of the Argentine political system. Argentina is a federal republic whose constitution borrowed heavily from that of the United States. As in the United States, power is divided into three branches of government (executive, legislature, and judiciary). Twenty-four provinces, which are the equivalent of states in other federal systems, are in charge of local affairs in Argentina. Traditionally, though, the presidency has had much more power than the other two branches. This trend intensified under dictatorships, which ruled the country on and off between 1930 and 1983. Presidents, including elected ones, have routinely made use of executive orders to a degree unknown in the United States. The executive's power rests in part on the fact that the provinces rely on the federal government for most of their funds because their tax base is small. However, governors do have some bargaining chips vis-à-vis the central government because they heavily influence the selection of candidates going to Congress.[11] In the event that the president's party does not control both houses of the legislature, governors can play a pivotal role in delivering the necessary votes. Consequently, this has led to the development of informal rules that presidents and governors use to compromise on important issues.

As for the Congress, it does not play the same assertive role as in the United States because most of the legislative agenda comes from the presidency. Nonetheless, the legislature is not supine as many people assume. Its importance and ability to force the executive to compromise increase if the president does not enjoy a stable majority in both houses. Yet the Argentine Congress is quite different from that of the United States. U.S. legislators tend to have strong ties to their constituents, whereas Argentine legislators do not. This is due to an electoral system in which the party leadership at the national and provincial levels picks the candidates on the basis of their influence within the party, and primaries take place only for presidential races. Voters must choose among lists, not candidates, according to a proportional representation formula, which allows for multiple members from the same district to be sent to the Chamber of Deputies (lower house). In short, people get into Congress based on their party loyalty, not constituent work. As a result, most legislators know how to dispense patronage to their party machine but have little skill in how to write a bill or read a budget. Adding to their weakness is the fact that a little

11. Up until 1994 provincial legislatures appointed federal senators and governors often had a decisive role in this matter.

more than 30 percent are usually reelected. Thus, legislators do not have incentives to specialize on issues; that is the realm of party bosses, who instead stay in Congress for long periods of time. In turn, this reinforces the power of party bosses who interact with the executive and among themselves according to informal rules. As a matter of fact, roll-call voting in the Argentine Congress between 1989 and 1995 shows a very high conformity of Radical and Peronist legislators to their leaderships' wishes (Jones, Sanguinetti, and Tommasi 2000). This explains why Congress is rarely an arena of public debate since the real deals are struck behind close doors.

Congress

According to some scholars, Argentine congressmen are usually uninterested in executive oversight because they are mostly "amateurs" in kind and their careers are controlled by provincial party bosses who are prone to "behind the scene deals" (Spiller and Tommasi 2003). This, in turn, plays into the hands of the executive branch, provided that the president can count on a steady congressional majority. Indeed, this was exactly the situation during Menem's tenure; not surprising, legislative oversight became much more constrained than under Alfonsín. As noted earlier, Argentina is characterized by a strong presidential system with extensive decree powers covering administrative rulings, statutory authority delegated by the legislature, and ad hoc decrees spelled out in the constitution. Nonetheless, during the Menem years the executive extended its powers even further to legislate at the expense of Congress, which in turn saw its ability to decide, debate, and oversee diminish rapidly.[12] What helped Menem in curtailing congressional resistance upon assuming office was the hyperinflation crisis that he inherited from President Alfonsín. To prevent the country from collapsing into total chaos Alfonsín, now a lame duck in office, allowed Menem to be sworn in six months ahead of schedule.[13] Menem accepted but forced the Radicals to make major concessions. Among them was the Radicals' pledge to withdraw a sufficient number of their 113 members in the Chamber of Deputies when crucial legislation was introduced. In so doing,

12. Humberto Roggero, the former whip of the PJ in the Chamber of Deputies, candidly admitted the emasculation of congressional powers and the lack of interest of many legislators to debate and oversee governmental decisions during the 1990s (La Nación, September 8, 2004).
13. Menem was elected in May 1989 but was not to assume office until December of that year.

the 97 Peronist representatives would become de facto the largest bloc in the legislature and could pass the president's emergency measures (Vidal 1995, 53). The Radicals also agreed to avoid a tough opposition on two laws that granted Menem broad emergency powers that were to become the cornerstone of his market reforms. Had they refused to live up to their pledge, Menem made it clear to the opposition in Congress that he was willing to use executive orders to bypass the legislature and enact his reform agenda.

Thus, using both threats and persuasion, Menem received from Congress emergency powers to act by decree on a host of issues that were the exclusive prerogative of the federal legislature.[14] In August 1989, after only a month and a half in office, Menem demanded Congress's approval of the State Reform Law (23.696), which authorized the executive branch to place trustees in charge of all state companies for 180 days, renewable for an additional 180. The law gave the executive the authority to immediately privatize some of the largest companies, although in some cases this required constitutional amendments. Most important, according to the new law, Congress delegated the power to privatize through decrees to the executive and left it with unlimited discretion on the criteria and means to be used (Ferreira Rubio and Goretti 1998). Furthermore, law 23.696 also eliminated many legal impediments and appeal procedures that might have been used to derail privatization. However, in so doing, it effectively withheld important tools that make privatization transparent and hold its managers accountable.

The following September Congress also passed a second piece of legislation, the Law of Economic Emergency (26.697). It gave the president the right to suspend costly industrial subsidies and tax breaks while sheltering the state from pending lawsuits and contractual obligations with government contractors. Technically, this granted the executive a host of prerogatives over taxation and other sensitive issues, which established an enormous discretionary power. Eventually, in the case of the State Reform Law Congress later expanded the extension to three years. With these two pieces of legislation Menem received the legal instruments for expediting his market reforms without legislative oversight in a matter of months (Lla-

---

14. Menem also warned the Radicals that had they tried to stop his reform agenda in Congress, his administration was ready to disclose to the press alleged corruption scandals that had taken place during the Alfonsín administration.

nos 2001). This gives us an idea of the magnitude of power concentration he acquired as a result.[15]

If there was any doubt about Menem's resolve, he quickly showed what he would do if congressmen still dragged their feet. At the time of the vote on the State Reform Law, some disgruntled legislators from both the opposition and the PJ tried to embarrass the administration by depriving the necessary quorum in the hope of winning some last-minute conces-sions. In response, government backers quickly rushed in some employees of the Chamber of Deputies (the Argentine lower house), who voted in place of the absent legislators. The impostors cast the decisive ballots, and despite the media exposure of this unprecedented event, the speaker of the house, a Menem supporter, refused to investigate the facts and nullify the voting session (Cerruti and Ciancaglini 1992, 98).

Although Menem repeatedly stated his respect for the independence of the legislative and judicial powers, in practice he rendered the oversight functions of these institutions ineffective. These efforts ran counter to Hay-ek's and Friedman's theories, which postulated that political power should be as dispersed as possible to guarantee effective checks and balances so as to prevent arbitrary government decisions in the economic arena. Follow-ing the same rationale, Saba (2000) noted that while market reforms under-line a presumption in favor of individual rights, market competition, and transparency, Menem systematically acted against them.

To appease criticism of his authoritarian tactics, Menem allowed Con-gress to form a Bicameral Commission on Privatization (BCP) in principle to bring accountability to the reform process. However, in reality the BCP could only request information and its recommendations were not binding. Thus, it had no real power and the Menem administration could ignore most of the attempts by opposition members within the BCP to stop ques-tionable privatizations (Natale 1993). To make things worse, the Peronists held a majority in such a committee from 1989 to 1997 and blocked any move from opposition parties to slow the process despite the many irregu-larities found by the committee (Natale 1993; Rigoli 2000).[16]

Between 1991 and 1997 the Peronists had a solid majority in both houses of Congress. Occasionally, however, maverick groups within the PJ threat-

---

15. On the legal inconsistencies and consequence of these laws, see Gordillo (1996).

16. Rigoli (2000) contends that several senators making up the BCP received bribes in order to give their support for the new patent law and the transfer to the private sector of water (Aguas Argentinas), federal highways, and the oil industry (Yacimientos Petroliferos Fiscales).

ened to defect unless the president compromised on pork barrel projects dear to them. This situation forced Menem to employ at times two additional powerful tools. Whenever the emergency powers described above were not sufficient to expedite his reform agenda, and his own legislators were slow in cooperating, the president employed decrees of necessity and urgency (decretos de necesidad y urgencia, DNUs) at a staggering pace. From the vantage point of the executive, DNUS were particularly appealing because they did not require any prior delegation or approval from Congress, as opposed to other forms of decree-laws. According to Ferreira Rubio and Goretti (2000), Menem's indiscriminate use of DNUS as a policy instrument allowed him to bypass constitutional checks and balances entrusted on other branches of government, effectively replacing the rule of law with "presidential fiat." The DNUS greatly expanded presidential legislative authority in areas reserved for Congress by the constitution. During his first term Menem issued a total of 335 DNUS. After the constitutional reform of 1994, which aimed at curtailing such decree power, he still managed 210 DNUS. They covered crucial policy areas that usually fell under congressional jurisdiction. During the 1989–94 period DNUS affected key issues such as taxation (72), salaries and wages (39), public debt (29), trade (10), transport (21), real estate privatization (22), litigation against the federal government (5), industrial promotion (8), civil and political rights (8), public agencies (32), and relations between federal and state government (6) (Ferreira Rubio and Goretti 1998).

Prior to Menem, by comparison, only thirty DNUS had been issued. This underscores the fact that since the approval of the constitution in 1853 the executive had abided to the rule that DNUS were to be limited to situations when Congress was not in session or the regular legislative process could not be used due to an impeding national crisis that demanded a quick response. Regardless, DNUS by law had to be submitted for legislative approval at later date, otherwise they would expire. Menem regarded all these requirements as mere formalities. Indeed, in 51 percent of the DNUS issued the government itself did not identify them as such, but nonetheless they were used to repeal or enforce laws without any clear legal ground or congressional delegation. Between 1989 and 1992 four out of ten DNUS were promulgated when Congress was in ordinary session and many remaining ones were enacted when Congress was convened in extraordinary session. Although the executive should have sent bills to Congress under both circumstances, Menem ignored the whole matter. As a result of the Olivos

Pact, the 1995 constitutional amendments aimed to curtail executive powers legislating through DNUS. However, Menem obtained that the expiration of laws so enacted would be postponed to the end of his mandate, thus keeping intact a lot of controversial legislation.[17]

Menem's second means to overcome legislative opposition consisted of presidential vetoes. Between 1989 and 1993 of the 625 bills passed by Congress the president vetoed thirty-seven completely and forty-one partially. In 1994–97 the president vetoed eighty-seven bills, fourteen of which Congress overran. During the same period Menem used line-item vetoes on thirty-eight occasions to enforce legislation. What is noteworthy in the case of partial vetoes is that Menem, by automatically promulgating parts of a given bill, was in clear violation of the constitution, which mandated that an amended bill be sent back to the chamber of Congress in which it had originated (article 72).

However, when Congress could not be circumvented through DNUS or vetoes, and the fate of a bill was very much in doubt, the Peronist leadership resorted to illegal means, such as the one described for the State Reform Law, to get things done. While debating the bill for the privatization of Gas del Estado in 1992, the Radicals tried to force Menem to bargain by depriving the necessary quorum for the vote to take place in the Chamber of Deputies. To overcome this delaying tactic, the Peronists had some impostors enter the voting session and take the seats of absent legislators. In so doing they provided the necessary quorum that allowed the Peronists to pass the bill notwithstanding the request of Radical legislators to annul the session and start an investigation (Vidal 1995, 122–28). In brief, these events are clear examples of an executive branch blatantly abusing its authority (Ferreira Rubio and Goretti 1998).

Other elements of the 1994 constitutional reform that could have helped restrain presidential powers turned out to be ineffective, in part because the Peronists dominated Congress and in part because a demoralized opposition seemed more prone to seek concessions through closed-door deals, as testified by the Olivos Pact, rather than through legislative action. For instance, despite having the power to question and receive written answers from gov-

---

17. Moreover, although one of the 1994 constitutional amendments mandated the creation of a bicameral commission to approve or reject DNUS and partial vetoes, the PJ majority in Congress purposely failed to act on it (Bowen and Rose-Ackerman 2003). This left Menem with a free hand to pursue his controversial agenda through DNUS and partial vetoes, just as before the 1994 amendments (*La Nación*, March 14, 2004).

ernment officials, congressmen largely failed to use such a prerogative (Bowen and Rose-Ackerman 2003). Although during Menem's second term Congress on occasion defied presidential authority on some important bills, such as social security reform (Llanos 2002), it often did so to preserve the benefits to political clienteles rather than to assert its accountability functions. In fact, rarely did Congress set up investigative commissions to assess wrongdoing, and when it happened it was done in a partisan fashion that allowed the Peronist majority to block any serious inquiry (Molinelli, Palanza, and Sin 1999). In fact, because the PJ was the majority party in Congress for most of Menem's tenure, it controlled the most important committees.[18] This explains, for instance, the lack of congressional oversight of budgetary expenditures. The last time Congress verified how the executive spent the federal budget was 1993. From that point on, the Peronist-dominated legislative commission in charge of monitoring budget execution failed to debate the issue, which basically meant that no one knew how the executive was actually spending the appropriations in the federal budget.[19]

Such an intimidating strategy paid off. During Menem's first term Congress was able to repeal only four presidential decrees out of 335. Moreover, in two cases the president succeeded in overriding legislative repeal through his veto powers (Jones 1997). Summing up, Menem from the start proceeded in concentrating power within the executive branch. Once he succeeded in acquiring broad legislative authority on socioeconomic matters from Congress, he neutralized both the judiciary and the independent agencies of the public administration that could have forced the executive to account for its highly controversial initiatives and shady deals. In less than three years the president had created a system of virtual impunity. I will now turn to the analysis of how Menem implemented his strategy to neutralize other accountability institutions.

The Courts

As noted in chapter 1, Hayek and Friedman hold that the courts, and their role in upholding property rights, constitute a fundamental institution in a

18. Moreover, the president of the Chamber of Deputies determines to which committee bills are sent, as well as which committee serves as the "lead" committee (responsible for managing the bill and the only committee, along with a budget if it is included, that can actually block a bill's passage).

19. This practice continued well into 2005. The AGN, which in principle was supposed to revise federal expenditures, usually did so several years later and sent its report to the Peronist-

market economy. Likewise, the WC urged Latin American countries to re-
vamp their judiciaries and bring them up to international standards. In
this regard, Argentina constitutes an interesting case. Following the U.S.
Constitution, Argentina's founding fathers established a clear separation of
powers among the three branches of government. The power of judicial
review is based on article 31 of the constitution and can be exercised by
both federal judges and the Supreme Court as in the United States. Indeed,
Argentine judges have used U.S. court rulings to justify their decisions. The
weakness of the Argentine civil law system, as opposed to that of the United
States, is that prior decisions on a similar case are not binding even in lower
courts (Bowman and Rose-Ackerman 2003). Precedents can only be used
as a reference, and each case must be filed individually, which deprives
defendants of class action suits.

How could this happen? During his presidency Alfonsín had serious
problems in convincing the Supreme Court to cooperate with some of his
own policies, particularly in the realm of prosecution of human rights

Nonetheless, from the 1880s until 1929 the Argentine courts slowly tried
to gain independence from the executive branch, which earned them a substantial amount of respect within the public. Unfortunately, this trend was
reversed between 1930 and 1983 when political instability ushered a series of
authoritarian and populist governments that subjugated judicial independence (Garay 1991; Nino 1993; Miller 1997). When the country returned to
democracy in the early 1980s, President Alfonsín allowed the Supreme
Court and the federal courts to regain some degree of political independence. However, this trend was short lived. Once Menem became president
in mid-1989 he took immediate steps that ran counter to the recommendations of Hayek, Friedman, and the WC with regard to property rights and
safeguarding the rule of law more generally. In fact, the independence of
the courts was immediately attacked and progovernment judges issued a
barrage of sentences that made a mockery of the rule of law throughout the
1990s (Miller 2001). Property rights became whatever Menem wanted them
to be, depending on the circumstances of the moment. Worse yet, sympathetic judges not only provided the government with the legal grounds to
defend its controversial policies but also guaranteed a system of impunity
for the wrongdoings committed by administration officials.

How could this happen? During his presidency Alfonsín had serious
problems in convincing the Supreme Court to cooperate with some of his
own policies, particularly in the realm of prosecution of human rights

---

controlled bicameral commission in charge, which failed to take any action even when the reports
cited possible wrongdoings (*La Nación*, September 20, 2005).

crimes. Keenly aware of the prestige and power that the Supreme Court had acquired during the Alfonsín administration, Menem proceed from the start to make sure that the highest court in the nation would be squarely in his camp. In doing so, he resurrected one of Alfonsín's aborted projects aimed at enlarging the Supreme Court membership. The official justification being that more justices were necessary to deal with the logjam of pending cases.

The attack on the court's independence started a few weeks after Menem took office. The strategy behind it was exposed by minister of justice Jorge Maiorano when he candidly stated that by electing Menem the people had endorsed a new project to transform Argentina. This meant that it was "absolutely necessary that there be a Court that understands the [administration's] policy and be supportive of the program that the [Argentine] society had voted" (Morgenstern and Manzetti 2003, 161). Initially, to convince some justices to step down voluntarily the Menem administration offered ambassadorships abroad (e.g., justice Carlos Fayt). For those close to the Radicals, it used intimidation—as in the case of justice Augusto Belluscio, against whom the Peronists in Congress started an impeachment procedure on the grounds of an alleged conflict of interests. Four out of the five members of the court denounced Menem's attempt, but to no avail. On April 5, 1990, the Chamber of Deputies voted to increase the number of justices to nine. The Radicals charged that impostors cast the decisive votes to have the necessary quorum (Verbitsky 1993, 49), but the Peronist president of the chamber overruled the Radicals' request to annul the vote once again. One of the five justices, Jorge Bacqué, quit in protest before the measure became effective, giving Menem the opportunity to nominate not four but five new justices. Three weeks later the Judiciary Committee in the Senate approved in only seven minutes the new justices proposed by the executive.[20] The remaining original four, concerned with possibly losing their jobs given Menem's threat of impeachment procedures that could surely be approved in a Peronist-dominated Senate, instead reversed their initial hostility and decided to cooperate by lending crucial support for highly controversial government initiatives (Helmke 2002).

Indeed, once Menem succeeded in packing the Supreme Court with loyalists, Argentina's highest tribunal became overtly partisan and played a

---

20. On the weak qualifications of Menem's appointees to the Supreme Court, see Chávez (2004).

decisive role at critical junctures to support the administration's decision-making style (Saba 2000). On the one hand, it gave the executive branch the legal justification for its controversial reforms, and on the other, it threw out any challenges coming from the Congress, lower courts, and civil society. The five Peronist justices were so accommodating to the presidential agenda in issuing their rulings that they were quickly dubbed the "automatic" majority (Chávez 2004). Within this context, four rulings were fundamental in helping Menem overcome any legal opposition to his authoritarian decision-making style.

The first of such rulings was the *Peralta, Luis A. y otro c/ Estado Nacional*, issued on December 27, 1990. This decision is fundamental since it legitimized the executive's authority to legislate without congressional approval. Late in December 1989 the government issued DNU 36/90, which sanctioned that all bank accounts exceeding $610 were automatically turned into ten-year, dollar-dominated bonds (*bonos externos*), which at the time traded 30 percent below their par value. The reasoning behind this confiscation of assets was that it would help stem a new bout of hyperinflation by curtailing the amount of liquidity in the market. Later that month, the Supreme Court received about thirty cases challenging the constitutionality of such a measure, commonly referred as the Bonex Plan since it had been enforced without the approval of Congress, which had jurisdiction on this type of fiscal measures. The Supreme Court instead ruled in favor of the government decree. It asserted that in situations where the very existence of the nation is at stake, restricting property rights, protected by article 17 of the constitution, is not a violation of the constitution itself as long as an emergency situation persists and the decree does not favor specific individuals. The importance of this is that individual rights became subject to government limitations under circumstances decided by the executive. The second point is directly related to the first. That is, since Congress had established a situation of crisis by passing the Economic Emergency Law, the executive could legislate through DNUs and restrict constitutional rights as long as the causes that created the crisis continued. Of course, the court implicitly left to the executive the determination of whether or not the country was an emergency situation. As a matter of fact, Menem ruled Argentina through emergency powers until he left office in December 1999. There is a third, and equally important, point in the Supreme Court ruling. The court stated that in situations of "high social risk," which require the application of "swift measures, whose efficacy are not conceivable through other means," the president can issue DNUs as he see fit. The only condition in doing so is that the executive informs Congress, and Congress itself does not express its disapproval. In other words, in so doing the Supreme Court established a new doctrine that could be labeled of "tacit approval."[21] This ruling was tantamount to sanctioning the transfer of legislative powers from the Congress to the executive as it added: "Immersed in today's reality, not only Argentina's but the universal reality, we have to admit that some kinds of problems and the solutions that they demand can hardly be dealt with or solved efficiently and expeditiously by [a] multi-personal [legislative] body. Confrontation of interests that delay . . . the process of making decisions; special interest pressure on those decisions, which is also the norm since the [legislature] represents the provinces and the people; the lack of homogeneity [of the legislature] as the individuals and groups that it represents are moved most of the time by divergent interests—make it necessary that the President, whose role demands the maintenance of peace and social order, which [is] seriously threatened in this case, has to make the decision to select the measures that are unavoidable and this reality urgently demands with no delay" (Saba 2000, 265).

In justifying its ruling, the Supreme Court went further. It stated that although the constitution established the division of powers among the three branches of government, this should not be interpreted in a way to allow the "dismemberment of the State so that each of its parts acts in isolation to the detriment of national unity." What is ironic in this interpretation is that, if we stretch it to the limit, under emergency situations, and in the name of pursuing the national interest, even the Supreme Court has to subordinate itself to the executive.

The transfer of Congress's law-making powers to the executive was reiterated in 1994 in the *Cocchia* benchmark case. In writing the majority decision, Justice Boggiano stated, "There exists a modern and strong doctrine that admits, within certain reasonable limits, the delegation of legislative powers as a claim for good government in the modern State. 'Delegation of legislative powers from the Assembly to the Executive has become a universal manifestation of the technological age,' as argued by Lowenstein, without distinguishing between parliamentary and presidential systems, and indeed [Lowenstein] pointed out the new universal character of the trend" (Saba 2000, 265).

---

21. As we saw in the previous chapter, Yeltsin tried the same approach to corner the Duma in 1992.

While the *Peralta* and *Cocchia* cases gave legal justifications to the executive in its quest to advocate to itself the role of the legislature, the case of *Fontela, Moisés Eduardo c/ Estado Nacional* of September 1990 was significant in that it made clear, from the start, that individual legislators could not use the court system as an alternative to Congress to make the Menem administration accountable for its policies. In July 1990, adopting the same arguments expressed earlier by the inspector general Alberto González Arzac with regard to legal and administrative irregularities in the upcoming privatization of the national flag carrier Aerolíneas Argentinas, Congressman Moisés Fontela filed an injunction before federal judge Oscar Garzón Funes to stop the sale until an investigation could ascertain the legality of the transaction. Garzón Funes, who was known for being quite an independent-minded judge, accepted the case and ordered the minister of public works Roberto Dromi, who was in charge of the privatization program, to restructure Aerolíneas according to law 19.550. In response, Dromi pleaded for the Supreme Court to take up the case. The court accepted the minister's request less than an hour after Grazón Funes had issued his order. This move was in open violation of article 257 of the Civil and Commercial Procedural Code, which allowed appeals to be filed only to the tribunal that had issued the ruling regarding the case. Using an obscure legal procedure called *per saltum,* the Supreme Court claimed the case for itself due to the "institutional gravity" of the matter without actually specifying what was so critical about selling an SOE from a constitutional standpoint. However, Menem badly needed this ruling. Aerolíneas was his first privatization. Had it failed, the whole divestiture process could have collapsed, putting into question his administration's ability to overcome the opposition that had earlier derailed Alfonsín's attempts in the late 1980s. It took only a few minutes for the Supreme Court to void Garzón Funes's injunction, thus paving the way for the airline transfer a few days later. The court justified the use of the *per saltum* citing that the U.S. Supreme Court had ruled on cases without previous sentences. Yet in his dissenting opinion, Justice Fayt pointed out that the Evart Act of 1891, which had established the U.S. Supreme Court's right to advocate cases in lower courts, was not applicable since the Argentine law 4055, inspired by the U.S. jurisprudence, did not contain any *per saltum* clause. Nonetheless, Menem obtained what he wanted, and the message behind the ruling was clear: the Supreme Court was solidly behind the president and could not be counted on to challenge his initiatives, no matter how unconstitutional they may be (Verbitsky 1993, 140).

The fourth case, *Alejandro Nieva y otros, c/ Poder Ejecutivo Nacional,* revolved around the use of DNUs under the 1994 constitutional amendments. In 1997 Menem launched the last large privatization, which sold the concession rights to manage thirty-three of the country's airports. As in past divestitures, allegations of corruption and irregularities abounded. Concerned with the necessity of speeding up the process and to avoid the mounting of an effective opposition, Menem issued a DNU that established the terms of transfer and the regulatory framework. Claiming that this was an abuse of presidential powers under the 1994 constitutional amendments establishing the parameters for the use of DNUs, some opposition members of Congress succeeded in having a lower court nullify the decree. Undeterred, Menem issued a new DNU that validated the old one, but a lower court again struck it down. Since the Peronist-dominated Congress had failed to create a bicameral commission regulating the use of DNUs, the case ended up in the Supreme Court, which promptly sided with the government and nullified the lower court's decision. As Bowen and Rose-Ackerman (2003, 176) explain, "the Court ruled that the second decree had rendered the first one moot, and that the legislators lacked legal standing to bring the second suit. The Court also argued that the dispute over the [DNU] was inherently political and thus inappropriate for judicial interference."

The president also appointed new federal appeal court judges who dealt with administrative law and could play an active role in thwarting the reform process. This was not a casual move since the many irregularities committed in the implementation of the reform program were likely to be challenged in lower courts. Menem also removed Andrés D'Alessio, the chief of the Federal Prosecutor's Office by decree. By constitutional provision such an office had both functional and budgetary autonomy, and its head had traditionally enjoyed the same status as the Supreme Court justices. This gave the president the opportunity to appoint, in his place, a person loyal to him who in turn purged the office of recalcitrant prosecutors and hired new ones who would not cause problems to the administration's agenda.[22] Many of these appointees had dubious qualifications.

22. Interview with former state prosecutor Luis Moreno Ocampo, Buenos Aires, March 20, 1996. Several of Menem's judges in later years were impeached on charges of corruption and administrative irregularities.

Justice minister León Arslanian, who opposed such a bold move, eventually resigned in protest (Larkins 1998). These events, as well as others that took place under Duhalde and Kirchner, further affected people's confidence in an institution that in the mid-1980s had regained a fair amount of popular respect. In 2001 only 23 percent of respondents showed trust in the judiciary, the second lowest score among major Latin American countries (Figure 4.1). In 2004 another poll showed that 46 percent of Argentines believed that it was very likely that one had to bribe a judge to receive a favorable sentence—the fourth highest score among Latin American countries—as opposed to 20 percent in Chile, which represented the lowest score (Latinobarometro 2004). These results were confirmed in 2005 by a local poll showing that 80 percent of respondents considered the judiciary untrustworthy and little/not honest at all ("Sin confianza en la justicia," *La Nación,* November 27, 2005).

Oversight Institutions

There are two broad categories of oversight institutions. The first consists of agencies and departments enjoying some degree of independence, at least in theory, from executive interference. The second is represented by departments directly under executive control and therefore unable to shelter themselves from presidential control. By 1992 Menem had either eliminated or neutralized all departments and special agencies by putting loyal supporters at their helm.

In the former category of agencies enjoying some independence was the Accounting Court (Tribunal de Cuentas), which was established after 1955 as a means to address administrative corruption during Perón's first two terms (1946–55). Modeled after its French and Spanish equivalents, the tribunal had substantial powers to conduct ex-ante investigations on government spending. The tribunal could also veto funding and initiate criminal prosecutions of acts perpetrated against the federal treasury. A board of five federal judges with life tenure specializing in fiscal and accounting matters managed the institution. In turn, the board members were nominated by the executive and appointed after being approved by the Senate. Despite having wide powers, the performance of the tribunal was very poor during the course of its history. While it denounced excesses, it rarely prosecuted prominent offenders.

Nonetheless, relations between the tribunal and Menem became rocky shortly after the president took office, not so much because the tribunal was actively pursuing suspects, but because the financial improprieties committed by administration officials were so egregious. For example, in March 1990 decree 477 required the Ministry of Health and Social Action to purchase 1.3 million aprons for school children at $5.90 per unit when the market average price was $4.30. Radical Congressman Antonio Berhongaray believed the tender to be suspicious and alerted the tribunal. Not only was the base price inflated but, as later discovered by the press, no company in the country was capable of producing that large an amount of aprons in the specified time. Also suspicious was that although the Economic Emergency Law had set strict limits on public contracts, interior minister Eduardo Bauzá, Menem's most trusted adviser, created a loophole to allow direct contracting because of its "emergency" nature (Verbitsky 1993).

Eventually, the company Herrera Hermanos S.A., which had never made an apron and had no real capital, won the contract. Its only qualification seemed to have been the political connection of its owner, a Buenos Aires Peronist politician by the name of Juan Ricardo Mussa, who had been spotted in the group of dignitaries at the time of Menem's inauguration ceremony. Mussa's other notable distinction was a pending trial for fraud. As the scandal evolved, high-ranking administration officials threatened to reopen cases of alleged corruption under President Alfonsín (Verbitsky 1993, 91). In the meantime, and against the terms of the contract, the Ministry of Health and Social Action paid $3 million in advance without having received any aprons. Upon discovering these irregularities, the tribunal started a criminal investigation for fraud. Shortly thereafter, as the media began to publicize the scandal, Menem signed a decree in which he rescinded the contract with Herrera Hermanos S.A. for lack of compliance.[23]

The tribunal discovered and denounced flagrant financial irregularities in other instances in 1990. Thanks to the media uproar some shady deals stopped in their tracks. One case involved the privatization of the reading of meters, billing, and collection of fees for three large SOES in public utilities: Gas del Estado, Segba, and Obras Sanitarias. The administration issued a DNU in this regard that contemplated a bidding process for the contract

---

23. In 2005 a federal court found two former government officials and two businessmen guilty of fraud, but the mastermind behind the apron's scandal, Bauzá, suffered no consequences as Judge Maria Servini de Cubria, a close friend of Menem's, had acquitted him years earlier (*La Nación*, May 14, 2005).

award. However, the Ministry of Economy later issued another decree that replaced the bidding process with a direct negotiation that would benefit a consortium having direct connections with some of Menem's old friends in his native province of La Rioja. The tribunal found the 15 percent fee that the consortium charged the government for the billing procedures of the three SOES excessive, and nullified the contract. Unfortunately, these actions hastened the tribunal's demise. Vice President Duhalde signed a decree in which he dismissed the tribunal board members, in violation of law 20.677, which required the Senate to start impeachment proceedings for the removal of any of its judges. Four of its five members were replaced with people close to the president (Larkins 1998). Not surprising, after 1990 the tribunal ceased to create problems for the administration and was dissolved in December 1992.[24]

The national investigative prosecutor (Fiscalía Nacional de Investigaciones Administrativas, FNIA) is in charge of investigating public officials suspected of having perpetrated crimes against federal property. The federal judge in charge of the FNIA has substantial powers to investigate and can submit his findings to a federal prosecutor for criminal or civil proceedings. At the time Menem took office, Ricardo Molinas directed the institution. Molinas had a solid reputation as a human rights lawyer. Although considered a maverick by some, he was appointed to his post as a federal judge by President Alfonsín. Molinas soon acquired a reputation for being very active in pursuing offenders—he investigated three times as many cases as his predecessor. Once Menem came to power, Molinas began to look into several allegations ranging from subsidies granted to companies in violation of the Economic Emergency Law to irregularities in the privatization of the federal highways and the telecom SOE ENTel (Ente Nacional de Telecomunicaciones). In early 1991 Menem removed Molinas by decree despite the fact that, as a judge, the latter had to first undergo an impeachment process in the Senate.[25] In a split decision, the Supreme Court upheld Molinas's removal and in his place the president appointed a loyalist who made the FNIA completely ineffective until a new judge took over in 2003.

Let us now turn to those institutions directly dependent on the executive branch. The most important one in 1989 was the General Accounting Agency for State Corporations (Sindicatura General de Empresas Públicas,

---

24. *Revista Argentina del Régimen de la Administración Pública* (December 1999).

25. Interviews with professors Roberto de Michele and Roberto Saba, University of Buenos Aires Law School, Buenos Aires, May 1994.

SIGEP), in charge of auditing the financial and legal procedures of SOEs. It had been created by the 1976–83 military government and in theory had substantial powers. It could use a variety of means ranging from simple observations to formal warnings up to the suspension of any financial and/ or administrative decision made by an SOE. Suspensions had to be ratified by the president. Menem appointed Mario Truffat, the manager of his presidential campaign, as head of SIGEP. Nonetheless, in the two years that Truffat was in charge of SIGEP he drafted six hundred objections to executive initiatives (Verbitsky 1991). His activism came in response to the many improprieties in the way administration officials were managing the privatization process and other issues affecting SOEs.[26] Truffat's collision course with several of Menem's ministers started in the fall of 1989, when he suspended the sale of the shopping mall Galería Pacifico because its contract was riddled with irregularities. However, the incident that delivered the coup de grace to Truffat came when the Argentine engineering company Impsa demanded that the government pay for $70 million worth of public contracts. Menem and his cabinet actually decided to award Impsa $200 million and told SIGEP to justify the $130 million in excess. Reluctantly, Truffat complied, but Menem and the Ministry of Economy had by then concluded that SIGEP constituted an "obstacle" to the privatization process (Verbitsky 1993). Using another decree, in August 1991 the president downgraded the SIGEP from Secretería de Estado (State Secretariat) to National Bureau (Dirección Nacional). In practice this meant that SIGEP's ability to suspend dubious contracts was terminated and its functions were relegated to nonbinding admonitions (Truffat resigned before these events took place).

The inspector general of the public administration (Inspector General de Justicia) was yet another office entrusted with the authority of making sure that new rules and requirements affecting the public administration conformed to existing legislation. Upon becoming president, Menem appointed at its helm a longtime friend and supporter, Alberto González Arzac. Unexpectedly, the new inspector general took his role seriously. In June 1990 Arzac warned Menem that Aerolíneas Argentinas could not be privatized as planned. In fact, the government intended to become a minority shareholder with veto rights and change the corporate structure of Aerolíneas. Yet Arzac contended that this scheme was legally unfeasible because

---

26. Interviews with former staffers of the SIGEP, Buenos Aires, May 1994.

the existing commercial codes did not contemplate such a company arrangement. In September of the same year, the inspector general had
warned the Ministry of Justice that ENTel had not fulfilled some of its obligations prior to its transfer to private operators. Days later Arzac admon-
ished María Julia Alsogaray, whom the president had chosen to organize
the ENTel divestiture, to the effect that she could not be on the board of
one of the firms managing the proceeds of the telephone privatization at
the same time. Although none of Arzac's legal opinions were binding, they
had embarrassed the administration enough to prompt his dismissal (Verbitsky 1993).

After neutralizing most oversight institutions Menem came under pressure from the World Bank, which had grown increasingly worried about
the numerous allegations of corrupt practices. Thus, he reorganized the
executive and congressional oversight institutions, but he did so in a way
that practically made the reorganizations ineffective. On October 30, 1992,
Congress approved law 24.156 (Law of Financial Administration and National Public Sector Control). However, it is important to note that the law
only came into effect at the end of 1993, when the administration had already carried out a number of crucial and highly controversial reforms
without any true oversight institution that could block possible wrongdoing. The new law streamlined auditing procedures by creating two new
separate agencies: the General Auditing Office of the Nation (Auditoria
General de la Nación, AGN), under the control of Congress, and the General
Accounting Agency of the Nation (Sindicatura General de la Nación,
SIGEN), under the control of the executive.

The AGN reports to Congress and serves as the external auditing institution for the public sector. Congress sets the AGN budget. The AGN has a
board of seven members elected for an eight-year term. The Chamber of
Deputies and the Senate appoint three each. The appointments mirror the
composition of the congressional membership, with the largest party nomi-
nating the largest number of board members. This meant that in 1993 the
PJ, which controlled both houses of Congress, had four members out of
seven on the board. The president of AGN is appointed jointly by the president of the republic and the speakers of the Chamber of Deputies and the
Senate. As a result of the Olivos Pact the AGN presidency goes to the largest
minority party in Congress. Thus, between 1994 and 1999 Enrique Paixao,
a Radical, was in charge of the institution and staffed the agency with people coming primarily from his party. The AGN board executes the action

plan previously approved by a bicameral congressional committee but has discretion in its internal hiring, contract consultation, and internal organization procedures.

On paper, the AGN is a powerful institution. It has jurisdiction over budgetary, economic, financial, legal, and inventory management of the public administration as well as the federal district of Buenos Aires. Moreover, it audits the fulfillment of privatization contracts as well as private companies and foundations that receive public funds. Section 118 of law 24.156 specifies AGN's duties, which are widely conceived, and section 119 defines its powers. The AGN can solicit information from all public administration offices, pursues investigations whenever it sees fit, and then transmits the results to the bicameral congressional committee mentioned above. It also establishes the criteria for control and auditing, submits a report to the bicameral congressional committee, and may receive from Congress auditing powers for entities that are not state owned and are governed by private law.

Nonetheless, several factors undercut the AGN's broad powers. First, the AGN's board makes decisions by a simple majority. This means that if the president's party holds a majority within the board, as happened between 1994 and 1999, it can effectively stop any initiative that can potentially damage the executive. According to my interviews in 1998 with senior AGN managers belonging to the UCR, Paixao wanted to continue an investigation regarding the National Pensioners Health Care Agency due to a massive corruption scandal into 1999. When the AGN president submitted his request to the board, the PJ board members vetoed it due to the potential embarrassment to the Menem administration that a thorough investigation could create. A second limitation came from the fact that the congressional committees overseeing the AGN drew up the agency's action plan and could make changes to the AGN's reports. Because the Peronists held a majority in those committees, these powers were used to thwart the AGN's ability to fulfill its duties. Third, the AGN's auditing mechanisms were patterned after Canadian and Puerto Rican models in which oversight is done according to a post-facto approach, as opposed to the prereform ex-ante method used by the Tribunal de Cuentas (see above). This seriously limited the AGN's ability to stop government abuses in the making. Fourth, in the last two years of his second term President Menem, citing the imperative of cutting the fiscal deficit, unilaterally reduced the AGN budget even though the authority to do so was within the realm of Congress. Not surprising, the

Peronist-dominated legislative committee overseeing the AGN did not pro-test the presidential initiative in this regard.

SIGEN is the auditing institution operating within the public administra-tion. Like the AGN, on paper SIGEN has broad powers. It oversees the presi-dency; all government departments and secretariats dependent on the presidency; about 105 public entities, including 36 universities, and all re-maining SOEs. However, under Menem it only went after small offenders. This is because the presidency selects the director and management of SIGEN, which in turn finds it hard to act independently. For instance, when I asked the Menem-era director of SIGEN what happened in those instances when SIGEN discovered flagrant cases of misuse of public funds and proce-dures, he replied, "I immediately call Carlitos!" He added, by way of clari-fication, "But of course, Carlitos Menem, he is a dear friend of mine!" Obviously, it is hard to believe that given these close personal ties the SIGEN could effectively pursue its tasks when the executive branch or people/pub-lic entities close to the president were at fault.

President De la Rúa, upon taking office in December 1999, appointed Rafael Bielsa to head the SIGEN. Bielsa found an agency with low morale, as SIGEN's managers kept the money allocated for merit-based salaries to all employees for themselves. Furthermore, there was a strong suspicion that some of SIGEN's top-level managers engaged in collusive activities with the business and government agencies they were supposed to control. Indeed, Bielsa admitted that the whole staff had been appointed according to politi-cal criteria. Even well-intentioned staffers understood that any audit that could question the behavior of high government officials was going to be stopped.[27]

Corruption

Having successfully muted opposition in Congress, the Supreme Court, and oversight institutions, by the end of 1992 Menem had created a system that offered him virtual impunity since all institutions entrusted with the enforcement of horizontal accountability had ceased to operate effectively. It is no coincidence that this lack of accountability corresponded with a mounting number of alleged corruption scandals involving ministers and

27. Interview with Rafael Bielsa, Buenos Aires, May 2000.

close presidential aides and friends. Indeed, although government corruption has always been an issue in Argentina, by most accounts it reached record levels during Menem's tenure. According to Cerruti and Ciancaglini (1992, 28–29), what struck foreign diplomats at the time was not so much corruption but the large amounts of bribes demanded and the high number of government officials involved. Such scandals were revealed by the only institution still escaping Menem's grip: Argentina's independent press.

In 1991 Horacio Verbitsky, Argentina's best-known investigative journalist, published what became the best seller of all times, "Robo para la Corona" (I steal for the crown), in which he painstakingly described Menem's corruption strategy as well as the deals behind it. Among other things, Verbitsky (1991) detailed how economic deregulation, as well as the privatization of Aerolíneas Argentinas, the telephone monopoly ENTel, the steelmaker Somisa, the federal highways, and the petrochemical company Petroquímica de Bahía Blanca, were rigged to obtain bribes on the order of an alleged $150 million.[28] At the center of many scandals were consortia led by foreign companies in association with local investors.

Despite the clamor that these disclosures provoked in Argentina, neither judges nor state prosecutors bothered to investigate the facts. Instead, the Menem administration launched a major campaign to discredit its critics. However, a major blow to the government campaign came from within. In August 1995 economy minister Domingo Cavallo publicly alleged that market reforms were put to corrupt use. Cavallo accused several of his fellow ministers, as well as many federal legislators, of rigging the privatization of the post office to favor what he labeled as a mafialike cartel owned by Alfredo Yabran, an Argentine businessman and a personal friend of the president (Llanos 2002). As a result, Menem forced Cavallo to resign. However, his accusations could not be dismissed as easily, and eventually Yabran had to withdraw from the public tender (Cherashny 1997).

Allegations of serious irregularities continued to surround even the last large privatization affecting the national airports in 1998 (Llanos 2002). The World Bank, which had initially advised the Argentine government on this matter, suddenly pulled out due to the lack of transparency that characterized the whole process.[29] Coincidentally, the most controversial privatiz-

---

28. In the case of Aerolíneas Argentinas alone, the Spanish airline Iberia allegedly paid $68 million (*La Nación*, November 22, 2003).

29. Interviews with World Bank staffers, Washington, D.C., April 1998.

ations ended by providing mediocre services for telephones and water supply at prices well above international levels. In several cases privatized companies failed to live up to their contractual obligations on investments and service provision, and a few ran into serious financial problems. By the end of 2001 Aerolíneas Argentinas was bankrupt, forcing the government to find another private investor to rescue it. Moreover, the consortia handling the post office (Macri Group) and the national airports (Aeropuertos Argentina 2000) owed the federal government $257 million in unpaid concession rights.[30]

Only after Menem left office in December 1999 could state prosecutors, no longer fearful of government retaliation, slowly but steadily begin to uncover some of the scandals that occurred in the 1990s.[31] In point of fact, first De la Rúa and later Kirchner encouraged such proceedings, but it was clear that investigations were welcome as long as they were confined to their political enemies. In 2003 a weekly magazine reported that the French company Thales Spectrum had paid $25 million in bribes to win the concession contract for control of Argentina's broadcasting system in 1997. A year later the Anti-Corruption Office (ACO) filed criminal charges against Thales Spectrum, which Kirchner used as justification in terminating the concession contract shortly thereafter.[32] In 2004 federal prosecutors requested several indictments with regard to the national highways concession contracts awarded between 1990 and 1992, charging that government officials had committed fraud by awarding illegal subsidies to private companies, which had cost the federal government an estimated $420 million. In May 2004 María Julia Alsogaray, who played a key role in the privatizations of ENTel and Somisa, was sentenced to three years in prison for illicit enrichment

30. The Correo Argentino by itself owed the federal government $206 million in back fees, whereas the Aeropuertos Argentina 2000 was seeking a 60 percent reduction of its annual fee worth $171 million (*Clarín*, August 8, 2001; *La Nación*, September 11, 2001).

31. The press was able to find out that the AGN audits on privatization revenues during the mid-1990s were seriously incomplete primarily because it could not obtain the necessary information from the executive branch (*La Nación*, November 12, 2003).

32. *Le Point*, October 2, 2003. President de la Rúa created the ACO in December 1999 as a special investigative unit within the Ministry of Justice. The ACO, on the one hand, investigates cases of corruption in the public administration, and if its officers conclude that the case has merit its conclusions are transmitted to a federal prosecutor to start a formal inquiry. On the other hand, it develops and helps implement new legislative and administrative anticorruption strategies. Staffed with highly competent and independent personnel, under de la Rúa the ACO was responsible for investigating and bringing to trial some of the most notorious cases of corruption in the 1990s. However, under Duhalde and then Kirchner the ACO budget was cut and presidential loyalists were put in charge primarily to investigate cases affecting political opponents.

and tax evasion.[33] Former minister Erman González was also indicted for the illicit management of the privatization of Tandanor. By 2005 two dozen high-ranking members of the Menem administration had been indicted or were under investigation on a variety of corruption charges.[34] The former president was briefly put under house arrest between June and November 2001 on arms-smuggling charges and also came under investigation for not having disclosed a Swiss bank account worth $600,000.[35]

This barrage of scandals took its toll economically as well as politically. A Gallup poll taken in June 2001 in Buenos Aires showed that, regardless of socioeconomic class, 60 percent of the respondents identified the corruption of the political class as being the country's number one problem. About 92 percent of the respondents also believed that reducing the "cost" of politics was very or fairly important. Gallup also detected a generalized sense of pessimism, as eight out of ten people surveyed expressed "little or no confidence" that politicians could reduce their "costs" of "doing politics." Political analysts and pollsters also believed that these events were responsible for the increasing public alienation from politics. In 1984, shortly after Argentina returned to democracy, 43 percent of the respondents were either "very" or "fairly" interested in politics, but in 2001 only 23 percent were.[36]

Likewise, Argentines' satisfaction with their government institutions was just as alarming. In 2001 public opinion polls showed how Argentines, more

33. In addition to mismanaging aspects of the telephone privatization, Alsogaray could not justify assets for $2.5 million in excess of her sworn declaration (*La Nación*, January 6, 2004).

34. Two ministers of the economy (Domingo Cavallo and Roque Fernández), one minister of defense (Jorge Dominguez), one minister of justice (Raúl Granillo Ocampo), and the former head of the internal revenue service (Ricardo Cossio), among others, were under investigation (*La Nación*, April 23, 2003).

35. Argentine and Swiss federal investigators found two different accounts in Switzerland linked to Menem—something the former president denied until 2002. As the inquiry expanded, state prosecutors found that Menem owned at least $1 million exceeding his own sworn declaration while in office and asked him to explain how he obtained those assets (*La Nación*, March 27, 2004). Moreover, Menem was investigated for having approved the smuggling of Argentine military equipment to Ecuador and Croatia between 1991 and 1995. According to the state prosecutors, of the $120 million netted in this illegal transaction, only $80 million could be accounted for, which raised the suspicion that the rest went to bribes for government officials. The former president was also accused by an Iranian defector of having received $10 million (deposited in Switzerland) from the Iranian government to cover up a terrorist attack against an Argentine Jewish association in Buenos Aires in 1994 (*New York Times*, July 21, 2002).

36. The public disgust with corruption is also illustrated by the fact that a month later about 80 percent of the people surveyed believed that Menem should be kept on house arrest (*La Nación*, June 10, 2001; *Pagina 12*, July 8, 2001).

than any other people in Latin America, displayed among the lowest levels of confidence in Congress, political parties, private business, and the judiciary (Table 4.1). A Gallup poll taken just prior to the financial crisis of December 2001 showed that 50 percent of the respondents believed that the solution to the country's problems was greater honesty from their politicians. Subsequent data released by the polling agency Latinobarometro confirmed that Argentines' support for democracy had dropped from 71 percent in 1996 to 65 percent in 2005. Similarly, Argentines displayed one of the strongest scores of distrust toward government institutions in Latin America, as opposed to neighboring Chile, which had some of the best ratings while implementing similar market reforms. Argentines did display strong confidence in President Kirchner (71 percent) but much lower levels of trust for the country's socioeconomic elites (34 percent), Congress (26 percent), the judiciary (26 percent), and political parties (20 percent). The same survey also showed that Argentina was one of the worst countries in terms of enforcing the law, spending taxpayer money appropriately, relying on a fair and expeditious justice system, and experiencing government corruption.[37]

Over the years several estimates appeared with regard to the cost of corruption during the 1990s. During that decade, according to high-ranking officials in the Ministry of Justice, corruption cost Argentina $5 billion annually, but official figures were never disclosed.[38] While there is no way to quantify with any degree of confidence the economic resources that corruption took away from the country, international corruption indexes provide additional evidence that the problem was very serious and hurt Argentina badly. One broad measurement is the Transparency International (TI) corruption index, which consistently ranked Argentina among the most corrupt countries in Latin America during the 1990s. Moreover, a study by Pricewaterhouse Coopers (PWC) estimated that the lack of transparency in business transactions cost Argentina about $18.7 billion in possible foreign investments that went elsewhere. Table 4.2 portrays the level of corruption

37. *La Nación*, November 4, 2001, and Latinobarometro (2007).

38. For the Ministry of Justice estimates, see *La Nación*, August 8, 2003. In 2004 the NGO Polo de Desarrollo Educativo Renovador put the cost of corruption and bad administration at two percentage points of the country's GDP and a loss of 150,000 jobs annually (*La Nación*, March 14, 2004). In 2005 another NGO, the Centro de Investigación y Prevención de la Criminalidad Económica, using an incomplete number of judicial inquiries as its database, estimated the cost of corruption since 1980 to be $10 billion. In both cases, experts cautioned about the reliability of such figures.

by country as reported in personal interviews with private companies' chief financial officers (CFOs) as well PWC's own staffers. As can be seen, among Latin American countries, Argentina had the second worst mean score (3.54) after Guatemala among CFOs and the worst according to PWC's staffers. When asked about the impact of corruption on business plans, Argentina again came across as the Latin American country where CFOs were most concerned, with a mean score of 3.43 (Table 4.3). Needless to say, had $18.7 billion come to the country it would have generated major tax revenues and much needed employment.

Collusion and Lack of Competition

The early objectives of the privatization process were twofold. The first goal was to involve the largest Argentine economic groups with ties to the administration, even if they lacked the qualifications, since they were Menem's supporters. The second was to transfer the SOEs, particularly in the lucrative sector of public utilities, to private investors under monopolistic/oligopolistic clauses to receive higher prices (Aspiazu and Vispo 1994; Gerchunoff and Cánovas 1995) with the full support of the IMF and the World Bank.[39] A clear example of the first goal was the initial privatization law requiring foreign investors to form joint ventures with domestic companies, regardless of their technical and financial qualifications. Majul (1993, 1994) showed that the largest domestic groups obtained preferential treatment due to their "special" relationship with Menem, who in turn received generous contributions for his electoral campaigns in 1989 and 1995.

The second goal ran counter to economic theory, which postulates that whenever technology allows it, monopolistic SOEs in public utilities should be broken into smaller companies in order to create competition prior to the sale as a means to improve quality and lower costs. The privatization of the telephone company ENTel is a case in point. ENTel was geographically divided into two regions and then sold separately to two different foreign consortia enjoying a monopoly status in their respective areas until 1997 with the possibility of an extension option. This resulted in some of the

---

39. In the early stages of the privatization process the IMF and the World Bank put a strong emphasis on speed. Divesting quickly was financially important, as it could guarantee a quick reimbursement of the money that the two institutions had lent to Argentina (interviews with World Bank economists, Washington, D.C., March 1998).

highest long-distance rates in the world—a fact that was often cited by analysts as unduly increasing the cost of doing business in Argentina. For instance, in the early 1990s a minute call rate from Buenos Aires to New York was $3.69. In contrast, in Chile, where competition was introduced prior to state divestiture, a call from Santiago to New York was $0.75 (Guislain 1997). Due to the public backlash following the ENTel transfer, the World Bank and investment banks put pressure on the Menem administration to change its approach when the time came to divest the electricity sector. By most accounts, the divestiture of the SOEs in electricity created competition and an adequate regulatory framework prior to privatization (Artana, Navajas, and Urbiztondo 1999). However, it remained an isolated instance precisely because foreign pressure was limited to this sector.

In fact, in many cases the government failed to promote competition through regulatory policy as it should have (Urbiztondo et al. 1997; Artana, Navajas, and Urbiztondo 1999). This was particularly problematic in natural monopolies (highways, railways, airports, and water supply) where effective regulation to prevent abuses of companies' dominant position was a serious issue. Moreover, other sectors where competition was possible but required a good regulatory framework to enforce it (oil refinement and distribution, steel, and air passenger traffic) received lip service. Indeed, the great majority of the regulatory agencies fell captive to the interests of the companies they were supposed to keep in check (Abdala 2001). Most sectors continued to be regulated by secretariats directly dependent on the Ministry of the Economy, which for political reasons often decided to cut deals with interested companies behind closed doors. In those cases where independent regulatory agencies were created, the government often intervened by overruling their jurisdiction and siding with the interested company, as in the telecommunications sector (Abdala 2001). Although many privatized companies improved in terms of efficiency, labor productivity, investments, the breadth of service provision, and customer service (Chisari, Estache, and Romero 1997), quite a few also took advantage of the rent-seeking conditions allowed by the government (Petrazzini 1995; Abdala 2001; Rodríguez-Boetsch 2005). The result was that in markets such as air passenger cargo, telecommunications, petrochemicals, highways, railways, and water and sanitation services, the government surrendered efficiency in exchange for funding (Gerchunoff and Coloma 1993) and results were often poor or far below what could have been possible in the face of a more effective regulation. By contrast, in the few cases when competition was introduced into the market (natural gas and electricity), results were quite good.

To make things worse, privatization occurred in the context of trade liberalization, resulting in the creation of a dysfunctional two-sector economy. On the one hand there were medium- and small-sized domestic firms confronting foreign competition that were forced to make drastic adjustments in order to survive—something that became increasingly difficult as the Argentine peso appreciated during the 1990s. On the other there were foreign companies and a few domestic conglomerates controlling former state monopolies facing little or no competition that remained unaffected by the overvalued exchange rate. Because such companies operated in captured markets, they posted large profits while the rest of the economy suffered, particularly after 1994. This situation resulted in a drastic change in the ranking of the largest companies in Argentina between 1989 and 1999 (Table 4.4). By the end of that period the old SOEs had been supplanted by foreign companies and, to a lesser extent, domestic groups whose production was primarily geared toward the Argentine market.

Some early studies estimated the government losses ensuing from the poor regulatory environment in the oil field sector were about 32 percent of the total income earned (Petrecolla et al. 1993). A subsequent study (Chisari et al. 1997) came up with about $915 million worth of losses from ineffective regulation of public utilities, which on average resulted in a 16 percent additional tax per household to obtain such services. In 1997 an AGN report on privatized firms pointed out that many public utilities did not comply with their contract agreements and that regulatory agencies overseeing their activities failed to sanction wrongdoings. The situation, the report continued, was particularly alarming in the provision of telephone, gas, water, and railway service. However, neither Congress nor the regulatory agencies being criticized showed any interest in rectifying the problem for the political reasons already mentioned earlier in this chapter. Even the Ente Regulador de Energia (ENRE), considered by most to be the best of all regulatory agencies, came under serious attack. In 2001 the Secretariat for the Defense of Competition, staffed with new people once President De la Rúa took office in December 1999, found that ENRE had tacitly allowed the creation of a distribution monopoly in the most lucrative market of the country.[40] Moreover, the exten-

40. In 1997 the Spanish electricity group ENDESA acquired the Chilean company controlling EDESUR, one of the two electricity distributors of Buenos Aires. However, ENDESA was also the majority shareholder of the other Buenos Aires distributor, EDENOR. Despite the monopoly so created, ENRE decided not to intervene allegedly due to an intense lobbying from the part of

sion of the monopoly status to the telephone companies until 2000 and to the urban railway operators (for twenty years, which included a 90 percent tariff hike to finance infrastructures) generated widespread controversy. In fact, such decisions were made by the executive instead of the proper regulatory agency (Abdala 2001). This raised suspicions of collusion between government officials and the affected companies. In 2002 another AGN report strongly criticized the way airports, water and sanitation services, and trains had been privatized. It also added that the regulatory agencies overseeing these services had failed their tasks, particularly in the area of monitoring service quality and investment commitments.

As a result, situations such as these started to erode public confidence in the soundness of market reforms. Following the 2001–2 meltdown, disillusion and anger toward market reforms were pervasive. Public opinion polls showed that at the beginning of the privatization process in late 1989 more than 60 percent of respondents favored private ownership of public utilities and an economy driven by market forces rather than the state. By mid-2002 the mood had reversed itself. More than 60 percent favored state interventionism and 46 percent favored a return of public utilities to government hands. The trend can also be observed in Figure 4.2. When examined in comparative fashion, public satisfaction with the privatization of SOEs declined from 32 percent in 1998 to 12 percent in 2003, the second worst rating in Latin America (Table 4.5). In 2004, 75 percent of respondents were dissatisfied with the privatization of public utilities, and only 16 percent were satisfied with the market economy. However, 56 percent thought that a market economy was the only system to promote development (Latinobarometro 2004). This would indicate that while the majority of Argentines still supported a market economy, they were very dissatisfied with the way reforms were implemented.

This substantial change in public mood allowed Kirchner to implement his nationalist, progovernment intervention approach and reverse some of the market reforms of the 1990s. In one case Kirchner revived the old state entrepreneurial model by creating a new company, Enarsa, in the strategic oil business, claiming that foreign oil companies were not investing enough to meet Argentina's energy needs. Frequently, the president used disputes with private companies over tariffs and concession issues to terminate exist-

ENDESA. Interview with Carlos Winograd, head of the Secretariat for the Defense of Competition, Buenos Aires, March 2001.

ing contracts. In some cases this led the government to again take the ownership of major companies, such as the post office, some train lines, and Aerolíneas Argentinas. However, more often than not, Kirchner orchestrated complex operations to replace foreign with domestic investors sympathetic to his agenda and willing to comply with his political demands. This was true in key sectors such as electricity (Tansener and EDENOR), telecommunications (Telecom), and water and sanitation (Aguas Argentina). While Menem welcomed foreign investors with open arms, Kirchner openly antagonized them using the argument that during the 1990s they had used their monopolistic/oligopolistic market shares at the expense of the Argentine consumers. This confrontational style led to a strain in diplomatic relations with Spain and France, whose companies were major targets of Kirchner's renationalization agenda.[41]

Patronage Politics

Menem accomplished the seemingly impossible during his first term (1989–95). He reduced inflation to a single digit and was able to generate sustained economic growth until 1994. However, the trends of the 1991–94 period, rather than encouraging the Menem administration to pursue with greater vigor its early efforts to control spending, actually created a false sense of euphoria and overconfidence. Record levels in privatization, FDIS, and federal revenues deceived policy makers. Assuming that such a trend would continue well into the second half of the 1990s, Menem's economic teams thought that sustained growth would bring in the necessary tax money and foreign investments to fund increasing government spending. During the first phase of the stabilization effort, Menem won wide praise abroad for his attempt to downsize the public sector. While in 1989 federal government employees numbered 874,182, by 1994 only 190,414 were left (Gibson and Calvo 2000). Through privatization alone, the government transferred about 280,000 employees to the payroll of the private sector, thus freeing important economic resources for other purposes.

41. The French ambassador in Argentina, in an unusual move, branded Kirchner's strategy as "populist." France's major companies (Electricité de France, France Telecom, and Suez) won important utility concession contracts in the early 1990s, but by 2005 they had left Argentina citing the lack of rule of law in enforcing existing contracts on the part of both the courts and regulatory agencies (*La Nación*, October 6, 2005).

Unfortunately, once Menem's Peronist Party won a congressional majority in the 1991 midterm elections, and the economic situation turned increasingly positive, fiscal restraint gave way to the need of rewarding political supporters. Indeed, thanks to the leniency of the IMF and the World Bank, and some creative bookkeeping, Menem managed to finance its ballooning fiscal deficit until the end of his second term. According to Veigel (2009, 187):

> For example, revenues from privatization of public companies were counted as current incomes while payments, which were realized with bonds and the capitalization of interest payments on outstanding debt, were not counted towards the current expenditure. Similarly, the central government failed to report deficits of provincial governments for which it would ultimately take responsibility. Mario Teijero calculated that the difference between the "official" and adjusted deficit amounted to more than US$75 billion over the period between 1991 and 2000 and that far from the rhetoric of orthodoxy of the Menem administration, the fiscal deficit amounted to between 4 and 6 percent of GDP throughout most of the 1990s.

As a matter of fact, according to official figures, current expenditures rose from $44 billion to $60 billion between 1993 and 1999 (Table 4.6). Where did all this money go? During this period, once we exclude money paid for subsidies and to service interest payments on the debt, two expenditure items increased steadily: federal transfers to the provinces and social security. By themselves these expenditure items accounted for 55 percent of the increase during this period.

Why are these two statistics important? Previous studies (Sawers 1996; Jones, Sanguinetti, and Tommasi 2000; Remmer and Wibbels 2000) point out that these budget items were a major source of clientelism in the 1990s. Recent research on Argentina shows the importance for the Peronists to pursue clientelistic strategies in order to retain and even expand their electoral base (Auyero 2000; Levitsky 2003; Calvo and Murillo 2004; Stokes 2005; Brusco, Nazareno, and Stokes 2005; Jones and Hwang 2005). The derailing of economic resources into political patronage can be identified in the federal funding to provincial governments. In turn, this became a major drain for the national budget.

For instance, Gibson and Calvo (2000) showed how Menem used clientelistic spending to secure congressional support during his first term. This was done to offset the potential opposition of representatives from industrial districts that were going to suffer the most from privatization and market deregulation (i.e., Buenos Aires, Cordoba, and Rosario). According to Gibson and Calvo (2000), Menem cleverly exploited the overrepresentation in Congress of what they call "peripheral" provinces by co-opting the support of their representatives. Such provinces controlled 83 percent of the seats in the Senate and 52 percent of the seats in the Chamber of Deputies, thus holding the key to the legislative approval of any reform agenda. Dispensing generous federal funds to guarantee their legislative support was, on a cash basis, much less expensive than trying to sway the votes of urban areas where party competition was more intense and required greater infusion of funds to appease voters. Two factors helped Menem's effort: (1) peripheral provinces were cash starved and (2) many provinces were either Peronist or controlled by local parties willing to cooperate for federal pork barrel programs.[42]

Consequently, the president transferred large amounts of federal funds to poor, peripheral provinces, which not only escaped the harshness of the 1989–91 stabilization policies but actually saw their finances increase appreciably. This was accomplished through (a) a revenue-sharing scheme of federal taxes, also referred to as the co-participation law, first enacted in 1988; (b) provincial guarantees; (c) special laws; (d) discretionary funds (among which the Aportes Nacional del Tesoro, ATNs, figured prominently); and (e) capital outlays (Table 4.6). The bulk of transfers to the provinces, which averaged 32 percent of federal spending between 1989 and 1995, were eventually formalized into law in 1993 through the Federal Pact and the Fiscal Pact, the latter of which was amended in 1995, 1996, 1998, and 2000. Through the Fiscal Pact, provincial governors pledged to support the market reforms of the Menem administration and start reforming their own economies.[43] The revenue-sharing funds were meant in principle to

---

42. With the exception of Buenos Aires, Cordoba, Mendoza, and Santa Cruz, the rest of the Argentine provinces are characterized by small economies that cannot sustain the level of local government spending. According to Jones and Hwang (2005), during 1989–2001 the median province obtained 72 percent of its revenues from federal transfer programs, which the executive disbursed in a highly discretionary fashion. Although one of the 1994 constitutional amendments mandated that within a year such transfers had to be regulated according to transparent and accountable processes, Congress has yet to act on it.

43. The provinces pledged to cooperate with the federal government in (a) limiting taxes on real estate and car registration; (b) limiting some municipal taxes; (c) eliminating some provincial

empower local government and enhance democratic policy making. Unfortunately, they ended up creating more opportunities for clientelistic practices as governors and their party machines weakened accountability procedures and used such funds in a very discretionary ways (Rezk 2000). For instance, Gibson and Calvo (2000) pointed out how federal transfers more than doubled between 1990 and 1995, which boosted local government programs and employment levels.[44] Their regression analysis showed that the electoral fortunes of the Peronists improved significantly as such funds were utilized to increase the size of the public sector employment.

My data confirm Gibson and Calvo's early findings. During the 1990s between 25 to 40 percent of federal outlays were disbursed to the provinces. In turn, these funds accounted on average for 70 percent of the provinces' income. Under President Alfonsín the federal contributions grew from $5.6 billion in 1984 to $7.5 billion in 1988. During Menem's first half year in office in 1989 (July–December) federal funds were momentarily cut down to $6.6 billion as part of the effort to control hyperinflation, but fiscal austerity was short lived. By 1991, as inflation abated, federal funds to the provinces surpassed the 1988 levels ($8.4 billion) and grew much faster thereafter, reaching $15.6 billion in 1999.

Gibson and Calvo's (2000) analysis covers Menem's first term in office (1989–95), but the trend continued during the second term (1995–99) as well. The reason is that Menem's successful attempt to amend the constitution so he could run for a second consecutive term in 1995 cost him dearly. Peronist governors and legislators, whose support was essential for this controversial initiative, demanded greater federal funds for their own patronage networks.[45] Although tax collection shrank in 1996 and 1999, federal transfers to the provinces increased during Menem's second term. Conversely, the fiscal deficit of the federal government kept climbing steadily from 1994 onward (Table 4.6). Most of the money that the provinces received went to additional employment and higher salaries, which in turn

---

taxes; (d) deregulating many economic activities; (e) privatizing provincially owned companies and banks; and (f) diminishing employers' compensations from 80 percent to 30 percent.

44. The Co-Participation Law fixed the amount of federal taxes going to each province. However, based on the interviews with senior civil servants in the Ministries of the Economy and the Interior, Menem often delayed payments to provinces controlled by opposition parties while granting to Peronist provinces higher shares of the tax base when new negotiations took place to reconfigure the tax-sharing mechanism (interviews with Argentine government officials, Buenos Aires, March 2002).

45. Interview with former minister and presidential adviser Roberto Dromi, Buenos Aires, March 2002.

bought votes. Between 1989 and 1998 provincial personnel spending rose from $6.5 billion to $16.8 billion, which constituted a net increase of 157 percent. In percentage terms, personnel spending, as a share of provincial current expenditures over the same period, increased from 58 percent to 81 percent.[46] Table 4.7 gives us an idea of which provinces were more "labor intensive" between 1989 and 1993. Not surprising, seven of the top ten were controlled by the Peronists, with Menem's home province, La Rioja, ranking number one.[47] These provinces tended to be among the poorest in the country, whereas the richest ones (Buenos Aires, Cordoba, and Mendoza) were at the bottom of the scale.

Some of the money that provincial governments spent also went to support their legislatures. In the late 1990s on average a provincial legislator spent $655,000 as compared to $360,000 in the United States (Manzetti 2003, 353). The German state of Bayern (Bavaria), with a population of twelve million people, spent annually a little less than the province of Formosa, which had a population of 504,000. Similarly, the autonomous community of Catalonia, Spain, with a population of six million, spent less than the province of Chaco, although the general domestic product of the latter is thirty-nine times less than that of the former (Manzetti 2003, 353). Again, not surprising, the provinces with the highest debt are also those that spent more, per capita, on their legislature (Grupo Sophia 2001).

In addition to co-participation (federal revenue sharing) and provincial guarantee funds, another major source of patronage was the ATNs, which were originally designed to help fiscal imbalances and emergency situations in the provinces (Tommasi, Saiegh, and Sanguinetti 2001).[48] In 2002 a congressional inquiry found out that most of the $2.7 billion spent in this way between 1990 and 1999 was schemed away to finance Peronist politicians and their clienteles at the municipal level.[49] The president's home province,

46. Data mentioned above comes from the Dirreción Nacional de la Coordinación con las Provincias.

47. In La Rioja the biggest beneficiary was the Yoma group, owned by Menem's former brothers-in-law. Between 1995 and 1998 the Yomas obtained $180 million in unsecured loans from government-owned banks in part through a presidential decree. In 2005 tax auditors also demanded the return of $8.5 in export refunds that the Yomas had improperly received (*La Nación*, June 25 and August 31, 2004).

48. The ATNs were created in January 1988 under Alfonsín. Law 23.548 appropriated 1 percent of federal taxes to fund such programs.

49. A typical case was that of former Peronist deputy Miguel Nacul, who in 1995 solicited the immediate transfer to him of $550,000 in ATNs, supposedly to attend the needs of several towns in the province of Tucumán. Yet in a handwritten letter addressed to the Ministry of the Interior, Nacul mentions that $275,000 were to cover his own expenditures without specifying

La Rioja, was by far the largest recipient of ATN funds, netting $865 million ("ATN: Un Agujero Por el Que se Escaparon 2.700 Millones," *Clarín*, May 20, 2002), or 32 percent of the total disbursed. Menem's misuse of federal funds during his tenure to strengthen his patronage networks with politicians of the interior was acknowledged only after he left office. In 2001, for instance, the Inter-American Development Bank (IDB) warned the Argentine government to properly utilize its credit supporting ATN funds to the provinces. The IDB, in an official document, made it clear that this was not the case under Menem ("La Carta de un Diputado Revela Cómo se Gestionaban los ATN," *La Nación*, October 22, 2001), who had misused these funds (although he was not mentioned by name). In 2005 the SIGEN released a report detailing how, in many cases, ATNs had indeed been disbursed without any valid reason and in a highly irregular manner.

Interestingly, despite the increasing federal outlays, the provinces were unable to function. As spending kept exceeding revenues, many of them borrowed heavily, mostly from government and private banks and to a lesser extent from IFIS and the bond market. This led to a doubling of provincial debt exposure between 1997 and 2001 (Table 4.8) and could occur because Argentina's provinces have the largest degree of borrowing autonomy in Latin America (Figure 4.3). In 2002 under pressure from the IMF, interim president Eduardo Duhalde forced the provinces to drastically cut their expenditures. The following year, despite the termination of additional loans and most pork-related programs (including ATNs), the provinces were all of a sudden able to cut their operating deficit by 72 percent (Manzetti 2003).

The other major burden in the federal budget was social security, which grew from $12.5 billion in 1993 to $17.4 billion in 1999 (Table 4.6) and Medicare. After 2000 the judiciary uncovered a number of alleged frauds committed by high-ranking officials of the Menem era that cost the public coffers millions of dollars. The first case involved the social security agency ANSES (Administracion Nacional de Seguridad Social). According to pre-

---

their nature. About $300,000 was eventually disbursed, but the problem is that ATNs could not be sent to individuals, thus prompting the charge of illegal use of federal funds (*La Nación*, October 22, 2001, and December 19, 2005). Furthermore, the powerful union leader and PJ senator Luis Barrionuevo received in 1997 some $200,000 to remodel a swimming pool at a private club (*La Nación*, May 20, 2002). Another notorious case was that of the Peronist congresswoman Norma Godoy, who asked for almost $1 million in ATNs to finance foundations helping handicapped people. Later it was discovered that Godoy and her husband managed such foundations as fronts for their own private interests (*La Nación*, May 14, 2005).

liminary investigations, Luis González, the son of the former minister of labor, Erman González, in his capacity of ANSeS manager for the province of La Rioja granted his father a retroactive bonus for $220,000 after the minister retired in March 2000. A few months earlier, before the Menem administration went out of office, the thirty-eight-year-old Luis obtained for himself an early retirement pension of $1,800 monthly even though he did not qualify for it (Manzetti 2003, 355). Further, state prosecutors found that ANSeS had awarded some three hundred special pensions worth between $5,000 and $15,000 monthly to former employees of the Banco de La Rioja. The bank, which became insolvent in 1991 since it could not collect the $840 million that the provincial government owed to it, was eventually privatized. State prosecutor Guillermo Marijuan estimated that the fraud could have possibly cost ANSeS more than $50 million. Among other people who received special pensions despite having never worked at the bank were Menem's physical trainer and chauffeur, the tennis trainer of Menem's daughter, a former federal congresswoman from La Rioja, and a host of friends and relatives of the Menems and the Gonzálezes. Many more received pensions for pure clientelistic reasons.[50] In 2002 an internal audit of the ANSeS under a new managing team uncovered that as many as ten thousand pensions had been illegally awarded in the 1990s, particularly to people living in poor Peronist strongholds, costing the agency substantial losses (La Nación, March 7, 2002).

The Medicare agency PAMI (Programa de Asistencia Medica Integrado) and its affiliate INSSJP (Instituto Nacional de Servicios Sociales para Jubilados y Pensionados) were also the object of fraudulent behavior during the Menem years. According to the agency itself, by 2001 its deficit had reached $3.3 billion mainly due to "great administrative disorder, without adequate controls and characterized by direct contracts that affected the budget as well as the service rendered."[51] In the same document the agency noted that out of the twelve thousand employees under contract, between four thousand and nine thousand were in excess due to the clientelistic hiring policies of the previous administration. In July 2000 a federal judge issued an arrest warrant for Victor Alderete, PAMI's former director under Menem, for hav-

---

50. As one of the beneficiaries testified before a judge, "Some fellows approached me and said that I could have received a pension had my family and I voted for the Peronists" (La Nación, September 3, 2001). Equally troubling were early indications that similar frauds had been perpetrated in different parts of the country (La Nación, March 7, 2002).

51. Clarín, July 1, 2000.

ing organized a scheme bypassing the control mechanisms for purchases and contracts.[52] In yet another instance INSSJP paid $16 million to a travel company for services that could not be proved to benefit people for whom they were intended. The company had committed flagrant irregularities in 60 percent of the verified cases.[53] In 2002 the new director of PAMI admitted that the agency he had inherited was paralyzed by corruption, hundreds of political appointees who failed to perform any meaningful task, and the absence of basic internal control mechanisms, which cost millions of dollars.

According to some estimates, the use of the national health care system for patronage purposes cost approximately $1 billion. In all, the magnitude of the money squandered through political patronage jobs alone was calculated to be around $2.2 billion a year (Grupo Sophia 2001). Another notorious form of clientelism came from Congress itself. In the 1990s congressmen could award discretionary pensions, grants, and subsidies as they pleased. In 1996 legislators spent $25 million monthly in special pensions alone.[54] As tax revenues could not keep up with spending, Menem bridged the fiscal deficit by borrowing more from abroad and allowed the provinces to do the same. Coincidentally, between 1989 and 1999 Argentina's external debt rose from $65 billion to $121 billion (Table 4.8).

Concluding Remarks

Argentina's experience under the Menem administration is similar to Russia's and lends support to the thesis that when market reforms take place in an environment where accountability institutions are weak, corruption, crony capitalism, and political patronage thrive, contributing to the deterioration of the overall economic situation by wasting important financial resources often obtained through foreign loans.

The financial collapse of 2001/2002 was a far cry of what most people had predicted only a decade earlier. In 1989 Menem had a unique opportu-

52. In one case, Alderete was accused of having approved the payment to the Federación de Clínicas de la Provincia de Buenos Aires for $7 million when the actual amount due was only $2.9 million. In another case, the PAMI's director awarded a contract to the cleaning company Linser for $5.9 million, which was $4 million more than the market price at the time (*Clarín*, February 13, 2001).

53. Data provided by the ACO, September 2001. See also *La Nación*, February 12, 2002.

54. This congressional privilege was briefly interrupted in 2001 but resumed again in 2005.

nity to reshape Argentina politically and economically. Frustrated by decades of economic decline and political instability, many of his fellow Argentines were more than willing to embrace the promise of market reforms since the economic protectionism and widespread government intervention started in the 1940s had failed miserably. Menem's adoption of the neoliberal model was a watershed in Argentine history as it ran counter to what Perón had stood for in the minds of most Peronists. His bold move in the short term paid off handsomely. All of a sudden Argentina became the darling of the international financial community and Menem received steady political and economic support from the United States, the IMF, the World Bank, and the IDB throughout his decade in office. Menem's success in eliminating inflation and privatizing most economic activities while opening up the country to foreign trade and investments resulted in high praise at home and abroad (Veigel 2009). In the early 1990s the economy grew at a rate not seen since the 1950s. In October 1998 Menem's "achievements" earned him an invitation to address the annual IMF/World Bank board of governors meeting, which at the time was considered a rare honor for the head of state of an emerging market.[55]

However, it was clear from the beginning that Menem embraced the neoliberal credo not out of a true conversion to market principles but rather out of pragmatism. In mid-1989, with the federal coffers empty and the country's creditworthiness destroyed, he simply had no choice. His paramount goal was, first and foremost, to consolidate political power by whatever means possible. Thus, market reform was not an end in itself but rather a means to achieve political goals. In the 1940s ISI and the establishment of a welfare state were the policy instruments that endeared Perón to labor and the urban middle classes. In the 1990s market reforms (the antithesis of ISI) served the same political goal for Menem, but its main beneficiaries were large domestic and foreign entrepreneurs.

This explains why market reforms were not designed, as they should have been at least in theory, to foster competition and property rights. Instead they often reallocated rents among Menem's supporters, as was the case in Yeltsin's Russia. In fact, state divestiture had allowed some of the most important markets to become captive to monopolistic or oligopolistic control (similar to Russia), which prevented true competition. Moreover,

---

55. The only other head of state addressing the IMF/World Bank plenary session was Bill Clinton.

because Menem's overall strategy implied breaking the law, it was imperative to destroy or make inoperative those accountability institutions that stood in the way. Indeed, the way market reforms were implemented in Argentina, very much like in Russia, actively conspired against the very principle of good governance. In this regard Menem was extremely successful, but in the process, like Yeltsin, the Argentine president irremediably undermined the credibility of market reform since his policies became associated with corruption, clientelism, and crony capitalism. Moreover, as the foundations of the new economic model were flawed from the start, once the most lucrative privatizations were over by 1994 foreign investments began to steadily decline as business opportunities were restricted by new entry barriers. To make things worse, the decline in foreign investments not only affected economic growth but also coincided with an increase in government spending from 1995 on, which was in part caused by accountability-related problems.

The U.S. government and the IFIS were quite aware of the way Menem manipulated the reform agenda. Although World Bank and IMF financial support contemplated a certain degree of transparency in transferring SOEs to the private sector and establishing new regulatory frameworks, in the end the urgency to privatize as quickly as possible led them to tolerate major government abuses in this regard. Their underlying hope was that eventually the president would clean up his act and the market would weed out the distortions created in the early 1990s.[56] It never happened. Having invested so much in the "Argentine miracle," the IFIS continued to lend money until the end of 2001 when a new administration in Washington with different priorities concluded that throwing good money after bad did not make sense any longer. As a result, in December 2001 the bubble (so created) burst in the worst possible way as angry crowds took control of the streets chanting, "Que se vayan todos" (they all must go), forcing President De la Rúa to flee the presidential palace by helicopter. In 2004 the IMF and the World Bank recognized that they had been too lenient toward the Menem administration, but it was too little too late since their reputations had been badly tarnished. The Independent Evaluation Office of the IMF issued a report sharply critical of the IFI's role in Argentina (IMF 2004). Aside from the mistake of endorsing the fixed exchange rate, the report

56. This interpretation is based on interviews with U.S. State Department and World Bank officials.

underscored how its top executives were too lenient on Menem by failing to enforce conditionality clauses. The IMF tolerated for too long the lack of fiscal discipline and the weak commitment to structural reforms. In particular, it did not pay enough attention to the provincial debt and allowed a steady increase of the federal debt as well, which was clearly unsustainable over time. As in Russia, although staff managers expressed their concerns the IMF executive board, under pressure from major shareholders (e.g., the United States and other major European governments), overruled their objections.

In the end, similar to the Russian case, the cost that Argentines paid for the corruption, crony capitalism, and political patronage that took place during Menem's reforms will never be assessed accurately since wrongdoings were not prosecuted and we do not have detailed court accounts. Nonetheless, in the previous sections I mentioned several estimates about such costs, which probably are only the tip of the iceberg. Some losses came from the inability of privatized firms to pay their concession fees. Several of the companies that won concession contracts early, despite a lack of expertise in the business for which they were bidding, had a close relationship with Menem and managed to get by until he stayed in office. Once he retired, the Kirchner administration demanded compensation in the hundreds of millions of U.S. dollars, as detailed above. Corruption, which served many politicians well, turned out to be a boomerang. Argentina earned such a bad reputation in this regard that foreign investors, once the privatization bonanza was over, looked elsewhere in Latin America for business opportunities. As noted, this was calculated to have cost the country $18.7 million in possible investments. If we look at political patronage, its costs were severe as well. If we assume (as many Argentine analysts do) that the amazing increase of provincial government employment levels to be the result of political patronage, its cost (as reported earlier) was roughly $10 billion during Menem's two terms in office. If we add to this amount the estimated cost of only a handful of cases described in previous sections, such as poor regulation ($915 million), illegal subsidies ($420 million), and the discretionary expenditures issued through ATNs ($2.2 billion), the government may have wasted $13.5 billion. Considering that between 1993 and 1999 Argentina spent $33.8 billion in servicing its external debt alone, and assuming that the estimates just mentioned are accurate, $13.5 billion could have cut interest payments by a third and possibly averted the economic meltdown of 2002.

Of course, this does not mean that economic factors did not play a major role in the financial crisis of 2002. Many observers underscored the negative consequences of the fixed exchange parity with the U.S. dollar established in 1991 as a major problem. As the dollar kept appreciating in the 1990s, Argentine exports lost important markets, weakening the country's balance of payments, which were already hurting due to a massive influx of cheap imports resulting from trade liberalization. Yet the costs associated with the lack of accountability contributed to the deterioration of the fiscal situation, precisely because Menem was left free to spend money that he could not acquire through export earnings. He found a temporary solution to finance the fiscal deficit by borrowing abroad, but in the end even this gimmick proved unsustainable, although it was President De la Rúa who would face its consequences.

Between 2003 and 2008, however, the macroeconomic situation changed dramatically. During this period Argentina's GDP grew almost 9 percent a year. Kirchner should be credited for skillfully forcing his creditors to accept a two-third reduction on part of Argentina's foreign debt in order to end the debt moratorium started in 2002. However, a fair amount of this success was not due to Kirchner's claim that his decision to return to economic protectionism and rescind many privatization contracts turned the economy around. As in Putin's Russia, high GDP growth between 2003 and 2008 was largely attributable to record-level prices for Argentine commodities (particularly soy), not sound economic policy (Zarazaga 2006). The moratorium on much of the country's debt for almost four years also helped. Indeed, even after four years of strong growth, the country's GDP in 2006 was $214 billion, as opposed to $260 billion in 2001.[57] Foreign investments during Kirchner's term averaged $3.7 billion a year, as opposed to $7.1 billion during the 1990s, which clearly showed that much of the growth during the Kirchner years was driven by unusually high prices for Argentine commodity exports, not the result of an investment boom (UNCTAD 2007). In turn, the unusual lack of FDIs in part may be due to Kirchner's manipulation of the courts and his antagonistic approach to

57. "Argentina Economic Structure," *The Economist*, http://www.economist.com/countries/Argentina/profile.cfm?folder=Profile%2DEconomic%20Structure.

contractual disputes with privatized companies. The latter resulted in Argentina having the largest number of lawsuits pending before the World Bank's International Center for Settlement of Investment Disputes between 2003 and 2008.[58]

It is no wonder that many of the consequences of the 2001/2002 economic crash were still hard felt years later. In fact, in 2005, despite Kirchner's self-congratulatory achievements, salaries' purchasing power were still 10.8 percent less than in 2001 and the GDP was still 5 percent less than in 1997, when only 28 percent of Argentines lived in poverty. Retirees were hit even harder, as their purchasing power in 2005 was still 40 percent less than in 2001.[59] By the time Kirchner left office in 2007 about 30 percent of the population was still living in poverty, after peaking at 57 percent in October 2002, inflation was accelerating, and Argentina's debt had reached $144 billion (56 percent of GDP), very similar to the level of December 2001 when the country went into default.[60]

In 2009, similar to Russia, market reforms in Argentina were in complete disrepute and their failures had given new life to government intervention in the economy, which was exactly the opposite of what the international community had hoped for when it enthusiastically endorsed Menem's conversion to market economics in 1989. By then Menem had become a political pariah as he was abandoned by most of his former allies.

Unfortunately, even after Menem's exit from power democratic governance remained as weak as ever. While relentlessly exposing Menem's failures, Kirchner employed much of the same means to strengthen his personal power, while harassing the independent media and keeping at bay any form of accountability.[61] Under pressure, Congress renewed the delega-

58. By 2008 disputes over privatization contracts led twenty-six companies (primarily foreign) to ask the arbitration of the World Bank since Argentine regulatory agencies and domestic courts ruled in line with presidential wishes (*La Nación*, February 4, 2008).

59. The situation was worse for minors, with 56.4 percent living below the poverty line (*La Nación*, May 21, 2005). Moreover, a good amount of the decrease was not due to new jobs but rather government handouts, which were granted in a highly clientelistic fashion (*La Nación*, August 8, 2005).

60. Toward the end of his term Kirchner began to temper official statistics as he replaced most of the technical staff at the government agency in charge of statistical analysis (Instituto Nacional de Estadística y Censos, INDEC) with political appointees. As a result, according to most independent analysts, INDEC began to underreport the level of inflation, poverty, and unemployment and other key economic indicators, making official statistics unreliable (*La Nación*, September 8, 18, 2005, and April 28 and September 19, 2008).

61. Using the threat of withdrawing government advertisements, President Kirchner was able to mute and co-opt much of the independent media, creating a situation of self-censorship that had not taken place even during Menem's tenure (*The Economist*, January 12, 2006).

tion of legislative prerogatives to the executive on key economic issues.[62] Moreover, Kirchner showed an even greater tendency than Menem to use DNUs.[63] The presidential use of ad hoc programs for clientelistic goals continued unabated and controversial provisions like the ATNs, which were temporarily eliminated in 2002, were resumed in 2005. Kirchner forced out Menem's appointees from the Supreme Court and replaced them with others sympathetic to his own agenda.[64] Yet again, with accountability institutions under siege, corruption continued to thrive. When in late 2005, economy minister Roberto Lavagna acknowledged that government contracts were being fixed to favor companies close to the president, Kirchner promptly discharged him. By 2007 the Argentine government was rocked by a stream of corruption scandals, forcing out of office high-profile officials, including Lavagna's successor ("A Corruption Scandal in Argentina," *The Economist*, May 10, 2007). Rather than taking the opportunity to reassert its role, Congress (where Kirchner's backers had a comfortable majority in both houses) reformed the criminal law code to make corruption crimes more difficult to prosecute and allowed hundreds of pending trials to be dismissed.[65] In short, while a "conservative" Menem had made great strides to destroy political accountability, the "left-leaning" Kirchner was finishing the job. Thus, the hope that the 2002 crisis would regenerate Argentine politics and prompt the emergence of a new, honest, and well-meaning political class proved short lived.[66] The Peronist bosses who had cheered Menem and his market reforms had changed their tune but were still solidly in power and prevented any meaningful democratic progress.

62. In August 2004 Congress extended for two years two thousand delegated laws enacted by the executive since the 1990s, and in November of the same year it granted emergency legislative powers to Kirchner on a wide array of fiscal issues.

63. During his presidency Kirchner signed 249 DNUs and only sent to Congress 176 bills. By way of comparison Kirchner signed in an average year 60 DNUs, as opposed to Menem's 54 (*La Nación*, September 10, 2007).

64. In a very controversial decision, the pro-Kirchner justices on the Supreme Court upheld the government's decision to convert all dollar deposits into pesos in 2002, which was a de facto confiscation of property since former dollar-dominated financial assets had lost 70 percent of their value due to the peso's devaluation.

65. In February 2005 the modification of article 67 of the criminal code put into prescription most judicial investigations for crimes against the public administration and shortened the time of judicial inquiries.

66. In 2002 Duhalde proposed to reduce congressional seats by 25 percent and reform the electoral law to make it less dependent on party bosses, but Congress did not go along.

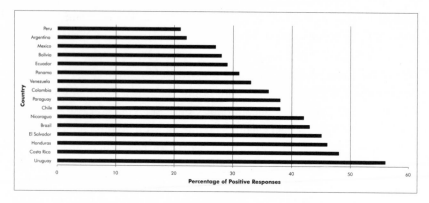

Figure 4.1 Trust in the Judiciary in Argentina Versus Latin America
SOURCE: Inter-American Development Bank (2000).

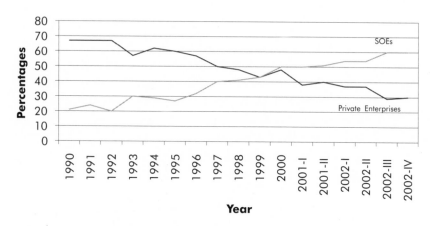

Figure 4.2 Argentina Support for Private Enterprises Versus SOEs
SOURCE: Ipsos Argentina-Mora y Araujo.
NOTE: Responses to the question, "Would you say that a better country is one where the vast majority of things are made by SOEs or private enterprises?"

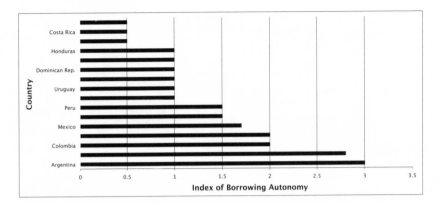

Figure 4.3 Argentina Versus Latin America Subnational Government Borrowing
Autonomy
SOURCE: Inter-American Development Bank (1997).

Table 4.1 Latin American Popular Confidence in Public Institutions, 2001 (%)

All Government Institutions		Political Parties		Private Enterprise		Congress	
Puerto Rico	66	Uruguay	27	Venezuela	83	Puerto Rico	42
Uruguay	55	Portugal	25	Puerto Rico	69	Uruguay	40
Portugal	55	Puerto Rico	24	Panama	68	Spain	40
Colombia	53	Spain	22	Paraguay	67	Mexico	37
Venezuela	52	Colombia	20	Mexico	63	Portugal	33
Spain	50	Peru	18	Portugal	62	Chile	28
Chile	50	Mexico	17	Guatemala	62	Peru	28
Bolivia	44	Venezuela	17	Colombia	61	Colombia	21
Mexico	41	Panama	16	Uruguay	58	Bolivia	17
Paraguay	40	Chile	13	Chile	54	Paraguay	11
Guatemala	40	Argentina	10	Spain	49	Argentina	11
Peru	40	Brazil	10	Ecuador	48	Guatemala	11
Argentina	39	Paraguay	9	Peru	45	Venezuela	10
Ecuador	38	Guatemala	9	Bolivia	38	Brazil	8
Brazil	34	Bolivia	8	Argentina	33	Ecuador	3
		Ecuador	3	Brazil	32		

SOURCE: Consorcio Iberoamericano de Empresa de Investigación de Mercado y Asesoramiento (2001).

Table 4.2 Presence of Corruption, January 2001

	Corporations				PwC Staff		
	Sample Size	Mean	Min.	Max.	Sample Size	Mean	Min.	Max.
All Countries*	689	3.00	1.00	10.00	209	2.81	1.00	8.75
Argentina	**21**	**3.54**	**1.00**	**8.33**	**6**	**3.48**	**1.38**	**8.75**
Brazil	22	2.77	1.00	7.33	9	2.36	1.38	3.38
Chile	20	2.59	1.00	8.00	3	2.04	1.75	2.50
Colombia	19	2.91	1.00	6.60	8	3.48	2.13	5.38
Ecuador	20	3.01	1.00	7.20	5	3.04	1.71	6.25
Guatemala	23	4.34	1.00	7.80	7	2.55	1.50	4.13
Mexico	24	3.04	1.00	7.60	5	2.55	1.88	3.50
Peru	20	2.22	1.00	6.20	8	2.80	1.00	8.50
Uruguay	20	3.33	1.00	10.00	7	3.23	1.25	6.00
Venezuela	21	3.31	1.00	7.80	7	2.89	1.38	4.50

SOURCE: The Opacity Index (Pricewaterhouse Coopers, 2001).

*The full report includes 36 countries worldwide.

Table 4.3 Corruption's Impact on Decision Making, January 2001

	Corporations				PwC Staff			
	Sample Size	Mean	Min.	Max.	Sample Size	Mean	Min.	Max.
All Countries*	693	2.66	1	4	212	2.51	1	9
Argentina	**21**	**3.43**	**2**	**4**	**6**	**2.67**	**2**	**3**
Brazil	23	2.83	1	4	9	2.78	2	4
Chile	19	2.21	1	4	3	2.00	1	3
Colombia	20	3.30	2	4	8	3.13	3	4
Ecuador	19	3.00	1	4	5	3.20	3	4
Guatemala	23	2.87	1	4	7	3.00	2	3
Mexico	24	2.63	1	4	5	2.40	2	3
Peru	20	3.05	1	4	8	2.88	1	3
Uruguay	20	2.55	1	4	7	2.57	2	3
Venezuela	21	3.10	2	4	7	2.86	2	3

SOURCE: The Opacity Index (Pricewaterhouse Coopers, 2001).

*The full report includes 36 countries worldwide.

Table 4.4 Argentina's Top Ten Corporations, 1989 and 1999 (by sales)

Company (1989)	Majority Shareholder	Company (1999)	Majority Shareholder
Yacimientos Petrolíferos Fiscales (oil)	SOE	REPSOL-YPF (oil)	foreign
Gas del Estado (gas)	SOE	Exxel Group (financial services)	Argentine*
Aerolineas Argentinas (air cargo)	SOE	Techint (steel)	Argentine*
Shell (oil)	foreign	Telefonica de Argentina (telecoms)	foreign
Somisa (steel)	SOE	Telecom (telecoms)	foreign
Empresa Nacional de Telecomunicaciones (telecoms)	SOE	Perez Companc Group (oil, banking)	Argentine*
Massalin (tobacco)	Argentine*	Supermercados Norte (food distribution)	foreign
Segba (electricity)	SOE	Cargill (food production)	foreign
Sevel (automobiles)	Argentine	Grupo Disco-Ekono (food distribution)	foreign

SOURCE: Manzetti (2003, 347).

*Argentine and privately owned

Table 4.5   Latin American Support for the Privatization of Public Companies (%)

	1998	2002	2003
Brazil	51	38	33
Venezuela	51	38	32
Mexico	49	28	31
Chile	51	22	29
Honduras	47	34	25
Colombia	39	23	24
Paraguay	46	19	23
Peru	44	32	22
Ecuador	52	40	20
Nicaragua	46	30	20
Bolivia	49	23	19
Guatemala	62	29	16
Uruguay	29	16	16
El Salvador	54	35	15
Argentina	**32**	**14**	**12**
Panama	20	31	10
Latin America	46	28	22

SOURCE: Latinobarometro (2003).

Table 4.6 Argentina Public Finances—Nonfinancial Public Sector, 1993–99 (in US$ millions)

	1993	1994	1995	1996	1997	1998	1999
I. Current Revenues	**50,058.70**	**50,271.30**	**49,037.80**	**46,917.70**	**54,641.10**	**56,217.30**	**55,676.70**
Tax Revenue	29,007.2	31,614.1	31,034.7	33,176.0	38,352.3	40,362.8	32,625.6
Social Security	13,345.0	14,083.8	13,704.8	10,281.0	12,201.7	11,990.0	10,891.8
Non-tax revenue	2041.3	2103.3	1709.6	1350.9	1505.7	2148.4	3472.3
Sales of Goods and Services	252.1	345.6	322.3	168.8	149.3	203.8	196.8
Operating Income	5016.4	1439.4	1091.0	917.6	851.6	276.8	1073.3
Property Rentals	331.0	579.1	1072.3	958.6	1514.6	1054.2	1155.1
Current Transfers	0.0	12.0	55.5	62.8	65.9	181.3	261.8
Other Income	65.7	94.0	47.6	2.0	0.0	0.0	0.0
II. Current Expenditures	**44,245.80**	**47,477.20**	**48,449.40**	**49,369.80**	**55,858.60**	**57,032.40**	**60,047.10**
Consumption and Oper. Exp.	12,327.5	10,259.7	9850.2	9862.7	10,278.6	9350.3	10,455.5
Wages and Salaries	7626.8	7642.2	7249.7	7213.3	7554.2	6844.3	7353.9
Goods and Services	4084.1	2444.7	2482.3	2472.9	2659.9	2477.1	2877.6
Other Expenses	616.6	172.8	118.2	176.5	64.5	28.9	224.0
Property Rentals	2914.0	3150.8	4086.6	4609.5	5747.3	6661.2	8223.9
Interest	2914.0	234.7	4083.5	4607.9	5745.0	6660.3	8223.6
Interest on Domestic Debt	362.1	234.7	193.0	147.6	247.8	215.0	223.6
Interest on External Debt	2551.9	2915.6	3890.5	4460.3	5497.2	6445.3	8000.0
Other Income	0.0	0.5	3.1	1.6	2.3	0.9	0.3
Social Security Benefits	12,513.3	15,241.1	15,627.8	15,443.9	17,199.3	17,480.6	17,436.4
Other Current Expenses	0.2	0.5	11.6	1.4	0.5	0.8	0.9
Current Transfers	16,440.6	18,742.3	18,684.0	19,452.3	22,632.9	23,539.5	23,930.4
To the Private Sector	3249.9	4567.7	4679.6	4444.7	5700.3	5909.8	6411.0
To the Public Sector	13,166.3	14,133.0	13,983.8	14,903.0	16,848.8	17,541.0	17,438.6
Provinces and Federal District	11,808.6	12,535.3	12,428.7	13,335.8	15,176.1	15,832.8	15,640.7
Shared Revenue	9917.8	10,673.2	9966.1	10,854.4	12,544.4	13,353.4	12,889.7
Provincial Guarantee Pact	746.6	263.3	748.9	421.9	229.6	4.4	0.0
Special Laws	319.9	375.1	328.0	277.6	436.8	600.8	573.9
Others	824.3	1218.7	1385.7	1781.9	1965.3	1874.2	2177.1
Universities	1290.3	1412.1	1410.2	1528.6	1614.8	1645.4	1779.9
Others	67.4	185.6	139.3	38.6	57.9	62.8	18.0
To the External Sector	24.4	41.6	26.2	104.6	83.8	88.7	80.8
Other expenses	50.2	82.8	189.2	0.0	0.0	0.0	0.0

Table 4.6 (Continued)

	1993	1994	1995	1996	1997	1998	1999
III. Current Savings (I–II)	**5812.9**	**2794.1**	**588.4**	**–2452.1**	**–1217.5**	**–815.1**	**–4370.0**
IV. Capital Resources	**667.8**	**806.9**	**1255.8**	**751.2**	**735.6**	**508.8**	**2778.7**
Privatizations	523.3	732.9	1171.2	374.9	305.7	96.3	2579.1
Others	144.5	74.0	84.6	376.3	429.9	412.5	199.5
V. Capital Outlays	**3750.2**	**3886.9**	**3217.5**	**3563.5**	**3794.7**	**3767.2**	**3176.7**
Direct Real Investment	1666.0	1214.8	871.7	757.6	855.1	888.8	634.8
Capital Transfers	1992.9	2514.8	2262.2	2765.4	2791.0	2821.8	2487.0
Provinces and Federal District	1908.4	2236.3	2080.4	2550.4	2499.1	2500.5	2203.7
Special Laws	826.3	1032.2	1003.1	1178.8	1169.4	1129.5	1098.6
Miscellaneous	1082.1	1204.1	1077.3	1371.6	1329.7	1371.0	1105.1
Other	57.3	107.2	55.7	37.2	143.5	54.8	51.8
VI. Total Income (I + IV)	**50,726.5**	**51,078.2**	**50,293.6**	**47,668.9**	**55,376.7**	**56,726.1**	**58,455.4**
VII. Total Expenses (II + V)	**47,996.0**	**51,364.3**	**51,666.9**	**52,933.3**	**59,653.3**	**60,799.6**	**63,223.8**
VIII. Overall Surplus (VI – VII)	**2730.5**	**–285.9**	**–1373.3**	**–5264.4**	**–4276.6**	**–4073.5**	**–4768.4**

SOURCE: Ministry of the Economy (2001).

Table 4.7 Provincial Public Employment Trends in Argentina, 1989–93

Province	Governor's Party*	Employment Per 1000 Inhabitants	Growth of Public Employment (%)
La Rioja	PJ	97	92.2
Catamarca	PJ/UCR	81	69.4
Santa Cruz	PJ	76	43.9
Formosa	PJ	72	72.9
San Juan	PJ/Bloquista Party	64	107.8
Neuquen	Mov. Popular Neuquino	62	106.2
La Pampa	PJ	57	69.0
Santiago del Estero	PJ	56	45.6
San Luis	PJ	54	25.1
Tierra del Fuego	Mov. Popular Fuegino	53	192.3
Rio Negro	UCR	53	60.8
Jujuy	PJ	51	45.1
Chubut	UCR	47	60.0
Tucuman	PJ	45	69.2
Corrientes	PJ/Autonomo Liberal P.	45	29.6
Salta	PJ/Renovador de Salta	44	63.3
Entre Rios	Peronist	41	65.6
Chaco	PJ/Accion Chaquena	41	60.8
Misiones	PJ	33	55.1
Santa Fe	PJ	31	37.3
Cordoba	UCR	28	34.5
Mendoza	PJ	27	23.7
Buenos Aires	PJ	21	59.0

SOURCE: Ministerio del Interior, Subsecretaria de Asistencia a las Provincias (1996).

*Partido Justicialista (PJ), Union Civica Radical (UCR)

Table 4.8   Argentinian Federal and Provincial Government Debt, 1989–2001

Government Institution	Federal*	Provincial**
1989	65,256	2,431
1990	62,233	3,095
1991	65,396	2,385
1992	68,339	1,749
1993	70,565	1,589
1994	77,387	2,797
1995	89,747	5,367
1996	97,105	13,921
1997	101,001	11,802
1998	112,357	13,164
1999	121,877	16,565
2000	128,018	21,227
2001	132,000	21,795

*Ministry of the Economy (in US$ millions)
**Dirección Nacional de Coordinación Fiscal con las Provincias

five

CHILE

Introduction

The story of Chile is one of two tales. It shows us marked differences in terms of economic performance depending on the kind of institutional settings within which market reforms take place. The first tale is about the level of success of a military dictatorship (1973–90) that decided to adopt "technically" sound policies as advocated by neoliberal economists, within a context of complete lack of accountability and transparency. The second tale is about the performance of democratically elected governments (1990–2006) in applying many of the same policies. Yet there was an appreciable difference in the overall environment that characterized the reform process. The Chilean democratic governments after 1990 implemented market reforms but faced strict institutional constraints and political accountability, which the previous military regime had systematically eliminated to have a free hand. Even more interesting for the purpose of this book is that democratic governments actually made a deliberate effort to improve accountability, transparency, and competition, resulting in what I would argue contributed to superior economic performance.

Historically, Chile has been characterized by strong political parties that provided political stability and shared a commitment to the basic rules of the democratic game. This often made the country an exception in Latin America. Starting in the late 1930s a series of center-left governments began to actively promote ISI as a way to mitigate the economic downturns following sharp declines in the price of copper, Chile's most important export. In the 1950s and 1960s subsequent conservative and centrist administrations expanded ISI policies, making Chile one of the most regulated and protected economies in Latin America (Ffrench-Davis 2002). However, by the late 1960s Socialist and Communist political elites stepped up their demands for better standards of living and social reforms favoring the lower classes, which exacerbated political polarization. This situation created three major political blocs with conservative and left-wing political parties at the extremes, while the moderate center was occupied by the Christian Democrats.

In 1970 Salvador Allende's election to the presidency, supported by a coalition of Socialists, Communists, and smaller left-wing parties called Unidad Popular (UP), marked the climax of the polarization process. Allende wanted to promote Chile's "way to socialism" by empowering the state with most economic activities and relegating the private sector to a subsidiary and heavily regulated role. Despite lacking a congressional majority, Allende moved swiftly through a variety of administrative measures to deliver on his campaign promises. He nationalized "strategic" industries (copper, banking, telecommunications, and many manufacturing industries) either by compensation or outright expropriation.[1] He also redistributed land to rural poor by breaking up large estates and promoted prolabor regulations and income-redistribution policies benefiting the working class through wage hikes.[2] However, Allende's populism went too far, too fast and broke with the Chilean tradition of incremental policy change and respect for the legislative process. The UP expansionary policies had fueled runaway inflation (342 percent in August 1973) and a mushrooming fiscal deficit (24.6 percent of GDP by 1973) as the government resorted to printing money since it could no longer finance its debt through foreign borrowing.[3] As inflation soared to record levels, unions resorted to widespread strikes demanding wage adjustments, thus paralyzing economic activity. Shortages of basic goods became endemic, outraging even government sympathizers. Politically, as the country fell into chaos, Allende became increasingly incapable of restraining the most militant members of UP, who encouraged illegal land and factory takeovers. By August 1973 the situation had reached

---

1. The nationalization of the copper industry, though, was widely supported across the political spectrum.

2. In little more than a year the effects of wage hikes were washed out by runaway inflation.

3. The reported data are from Edwards and Cox Edwards (1987, 29). The Nixon administration played a crucial role in shutting down international lending through the IMF, the World Bank, and private financial institutions. Prior to Allende, Chile was one of the largest beneficiaries of U.S. financial assistance, but once UP took power, Nixon decided to topple Allende by any means to prevent socialism from spreading to other Latin American countries.

the point of no return. Even moderate Christian Democrats joined the conservatives and the business community in lobbying the military to intervene before the country fell into full-fledged Marxism and a likely civil war (Valdés 1995, 16).

Consequently, in September 1973 the armed forces had enough political support to depose Allende. What followed, though, was the establishment of one of the harshest military dictatorships in South America, which turned Chile into an international pariah until its demise in 1990. In fact, contrary to the expectations of the civilian supporters of the coup, who had hoped for a quick return to democracy, the military decided to retain power and in the process closed the legislature, banned political parties, and established martial law. Initially, a ruling committee (Junta), made up by the commanders of the three armed services plus the police, took over executive duties and ruled by decree. By December 1974 the army commander, General Augusto Pinochet, who had acted as the spokesman of the Junta, proclaimed himself president, and in 1978 forced into retirement most of the officers who had opposed the consolidation of his personal power and advocated a return to democracy (Huneeus 2006).[4]

Consistent with the national security doctrine, which emphasized the fight against "internal enemies," the foremost political goal of Pinochet and the military was the eradication of Marxism and other left-wing ideologies, which resulted in the execution or "disappearance" of an estimated three thousand people and the incarceration, and often torture, of an additional twenty-seven thousand people (Correa 1992). Economically, within its first year in power the military proceeded tentatively as navy officers took over the economic portfolios but with no clear ideas on how to solve the crisis. The military Junta's Declaration of Principles of March 1974 called for a reduction of the government's role in economic matters, stating that the "state should only assume direct responsibility for those functions which the [people] . . . are unable to deal with adequately," but still ascribed to the government a substantial role in shaping economic and social policy (Vergara 1985).[5] In point of fact, as Tironi pointed out, the initial measures

4. The chief casualty of the purge was a fellow Junta member and Air Force commander, general Gustavo Leigh, who had been Pinochet's main critic. In Chile the police was incorporated into the Ministry of Defense.

5. Cited from Edwards and Cox Edwards (1987, 93). The same document was somewhat contradictory as it also made reference to workers' possible involvement in the management of SOES following the Yugoslavian model.

"did not aim, not even implicitly, at producing radical changes in the economic system that Chile had up to the 1970s, but only attempted to normal-
ize its operations and introduce gradual reforms in part of the system."[6]
This apparent indecisiveness stemmed from the fact that important sectors
within the military opposed drastic measures, which could trigger a popular
backlash, and wanted to retain a prominent role for the state in "strategic"
industries such as copper and public utilities (Teichman 2001). Consequently, the first economic team under the military opted for a gradual
approach to tackle the crisis. Its main objectives were to drastically reduce
both the fiscal deficit and inflation, and return land and firms that had been
nationalized or expropriated under Allende to their original owners.

In 1974 these measures met with some success. The fiscal deficit declined
to 10.5 percent of GDP and inflation, which had jumped to 605 percent at
the end of 1973, dropped to 369 percent (Edwards and Cox Edwards 1987,
32). However, the macroeconomic situation again took a turn for the worse
when copper prices, which accounted for 80 percent of Chile's export earnings at the time, declined by 40 percent in the third quarter of 1974. This
deteriorating situation gave Pinochet the opportunity to make a cabinet
reshuffle that would bolster his control over economic policy. Rear admiral
Lorenzo Gottuzzo, who had been in charge of the Ministry of Finance, was
replaced by Jorge Cauas, a former Central Bank chairman and director of
the Institute for Economics at the Catholic University of Chile. Cauas's
appointment was a turning point and shortly thereafter was followed by
the arrival of a group of conservative reformers—many of whom had grad-
uated from the Catholic University and eventually went on to pursue post-
graduate training at the University of Chicago—to key positions, including
the Central Bank of Chile. Such a group was quickly dubbed the "Chicago
Boys."

The Chicago Boys made up an ideologically cohesive and close-knit
group of university professors and businessmen who espoused wholeheart-
edly the creed of the primacy of economic freedom as postulated by their
former professors at Chicago, among whom Milton Friedman and Arnold
Harberger were the most influential. In 1971 a small group of entrepreneurs,
some of whom represented the most important Chilean conglomerates
(Edwards and Banco Hipotecario de Chile, BHC), began to hold meetings
to devise a strategy to resist Allende's policies and in 1972 commissioned a

6. Cited in Valdés (1995, 94).

team of economists from the Catholic University to formulate an economic plan that could be readily used in the event of a military coup. The result was a coherent plan dubbed El Ladrillo (the brick), which became the blueprint of the market reforms that would be implemented between 1974 and 1989. Many of its authors were Chicago Boys who from 1974 to 1982 came to control the most important ministries, the Central Bank, and the budget office. Equally important, many of them had direct ties with some of Chile's largest conglomerates, which led to a cozy alliance between businessmen and government officials (Silva 1996).

The Chicago Boys were true believers in the primacy of the market and the necessity to reduce the government's role in economic activity to a subsidiary, minimal role. Once they took office, they put into practice Friedman's and Hayek's teachings to a degree unparalleled in any capitalist economy to this day. In fact, they were not content to just undo the Socialist policies of the Allende administration. Their ultimate goal was to eradicate five decades of ISI policies altogether. They also shared a deep-seated contempt for politics, which they regarded as prone to demagogic populism and monopolistic market arrangements that prevented competition and growth. Oddly enough, for people who found in government intervention the culprit of every problem, the Chicago Boys believed that only an authoritarian "government" could actually promote their market reforms since the democratic process was too permeable to lobbying by powerful groups. According to Sergio de Castro, the intellectual leader of the Chicago Boys and the man who succeeded Cauas as finance minister between 1976 and 1982, "a person's actual freedom can only be ensured through an authoritarian regime that exercises power by implementing equal rules for everyone."[7]

By the end of 1974, the Chicago Boys began to expedite their plans and lobbied Pinochet to embrace their recipe for radical market reforms (Silva 1996, 109). Why did Pinochet, who until then had not manifested any particular sympathy for market economics, find in the Chicago Boys' master plan a great deal of affinity with his own goals? This is a question that often even the most sophisticated and detailed economic analyses on Chile have omitted, but it is crucial if we want to understand the events that took place from 1974 until 1989. First, market reforms went beyond the economic sphere, as they aimed at radically transforming Chilean society in a conser-

7. Quoted in Valdés (1995, 30).

vative fashion, which appealed to Pinochet. Second, and even more important from the standpoint of consolidating Pinochet's personal authority,
the implementation of sweeping market reforms could emasculate the bargaining power of political parties that had used government resources to
create patronage networks, as well as diminish the political clout of vested
interests such as business organizations, professional associations, and trade
unions. The only institution left untouched by the reform process was the
military, which could then act as the undisputed master of the political
arena.[8] Third, the Chicago Boys argued that the success of market reforms
would establish a new class of entrepreneurs linked to them that were alien
to Chile's established business groups (whose influence Pinochet wanted
to reduce) and, therefore, could constitute an important support base for
Pinochet's long-term plans (Silva 1996, 110).

In March 1975 Javier Vial, chairman of the BHC conglomerate that would
benefit tremendously from the economic policies of the dictatorship until
1982, invited Friedman and Harberger to give a series of lectures at the
Catholic University.[9] During this time the two U.S. economists met privately with Pinochet and suggested he attack inflation through the adoption
of shock therapy.[10] This event tilted the balance of power in favor of the
Chicago Boys. The following month Pinochet gave them the green light to
apply shock therapy. The Ministry of Finance became a superministry and
in 1976 de Castro replaced Cauas at its helm. By then the Chicago Boys
controlled all the important positions related to economic policy making
in the cabinet and Pinochet insulated them from any lobbying pressure. In
so doing, the dictator allowed them to enforce tight monetary policy and
government spending to eliminate the fiscal deficit. The Chicago Boys pursued shock therapy while simultaneously enforcing fundamental structural
reforms. Following the blueprint envisaged in El Ladrillo, the pillars of their
economic program were the privatization of SOEs, trade liberalization, and
market deregulation. Price controls were lifted, tariffs were reduced to 10
percent by 1978, most subsidies were eliminated, and government employment was cut by 20 percent (Edwards and Cox Edwards 1987, 29). During

8. Interview with former finance minister Rolf Lüders (1982–83), Santiago de Chile, August
1996.
9. Vial was a Chicago graduate himself and had very close ties to the Chicago Boys in
government.
10. Public Broadcasting Service, "Commanding Heights: The Battle for the World Economy," http://www.pbs.org/wgbh/commandingheights/shared/minitextlo/tr_show02.html.

1975–79 through privatization the government shed 207 SOEs, including most banks, manufacturing industries, and service companies (Hachette and Lüders 1993, 47).[11] However, due to Pinochet's opposition, the government retained control of the most important SOEs concentrated in "strategic" industries in mining, public utilities, and oil.

Shock therapy caused the country to go into a tailspin as GDP dropped by a whopping 16 percent in 1975, the largest contraction since the Great Depression. Unemployment shot up to 15 percent, and real wages declined by 35 percent as compared to 1970 (Ffrench-Davis 2002, 48). By 1977, though, these draconian measures seemed to produce the desired effects. Inflation abated significantly and the government deficit turned into a surplus. The deregulation of financial services, the elimination of restriction on capital flows, and the adoption of a fixed exchange rate vis-à-vis the U.S. dollar allowed private companies to borrow heavily from abroad. These events fueled investments and a steady economic recovery that during 1980–81 turned into a boom, prompting some to describe it as a "Chilean miracle." Emboldened by such results, in 1979 de Castro decided to make a final push for even more profound reforms affecting Chilean society. That same year Pinochet announced the "seven modernizations," among which the privatization of social security, health services, education, and the elimination of collective bargaining and most prolabor laws were the most controversial. A year later Pinochet made the core elements of the Chicago Boys reforms permanent when they were enshrined in a new constitution, which was approved in a tightly controlled plebiscite in 1980. Moreover, in an effort to prevent a return to ISI and the "demagoguery" of the Allende years, the new constitution explicitly stated the subsidiary role of the government in economic development vis-à-vis the private sector and the inviolability of individual property rights. It also placed the budget process under the control of the executive, mandated a balanced budget, established the independence of the Central Bank, and prohibited the Central Bank from financing the government's deficit.[12] In brief, economically, the 1980 constitution created a host of institutional constraints that made the rever-

11. This added to 325 SOEs that were privatized in 1973–74. Many of such companies had been recent acquisitions as a result of Allende "nationalization" effort and were returned to their original owners.

12. Many of these constraints of course would not apply to Pinochet, who would still be in office. The independence of the Central Bank became effective only in 1989, shortly before the military withdrew from power.

sal of market reforms in the event of a return to democracy extremely difficult. However, all these constraints would not be applicable to the military government. In fact, under Article 24 the 1980 constitution came into effect only in 1990, thus leaving Pinochet with complete power until then. Strict checks and balances were enshrined in the constitution but would not be enforced under the dictatorship.

The euphoria came to an abrupt end during 1982–83. As noted, much of the recovery had been fueled by massive foreign borrowing. This was made possible by the good relations that Chile had with the United States until Jimmy Carter took office as president. Between 1974 and 1976 the U.S. government, along with the World Bank and the IDB, granted Chile $628 million (Angell 2007). The IMF and the World Bank stamp of approval also paved the way for much of the $10 billion borrowing that Chilean private banks received from Citicorp, Wells Fargo, Bank of America, and Chase Manhattan by 1981. As a result, private corporations took advantage of an overvalued exchange rate that made the price of U.S.-dominated dollar loans inexpensive and invested in highly risky portfolio ventures rather than fixed capital (Ffrench-Davis 2002; Yotopoulos 1989).

However, the decision of the U.S. Federal Reserve to tighten the money supply to combat inflation in late 1979 led to a 21 percent increase of the prime rate by 1981. This translated into much higher increases in the interest rates for Chilean foreign loans, which, coupled with a deterioration of terms of trade, began to put hundreds of highly leveraged companies out of business. Consistent with Friedman's and Hayek's laissez faire teaching, de Castro argued that this was a physiological problem that would help the market rid itself of inefficient companies and chose to do nothing. Inaction only intensified the severity of the problem and cost de Castro his job in April 1982. That year 810 companies went bankrupt, twice as many as the average of the previous five years (Edwards and Cox Edwards 1987, 78). In 1982 stagflation settled in as GDP plummeted by 15 percent and unemployment rose by 30 percent (Larraín and Labán 1997, 4). The number of people living below the poverty line rose from 30 percent in 1981 to 55 percent in 1983 (Barandiarán and Hernández 1999, 1). By most accounts it was a crisis even more devastating than the one in 1975. In fact, as companies went under so did the banks that financed them. To avert a meltdown of the banking system, the government finally intervened in January 1983 by taking over eight financial institutions, including Chile's two largest banks (Barandiarán and Hernández 1999, 46). Ironically, in so doing the government not only renationalized the same banks that it had privatized in the mid-1970s, but it also reacquired most companies that it had privatized at that time since they had come under the control of the very banks and conglomerates, or *grupos*, that controlled the banks themselves. The government was left with picking up the pieces and had to orchestrate a massive bailout of those economic groups linked to the Chicago Boys that it had tried to promote in the mid-1970s. The rescue operation was possible thanks to the financial assistance of the IMF, the World Bank, and the IDB.[13] Between 1983 and 1987 these three IFIS provided Chile with $760 million annually and interceded with the international banks to reschedule foreign loans and grant additional credit to allow Chile to make its debt-servicing payments (Valdés 1995, 263). In return Pinochet agreed to repay to foreign banks the debt contracted earlier by the domestic conglomerates.

As postulated in chapter 1, the lack of political accountability fed into the lack of transparency and produced bad policies and collusion. The crisis, so generated, prompted massive protests in 1983, which shook the regime. As Valdés (1995, 264) noted: "After 1983, IMF strategy defined and guided Chilean economic policy, something that continued to provoke opposition in the business sector. Indeed, business groups had been among the strongest critics of the regime's handling of the crisis and had laid much of the blame for their predicament on the 'Chicago model. They regarded this option as designed exclusively for the benefit of the financial sector and speculators . . . As a result, from 1983 to 1984, the Central Bank provided around US$6,000 million—then equivalent to 30 percent of GNP—in relatively generous subsidies to debtors in foreign currency, to the private banks, and to those owing Chilean pesos.'" Notwithstanding the severity of the crisis, given the authoritarian nature of the political regime, Pinochet was skillful enough to weather the storm. Still, the price paid by average Chileans, to quote the former finance minister Alejandro Foxley, was "very, very high" in economic terms alone and could have been avoided.[14]

As a consequence of the 1982–83 debacle, the most ideological members of the Chicago Boys left government. Their replacements kept the basic elements of the free-market model intact but were more flexible in their

13. As part of this rescue operation, in the mid-1980s Chile agreed on an Extended Fund Facility Program with the IMF and on a Structural Adjustment Program with the World Bank.

14. Public Broadcasting Service, "Commanding Heights: The Battle for the World Economy," http://www.pbs.org/wgbh/commandingheights/shared/minitextlo/tr_show02.html.

approach than their predecessors.[15] After 1985 the government again launched a new privatization program and a series of policies aimed at tax reform and diversifying the export sector, which proved very successful. Moreover, the fixed exchange regime, which many believed to be a major cause of the financial collapse, was replaced by a flexible one, which allowed Chilean exports to become competitive. The inadequate regulation of the financial sector, which for many was another major factor behind the crisis, was also addressed as the government imposed strict controls on foreign borrowing and large reserve requirements. The current account deficit, which the Chicago Boys had downplayed early even after reaching 10 percent of GDP, was brought under control. Equally interesting was the fact that new measures reversed some of the neoliberal policies set in motion since the mid-1970s. For instance, the government imposed controls on short-term capital inflows to avoid speculative operations and the appreciation of the peso. Import tariffs and restrictions were also reinstated, as well as an array of selective export subsidies.[16]

These changes brought about the desired effects. Between 1986 and 1989 Chile experienced a period of strong recovery and a fiscal surplus, making it the best performing economy in Latin America. Reassured by such results, Pinochet called for a plebiscite in October 1988, as stipulated by the 1980 constitution, according to which Chileans were asked whether they wanted him to stay in power for another seven years.[17] Much to the dictator's disappointment, the majority of the people voted against him, prompting the scheduling of free elections at the end of 1989. What Pinochet had not realized was that despite the economic turnaround, poverty and income

15. On the pragatism of Pinochet's economic team after the 1982 crisis, see the opinion of Martin Wolf, Sebastian Edwards, Dani Rodrik, and Javier Santiso in "Chile Blazes Trail for Latin America," *Financial Times*, December 13, 2006. According to Rodrik, "Martin Wolf and Javier Santiso are right that pragmatism has been the key to Chile's success. When Pinochet slavishly followed some textbook theory of how macroeconomics worked, the results were a disaster. In 1982–83, Chile experienced the largest collapse of any country in the region. Under Pinochet, Chile's per-capita GDP growth averaged no more than 1 per cent per year, which hardly makes the Pinochet period an economic success. The economy took off only when Pinochet jettisoned economic orthodoxy in the aftermath of the 1982–83 crisis, engineered an undervalued exchange rate and jacked up import tariffs to 35 per cent." Economists' Forum, "Chile Blazes Trail for Latin America," http://blogs.ft.com/economistsforum/2006/12/chile-blazes-trhtml/.

16. As a result of the crisis, import tariffs jumped to 35 percent but were progressively reduced to 15 percent once the situation stabilized after 1985.

17. The 1980 constitution stipulated that Pinochet would serve eight years as president, with a plebiscite to be held during the eighth year to select the new head of state. However, only the Junta could pick the new presidential candidate, which in 1988 happened to be Pinochet again.

concentration had soared tremendously. In turn, these factors played an important role in swinging the vote of the middle and poor strata of society against him (Larraín and Labán 1997, 12).

Having learned from seventeen years of harsh repression Christian Democrats and Socialists, who had been bitter rivals prior to 1973, resolved that the only way to return to democracy was to reconcile their differences and promote a multiparty alliance, which was dubbed Concertación. In a remarkable display of unity and sense of purpose, Concertación candidates won the presidency in 1989 and again in 1994, 2000, and 2006. The first Concertación president, Christian Democrat Patricio Aylwin (1990–94), set the tone for what would become the hallmark of the governing coalition, which included not just the acceptance but the improvement of the market-friendly policies of the military regime, along with the strengthening of democratic institutions and a deliberate attempt to use government programs to diminish income inequalities, or what came to be known as "growth with equity." Although many analysts credit Pinochet and the Chicago Boys for the economic success that Chile has experienced since the late 1990s, making it an example for the rest of the developing world, most of the policies aimed at fostering competition and transparency were actually promoted during the Concertación. As we shall see in the following sections, this effort to make political and economic processes more transparent and competitive through a proactive government made Chile the success story that it became. Through competition the Concertación unleashed market forces still trapped in the cozy economic arrangements that under the military allowed some powerful companies to dominate important markets. Privatization, which was the hallmark of the military regime, continued. In fact, the Concertación administrations transferred fourteen SOEs to the private sector between 1994 and 2000 (Fischer, Gutiérrez, and Serra 2002), but compared to the military regime the process was transparent as it used public auctions as opposed to direct sales. Through greater accountability and transparency the democratic governments of the post-Pinochet era earned popular support and the type of legitimacy necessary for market reforms to consolidate and thrive.

The results in the post-Pinochet regime were impressive. GDP growth went from an average of 3.1 percent during 1974–89 to 6.4 percent in the 1990–2000 period and 5.1 percent during 2001–5.[18] Poverty, which ac-

---

18. Central Bank of Chile yearly statistics on GDP growth.

counted for 45 percent of the total population in 1987, declined to 19 percent in 2003 (Angell 2005, 11). Real wages, which at the end of the military regime were still 35 percent below their 1980 level (Larraín and Labán 1997, 12), increased by 38 percent between 1993 and 2005.[19] According to Angell (2005, 12) between 1990 and 2000 the Concertación improved the social conditions of the lower classes by annually increasing investments in health (9.4 percent) and education (10.6 percent). Moreover, the Concertación administrations' effort to improve the quality of government institutions paid off. Between 1996 and 2006 Chile made great strides in terms of economic competitiveness and the quality of government institutions, as measured by international indexes, scoring well ahead of most developing countries and slightly below the United States and the United Kingdom (Angell 2005, 13). In the next sections I will examine the role that accountability institutions played in shaping market reforms in Chile during the Pinochet regime and the subsequent Concertación period.

Accountability in the 1973–2000 Period

As noted earlier, the military regime ruled Chile by fiat and was unrestrained in its exercise of power. Between 1973 and 1980 the Junta closed Congress, suspended the constitution that had governed the land since 1925, and purged members of the judiciary unwilling to cooperate. The new constitution drafted in 1980 not only meant to enshrine into law the neoliberal economic policies that the Chicago Boys had enacted in the previous years but also created severe institutional constraints in the event that the country returned to democracy in the future. Also noted earlier, the peculiarity of the 1980 constitution, though, was that its content would not affect the military government for nine years after its approval, which occurred in September 1980 through a popular plebiscite. During that period Pinochet used "transitory" articles, which the dictator of course applied as he saw fit.[20] As Angell (2005, 6) aptly put it, the 1980 Constitution "gave the state a limited [economic] role, but with authoritarian controls over democratic processes." The new constitution made the bicameral legislature weak on

19. Ibid.
20. The most controversial measure of the transitory rules was Article 24, which gave the president the power to restrict the right of free association and assembly. Under the same clause, people could be arrested and exiled without appeal save for a petition to the president himself.

purpose and gave the executive a tremendous amount of power vis-à-vis the Congress.[21] As opposed to the 1925 constitution, the new law of the land significantly reduced legislative oversight prerogatives (Siavelis 2000a).

Another factor strengthening executive authority was the fact that the president could appoint a large number of senators with life tenure. This clause allowed Pinochet and the National Security Council (NSC) to name for life nine loyalists as senators before the country returned to democracy in 1990, which gave the pro-Pinochet conservative parties in Congress a virtual veto power over legislation.[22] The 1980 constitution also incorporated the main articles of the national security doctrine and made the military the "guarantor" of the "integrity" of the new political institutions. The most visible institution of this approach was the NSC, which was dominated by members of the military and was allowed to "express to any authority established by this constitution its opinion regarding any deed, event, or act, or subject matter, which in its judgment gravely challenges the bases of the institutional order or could threaten national security" (Article 96). Article 93 also insulated the military from civilian control.[23] Moreover, Article 32 denied the popular election of local administrators, which had been a mainstay of the Chilean democracy until 1973. In fact, the president received exclusive authority over the appointment of provincial governors, mayors of large cities, and regional administrators, which was a prerogative that Pinochet used extensively before relinquishing power. In 1989 Pinochet also issued a series of "binding laws," which were aimed at restricting the discretionary power of the Concertación government. One of such laws granted life tenure to public employees who had served under Pinochet, thus limiting President Aylwin, who succeeded him, in his ability to staff the public administration with technocrats of his liking (Angell 2000).

In short, while the military ruled without any constraint for seventeen years, it made sure the democratic governments that would follow had little room for maneuvering if they wanted to alter the conservative institutional

21. The Chamber of Deputies and the Senate operate in similar fashion. Chile adopted a binomial electoral system, which allows the election of two senators and two deputies from each district. This system discriminates against small parties that are not members of a large coalition and was designed to prevent representation of small, radical parties from the left.

22. The president selected five new senators, whereas the National Security Council named four. The NSC also named two of the seven members of the Constitutional Tribunal.

23. The president could name the commanders of the armed forces and the military police only from a list submitted by the military and they could only be removed from their post by the NSC.

framework spelled out in the 1980 constitution.[24] Last but not least, before relinquishing power Pinochet issued a law banning all congressional inquiries of events that took place under the military regime.[25] This added to a decree enacted in 1978 that through an amnesty shielded military personnel from prosecution for possible human rights violations.

Given the restrictions imposed by the outgoing military regime, many governments would have been tempted to use the questionable legitimacy of the referendum that approved the 1980 constitution and act unilaterally to change it, but this was not the case in Chile. Instead, the Concertación presidents showed an unusual degree of restraint and respect for due process as they opted to work with the conservative opposition to find a common ground so that the most authoritarian aspects of the constitution could be eliminated. The process of amending the constitution was lengthy. Through bipartisan agreements the Chilean Congress passed constitutional amendments in late 1989, 1993, and 1997, and finally in 2005 when the last draconian elements of the 1980 constitution were eliminated. Only then could president Ricardo Lagos (2000–2006) finally announce that Chile's transition to democracy, which had started with the 1988 plebiscite, was finally complete.[26] Most notable, the latest changes also strengthened the investigative powers of the Chamber of Deputies.

Congress

Prior to the 1973 coup Congress was able to exercise some oversight over the executive branch, particularly on matters regarding the budget process, but after the 1980 constitutional reform this was no longer the case. As legislative checks and balances over the executive were greatly weakened and made the Chilean presidency the strongest in terms of legislative prerogatives in all of Latin America (Siavelis 2000a). Under the new basic law the executive had a variety of powers to determine on which policies Congress can decide, when, and under what conditions. The most important of

24. Pinochet made constitutional amendments extremely difficult as they required the approval of two succeeding legislatures by a three-fifths vote of both houses of Congress.

25. Law No. 18.918, Ley Organica Constitucional del Congreso Nacional, Article 2, Transitory Provisions (Siavelis 2000b, 78).

26. Congress approved fifty-eight new amendments in 2000, which eliminated the "appointed senators," reinstated the presidential right to dismiss the commanders-in-chief of the armed forces, and eliminated Senate seats for former presidents, and the presidential term was shortened from six to four years starting in 2006.

such powers was the prerogative to introduce the budget, which Congress could alter only within a very limited period of time and under strict conditions.[27] The same applied to issues related to social security, taxation, social policies, remuneration and collective bargaining, and the public administration, where the president retained exclusive authority to propose changes on existing legislation. Moreover, by identifying any given bill as urgent, the executive could expedite its approval in Congress (Cea Egaña 1994). Presidents also exercised extensive veto powers, which could be overturned only with a two-thirds congressional majority. As opposed to the pre-1973 period, these changes deprived legislators of their ability to delay voting on presidential bills so as to force concessions.

Although the 1980 constitution explicitly states the role of the Chamber of Deputies (lower house) in overseeing the activities of the executive branch (Article 48, No. 1), in practice legislators have very limited tools at their disposal to inquire and prosecute offenders. To compound matters, the partisan divisions in Congress have politicized inquiries, thus undermining most oversight efforts. In his analysis of legislative oversight in Chile, Siavelis (2000b, 77) identified three major areas in which the Congress's prerogatives were eroded as opposed to the pre-1973 period. The first relates to the fact that the president is no longer required to personally answer inquiries from members of the Chamber of Deputies. Instead, ministers can do so in the president's place. Second, as opposed to the 1925 constitution, resolutions passed in the Chamber of Deputies under no circumstances may "affect the political responsibility of the ministers" (Article 48, No. 1). Third, when congressmen present written requests soliciting information (oficio), the executive is mandated to provide an answer, but there are no clear rules with regard to their substantive content. Moreover, for some legal scholars the definition of what parts of the executive branch are accountable is vague enough that congressional investigative inquiries over the public administration may be based on shaky constitutional grounds (Cea Egaña 1994, 12).

In general, the most common form of accountability in the hands of the legislature remained the oficio. The oficio simple, as the name suggests, is a basic request of information that a legislator sends to a specific ministry or

---

27. Congress has sixty days from its submittal to vote on the budget, after which it is automatically approved. Congress can reduce spending but cannot increase it, and it can only decrease proposed presidential spending. As a result, during the 1990s Congress approved presidential budgets with very minor changes.

bureaucratic agency. The *oficio de fiscalización*, instead, entails some degree of control and possible sanction but requires a simple majority in the Chamber of Deputies to prompt an inquiry about possible cases of wrongdoing. As Siavelis (2000b, 77) noted, the *oficio simple* has proved to be a very weak accountability tool and has been used primarily for pork-barrel-related issues, which has weakened its credibility. During the Aylwin (1990–94) administration, 18,532 were filed and 14,700 received a written response, but government officials complained about their poor quality and occasional trivial nature, leading to the perception that their reply was more often than not a waste of time and did not serve any accountability purpose (Siavelis 2000b, 84–85).

The *oficio de fiscalización* is, on paper, a stronger accountability tool than the simple *oficio*, but it suffers from the fact that the executive is not required to comply with the recommendations that the Chamber of Deputies may have presented once it has received a written reply from the government. The Chamber of Deputies has the option to start a constitutional accusation procedure against individual ministers or the president if they fail to reply, but such an option has been hardly exercised. In fact, during the first four years of the Eduardo Frei administration (1994–2000) only eight *oficios de fiscalización* were sent to the government, which, in turn, replied to six (Siavelis 2000b, 86). The low use of the *oficios de fiscalización* can be explained with the high degree of congressional party discipline in Chile. Since the Concertación presidents have enjoyed a majority in the Chamber of Deputies since 1990, their back benchers did not have the necessary incentive to join the opposition and use the *oficios de fiscalización* to investigate cases of corruption and questionable administrative behavior, which could have embarrassed their governing coalition. In point of fact, Congress did not show a greater propensity to use this particular tool of accountability than it did prior to the 1973 coup (Gil 1966).

Under the old 1925 constitution the Chamber of Deputies could set up special investigative committees to look into wrongdoings in the executive branch, including the public administration. The 1980 constitution does not mention them, but special committees were reintroduced after 1990 through the internal by-laws of the lower house. However, as it was true in the pre-1973 period, these committees turned out to be largely ineffective as a means to pursue legislative accountability over the executive (Cea Egaña 1994; Siavelis 2000b). On paper these committees have broad powers to summon government officials, bureaucrats, and representatives of pri-

vate companies who have contractual obligations with the national administration. During the 1990–98 period the Chamber of Deputies authorized
thirty-five special committees, but of these only ten were able to issue reports; their findings often followed partisan lines and did not lead to any
tangible action. In his analysis of special committees, Siavelis (2000b, 87–
88) pointed to several factors that undermined their potential role in assert-
ing legislative prerogative to hold the executive accountable. First, their
constitutional legitimacy is unclear since they are not included in Article
48 of the constitution, which details the congressional oversight authority.
Second, committees cannot protect their witnesses nor can they ensure the
truthfulness of the information gathered since people do not testify under
oath and cannot be prosecuted for false statements. Third, the opposition
often used them simply as vehicles to embarrass the sitting president rather
than as a means to find out the truth, and in so doing many committees
lost credibility. On occasion some committees issued final reports containing split assessments that reflected partisan lines and made them just as
ineffective. Fourth, many committees took a long time to be organized,
proceeded with their investigations just as slowly, and in some cases could
not reach a final conclusion.

The most powerful form of legislative accountability was the possibility
of an impeachment procedure against mayors, regional governors, judges,
army officers, ministers, and the president. This prerogative, which was
used occasionally prior to 1973, escalated during the last two years of the
Allende administration when the opposition in Congress failed to impeach
the president. The 1980 constitution ascribes Congress the same prerogatives, but during the 1990s they were never used against ministers. The
only noticeable case was when an impeachment succeeded against Supreme
Court Justice Hernán Cereceda Bravo for his handling of a human rights
case. The second major case was against Pinochet himself, who became a
senator after his retirement from active duty in 1998, but this proceeding
was abandoned in the late 1990s.

Despite many limitations, Congress did exercise a restraining role on the
executive under the Concertación administrations. Until 2006 the opposition controlled the Senate due to the fact that Pinochet appointed legislators in the upper house who invariably formed a majority with the
conservative delegation. Moreover, as the 1990s progressed even Concertación legislators began to put pressure on the executive to be more receptive
to congressional input on economic policy and making the budget process

more transparent. Since 1993 Congress maintained that the executive limited its ability to change the budget without issuing a new law. In 1995 the executive agreed to brief congressional budget committees on quarterly bases about the government public finances, while SOEs were required to do so every semester. In 1997 new norms increased congressional oversight over most state agencies and made the approval of future spending dependent on a positive evaluation of ongoing appropriations. Congress also tightened its control over the execution of the budget and diminished the ability of the Ministry of Finance to transfer budgeted funds without legislative approval. In 2001 congressional subcommittees were granted two months to evaluate the budget instead of a few legislative sessions (Montecinos 2003, 21–22). Moreover, under the Concertación administrations, the executive gradually began to engage Congress in policy negotiations, which allowed legislators to soften the executive dominance over economic policy. This prompted the Concertación to "adhere to rigorous fiscal policy principles and . . . to improving quality and efficiency standards within the public sector" (Montecinos 2003, 22). Thus, by the late 1990s Congress had made considerable strides in diminishing the iron control over the budget process, which the executive enjoyed early in that decade.

It is also worth noting that the constitutional amendments approved in 2005 granted congressional committees greater investigative powers over issues that previously had been barred. For instance, as we shall see later, the Chamber of Deputies was allowed to set up a special committee to assess alleged cases of corruption involved in the privatization policies of the military regime. Such an inquiry was a major breakthrough and was fully supported by president Ricardo Lagos (2000–2006) at the time. In fact, it finally shed some light into a shady policy process that Pinochet had explicitly tried to cover up through transitory legal measures right before President Aylwin took office in March 1990.

The Courts

Although upon independence Chile looked to the United States to draft its own constitution, it adopted a very hierarchical organization of its judicial system, which was patterned after the Spanish model. Further, the Chileans developed their criminal and administrative laws following the Roman/Napoleonic legal traditions. The judiciary has usually been regarded as a very conservative-minded institution functioning in an almost archaic fashion

(Matus 1999). Throughout most of its history it adopted a very strict interpretation of the law and avoided actively participating in political matters. From 1925 until the 1973 coup the Chilean judiciary was fairly independent from political power but did not distinguish itself in terms of competence, efficiency, or defense of civil rights. In 1972 it collided with the Allende administration over property rights issues when the Supreme Court refused to legitimize the UP's nationalization and expropriation policy agenda.

The 1980 constitution strengthened the independence of the judiciary.[28] As in the past, the Supreme Court was granted administrative and economic control over the lower courts. However, the new constitution created the Constitutional Court, whose role was to provide an ex-ante control over the constitutionality of congressional bills, executive orders, and constitutional amendments. The jurisdiction of the Constitutional Court was limited to cases after the new constitution came into effect. Prior cases remained under the control of the Supreme Court and lower court judges. Moreover, its weaknesses stem from the fact that it can only take up a case if the presidency or one of the two chambers of Congress formally asks to do so; individual citizens cannot (Gómez 1999).

During the military regime, the attitude of the courts was passive and subordinated to the wishes of the government (Hilbink 1999). As often happened in Latin America under authoritarian governments, the Supreme Court accepted the constitutionality of the Junta's decisions and refused to review human rights cases. In the meantime, while in power Pinochet appointed a large number of sympathetic judges to the bench in lower courts. The "politicization" of the courts became overt when Pinochet packed the Supreme Court with loyalists right before leaving the presidency. He replaced many old judges, who took advantage of a very generous retirement package, with much younger ones (Matus 1999). These events severely eroded the prestige and credibility of the judiciary, which along with the military came to be regarded as the most visible bastion protecting Pinochet's authoritarian legacy after the country returned to democracy (Muhlenbrock 1996). In fact, the 1980 constitution, which began to be fully operative only shortly before Pinochet stepped down from the presidency, granted the Supreme Court important prerogatives to preserve the status quo. Among such prerogatives were the nomination of judges to

28. In terms of independence, the Chilean judiciary ranks second according to the World Economic Forum index (2004), and third according to the Feld and Voigt index (2003) when compared to the rest of Latin America.

the Constitutional and the Electoral Qualification Tribunals and a representation in the National Security Council and the Senate (Galleguillos 1999).

As a result, while the judiciary in general and the Supreme Court in particular acted as docile institutions that rubberstamped Pinochet's reforms during the dictatorship, they often played an antagonistic role under the Concertación administrations. A clear indication of the Supreme Court bias came in 1990 when it upheld the constitutionality of the 1978 Amnesty Law, which protected military and police personnel from possible lawsuits for human rights violations (Loveman and Lira 2000). Another example was when the Commission for Truth and Reconciliation issued a report to President Aylwin regarding violations of human rights during the military regime. The Supreme Court released a statement charging that the report was biased and vindictive and that the commission had unduly intruded into matters that were the sole responsibility of the judiciary to investigate.

In the 1990s it became apparent to the Concertación presidents that the judiciary had turned into a major stumbling block to political and economic reforms. During Aylwin's tenure the government was particularly concerned with the judiciary's dismal record on human rights, opaque internal administration, and poor training. Thus, it appointed a commission to draft a legislative proposal to overhaul the whole system of justice administration.[29] However, the Supreme Court reacted vehemently and made no apologies for its behavior under the military regime. Moreover, it charged that the government was breaching the constitutional separation of powers and enlisted the support of conservative parties in Congress and the military to stop the reform in its tracks. However, it was a pyrrhic victory as the partisan behavior of the judiciary began to undermine its credibility even among former allies. Alleged cases of incompetence and corruption did the rest. By the mid-1990s large sectors within the conservative parties in Congress and the business community had come to the conclusion that judicial reform was not just unavoidable but actually overdue.[30] As Correa (1999, 292) noted, "the right wing, although it considered the Supreme Court one of the core enclaves for the defense of the new institu-

29. One key feature of the Judicial Reform Commission was a recommendation to create a National Council of Justice entrusted with the appointment of future judges, thus taking away a major prerogative from the Supreme Court. The proposal also included the provision that one-third of the Supreme Court justices be lawyers from outside the judiciary. Furthermore, the commission called for improved training through the establishment of a Judges' College.

30. In 1991 the conservative think-tank Centro de Estudios Públicos published a report advocating a major reform of the judicial system.

tional order, perceived it as a body that was unable to modernize itself. Particularly within entrepreneurial circles the judicial branch was perceived as inadequate for the resolution of [business] disputes." What concerned the business community and the conservative parties was the need to update existing legislation to integrate Chile farther into the global economy. While the courts had played an important political role in keeping the authoritarian articles of the 1980 constitution in the early years of the transition to democracy, they appeared awfully unprepared to deal with the complexities of the country's fast-growing economy, which now competed regionally to attract foreign investments (Saavedra and Soto 2004). Chile's attempt to join the North American Free Trade Agreement and the legal and business requirements that such an effort entailed also played a part in the changed mood of many conservatives. This new economic scenario required a different type of judiciary that would be professional, honest, and could guarantee a fair interpretation of a rule of law and the respect for the due process. In sum, politically correct judges had proved themselves useful in going along with Pinochet during the early stages of market reforms, but as the economic model consolidated and the stakes to be internationally competitive grew higher, a new type of judiciary was in order.

President Frei, who succeeded Aylwin in 1994, took full advantage of the changing mood in the conservative camp. As opposed to his predecessor, he downplayed human rights issues and instead pitched his judicial reform plan as a key element to improve the competitiveness of the Chilean economy. A series of alleged scandals implicating members of the Supreme Court also softened the resistance of the conservative bloc in Congress. As the reputation of the courts became increasingly tarnished, conservative politicians did not just distance themselves from the judiciary but actually found it politically expedient to lead the charge against corrupt judges. In 1992 members of the opposition in Congress joined the Concertación and impeached four Supreme Court justices on charges of corruption.[31] In 1997 the conservative party Unión Demócrata Independiente (UDI) sponsored an impeachment proceeding against the chief justice Servando Jordán on corruption charges. Its attempt failed but showed how strained the relationship between the judiciary and conservative political parties had become.

Moreover, as much as Hayek and Friedman stressed the importance of

---

31. The four were Hernán Cereceda, Lionel Beraud, Germán Valenzuela, and Fernando Torres Silva. As mentioned earlier, only Cereceda was found guilty and expelled.

the judiciary in upholding individual rights, particularly in the economic realm, the Chilean courts displayed a conservative and often reactionary tendency in this regard. This was particularly noticeable in the area of free speech as the Supreme Court actively pursued a strategy of censorship when investigative journalists began to publish reports exposing the corrupt behavior of several prominent members of the highest court, including allegations of money laundering. The most notorious case in this regard was that involving journalist Alejandra Matus (1999), who was induced to leave the country to avoid arrest after her book was confiscated.[32] In the 1990s, unlike in many other Latin American countries, the executive and legislative branches, not the courts, began to expand constitutional rights in Chile. As a result, the judiciary became the least trusted of the three branches of government in the second half of the 1990s.[33]

In 1997 Frei finally succeeded in drafting the support of the conservative bloc in Congress to amend the 1980 constitution in areas affecting the role of the Supreme Court.[34] Moreover, Congress approved the most sweeping legal reform in over a century, particularly in the area of criminal law. It created the office of the Public Ministry (equivalent to the U.S. Public Prosecutor's Office), introduced oral proceedings and a public defender, and established a jury system while making judges more accountable for their actions.[35] Subsequently, the government introduced new legislation on intellectual property rights and business regulation to enhance competition policy in an effort to comply with the requirements of a Free Trade Agreement with the United States, which was signed in 2003.

32. Supreme Court Justice Servando Jordán filed a suit against Matus invoking the State Security Law, according to which insulting government representatives is a crime against public order. Earlier in 1993 the Supreme Court had banned a book by Francisco Martorell on similar grounds.

33. Between 1996 and 2001, 38 percent of the respondents showed confidence in the judiciary as opposed to 42 percent for the Congress and 56 percent for the presidency (Payne et al. 2002, 36). This source uses data from the Latinobarometro.

34. It increased the number of justices to twenty-one with five of them coming from outside the judiciary, imposed the retirement of Supreme Court justices over seventy-five years of age, and the chief justice's tenure was reduced to two years. Furthermore, the number of new potential candidates that the Supreme Court could submit to the president was increased from five to ten, giving greater choice to the executive, and the Senate was put in charge of confirming nominees. These changes significantly altered the composition of the Supreme Court, allowing the incorporation of eleven new members by 2000 (Galleguillos 1999).

35. Previously, Chile adopted the inquisitorial system, according to which defendants were regarded guilty until they proved their innocence. Moreover, judges were in charge of the entire proceeding since they were in charge of gathering evidence, prosecuting, and sentencing at the same time.

Although the judicial system left much to be desired and some of its features continued to impede the functioning of the Chilean market (Saavedra and Soto 2004), the reforms that the Concertación administrations introduced after 1990 attempted to remedy several of the problems inherited from the military regime. The Chicago Boys did make a deliberate effort to protect property rights by inserting clear-cut articles in the 1980 constitution to that effect, but they completely ignored the need to reform the judicial system accordingly because this could have run against Pinochet's intention to keep the judiciary subjugated to his wishes. Whether judges were incompetent or corrupt, as they turned out to be on several occasions, it did not matter to Pinochet (Matus 1999)—their unconditional loyalty did. This situation also explains why despite the fact that the market reforms of the military regime were marred by collusion and preferential treatment, which defied the very definition of market competition, the judiciary failed to prevent such practices from taking place in many cases. These very issues were only—and slowly—tackled under the Concertación era since the legal obstacles contained in the 1980 constitution required the cooperation of the opposition in Congress, which materialized only through a prolonged period of time. In sum, it was the Concertación administrations that made a serious effort to improve the rule of law, and the judiciary entrusted on its administration so that the design and enforcement of property rights would be consistent with the spirit of free markets. The military regime instead kept the judiciary subjugated and allowed the courts to enforce the law only when it was politically expedient while preventing them to go after cases that defied the very essence of competition.

Oversight Institutions

Starting in 1927 Chile established a highly centralized system of administrative control under the Contraloría General de la República (CGR), and in 1947 the institution became an autonomous agency of the public administration. The CGR had broad powers from its inception (Valenzuela 1977). It exercised an ex-ante oversight function by assessing the legality of all acts of the public administration, including laws and decrees. All such measures had to be sent to the CGR for an opinion before being issued. The CGR also controlled tax collection and the execution of budgetary expenditures and funds of ministries, municipalities, government agencies, and SOEs. Only the president could overrule the CGR's negative opinion, provided that all cabinet members countersigned such a decision. This endorsement, however, made cabinet members susceptible to a possible censure on the part of the legislature. The president appointed the comptroller general upon the approval of the Senate. Once in office the comptroller general could not be removed until the retirement age set at seventy-five. The 1980 constitution reiterated such characteristics and the privileged status of the CGR within the public administration. Indeed, the CGR quickly earned a fearsome reputation for its thoroughness, integrity, and high professional standards.

Historically, the CGR was particularly effective in controlling municipalities and government agencies, although it lacked the authority to punish elected officials or bureaucrats. It could declare the illegality of a given act, but in the case of criminal activity it had to turn the evidence to the courts for prosecution. However, as Valenzuela (1977, 42) noted, "in an indirect way the Contraloría did exercise much influence over Chilean local government. Highly publicized instances of the Contraloría's indictments resulting in punishment of functionaries as well as elected officials gave the agency an awesome reputation of efficiency."

During the military regime the CGR behaved similarly to the judiciary in that it limited itself to assessing the legality of military initiatives from a purely formal point of view. Once the country returned to democracy, the CGR again took an active role by investigating several cases of corruption at the municipal, administrative, and SOE level. During the 1993–94 period alone, the CGR investigated 241 cases of corruption, and the trend continued well into the 2000s as the comptroller general recommended drastic measures against a score of public officials, including some former ministers involved in major scandals (Rehren 2002). In 2002 Congress modified the legal statute of the CGR to make its functions compatible with the changes in the administration of justice introduced between 1997 and the early 2000s, but its prerogatives remained essentially the same. Therefore, unlike under the military regime, the CGR did play an important role in keeping public administrators and politicians accountable for their actions after 1989 and, as in the past, its investigations led to well-publicized judicial proceedings, reasserting its reputation as a reliable watchdog.

What is actually interesting in the Chilean case is that the Concertación administrations took the lead in strengthening government accountability and transparency procedures, particularly from the second half of the 1990s onward, as the authoritarian articles of the 1980 constitution began to be phased out. In the late 1990s the Chilean government was one of the first in Latin America to adopt a freedom of information act patterned after but not as comprehensive as the U.S. model. The IMF (2005, 23) acknowledged Chile's achievements in this regard as follows: "Particularly impressive is the rapid progress made recently toward enhancing transparency, and the authorities' responsiveness to new demands—both from within Chile and from international markets." In the IMF view, not only had Chile made important progress in institutionalizing its fiscal transparency, but "government accountability to Congress and the public is demonstrably being strengthened" (IMF 2005, 23). These institutional features clearly contrast with the secrecy and authoritarian behavior of Pinochet era and, although the IMF does not make the connection explicitly, they contributed to Chile's economic success under the Concertación.

Corruption

As noted, when the military regime drew to a close Pinochet enacted a number of economic and legal measures that, among other things, prevented inquiries into the privatization process. During his years in power Pinochet had effectively portrayed himself and his government as incorruptible and justified the measures taken to stop inquiries as a means to prevent subsequent governments from pursuing political retribution. However, once democracy returned rumors began to surface about alleged kickbacks to members of the Pinochet regime, as well as to his sons (Siavelis 2000b). The dictator's incorruptible aura came to an end in July 2004 when the U.S. Senate Permanent Subcommittee on Investigations, which was inquiring into money-laundering activities, released a report detailing how Pinochet used the Washington-based Riggs Bank, from 1994 to 2002, to hide millions of dollars from Chilean tax authorities through the establishment of more than 125 bank accounts under false names. In 2006 a subsequent investigation by the Chilean tax authorities found ten tons of gold worth $160 million in a Hong Kong bank account belonging to the former dictator. After this latest discovery Pinochet's personal fortune was estimated to be worth at least $200 million, an amount that was not justifiable on his annual salary of $40,000 while in office.[36] In June 2005 the Supreme

---

36. *Washington Post*, October 25, 2006. Pinochet's lawyers claimed that much of the money came from investments, donations, and royalties received from books the dictator had previously published.

Court stripped the former dictator of his parliamentary immunity and ordered him to stand trial for money laundering, document falsification, and tax evasion.[37] Government prosecutors served similar indictments in 2006 to Pinochet's wife, four of his children, and several of his closest aides.

Although none of the money that Pinochet had hidden away could be traced back to possible illegal deals committed in implementing market reforms, a 2005 Chilean congressional report on privatization cast further doubts about the honesty of the process. In 2004 the Chilean Congress established the Comisión de Privatizaciones (henceforth CP) to investigate the way privatization was carried out during its second phase (1985–89) as the country began to recover from the financial collapse of the 1982–83 period: "The most lucrative privatizations were from 1985 to 1990, when it was clear that the Pinochet government's days were numbered and when even some military officials questioned the wisdom of rapidly selling companies in industries vital to Chile's national security and economic well-being. Privatizations were largely controlled and overseen by a small group of senior Chilean military officials, civilian cabinet members, and economic advisers, a number of whom later got shares and high-paying positions at the very companies they helped privatize. Equally embarrassing was the public disclosure that even the general's family had profited from the privatization process" ("The Pinochet Money Trail," New York Times, December 12, 2004).

Some of the CP's most important findings concluded that the government (a) had granted loans under the privatization law to people who did not exist or had provided false information; (b) allowed credit to be disbursed under irregular conditions as they were used for speculation and personal interest; (c) failed to control whether loans were actually used for the purpose that they had been approved; (d) renegotiated loans in an irregular manner; and (e) never collected some loans issued by the Corporación de Fomento (CORFO), the agency in charge of managing the privatization process.[38] The CP also found that members of Pinochet's family owned insurance companies that had the exclusive rights to serve some privatized companies.

A prominent beneficiary of privatization within the Pinochet family was

---

37. After retiring as army commander-in-chief in 1998, Pinochet became a senator with lifelong tenure.

38. Informe Comisión Privatizaciones Cámara de Diputados 2004, http://www.purochile.org/privatizaciones1.pdf.

one of the dictator's sons-in-law, Julio Ponce Lerou. Despite being a recent college graduate and lacking any proven experience, Pinochet appointed him executive director on the forestry and parks department in 1974. From there Ponce Lerou managed to acquire a large number of estates, which were eventually privatized. While on government payroll Ponce Lerou obtained a loan from CORFO in the mid-1980s but failed to reimburse two-thirds of it. In the early 1980s Ponce Lerou's spectacular ascendancy led him to be the general director of CORFO and other important executive positions at some of Chile's major SOEs, including Chilectra, Endesa, Soquimich, Iansa, Compañia de Acero del Pacifico, and Celulosa Arauco y Constitución. In this capacity Ponce Lerou acquired crucial inside information, which he used when such SOEs were privatized. In the most noticeable transaction, Ponce Lerou led a group of investors who acquired the highly profitable fertilizer company Soquimich at a rock-bottom price. As Soquimich expanded rapidly into a powerful export-oriented conglomerate in the 1990s, Ponce Lerou became one the wealthiest Chilean entrepreneurs and expanded his investment portfolio in a host of other lucrative businesses ("The Pinochet Money Trail," *New York Times,* December 12, 2004). Interestingly, he appointed to the board of his companies a score of former government officials, including Hernán Büchi, who as finance minister between 1985 and 1989 orchestrated the privatization program during that period, and former finance minister Sergio de Castro.

According to the CP report, investigators discovered that essential records detailing bidding terms, transfer procedures, company assets, sale prices, and money actually collected once privatization was completed were often missing, raising suspicions of wrongdoing. Likewise, the commission found that important information with regard to the large amounts of loans and subsidies that CORFO granted to private companies and entrepreneurs to facilitate the privatization process was also missing on many occasions. In addition, the CP uncovered that CORFO and other ministries within the public administration often "donated" physical assets to private companies or individuals without much of an explication.

The congressional investigation tried to assess the damage suffered by the national treasury due to questionable divestitures. Based on the analysis of only thirty companies privatized between 1978 and 1990, the legislators calculated that losses amounted to $2.2 billion. Many of such losses, according to the CP, resulted from undervaluing the assets being sold. A similar conclusion had been reached years earlier by the CGR, which cited that most of the companies privatized had been sold at a price well below their market value. For the congressional commission, some of the biggest losses that occurred in this way came from the privatization of the largest SOES sold between 1985 and 1989, which included the Compañia de Aceros del Pacífico ($706.4 million), Endesa ($895.6 million), Chilgener ($171.1 million), Chilectra ($96.4 million), and Banco de Chile ($66.9 million).[39] The suspicion of assets being willfully undervalued rested on the fact that many government officials who designed the state divestiture between 1985 and 1989 passed privileged information to potential buyers, then retired and became members of the board of directors of the privatized companies. In other cases the situation was even more overt as public managers at CORFO arranged things in a way that allowed them to acquire at bargain prices the SOES whose privatization they had helped organize. In yet another set of cases, the CP believed that the procedures used to privatize were simply irregular.

In a best-selling book, Monckeberg (2001), an investigative journalist who researched the privatization process prior to the congressional inquiry, hypothesized that the collusive way in which the 1985–89 privatizations were arranged had two deliberate goals. It first aimed to create a core group of businessmen who would exercise a tight control on economic and political matters to shape Chilean society after the demise of the military regime. Secondly, it ensured the quick enrichment of loyal entrepreneurs and family members of the Pinochet clan. For its part, in concluding its analysis of the privatization process under Pinochet the congressional commission stated in rather sarcastic tone that "it was legal to sell without a public auction. It was legal that the same people who designed the privatizations and fixed prices of stocks could later buy them. It was legal that government loans remained unpaid or that they were renegotiated when it was convenient [to the borrower]. Thus, one must conclude that the whole privatization process developed in Chile through legal norms that were established in ad hoc manner by a dictatorship."[40]

However, Carlos Montes, the chairman of the congressional commission, added in an interview, "We have not yet uncovered proof [of bribes and kickbacks], in part because of missing records. But our hypothesis is the same that you hear repeated until exhaustion in the rest of Chilean

39. Ibid.
40. Ibid.

society: that those who benefited the most from the privatizations were generous with General Pinochet" ("The Pinochet Money Trail," *New York Times*, December 12, 2004).

What about the postauthoritarian period? Since the return to democracy Chile has been rocked by a series of highly publicized scandals that shocked a nation where corruption has been historically modest in breadth and scope when compared to most developing countries. The alleged scandals took place through traditional channels such as government contracts and the manipulation of SOES' finances. Irregularities began to surface in the operations of the few SOES still in government hands, such as the mining giant Codelco, the Concún Oil Refinery, the National Coal Corporation (Enacar), the National Shipping Industry (Empremar), and the Maritime Corporation and Port Authority. Other cases were connected with government agencies and departments such as the National Housing Service, the Sports and Recreation Department (Digeder), the Customs Agency (Aduanas), the National Emergency Office (Onemi), and the National Police Retirement Service. The worst case involved the Ministry of Public Works, in which millions of dollars were embezzled as construction companies were allowed to overcharge the government. This was allegedly done to supplement the salaries of high-ranking officials within the ministry and pay for the 2000 presidential campaign. The scandal resulted in the indictment of several contractors, ministry staffers, and the former minister of public works Carlos Cruz (Rehren 2004). In 2002 another scandal rocked the Concertación as six of its members in the Chamber of Deputies were stripped of their parliamentary immunity and three of them were later sentenced to jail terms for having solicited bribes in return for government contracts. However, Chilean analysts remarked that many of these scandals tended to be white-collar crimes, traditional forms of clientelism, and illegal campaign financing (Rehren 2002; Brinegar 2006).

There is no evidence to suggest that corruption affected the Concertación's own brand of market reforms and in particular privatization, which continued to be carried out in the 1990s. Indeed, the popular perception of corruption in Chile remained quite low by Latin American standards. A Latinobarometro (2003) survey showed that although people's perception of corruption increased, only 6 percent were personally aware of a corruption act, the lowest rating among Latin American countries. Nonetheless, President Lagos tried to address the problem. In November 2002 he announced a number of measures to combat corruption, including greater transparency in campaign financing, higher salaries for civil servants, greater controls on public contracts, and a strengthening of the auditing role of the CGR (Brinegar 2006). In January 2003 the president also appointed a Transparency and Probity Commission to make recommendations and devise a concrete proposal to fight corruption. Many of the commission's suggestions were incorporated into law later that year. According to Rehren (2004, 15), Lagos promoted the law not only to take the corruption issues away from the conservative opposition but also because he believed that it was necessary in "complementing the successful implementation of market economics in the 1980s."

Collusion and Crony Capitalism

Over the years plenty of sophisticated macroeconomic analyses have explained the 1982–83 financial meltdown in Chile. However, for the most part such analyses failed to address the core question about the roots of the crisis. How could a government presumably fostering market competition permit, in practice, so much market power in the hands of a few conglomerates with such a shallow financial base?

As noted earlier, the authoritarian nature of the military regime allowed an unprecedented amount of freedom to policy makers to pursue their goals, as they were only accountable to the Junta. The Chicago Boys, who took the helm of the reform process in many cases, not only had been academics but were also former executives of Chile's largest conglomerates. When they departed their business positions they left behind many fellow Chicago Boys with whom they kept in close touch. The link between the Chicago Boys in government and in business was based on ideology and employment (Silva 1996, 107). Once in government the Chicago Boys invited their friends and leaders of the largest conglomerates to bring their expert opinion in drafting the specific content of key reforms. The coincidence of opinions with the Chicago Boys in government about the nature and content of future policies enabled selected conglomerates to anticipate the implications of crucial reforms and devise investment strategies that allowed them to beat the competition and acquire dominant market shares. This was particularly true of two conglomerates that emerged out of nowhere in the mid-1970s to become the most dominant players in the Chilean economy: the BHC, headed by Javier Vial, and the Cruzat-Larraín group, owned by Manuel Cruzat.[41] The adoption of radical market reforms was mutually beneficial for the goals of the Chicago Boys and the emerging conglomerates. For Pinochet's technocrats such policies were the opportunity to shape the economy according to their ideological principles, whereas for the up-and-coming conglomerates radical reform represented a once-in-a-lifetime chance to dominate Chile's most lucrative markets. The Chicago Boys in government needed the new conglomerates to succeed if they wanted to bring about a new brand of capitalists sympathetic to their agenda, and, of course, the new conglomerates needed friendly policies to get ahead of the competition. It was an alliance based on convenience, not just ideas. The result was that "collusion between policymakers and economic elites who benefited from privatization drove [the] reforms" (Schamis 2002, 5). Indeed, according to Schamis, the coziness between the Chicago Boys in government and the conglomerates' representatives led to the "capture of key policy-making posts by the large *grupos* [and] to the implementation of an economic reform program by which these firms took over market reserves" (2002, 55). Interestingly enough, the Chicago Boys-turned-entrepreneurs were not interested in a level playing field and pro-competition policies but rather in rent seeking and through behind-the-scenes lobbying so they could acquire dominant market shares.

Two policies became crucial to the extraordinary growth of the BHC and Cruzat-Larraín groups: financial deregulation and privatization. Both conglomerates in the mid-1970s were upstarts with very little capital of their own. Nonetheless, they understood that the key to their success was to acquire a large segment of the financial industry that would be the means in seizing control of some of the most lucrative companies that were about to be privatized. In fact, both BHC and Cruzat-Larraín would in the years to come make financial institutions the core companies of their conglomerates. Their expansion plans received a tremendous boost in early 1974 when the government began the liberalization of financial markets by lowering reserve requirements and allowing the creation of nonbank financial institutions, commonly referred as *financieras*.[42] These new financial institutions

41. Both businessmen attended the University of Chicago. Vial was instrumental in convincing Friedman to visit Chile in 1975.

42. Reserve requirements were drastically lowered, dropping from 100 percent in 1973 to only 10 percent by 1980 (Edwards and Cox Edwards 1987, 55). *Financieras* were basically unregulated entities and had no restrictions on debt-to-asset ratios, whereas commercial banks had to maintain a debt-to-capital ratio at or below 20:1, which put them at a clear disadvantage. *Financieras'* maximum monthly interest rate was set at 25 percent against the 9.6 percent to be paid by

had an advantage over traditional banks as they could charge much higher interests and could issue short-term loans, which became very popular. According to Foxley (1983, 55), this was done on purpose so that the *financieras* could lure away depositors from traditional banks, which were still in government hands. Having advance knowledge of the government plans for financial liberalization, BHC and Cruzat-Larraín were the first conglomerates to establish *financieras*. Thanks to their good relations with U.S. commercial banks, they were able to fund their initial operations through foreign loans at cheap international rates.[43] At a time when capital was very scarce and many Chilean companies faced severe liquidity problems, BHC and Cruzat-Larraín's *financieras* made hefty profits and began to take large market shares in terms of deposits and borrowing customers from traditional banks. Moreover, as Silva (1996, 106) noted, "two additional factors strengthened [BHC and Cruzat-Larraín's] position. The traditional conglomerates were still struggling to regain control of assets they had sold to the government [under Allende], and . . . did not have financial service companies and banks of their own."

By 1975, when the privatization of large SOEs started, the conglomerates allied with the Chicago Boys in government were in a strong position to be major players in the divestiture process. The privatization of Chile's top banks offered BHC and Cruzat-Larraín a crucial boost as they were the first large companies to be put on the auction block. An additional break came in the form of government financing to help bidders who could obtain two-year loans at 10 percent for bank purchases and ten-year loans for nonfinancial companies (Edwards and Cox Edwards 1987, 96). To understand the magnitude of the subsidy involved, during 1974–78 government loans to the private sector amounted to roughly $300 million while privatization revenues reached $582 million (Hachette and Lüders 1993, 50).[44] Moreover, sale prices were particularly enticing and explained what some analysts believed to be an "additional" subsidy that accounted for as low as 27 percent (Vergara 1981) and as high as 40 percent of book value (Dahse 1979).

---

government banks (Foxley 1983, 55). In October 1975 limits on interest rates for commercial banks were also lifted (Yotopoulos 1989, 691).

43. Real interest rates from 1976 until the early 1980s were between two to six times higher than international rates, thus representing a huge windfall for the *financieras*, which Zahler (1980) estimated to be more than $800 million during 1976–79.

44. In spite of these large subsidies, conglomerates had to borrow money from abroad, which increased their overall debt exposure.

BHC and Cruzat-Larraín were the big winners of the bank privatization process that further consolidated their lock on the financial services market. Although in theory the government had placed restrictions on purchases of bank shares, conglomerates bypassed them by having several of their companies buy blocks of shares separately, which allowed them to acquire ownership control.[45] Government regulators, who were quite aware of such schemes, conveniently looked the other way (Edwards and Cox Edwards 1987, 96). Yet in the end, the Chicago Boys achieved their goal. By 1978 only one major bank was still under government control. This situation left the largest conglomerates with as much as 80 percent of privately owned bank equity (Edwards and Cox Edwards 1987, 99). BHC and Cruzat-Larraín had achieved their goal of becoming Chile's most powerful conglomerates, controlling 37.9 percent and 14.4 percent, respectively, of private banking assets (Silva 1996, 116), which together amounted to 52 percent of the total. Foreign credit, government subsidies, and the control of banking assets were pivotal factors in the bidding on the most important SOEs put up for sale. By 1978 BHC and Cruzat-Larraín controlled 24.7 percent and 12.6 percent, respectively, of the assets belonging to the top 250 Chilean firms, or 36.3 percent of the total (Silva 1996, 116). If we include the next three conglomerates, their asset control over the top 250 firms reached 53 percent. Suffice to say, to understand the economic clout so reached by the top five conglomerates, in a sample of one hundred firms, their assets increased 97 percent between 1969 and 1978, whereas the remaining firms grew by only 14 percent (Dahse 1979). Hachette and Lüders (1993, 49) stylized the new conglomerates' financial engineering that took advantage of privatization in the following terms:

The public sector would offer a financial institution for sale. One person or a small group of people would buy those shares with a small down payment, financing the difference either with direct credit offered by the public sector as part of the divestiture process itself, or with credit granted by the divested financial institution to one of their holding companies. In either event, the credit was guaranteed, at least in large part, by the shares being acquired. Next, encouraged by the capital gains realized, as share prices rose rapidly on the stock ex-

---

45. Individuals were limited to 3 percent of total shares, whereas private firms could buy up to 5 percent.

change, the same group would participate, perhaps through a holding company, in bidding for other enterprises being divested by the public sector. The controlling group would finance the required down payment in these cases with profits they had made from operating the financial institutions acquired earlier, or from other enterprises they owned, although they would, more often than not, complement those resources by using new credit granted by the financial sector to the holding company.

The government provided further help to BHC and Cruzat-Larraín, as well as other conglomerates, when it decided to privatize the social security system in 1980. In terms of assets, pension funds were particularly lucrative as most Chileans began to transfer their retirement contributions from the state-run system into them. In the first two months BHC and Cruzat-Larraín pension funds took control of 75 percent of the market and much-needed long-term investments estimated to be as much as 20 percent of GDP at the time (Schamis 2002). In short, the way the government carried out financial deregulation, privatization, and social security reform was a bonanza for the country's conglomerates and produced an acute concentration of assets in a few hands (Foxley 1983). As a result of these reforms, by late 1982 BHC and Cruzat-Larraín controlled Chile's two largest private banks, some of the most important insurance companies, mutual funds, and the largest pension funds (Yotopoulos 1989, 691).

Nevertheless, much of the conglomerates expansion was made possible through debt, contracted mostly from abroad at a low cost due to an overvalued exchange rate. The euphoria generated by fast growth in the late 1970s and early 1980s all too often hid the fact that the foundation of the economic recovery was based more on sophisticated financial engineering rather than increased output and revenue performance. Indeed, many newly privatized companies kept losing large amounts of money. This was particularly true at BHC and Cruzat-Larraín and induced them to engage in highly risky financial speculations as their banks borrowed even more from abroad so that they could lend to their troubled firms to keep them afloat. In some cases, such as Cruzat-Larraín's Banco de Santiago, loans to firms of the same conglomerate reached 42 percent of the bank's portfolio (Edwards and Cox Edwards 1987, 102). The widespread practice of "self-lending," as it came to be known in Chile, constituted a moral hazard of dramatic proportions and was made possible thanks to de Castro's economic team, which lifted controls on capital flows in 1979 and failed to enforce bank supervision procedures still in the books.[46] Not surprising, the private sector took full advantage of lax bank regulations as its foreign debt exposure went from $3.4 billion in 1979 to $10.4 billion in 1982 (a net increase of 68 percent), whereas the public debt rose only by $1.6 billion over the same period (Edwards and Cox Edwards 1987, 71). De Castro resisted mounting pressure to devalue, which would have spelled disaster for his fellow Chicago Boys in the largest conglomerates who had large debt exposure in dollar-dominated loans owned abroad. However, the quick unraveling of the crisis convinced Pinochet that de Castro and his team had become a liability. He first began to distance himself from them and eventually forced de Castro to resign in April 1982, which doomed the conglomerates allied to the Chicago Boys in government, as they were left unprotected and let to collapse. In fact, in January 1983 the dictator instructed a new economic team to intervene and prevent a total implosion of the financial industry. The government took over five banks, including the two largest (Banco de Santiago and the Banco de Chile, owned by the BHC group), and closed three more. Shortly thereafter the BHC and Cruzat-Larraín conglomerates and a few smaller ones that had flourished rapidly in the mid-1970s crashed, leaving the government to pay for their debts.

In taking over the bankrupt conglomerates, the government inherited 67 percent of bank deposits, 57 percent of pension funds, and repossessed 70 percent of companies that it had privatized after 1973, as the failed conglomerate-controlled banks owned most of them (Schamis 2002, 60). As noted earlier, under pressure from international banks, the IMF, and the World Bank, Pinochet agreed to honor the massive debt that the conglomerates owed abroad. The cost of this operation was enormous given the size of the Chilean economy. As a consequence, the percentage of the government debt rose from 35 percent in 1981 to 85 percent in 1988 (Larraín and Velasco 1990, 13). According to Schamis (2002, 60), the bailout cost the equivalent of 5 percent of GDP for five consecutive years. By 1988 Larraín and Velasco (1990, 17) estimated that the government owed $6.8 billion of medium- and long-term commercial debt and an additional $2.1 billion

46. In one instance, Javier Vial lent out $48 million to companies he owned and were connected with BHC, which severely depleted Banco de Chile's reserves.

of state-guaranteed private debt. Other scholars believed that by the end of 1990 the final accumulation of the debt may have reached as much as $9–10 billion (Barandiarán and Hernández 1999, 39; Ffrench-Davis 2002, 139).[47]

Ironically, the Chicago Boys' supposed quest for economic freedom, competition, and impartial rules of the game gave way to political exigencies and crony capitalism, producing an economic collapse of historical proportions. As the details of the conglomerates' bankruptcy began to surface, it became clear that the economic freedom ushered by the Chicago Boys turned into a license to do what one pleased irrespective of the law. For instance, when government regulators took over the Banco de Chile they found out that its largest debtor was its chief executive officer (Schamis 2002, 60). More broadly, "the rent-seeking opportunities created by privatization-cum-liberalization program led to a familiar moral hazard scenario, though one of monumental proportions" (Schamis 2002, 60). Even two prominent Chicago Boys, in describing the Chilean crisis of 1982–83, had to admit that "the most repeated error . . . appears to be the lack of transparency in divestitures . . . it raised eyebrows, to say the least, and provided ammunition to groups that felt that they were not given fair access to SOE stock being divested . . . The lack of transparency appears to have been, in retrospect, the main shortcoming" (Hachette and Lüders 1993, 6).

In 1985, as the economic situation began to stabilize, the government ushered a new wave of privatizations. The new finance minister, Hernán Büchi, put on the auction block not only the companies taken over during the 1982–83 period but also some of the crown jewels of the state sector— that is, the "strategic" SOEs in telecommunications and electricity that the military had decided to keep in government hands after the coup. Although Pinochet hailed this second round of privatizations free from the flaws of the 1970s, and in some cases allowed shares to be sold to company employees and small shareholder under what came to be known as "popular capitalism," collusion between government officials and privileged businessmen continued to be the name of the game, creating new opportunities for rent-seeking behavior (Monckeberg 2001). In fact, save for the privatization of the Banco de Santiago and Banco de Chile, by 1988 the overall impact of popular capitalism was negligible as the number of workers-turned-shareholders rose by only forty thousand, or 1.8 percent, in 1988 (Marcel 1989;

---

47. By themselves, the Banco de Santiago and the Banco de Chile accounted for $3 billion of defaulted debt (Barandiarán and Hernández 1999, 36).

Schamis 2002, 61). As a result, the main beneficiaries of the 1985–89 privatization process were large conglomerates, pension funds, and, most of all, government officials-turned-entrepreneurs (Murillo 2002). As noted in the previous section, high-ranking government officials working for CORFO or some of the most important SOES designed the privatization program, and then through generous government subsidies and the association with well-connected domestic groups ended up among the owners of the most important public utilities under monopolistic conditions (Marín and Rozas 1988).

Meanwhile, it became clear that shareholders were unable to make management accountable because their voting rights were restricted, leaving the former government-managers-turned-entrepreneurs with complete discretion (Bitrán and Sáez 1994). For instance, José Yuraszeck had worked at CORFO in planning some major privatizations and then moved to the electricity distribution company Chilectra prior to its divestiture. In 1986 Yuraszeck created Enersis and in association with other company managers gained control of Chilectra thanks to a loan from the Banco del Estado.[48] Another case involved the former minister of labor José Piñera, the architect of the social security privatization under Pinochet who became president of the electricity generation company ENDESA. After privatization a large numbers of former government officials and managers ended up staffing the board of directors of many privatized public utilities.[49]

The transfer of public utilities in electricity under monopolistic conditions was no coincidence (Monckeberg 2001). It was also reinforced by the fact that the regulatory framework put in place prior to state divestiture was weak, limited in scope, and allowed rent seeking under private ownership (Bitrán and Sáez 1994; OECD 2004). In point of fact, the regulatory institutions that the military regime left behind were in many cases regarded as incapable of stimulating market competition, were poorly staffed and funded, and lacked the necessary autonomy to resist lobbying efforts (Paredes Molina et al. 1998; Saavedra and Soto 2004; OECD 2004). Thus, once they acquired such rents, the new private owners tried repeatedly to

48. Although some shares were sold both to workers and the general public, Yuraszeck structured the deal so that he and his closest associates could retain control of the company.

49. For a detailed list of the government officials involved in these privatizations, see Schamis (2002, 64) and Murillo (2002, 482). To understand the magnitude that former managers acquired in this fashion, according to a 1996 listing of the top twenty companies, ENDESA ranked second, CTC (telecommunications) was fifth, Enersis was sixth, and ENTel (telecommunications) eighteen (Fazio 1997, 31).

capture government regulators and lobbied hard to maintain existing entry barriers in place to keep potential competition at bay. In 1990s the Concertación attempted to end the monopolistic status of Enersis, the largest electricity group. The case went all the way to the Supreme Court, which at the time was still dominated by Pinochet's appointees. In a controversial decision, the Supreme Court found the government case unconvincing. In June 1997 the government brought a similar case before the Anti-Trust Commission, arguing that Enersis's monopolistic behavior was responsible for the absence of new power companies in Chile. Again, Enersis won the legal battle, leading Concertación legislators to charge that the Anti-Trust Commission was virtually hostage to Enersis interests. Two years later the issue was partially rendered moot when Endesa of Spain bought Enersis in a very controversial transaction.[50]

In assessing Pinochet reforms Schamis (2002, 66) convincingly underscored that contrary to much neoliberal rhetoric, "rent-seeking behavior is not restricted to contexts of state intervention, and it may also occur under comprehensive marketization." Chile, during the military regime, was an example of this phenomenon as it showed how "collusion between political power and economic power, revolving-door relationships between corporate executive posts and government executive posts, and policymakers simply taking over state assets and reproducing parasitic behavior are key characteristics of state divestiture" (Schamis 2002, 66).

Patronage Politics

Political patronage was quite pervasive in Chile and was a means that all political parties that occupied government positions used to reward and mobilize their voters (Valenzuela 1977). This was true both during the period of the "Parliamentary Republic" (1891–1924), when the oligarchy still controlled the political process, as well as between 1925 and 1973, when mass-based parties emerged and the presidential system was again made the centerpiece of the Chilean polity. However, there is no tangible evidence

50. The conservative daily *El Mercurio*, Chile's largest newspaper, labeled the deal as "the scandal of the century" because Yuraszeck and some of his associates received some $350 million through a hidden clause. This led government regulators to fine Yuraszeck $75 million in penalties (*New York Times*, December 12, 2004). After 1990 both Yuraszeck and Piñera became prominent politicians of the Unión Demócrata Independiente and Renovación Nacional, respectively, both of which were right-wing parties supporting the Pinochet legacy.

that patronage politics was clearly linked to market reforms either during the military regime or when the Concertación administrations took over power. As part of his campaign to eradicate the influence of political parties in Chilean society, Pinochet made an explicit effort to reduce presidential appointments before retiring from office. Moreover, the privatization and deregulation policies took away some of the most important sources of patronage politics of the precoup period. As Rehren (2004, 15) stated, "privatizations introduced deep changes in the dependent nature of political parties from the entrepreneurial state and dismantled former clientelistic mechanisms. A reduced and much less powerful state left political parties without the lubrication necessary to maintain the previous clintelistic machinery." Furthermore, even after parties returned to center stage after 1990 the incidence of patronage politics never returned to its pre-1973 levels (Brinegar 2006, 7). As noted earlier, although a series of corruption scandals emerged during the Concertación, they followed the pattern of traditional forms of contract manipulations usually meant to fund illegal party financing.[51] There is no evidence that budget allocations resulting from privatization revenues and foreign loans were misappropriated to foster clientelistic networks during the Concertación despite the fact that it could have been possible given the great presidential control over budgetary issues.

Concluding Remarks

For many years the conventional wisdom with regard to the Chilean experiment with market economics was that Pinochet and the Chicago Boys were the true heroes of the country's economic success. Moreover, Chile became the darling of neoliberal economists and enjoyed "privileged treatment by the International Monetary Fund and the commercial banks" (Váldes 1995, 2). Indeed, the Chicago Boys earned a strong endorsement from both Hayek and Friedman. Friedman, in an interview with *Newsweek* in January 1992, praised Pinochet for his decision to support the principles of economic freedom and described what happened in Chile under the military regime as an "economic miracle." The IFIs took a similar stance as they used the Chilean experiment in market economics as the blueprint to con-

51. For a detailed account of political patronage scandals under the Concertación administrations, see Juan Pablo Cárdenas, "Corruption Scandals Contrast with Clean Reputation," Inter-Press Service News Agency, November 29, 2006.

vince other developing countries to reform their economies, particularly after the second half of the 1980s. The IFIS also granted Chile crucial economic assistance both after the 1973 coup and in the aftermath of the 1982 financial crisis.

Politically, given the authoritarian nature of the regime, the return to economic growth in the second half of the 1980s drove many analysts and conservative pundits to the conclusion that market reforms could only be successfully implemented by a "benign" dictator. This was surely the belief of many prominent Chicago Boys. However, as time passed and the Concertación proved to be a much better policy performer, such wisdom came into question. In looking back at the country's experience Rodrik commented, "The myth is that Chile's success is purely the result of fundamentalist free-market policies. But the truth is more complex than that. Government activism and management in Chile did not stifle the power of the free market. It unleashed the power of the free market" ("A Smoother Road to Free Markets," *Washington Post*, June 21, 2004).

This chapter not only confirms Rodrik's statement but brings evidence that the increased transparency and institutional accountability during the Concertación administrations played a major role in "unleashing market forces" since investors were more likely to put their money in an environment where the rules were clear, property rights were protected, and government power was restrained by checks and balances. Indeed, the Chilean case shows the kind of variance that one would expect in terms of market reform performance as the policy style changes from authoritarian to democratic and accountable. Thus, the very fact that all economic indicators increased tremendously after 1990 while keeping the original neoliberal model intact suggests that increased political accountability had something to do with it. Also interesting in the Chilean case is that Pinochet imposed on the Concertación administrations severe institutional constraints, which of course he never applied to himself. Yet the Concertación presidents not only accepted such constraints but actually expanded them by creating greater transparency in the way the executive promoted reforms. Major steps were taken in reforming the judiciary and regulatory institutions to make them more attuned to the needs of the modern economy and less susceptible to collusion and corruption. Likewise, by the early 2000s Congress and the CGR gained a greater role in exercising their oversight functions. The other noticeable factor is that, unlike Pinochet authoritarian style, the Concertación presidents promoted many of these reforms in a bipartisan way, which in the end enhanced their political legitimacy. The moderation in which the Concertación presidents pursued policy reforms, matched by a canny ability to negotiate, averted a much-feared showdown with the military and the conservatives in Congress. By the early 1990s the debate in Chile was no longer whether market reforms were good or bad for the country, but rather what government could do to build on them while making the more marginal sectors of society enjoy the fruits of the neoliberal model. As government politicians made themselves more accountable for their actions in promoting the reform process, so grew the public trust in the benefits of the markets that operate according to clear rules. Indeed, there were no major scandals associated with privatization and deregulation policies in Chile after 1989.

Conversely, the reform effort under Pinochet was marred by moral hazards, rent seeking, crony capitalism, and possible corruption. In itself, this was quite surprising since the Chicago Boys had claimed that market reforms would eradicate all these problems at once by reducing government intervention to a minimal role. However, they never privatized the largest SOE, Codelco, whose revenues the military used to finance its own budget. Still more disturbing was their lack of ethical standards for people who had claimed to abide to neutral, technical mechanisms to problem solving based on solely scientific analysis. The leading ideologue of the Chicago Boys, Pablo Baraona, had declared that the new democracy established under the military regime would be, among other things, "impersonal, in the sense that the regulations apply equally to everyone; libertarian in the sense that subsidiarity is an essential principle for achieving the common good; technified in the sense that political bodies should . . . [leave] to the technocracy the responsibility of using logical procedures for resolving problems."[52] As it turned out, the Chicago Boys did promote reforms, but they were also keen to help their own friends and themselves. Rules and regulations did not apply to everyone, nor were they impartial, since they were actually designed to favor specific groups and individuals in society. The common good pretense clashed with a reality where the reforms overwhelmingly favored a small segment of Chilean society, including Chicago Boys, SOE managers, and military officers who ended up owning former government companies or sitting on their board of directors, while the bulk of society saw its standards of living plummeting. Similarly, the Chicago Boys' techni-

52. Cited from Valdés (1995, 33).

cal approach often did not stand for logical procedures but seemed to camouflage collusive behavior.

The cost of the lack of accountability under Pinochet, as in the previous cases, cannot be assessed with any degree of accuracy. Save for some judicial proceedings against the general's personal wealth, few government investigations of possible misconduct exist during the dictatorship due primarily to the accords that Pinochet stipulated in 1989 before transferring power to President Aylwin that banned ex-post inquiries. Nonetheless, if we consider the bailout of the conglomerates' banks after 1982 as the direct result of the Chicago Boys' collusion with privileged businessmen, Chile had to spend 5 percent of its GDP to subsidize such a rescue effort between 1983 and 1987 (Schamis 2002, 60). Another estimate, which we discussed previously, comes from the $2 billion potential losses from undervaluing privatization assets during the 1985–89 period. For a country with an average GDP of $23 billion during that period, $2 billion in losses was not a small amount.

In sum, the Chilean case shows that accountability makes reforms much more effective and plays a pivotal role in avoiding the collusive and corrupt behavior associated with authoritarian and opaque decision-making processes. Equally important, accountability contributes, as the Concertación administrations demonstrated, to creating the necessary political legitimacy that is essential for market reforms to be sustainable over time.

six

CONCLUSION

At the beginning of this book I argued that, macroeconomic factors notwithstanding, the major financial crises that hit emerging markets between 1994 and 2002 were also associated with accountability-related issues. Indeed, the empirical evidence presented in this book suggests that the less political executives were constrained in their actions by oversight institutions upholding accountability, the more financial crises were likely to happen. The cross-national analysis surveying eighty democracies/partial democracies that attempted market-oriented reforms shows a high degree of association between crisis countries and poor accountability, as opposed to other emerging markets that promoted similar reforms. Moreover, the statistical analysis detects the same clear-cut trend between crisis countries vis-à-vis corruption and regulatory quality, respectively. Once the analysis shifts down to the regional level, comparing those eight postcommunist countries vis-à-vis Russia, accountability displays a strong association with positive trends in key economic variables. Almost invariably the Eastern European countries in our sample, which had to comply with the EU's democratic governance demands to be considered for future membership, promoted market reforms while enhancing political accountability and, as postulated, economically outperformed Russia, which under Yeltsin instead progressively weakened accountability institutions.

In the country chapters these patterns are further confirmed through a thorough examination of the main thesis by using a process-tracing method that permits the incorporation of a wealth of information not captured by the statistical analysis. Here we saw how the lack of accountability allowed the presidents of Russia and Argentina to enact market reforms in such a way that undermined them from the start. Yeltsin and Menem rendered ineffective the power of accountability institutions that stood in their paths. Once left unchecked, these two presidents were free to pursue economically inefficient and corrupt policies. Instead of creating much-needed competition, the collusive nature of privatization and market deregulation reassigned rents to privileged members of the private sectors, thus hurting economic growth. At the same time, Yeltsin and Menem engaged in reckless borrowing abroad to bankroll their political clienteles and business cronies to an unsustainable level, eventually dooming their countries to defaulting their debt obligations.

The case of Chile is in itself most interesting as it shows considerable variance in the results of market reforms depending on whether they were executed with or without political accountability. Under Pinochet's dictatorship the government pursued radical policies, but it did so without any checks and balances. This allowed government officials to tailor the reforms to benefit their friends and former associates in the business community whose conglomerates, as a result, came to dominate the country's most lucrative sectors in the late 1970s. The government privatization and economic deregulation programs explicitly picked the winners and losers of the new economic order. They also allowed private conglomerates to borrow abroad well beyond their means and circumvent banking regulations to pursue speculative financial operations. The bubble so produced imploded in 1982, driving the country into its worst crisis since the Great Depression. In 1985 a new economic team introduced a new wave of privatizations, but, yet again, the process was characterized by collusion as many public officials ended up controlling important stakes in the SOEs they helped privatize. As Pinochet stepped down in March 1990, the political context changed radically as a coalition of center-left parties ruled Chile under a web of constitutional and institutional restrictions that never applied to the former dictator. In fact, Pinochet enacted them right before withdrawing from power so as to restrict his successors' room for maneuvering. The democratic administrations that followed not only respected such restraints but over time took several initiatives to increase the transparency of their actions and the oversight powers of the legislature and regulatory agencies. This deliberate move to enhance accountability coincided with an economic growth twice as high as the one that Chile experienced under Pinochet and with drastic improvements in socioeconomic indicators. After 1990 the free market economic model that under the dictatorship had benefited only the upper class began to trickle down as the number of poor was cut in half, while the middle class increased appreciably in size and purchasing power. Moreover, unlike the Pinochet regime, the post-1990 reform effort was not clouded by blatant cases of moral hazard and allegations of corruption. Thus, although Pinochet and his Chicago Boys should be credited for introducing the basic tenets of the "Chilean miracle," it seems clear that it was under a more accountable and transparent government that the deeds of market reforms came to fruition. I will now elaborate on some of the main issues raised in the preceding chapters and the lessons that we can draw from the evidence at hand.

The Contradictory Nature of Neoliberalism

The irony of the market reform experience is that once the neoliberal agenda, which Hayek and Friedman championed so passionately, was put into policy it took a life of its own and often conspired against the very concept of freedom. Reforms were steamrolled through executive orders, delegated legislative powers, and administrative acts that bypassed the due process. This was done on the premise that there was no time to waste because the antireform groups could have garnered momentum to stop the reform effort in its tracks. Unfortunately, this "pragmatic" argument opened the door for all kinds of abuses perpetrated in the name of economic freedom since accountability procedures were muted. As Rodan (2004, 4) noted, market reforms were "accompanied by a combination of more coercive state powers to politically protect economic reforms from popular challenges, and a new regulatory state that was increasingly concealing and insulating choices from the political process altogether." Thus, as much as neoliberals have consistently claimed that economic and political liberty go hand in hand, it is also clear that when push came to shove, they were just as willing to sacrifice democratic principles on the altar of "free markets." In a typical Machiavellian way, the end justified the means, but in so doing even the most well-meaning reformers lost their souls as the intellectual integrity of their argument went to pieces because their policies came to be associated with authoritarian means and collusive behavior.[1]

1. In describing how this scenario applied to Russia, Grigory Yavlinski, the leader of the *Yabloko* party, which has campaigned since 1993 for greater freedom and civil liberties, stated, "Always when you are using the formula that the goals are justifying the means, you are destroy-

How can we explain this contradiction between theory and practice? Actually, once we take a close look at both Hayek's and Friedman's thinking, we can understand why many of those who embraced their ideas did not find much of a problem in pursuing "economic liberty" at the expense of "political liberty." We have already seen in the case of Chile how Pablo Baraona, the intellectual leader of the Chicago Boys, found market reforms to be incompatible with the democratic process. Conversely, he believed that only a "benign dictatorship" could have the courage to resist selfish political pressure to pursue sound technocratic policies that would establish economic freedom.

Indeed, Friedman and Hayek highly praised the Chilean market experiment under Pinochet. In 1978 Hayek affirmed that "I have not been able to find a single person even in much maligned Chile, who did not agree that personal freedom was much greater under Pinochet than it had been under Allende."[2] He went further in his attempt to reconcile how authoritarian means can actually promote economic freedom when he stated that "it is at least conceivable that an authoritarian government might act on liberal principles" (Hayek 1978, 143). Friedman's views were similar. While he described Pinochet's regime as terrible, he credited the Chilean dictator for paving the way toward economic freedom, which in the end created the conditions for the return to democracy. However, Friedman grew worried about whether economic freedom could be retained under democracy. He went on to say that, in more general terms, "while economic freedom facilitates political freedom, political freedom, once established, has a tendency to destroy economic freedom."[3] Thus, based on Hayek's and Friedman's later writings, democracy constitutes a paradox because it contains the seeds that destroy economic freedom. This is why, for neoliberals, "democracy—even limited democracy—is by no means an intrinsically attractive proposition. . . . Indeed, when it threatens the security of 'economic freedom,' alternative political regimes may be more appealing" (Rodan 2004, 9).

This would explain why neoliberals in general, while repeatedly stating

---

ing the goals." Public Broadcasting Service, "Commanding Heights: The Battle for the World Economy," http://www.pbs.org/wgbh/commandingheights/shared/minitextlo/tr_show02.html.

    2. Quoted in Arblaster (1984, 342).

    3. See Friedman's lecture of November 1, 1991, at the Smith Center for Private Enterprise Studies, "Economic Freedom, Human Freedom, Political Freedom," http://www.cbe.csueastbay .edu/~sbesc/index(home).html.

that economic and political freedom are two sides of the same coin, in practice made very little effort to promote reforms in an accountable way based on democratic principles. Likewise, neoliberals agreed on the need for democratic institution building but in practice were short on specifics save for property rights, which have always been an important element of their theoretical argument. Consequently, according to Rodan (2002, 10), "political freedoms—including democracy—become important . . . in protecting private property rights and underscoring efficient market systems. However, the conception of democracy here is often procedural rather than substantive, with an emphasis on institutions that enforce accountability and restraint in the exercise of political and bureaucratic power." Consequently, political freedom is a function of, rather than an integral part of, economic freedom, and if it gets in the way it may be expendable. Thus, if it takes an authoritarian government to protect economic freedom, so be it, although of course neoliberals would add that it is not the best-case scenario. What is interesting to note is that following this rationale, once General Pinochet, the enlightened dictator, returned to the barracks the Chilean economy should have performed worse, but actually the opposite happened. As political accountability increased, so did the performance of the Chilean economic "miracle," as I posited in chapter 1.

Neoliberalism and Accountability Institutions

In the preceding paragraphs the analysis has shown that the narrow neoliberal conception of what constitutes freedom and how to attain it had serious and often negative consequences in the way market reforms were designed and implemented. First, it provided a justification for the bypassing of oversight processes by condoning, if not encouraging, undemocratic means in the hope that quick execution would, almost automatically, lead to free markets and economic freedom. It did not. Instead, by muting accountability institutions such an approach opened up a Pandora's box for all kinds of power abuses. As a result, the more political accountability was destroyed, the more countries were likely to plummet into dire financial crises.

Second, in the rush to implement market reforms neoliberals tolerated the fact that reforming governments neglected competition and a host of legal institutions protecting property rights. This, in turn, created collusive market conditions that penalized investments and growth while leading to high unemployment and poverty levels.

Third, the neoliberal bias against government institutions added to the problem. The basic idea was to dismantle the state, not to reinvent it in order to make it more efficient and technically capable. This approach ran counter to successful examples of market capitalism, which have always been associated with a highly competent state bureaucracy that not only provides strong legal institutions but also administers numerous services, from infrastructures to education, that reduce transaction costs and facilitate business operations. Moreover, strong states have usually been characterized by regulatory institutions, norms, and procedures aimed at creating a level playing field so that competition can thrive, consumers can be protected from unfair practices, and business rights can be shielded against the breaching of contractual obligations. Only in the late 1990s, when many reforming countries ran into serious problems, did IFIS start to address these issues, but it was too little too late as a lot of damage created in the process was beyond recall (World Bank 2005).

In their own defense neoliberals have usually contended that poor execution was at the heart of the problem, not political accountability. That may be true to some degree, but the international community was well aware of what was happening and failed to act when it could still have had the time to prevent major disasters. Instead, Western governments and IFIS kept supporting troubled policies until the end of the 1990s. Collectively, they had the clout to force at least some meaningful changes, but for the reasons I will discuss shortly they kept endorsing governments whose actions were clearly going astray. Only later, and rather conveniently, they stepped up their criticisms against "faulty" policies. Some neoliberals retrospectively acknowledged that the insistence on overvalued exchange rates, fiscal laxity, and hazardous borrowing practices played a large role in crisis countries (Kuczynski and Williamson 2003; Weller and Singleton 2003). This is certainly true, but there was already plenty of evidence coming from Chile following the 1982 financial crisis that should have suggested avoiding those policies from the start. The IFIS had the means to put pressure on reforming governments to change their course of action and again chose for political reasons not to do so.[4]

On the opposite side of the policy debate Stiglitz (2002) and other critics

---

4. For a defense of the IMF position, see Fischer (2001).

of the neoliberal model have also discounted the importance of account-ability as a smoke screen that IFIS recently used to put the blame on bor-rowing countries. For Stiglitz the neoliberal "market fundamentalism" of the U.S. Treasury and the IMF was at the core of the problem, as it assumed that markets, once freed from regulation, invariably lead to sustained growth. However, for this to work some initial conditions, which actually did not exist in the first place, had to be met. For instance, reforming countries lacked good property rights protection, procompetition policies, and a host of institutions that would empower economic agents with per-fect information to limit transaction cost problems—all things that neolib-erals took for granted. In his view the insistence of the U.S. Treasury and the IFIS on the adoption of capital market liberalization, privatization, trade deregulation, and fiscal austerity policies all at once led to disastrous conse-quences. The only ones who benefited from them were domestic insiders and foreign commercial interests, while the rest of the population saw its standards of living destroyed by the economic crises that eventually ensued.

Although Stiglitz's argument is well taken on a number of grounds, his point that accountability did not matter is overly simplistic. For in-stance, it does not explain why many Eastern European countries that, like Russia, initially lacked many of Stiglitz's necessary preconditions for market reforms to succeed outperformed their neighbor to the east. Why would Chile perform so much better economically in the 1990s than under Pinochet?

While economists remain deeply divided about the causes behind the financial crises in emerging markets, recent research in political science has emphasized that such crises seemed to share many negative political and institutional features. In this book I argued that by focusing on political accountability (or lack thereof) we can provide a powerful and complemen-tary insight to some of the best explanations coming from economics. Economists fail to explain why some governments pushed reforms and began to build promarket institutions while others did reform but neglected institution building. Usually, they address the puzzle by adding to their models a dummy variable called "political will" but fail to explain exactly what it means. Equally important, they do not explain what shapes such a will. Is it just pressure from the U.S. Treasury and IFIS? Obviously, that did not deter Yeltsin and Menem from engaging in reckless policies. On paper, every executive officer, be it a president or a prime minister, would love to enact his/her policies without having to bother with legislatures, the courts, and other oversight institutions, but in a truly democratic political system that is not possible precisely because the institutions just mentioned are there to make leaders accountable for their actions (Schmitter 2004; Diamond 2005).

The Role of Multilateral Lending Agencies

The preceding analysis points to the fact that the neoliberals' theoretical notion of economic freedom, once faced with hard choices, was prone not only to downplay but even ran against issues related to political freedom and accountability. Thus, it is not surprising that in the early 1990s the WC, and more specifically the U.S. Treasury, IMF, and the World Bank, exclusively prioritized policies aimed at "freeing" the markets from government intervention, no matter the means used. Issues related to the modernization of the administrative capacity of the state were relegated to the back burner because, as the neoliberal theory postulated, once the market forces were given free reign better institutions would emerge almost by fiat. The influence of the United States, and to a lesser extent other major industrial nations (Japan, Germany, the United Kingdom, France), on the IMF and the World Bank relations with many crisis countries in this regard cannot be underestimated. This is not to say that the major shareholders of the IMF and World Bank imposed their wishes on such IFIS. However, the evidence suggests that when a country represented a major concern for the United States' strategic interests, Washington had a large say in what the IFIS could or could not do. Indeed, in many financial crises from Russia to Mexico, from Argentina to South Korea, the United States interfered in such a way so that the IMF and the World Bank waved/watered down conditionality requirements and disbursed funds despite the serious reservations of many of their field officers and senior managers (Bluestein 2005; Woods 2006). This allowed countries enjoying a special relationship with the United States, such as Russia and Argentina in our particular case, to often have an upper hand in the negotiations with the IMF and World Bank.

For their part, the IMF, the World Bank, and other IFIS involved in the market reform effort had their own responsibilities ranging from poor diagnostics and policy advice to lack of proper loan supervision. Moreover, the IMF and the World Bank often decided to interpret incoming data in a very selective fashion, highlighting what they believed to be positive trends while ignoring early signals that things could deteriorate very fast and possibly lead to disastrous consequences (Woods 2006). This in part was due to the fact that once they had thrown their support to a given country they both found it more and more difficult, as time went on, to consider alternative scenarios and a change of course in policy advice.

Private investment banks had their own responsibilities as well since the urgency to become major players in the most lucrative emerging markets led to overoptimistic forecasts, self-censorship, and loose lending practices. On occasions, the same banks that published reports about the state of the economy of a given country were also managing, at a lucrative commission rate, the bonds that the same country sold in the international market to raise capital. Miguel Kiguel, who served as an undersecretary in the Argentine Ministry of the Economy depicted the situation in these terms: "I think that within the banks there was some censorship to avoid offending us. If they had something negative to say, they toned it down in public. . . . We were big issuers in the market. They wanted to have a good relation with us. My view is these people are not fully independent or objective" (Blustein 2005, 64).

However, that things were not going according the WC's initial assumption was evident from the start, but it took a long while for the United States and IFIS to recognize and act on it. When reports about corruption and collusion associated with privatization and deregulation began to surface, the initial response of the U.S. Treasury and IFIS was that these were transitory problems. Consistent with Hayek's and Friedman's theories, neoliberals in these institutions argued that eventually the market would weed out bad entrepreneurs and voters would punish corrupt politicians at the ballot box. Almost invariably this did not happen. Corrupt politicians used government funds, often obtained through foreign loans, to buy votes before elections took place to remain in office, as we saw in the Russian and Argentine cases, while inefficient but politically connected cartels retained large market shares thanks to their political clout. When U.S. State Department, IMF, World Bank, and investment bank analysts working in emerging countries plagued by thriving corruption and crony capitalism reported such activities to their superiors, the standard response was to look the other way as such matters could derail the reform process and denouncing them would have created diplomatic rifts.

Only in the second half of the 1990s, when large North American corporations complained to the Clinton administration that they were being hurt by monopolistic and corrupt practices in emerging markets, did the United States and IFIS agencies begin to pay attention to issues related to governance. This meant that "stronger, more transparent and less corrupt institutions of governance had to be developed alongside structural adjustment and economic reform. The Washington Consensus had to be expanded to include 'good governance'" (Woods 2006, 22). Accordingly, the IMF and the World Bank began to advocate "second generation reforms," but in practice they focused primarily on legal issues because attacking head on the roots of corruption and crony capitalism in the most important markets was still too sensitive an issue. Thus, the new good governance effort was pursued in a highly selective way. As Stiglitz (2002, 47) noted, the IMF cracked down on Kenya and denied loans for "petty theft" but kept ignoring grand-scale corruption in Russia. However, for that matter much of the same can be said about Mexico, Indonesia, and Argentina. In fact, on the one hand these were countries in which the Clinton administration had too much at stake strategically and, on the other, the IMF and the World Bank had already spent considerable financial and political capital once they had identified them as poster children for the diffusion of free markets at the regional level.

Given these limitations, tangible improvements in the second-generation reforms were negligible. Instead the end result was that corrupt politicians (and the business elites tied to them in the countries just mentioned) were very clever in manipulating the West, rather than the other way around. Stiglitz (2002, 168) summarized the situation in these terms: "Many of those with whom we allied ourselves were less interested in creating the kind of market economy that has worked out so well in the West than in enriching themselves."[5] As things went from bad to worse in Russia—but the same could be said for other countries that experienced major financial crises—officials of the U.S. government and the IMF hunkered down.[6] Their ap-

5. Stiglitz served as chairman of the Council of Economic Advisers during Clinton's first term. He then moved to the World Bank, where he took the position of chief economist and senior vice president for development policy until November 1999. During his tenure at the World Bank he clashed repeatedly with Lawrence Summers and the IMF over policy advice toward emerging markets.

6. Former IMF chief economist Michael Mussa explained his institution's unwillingness to confront Argentina's fiscal deficit problem as follows: "With the Fund under widespread criticism . . . for its involvement in Asia, it was particularly gratifying to be able to pint out at least one important program country where the Fund appeared to be supporting successful economic policies. In this situation, there was probably even more than the usual reluctance for the Fund to be the skunk at the garden party, by stressing the accumulating failures of the Argentine fiscal policy" (cited in Blustein 2005, 50).

proach was "to ignore the facts, to deny reality, to suppress the discussion, to throw more good money after bad" (Stiglitz 2002, 168).

According to Stiglitz, neoliberal market fundamentalism came to dominate the economic thinking of the U.S. Treasury, the IMF, and to a lesser extent the World Bank in the early 1980s with Ronald Reagan's rise to power in the United States. Because the United States is the largest shareholder of the IMF and the World Bank, Reagan made sure that these two institutions would follow the new economic philosophy of his administration. However, for the purpose of this book it is worth noting that the neoliberal theory embraced by the United States and IFIS by condoning and often tacitly supporting authoritarian means to promote market reforms, as well as the kind of collusive and corrupt behavior just described, became an incoherent approach. This not only affected accountability issues, which were willfully ignored, but also some core economic principles that Hayek and Friedman had always stood for, such as competition. Indeed, when IFIS began to push Latin American and former Communist countries to privatize, their top priority was speed. Tackling competition and regulatory problems was relegated to a second phase of the reform process. As Stiglitz (2002, 54) put it, "those who privatized faster got high marks." This approach, however, ran counter to existing works on state divestiture, which stressed the importance of having three conditions in place prior to privatization.

First was the creation of competition whenever technically possible in markets that had been under government monopolistic control. Second was the establishment of clear regulatory frameworks managed by agencies shielded as much as possible from political control to foster competition. In the initial wave of privatization none of these conditions were met and the expected efficiency gains not only were lost but turned into new and detrimental forms of rent seeking under private ownership. Many new private enterprises resulting from privatization, particularly in lucrative sectors such as public utilities, were able to operate under monopolistic or oligopolistic conditions. Equally damaging was the fact that once they captured their markets such companies effectively resisted any move toward competition, artificially increasing the cost of doing business and penalizing consumers. The country cases examined in this book all displayed these problems. Notwithstanding the fact that there was abundant theoretical and empirical evidence suggesting the perils involved in the quick and loose approach to privatization, IFIS felt that they had no option and provided political support, funds, and technical assistance for highly controversial state divestitures. For the IMF and the World Bank, as well as regional development banks, doing so was the lesser evil. Again, their rationale was based on the fear that had reformers not acted quickly, the antireform groups would have had enough time to organize and block privatization. Thus, once more political expediency prevailed over the "scientific" and "sound" principles to which the same IFIs claimed to adhere.

The third condition relates to property rights. As we saw in chapter 1, Hayek and Friedman believed that no market economy can adequately function unless property rights are clearly specified and enforced. However, when market-friendly administrations launched their reforms legal institutions were ill suited to support them, particularly in the former Communist countries, where legal codes contradicted the establishment of private property, and left the government with still abundant discretionary powers to expropriate. Likewise, the courts lacked the expertise and political independence to be reliable institutions in upholding whatever promarket legislation was in the books. As noted before, the second generation of reforms tried to address the problem posed by inadequate legal institutions. Unfortunately, they usually came up far short of what was needed, and often it was too late as much damage had been already done since the new legal codes could not be enforced retroactively. A typical case was the inadequacy of minority shareholder rights in the Russian privatization (and several Eastern European and Latin American countries) as people were left without any effective legal recourse against management controlling a majority stake in a company. Moreover, particularly in Russia, the absence of clear legal rules helped the new owners of privatized companies to engage in asset stripping rather than productive investments. Even when legal codes were updated to protect property rights, they clashed with judges who were often ideologically biased against them, incompetent to enforce them, corrupt, and easily manipulated by the government of the day.

Indeed, the barrage of criticism that arose from the East Asian and Russian financial crises in the late 1990s prompted the IMF and World Bank to focus on the issue of transparency. More specifically, multilateral lending agencies began to require aid recipients to (a) improve budget and accounting processes; (b) promote reforms enhancing corporate governance and accountability; (c) provide information on off-budget expenditures; (d) fully disclose Central Bank reserves and financing operations; and (e) upgrade bankruptcy laws (Anjaria 2002). The assumption on promoting financial transparency was that greater controls and information disclosure could strengthen market-based mechanisms for resource allocation. They would also provide the necessary police patrols and fire alarms on a global scale, which were sorely missing in the 1990s, to prevent future financial crises. However, this new effort remained confined to technical issues linked to financial transparency and, in fact, did not prevent the Turkish and Argentine crises that followed only a few years later.

A Historical Opportunity Turns Sour

As noted in chapter 1, in the late 1980s the simultaneous collapse of Communism in the Soviet bloc and ISI in the developing world gave neoliberals a once-in-a-life-time opportunity to reshape the world economy according to their ideas. Having already won the debate in North America and much of Western Europe over Keynesianism, neoliberals could count on the advocacy of the United States and the most important Western capitalist countries to spread their beliefs to the rest of the world. To make more politically acceptable the sacrifices involved in turning around the ailing economies of the former Soviet bloc and many developing countries, Western leaders repeatedly stated that democracy and free markets were inextricably intertwined. Thus, once economic freedom was consolidated prosperity would follow and, by association, democratic institutions would be strengthened as well. The WC, which symbolized this general argument, reassured that had its recommendations turned into policy action reforming countries would meet with success in a relatively short period of time.

Unfortunately, things worked out quite differently as many emerging markets experienced economic downturns in the late 1990s. By the early 2000s the WC and its policies came to be regarded as a failure and responsible for a host of problems, spanning from rising unemployment, increasing poverty, and provoking deindustrialization. As a result, the high expectations that it had generated in the early 1990s turned into a bitter resentment in the eyes of public opinion. Even more damaging was the fact that in many countries in Latin America, the former Soviet bloc, and East Asia market reforms came to be associated with corruption and crony capitalism, punctuated by decision-making processes that undermined people's faith in democracy (Clark, Goss, and Kosova 2003; Holmes 2006)—the very opposite of what the WC had envisioned. For instance, in Russia privatization and democracy began to be commonly dubbed as "briberization" and "shitocracy." Thus, not only did economic prosperity not materialize, but often the reforms were tainted by political and economic abuses that conspired against democratic consolidation.

The disappointment with too many unfulfilled promises led to serious backlashes around the globe. As it can be seen in Table 6.1, the aftermath of the economic crises that hit East Asia, Russia, and Latin America between the late 1990s and early 2000s coincided with some disturbing trends. In fact, while the majority of the people surveyed in emerging markets were still supportive of democracy, they were appreciably less satisfied with the way it worked, particularly in South Asia (-51 percent), Latin America and Eastern Europe (-24 percent), Africa (-11 percent), and Asia (-6 percent). If we look closely at the regional level, data from the Latinobarometro show that while in 1998, at the peak of the WC influence, 66 percent of Latin Americans agreed that the market economy was the best way to promote development in their country, in 2007 only 52 percent believed so.

Indeed, the impact of macroeconomic factors on Latin American public opinion is unmistakable, as it can be seen from the Panizza and Yanez (2006) regression analysis in Table 6.2. The dependent variables are the public's attitude toward privatization and the market economy based on the Latinobarometro surveys, and the independent variables are the GDP gap, unemployment, inflation, and the depth of the crisis (lagged by one year), plus a number of standard controls for, sex, income, and age. Overall, all the macroeconomic variables are statistically significant and with the expected sign, particularly the GDP gap. In discussing their results, Panizza and Yanez (2006) stated, "If we look at the relationship between the output gap and the support for privatization during the 1998–2003 period, we can see that support for privatization went from 52 to 25 percent. The average output gap was 3 percent in 1997, and -3 percent in 2002 (a change of 6 percentage points). By multiplying 6 by the estimated coefficient (0.012), we obtain 0.072, which is close to one-third of the total drop in support for reforms. The case of Argentina is a striking example of the importance of macroeconomic factors. In this country, the output gap went from 7 percent in 1997 to -14 percent in 2002. This alone explains a drop in support for privatization equivalent to 25 percentage points, which is about 80 percent of the observed drop in support for privatization in Argentina (which fell from 45 to 13 percent)." Indeed, the number of Latin Americans who believed that privatization had been beneficial to their country dropped from 48 percent in 1998 to 35 percent in 2007. Conversely, the failure of markets reforms led some people to reconsider the positive nature of state intervention. In 2007 about 38 percent of Latin American respondents believed that the state could solve all problems—up from 33 percent in 1998 (Latinobarometro 2007, 30). In Latin America this general malaise has helped the rise to power of a new brand of left-wing populists (Hugo Chávez in Venezuela, Evo Morales in Bolivia, Rafael Correa in Ecuador, and Nestor and Cristina Kirchner in Argentina) who have embraced economic protectionism and a return to government ownership of the commanding heights of the economy. In East Asia, Africa, and the former Soviet bloc popular dissatisfaction have induced governments to experiment with an array of economic nationalism and welfare policies that the wc had tried to terminate altogether in the 1990s. In short, the mismanagement of the reform effort seems to have backfired and given new life to antimarket and, in several cases, demagogic and authoritarian political leaders.

This is a rather dismal record and brings us back to the nexus between economic and political freedom discussed in chapter 1. The findings of this book do not support Friedman's assumption that economic freedom leads to political freedom. If anything, both Russia and Argentina, after experimenting with market reforms for a decade, regressed politically. Putin and Kirchner became very popular at home by reversing the economic policies of the 1990s, but, interestingly enough, they continued in their predecessors' efforts to curtail democratic checks and balances. In Chile, on the contrary, we saw the opposite trend. Economic success came only in the last five years of the Pinochet regime and only when some of its most controversial macroeconomic policies were abandoned (financial liberalization and fixed exchange rate). More important, the Chilean economy blossomed under the democratic governments that followed. This was accompanied by a public scrutiny and horizontal accountability that never existed under Pinochet. It is also noteworthy that the Chilean economic success has not been based on unusually high prices for commodities that propelled the Russian and Argentine recovery until 2007, but on a sound export diversification policy and the protection of property rights.

The fact that many people in emerging markets, and particularly Latin Americans, have elected antiglobalization leaders should not be interpreted as a major shift to the left though. Between 1996 and 2007 most people in that part of the world still identified themselves as centrist (Table 6.3), including countries that have elected left-wing populists (Venezuela, Bolivia,

Ecuador, and Argentina). This would suggest that the loss of confidence in democracy and market reforms is not due to an ideological change of heart but, rather, to the disillusionment with their results. In brief, people may not want less market and more authoritarianism but a better, more transparent and responsive democracy capable of promoting competitive and efficient economies that can create opportunities for all rather than corruption, collusions, and rents benefiting those close to political power.

Thus, these conclusions support Feng's (2003) earlier work, which shows how political freedom determines economic freedom, whereas economic freedom is only indirectly conducive to political freedom. Based on his extensive statistical analysis, Feng (2003, 274) contends that in developing and postcommunist countries, "a democratic system will be instrumental in creating and deepening economic freedom. Western countries should not only promote market economics in these nations, but also concurrently help develop political systems instrumental toward consolidating free-market economics." Needless to say, strengthening vertical and horizontal accountability institutions should be an integral part of this process. Indeed, some of the available evidence indicates that where reforms were implemented in a more accountable and democratic fashion, economic results were positive and earned good marks from the citizenry. Conversely, where reforms were executed by all powerful executives results were poor and so was their evaluation on the part of public opinion (Harris 2003).

Final Remarks

The findings of this book show the importance of political accountability in understanding the dynamics of financial crises ensuing from market reforms. Contrary to what many economists believed in the early the 1990s, governments that insulated themselves from political pressure performed disastrously. In a nutshell, constrained executives were more likely to produce better and longer-lasting reforms whereas countries with weak institutions of democratic accountability were strongly associated with poor reforms and financial crises. This is because, as we saw in the country chapters, accountability institutions in the latter group were less likely to prevent crucial mistakes and questionable initiatives than was the case in more accountable political systems.

In crisis countries oversight institutions could not provide a sort of insurance policy against reckless executive behavior. The other aspect that is worth noting is that checks and balances fostering political accountability were also more likely to induce governments toward policy convergence, thus enhancing the legitimacy of the reforms themselves as they could stand on a larger base of support than those policies based on unilateral decision-making. Chile is a case in point. The democratic administrations that followed the military regime not only accepted the institutional constraints placed on them but also negotiated all major reforms aimed at improving the policies they inherited with the opposition. This created a situation where market reforms enjoyed broad support across the political spectrum. It also contrasts quite strikingly with neighboring Argentina, where the highly authoritarian and corrupt fashion in which Menem operated undermined the reform's legitimacy and, once the country imploded in 2001, fueled the backlash against them.

The findings of this book also cast doubts on the "self-regulating" nature of free markets when the appropriate checks and balances are not in place. The global financial crash of 2008 is just a reminder of how even the most advanced capitalist economies can fail to regulate themselves without adequate supervision. The debate that emerged around the appropriate nature of the U.S. Treasury Department bailout of its financial system in October of 2008 underscored the necessity to enhance transparency and accountability procedures in the financial sector.[7] If the self-regulation fallacy came to be exposed in highly institutionalized environments such as the United States and Western Europe, one can only imagine its deleterious consequences in countries characterized by weak government institutions and lack of transparent processes. Thus, an explicit emphasis on the accountability aspects of democracy provides more key critical points in regard to economic neoliberalism. If markets are not self-regulating, then democratic practices are all the more valuable.[8] In point of fact, as imperfect as they may be, both vertical and horizontal accountability institutions serve precisely the purpose, at least in principle, of thwarting market forces from engaging in collusive activities when the market cannot regulate itself.

The realization that accountability matters recently led IFIS to not only admit past mistakes driven by the "market fundamentalism" but also to rethink their approach to market reforms (World Bank 2005; Woods 2006).

---

7. On Alan Greenspan congressional testimony and his admission of regulatory failures in the U.S. economy, see the *New York Times* (October 23, 2008).

8. I owe this point to Michael Johnston.

In a review of what went wrong an IMF paper concluded, "governments need to be made accountable, not bypassed . . . the focus should be on improving checks and balances on government discretion and putting in place conditions to better decision making" (Zagha, Nankani, and Gill 2006, 10). New estimates on the high costs associated with the consequences of the lack of accountability have also played a part in the IFIs' new attitude. The former World Bank president Paul Wolfowitz estimated the cost of corruption for developing nations at $80 billion a year, an amount that equals all development assistance.[9] Accordingly, the World Bank has made some positive steps forward by increasing its focus on "good governance" issues and, along with the IMF and other multilateral agencies, has introduced "good governance" clauses in recent loan agreements. In 2006 multilateral institutions developed units with legal and investigative powers to prevent corruption, fraud, and collusive practices as part of a common policy agenda.[10] These are just initial steps, but they testify that the same lending institutions that once tried to shrug off accountability issues are becoming increasingly aware that emerging markets cannot flourish without strong oversight institutions, which in itself is a major turning point. The question remains whether the largest capitalist countries in the world will commit themselves to enhancing political accountability in emerging markets through IFIs, even when this effort may hurt their own strategic and commercial interests.

As researchers, all we can do is to provide a better understanding of the problem and possible ways to solve it. This book has tried to make a small contribution in this direction. The process-tracing employed in the three case studies has highlighted the theoretical mechanisms by which the lack of accountability affects the likelihood of poor economic performance. However, we are still a long way from developing comprehensive theories testing the linkage between accountability and economic performance in a broader set of countries via both qualitative methods and more rigorous quantitative approaches that can overcome the endogeneity problems affecting institutional variables. Moreover, we need to develop precise mea-

9. Opening statement at the Research and Corruption and Its Control: The State of the Art Conference hosted by the Wharton School, University of Pennsylvania, Philadelphia, March 2–4, 2006.

10. The African Development Bank, Asian Development Bank, Inter-American Development Bank, European Investment Bank, European Bank for Reconstruction and Development, the International Monetary Fund, and the World Bank have recently developed legal and investigative units sharing information and a common plan of action in this regard.

surements of what constitutes institutional quality. As I showed in this study, political accountability is clearly associated with economic performance, but it remains to be seen to which degree it can determine by itself the final outcome of economic policy, and to do so improved institutional indicators are essential. The task ahead for future research is to come up with better theory based on better data and statistical analyses capable of overcoming the problems just mentioned, which, in turn, can help us develop better diagnostics.

In conclusion, there is little doubt that capitalism still remains the most successful economic system in promoting growth. Likewise, there is ample evidence that strong democratic institutions have been fundamental in promoting thriving market economies capable of spreading their wealth among most of their citizens. Thus, there is every reason to believe that the same can and should happen in the rest of the world. The challenge is to create the necessary political and legal institutions that enhance accountability to make economic policies transparent and, in the process, legitimate. Some may argue that this is easy to say retrospectively, but when reforms took place time was of the essence. My simple response is that of course blunders were bound to happen, and indeed often policies produce unintended effects, but there was no need to steal in the process and that could and should have been avoided.

The lesson of the experiences examined in this book is that there are no institutional shortcuts to achieving economic progress. As I stressed in other writings, market reforms can play a very positive role in this regard. However, it is the lack of accountability that demands scrutiny and action. Indeed, as Saint Augustine reasoned long ago, states without justice are but bands of thieves at large (*City of God*, 4).

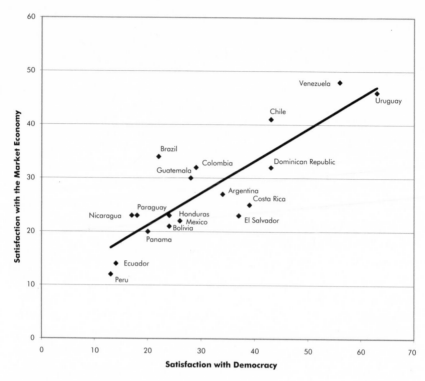

Figure 6.1 Satisfaction with Democracy and Market Economy in Latin America, 2005
SOURCE: Latinobarometro (2005).
(Pearson's r = 85**)

Table 6.1   Support for Versus Satisfaction with Democracy in Emerging Markets (%)

Regional Polls	Support	Satisfaction	Difference
Afrobarometer (1999–2001)	69	58	−11
Asianbarometer (1999–2001)	61	55	−6
Eastern Europe (2000)	53	29	−24
Latinobarometro (1995–2005)	56	32	−24
South Asia Barometer (2004)	62	11	−51

SOURCE: Lagos (2007).

Table 6.2 Macroeconomic Factors and Support for Market Reforms in Latin America

	1 Privatization	2 Privatization	3 Privatization	4 Privatization	5 Privatization	6 Market	7 Market	8 Market	9 Market	10 Market
GDP Gap	0.012 (5.36)***				0.014 (2.72)***	0.032 (5.22)***				0.04 (3.08)***
Unemployment		−0.023 (3.01)***			−0.000 (0.01)		−0.050 (2.16)**			0.022 (0.62)
Inflation			0.416 (1.35)		0.585 (4.18)***			1.826 (1.35)		2.146 (3.01)***
Depth of Crisis				−0.016 (4.63)***					−0.048 (4.66)***	
Age	−0.001 (2.87)***	−0.001 (2.33)**	−0.001 (3.00)***	−0.001 (2.91)***	−0.001 (2.35)**	−0.001 (1.58)	−0.000 (1.22)	−0.001 (1.94)**	−0.001 (1.62)	−0.000 (1.17)
Sex	−0.015 (2.78)***	−0.017 (2.89)***	−0.016 (2.78)***	−0.015 (2.78)***	−0.017 (2.86)***	−0.017 (3.28)***	−0.022 (3.96)***	−0.021 (3.71)***	−0.018 (3.53)***	−0.018 (3.07)***
Quintile = 2	−0.008 (1.06)	−0.002 (0.30)	−0.008 (0.99)	−0.008 (1.03)	−0.002 (0.24)	0.001 (0.12)	0.005 (0.53)	0.004 (0.44)	0.002 (0.21)	0.006 (0.65)
Quintile = 3	0.003 (0.27)	0.010 (1.12)	0.002 (1.16)	0.002 (0.25)	0.011 (1.29)	0.016 (1.61)	0.018 (1.85)*	0.014 (1.47)	0.015 (1.58)	0.021 (2.14)**
Quintile = 4	0.02 (1.80)*	0.029 (2.94)***	0.020 (1.79)*	0.020 (1.82)*	0.029 (2.97)***	0.023 (2.26)**	0.032 (3.38)***	0.030 (2.86)***	0.024 (2.25)**	0.030 (3.47)***
Quintile = 5	0.079 (4.84)***	0.089 (5.56)***	0.078 (4.78)***	0.079 (4.84)***	0.090 (5.66)***	0.039 (2.69)***	0.052 (3.56)***	0.043 (3.00)***	0.039 (2.67)***	0.050 (3.83)***
Constant	0.398 (23.09)***	0.622 (8.25)***	0.364 (10.14)***	0.425 (21.66)***	0.334 (2.37)**	0.558 (34.75)***	1.041 (4.68)***	0.391 (3.02)***	0.646 (33.13)***	0.122 (0.34)
Observations	65083	58013	65083	65083	58013	48009	42615	48009	48009	42615
R – squared	0.04	0.04	0.04	0.03	0.04	0.05	0.10	0.05	0.09	0.15

SOURCE: Panizza and Yanez (2006, 20).

Note: Robust t statistics in parentheses; all regressions include fixed effects and clustered errors.

*Significant at 10 percent
**Significant at 5 percent
***Significant at 1 percent

Table 6.3 Left-Right Ideological Scale in Latin America, 1996–2007

Country	1996	1997	1998	2000	2001	2002	2003	2004	2005	2006	2007	Average*
Dominican Republic								5.9	5.8	7.1	6.2	6.2
Costa Rica	6.0	6.1	5.5	6.4	6.9	7.4	5.7	5.2	5.6	6.3	6.1	6.1
Colombia	5.7	6.2	5.3	5.5	6.4	7.0	6.1	5.6	6.1	5.6	5.8	5.9
Honduras	7.1	7.2	7.0	5.6	8.1	7.6	6.6	5.8	6.0	6.2	5.8	6.6
Argentina	5.7	5.6	5.9	5.7	5.7	5.3	5.4	5.5	5.7	5.3	5.6	5.9
Mexico	4.6	5.3	5.5	5.4	5.8	4.9	5.0	4.8	5.1	5.6	5.3	5.2
Venezuela	5.2	5.3	5.6	5.0	5.0	5.1	4.9	4.8	4.5	5.6	5.3	5.1
Bolivia	5.1	5.0	4.8	4.6	5.2	5.1	5.1	4.6	4.7	4.8	5.2	4.9
El Salvador	5.4	5.3	5.5	5.3	6.4	6.5	5.9	5.9	6.3	5.3	5.2	5.7
Panama	4.0	5.5	7.4	5.9	6.1	5.3	5.1	4.1	4.8	4.6	5.2	5.2
Brazil	5.1	4.8	5.2	5.0	5.7	5.3	5.5	5.1	5.1	5.2	5.1	5.2
Ecuador	5.3	5.4	5.5	5.4	5.5	5.6	5.5	5.2	5.2	5.4	5.1	5.3
Nicaragua	5.3	5.5	5.1	4.5	5.4	6.3	5.9	5.3	5.5	5.0	5.1	5.3
Paraguay	5.9	5.1	5.2	5.1	5.5	5.7	5.8	5.0	5.4	5.2	5.1	5.3
Peru	5.6	5.6	5.5	5.4	5.6	5.4	5.3	4.8	5.1	5.1	5.1	5.3
Chile	4.8	4.8	5.0	5.0	5.2	5.1	5.3	4.9	4.8	4.9	4.9	5.0
Uruguay	5.2	5.4	5.7	5.2	5.2	5.3	5.0	5.0	4.5	4.7	4.8	5.0
Guatemala	4.8	4.2	5.2	5.0	5.8	6.3	6.1	4.9	5.3	5.3	4.6	5.2
Latin America	5.3	5.4	5.6	5.3	5.6	5.8	5.5	5.1	5.3	5.4	5.3	5.4

SOURCE: Latinobarometro (2007).

*0 = left; 10 = right

references

Abdala, Manuel. 2001. "Institutions, Contracts, and Regulations of Infrastructure in Argentina." *Journal of Applied Economics* 4, no. 2: 217–54.

Acemoglu, Daron, and James A. Robinson. 2000. "Political Losers and Barriers to Economic Development." *American Economic Review* 90:126–30.

———. 2001."Inefficient Redistribution." *American Political Science Review* 95:649–62.

Acemoglu, Daron, Simon Johnson, and James Robinson. 2001. "The Colonial Origins of Comparative Development: An Empirical Investigation." *American Economic Review* 91:1369–401.

Acemoglu, Daron, Simon Johnson, James Robinson, and Yunyong Thaicharoen. 2003. "Institutional Causes, Macroeconomic Symptoms: Volatility, Crises and Growth." *Journal of Monetary Economics* 50:49–123.

Addison, Tony, and Mina Baliamoune-Lutz. 2006. "Economic Reform when Institutional Quality Is Weak: The Case of the Maghreb." *Journal of Policy Modeling* 28, no. 9: 1029–43.

Ades, Alberto, and Rafael Di Tella. 1999. "Rents, Competition, and Corruption." *American Economic Review* 89, no. 4: 982–93.

Alesina, Alberto, Arnaud Devleeschauwer, William Easterly, Sergio Kurlat, and Romain Wacziarg. 2003. "Fractionalization." *Journal of Economic Growth* 8:155–94.

Aminzade, Ronald. 1993. "Class Analysis, Politics, and French Labor History." In *Rethinking Labor History*, ed. Lenard Berlanstein, 90–113. Urbana: University of Illinois Press.

Andalón, Mabel, and Luis F. López-Calva. 2002. "The Many Mexicos: Income Inequality and Polarization in Urban Mexico During the 90s." Paper prepared for the Cornell-LSE-WIDER Conference on Spatial Inequality, June 28–30, in London.

Anderson, Christopher, and Yuliya Tverdova. 2003. "Corruption, Political Allegiances, and Attitudes Toward Government in Contemporary Democracies." *American Political Science Review* 47, no. 1: 91–109.

Andrade, Jaime. 2003. "Evolución de la política social y de la reducción de la pobreza." Mimeo, Ministerio de Planificación y Cooperación, Santiago de Chile.

Angell, Alan. 2005. "Democratic Governance in Chile." Paper delivered at the Democratic Governability in Latin America Conference, October 7–8, at the University of Notre Dame.

———. 2007. *Democracy After Pinochet: Politics, Parties, and Elections in Chile.* London: Institute for the Americas.

Anjaria, Shailendra. 2002. "The IMF and Transparency—Moving Forward." Speech delivered October 28 in Washington, D.C., http://www.imf.org/external/np/speeches/2002/102802.htm.

Appel, Hilary. 2004. *A New Capitalist Order: Privatization and Ideology in Russia and Eastern Europe*. Pittsburgh: University of Pittsburgh Press.

Arblaster, Anthony. 1984. *The Rise and Decline of Western Liberalism*. Oxford: Blackwell.

Artana, Daniel, Fernando Navajas, and Santiago Urbiztondo. 1999. "Regulation and Contractual Adaptation in Public Utilities: The Case of Argentina." *Infrastructure and Financial Markets Review* 115:1–12.

Asian Development Bank. 2007. *Asian Development Outlook 2007 Update*. Manila: Asian Development Bank Press.

Åslund, Anders. 2002. *Building Capitalism: The Transformation of the Former Soviet Bloc*. New York: Cambridge University Press.

———. 2007. *Russia's Capitalist Revolution: Why Market Reform Succeeded and Democracy Failed*. New York: Cambridge University Press.

Aspiazu, Daniel, and Adolfo Vispo. 1994. "Algunas enseñanzas de las privatizaciones en la Argentina." *Revista de la CEPAL* (December): 129–47.

Auyero, Javier. 2000. *Poor People's Politics: Peronist Networks and the Legacy of Evita*. Durham: Duke University Press.

Baldacci, Emanuele, Luiz de Mello, and Gabriela Inchauste. 2002. "Financial Crises, Poverty, and Income Distribution." *Finance and Development* 39, no. 2: 24–27.

Barandiarán, Edgardo, and Leonardo Hernández. 1999. "Origins and Resolution of a Banking Crisis: Chile 1982–86." Working Paper 57, Banco Central de Chile, Santiago de Chile.

Barro, Robert. 1973. "The Control of Politicians: An Economic Model." *Public Choice* 14:19–42.

———. 1996. "Democracy and Growth." *Journal of Economic Growth* 1 (March): 1–27.

Bates, Robert. 1981. *Markets and States in Tropical Africa: The Political Basis of Agricultural Policies*. Berkeley and Los Angeles: University of California Press.

Bates, Robert, Avner Greif, Margaret Levi, Jean-Laurent Rosenthal, and Barry Weingast. 1998. *Analytic Narratives*. Princeton: Princeton University Press.

Beck, Thorsten, George Clarke, Alberto Groff, Philip Keefer, and Patrick Walsh. 2001. "New Tools in Comparative Political Economy: The Database of Political Institutions." *World Bank Economic Review* 15, no. 1: 165–76.

Bellamy, Richard. 1994. "'Dethroning Politics': Liberalism, Constitutionalism, and Democracy in the Thought of F. A. Hayek." *British Journal of Political Science* 24:419–41.

Bernstam, Mikhail, and Alvin Rabushka. 1998. *Fixing Russia's Banks: A Proposal for Growth*. Stanford: Hoover Institution Press.

Beyer, Harald, and Rodrigo Vergara. 2002. "Productivity and Economic Growth: The Case of Chile." Working Paper 174, Banco Central de Chile, Santiago de Chile.

Bitrán, Eduardo, and Raúl Sáez. 1994. "Privatization and Regulation in Chile." In *The Chilean Economy: Policy Lessons and Challenges*, ed. Barry Bosworth, Rudiger Dornbusch, and Raúl Labán. Washington, D.C.: Brookings Institution Press.

Blustein, Paul. 2005. *And the Money Kept Rolling In (and Out): Wall Street, the IMF, and the Bankrupting of Argentina*. New York: PublicAffairs.

Bonnet, Celine, Pierre Dubois, David Martimort, and Stephanie Straub. 2006. "Empirical Evidence on Satisfaction with Privatization in Latin America: Welfare Effects and Beliefs." Mimeo, University of Toulouse.

Bowen, Jeff, and Susan Rose-Ackerman. 2003. "Partisan Politics and Executive Accountability: Argentina in Comparative Perspective." *Supreme Court Economic Review* 10:157–210.

Boycko, Maxim, Andrei Shleifer, and Robert Vishny. 1995. *Privatizing Russia.* Cambridge: MIT Press.

Brinegar, Adam. 2006. "Partisanship, Information, and Economic Performance: Evaluating Citizen Attitudes about Corruption in Chile." Paper prepared for the Latin American Studies Association meeting, March 15–18, in San Juan, Puerto Rico.

Broadman, Harry, and Francesca Recanatini. 2000. "Seeds of Corruption: Do Markets Matter?" Policy Research Working Paper 2368, World Bank, Washington, D.C.

Brown, Archie. 2007. *Seven Years That Changed the World: Perestroika in Perspective.* New York: Oxford University Press.

Brusco, Valeria, Marcelo Nazareno, and Susan Stokes. 2004. "Vote Buying in Argentina." *Latin American Research Review* 39, no. 2: 66–88.

Busch, Andrew. 2001. *Ronald Reagan and the Politics of Freedom.* Lanham: Rowman and Littlefield.

Calvo, Ernesto, and Maria Victoria Murillo. 2004. "Who Delivers? Partisan Clients in the Argentine Electoral Market." *American Journal of Political Science* 48:742–57.

Camdessus, Michel. 1998. "Russia and the IMF: Meeting the Challenges of an Emerging Market and Transition Economy." Address by Michele Camdessus to the U.S.-Russia Business Council, April 1, in Washington, D.C.

———. 1999. "Governments and Economic Development in a Globalized World." Speech delivered at the Pacific Basin Economic Council international general meeting, May 17, in Hong Kong, http://www.imf.org/external/np/speeches/1999/051799.htm.

Carvalho Filho, Irineu de, and Marcos Chamon. 2006. "The Myth of Post-Reform Income Stagnation in Brazil." Working Paper 275, International Monetary Fund, Washington, D.C.

Cea Egaña, José Luis. 1994. "Reforma de la fiscalización parlamentaria en Chile." *Revista de Derecho de la Universidad Austral* 5:13–25.

Cerruti, Gabriela, and Sergio Ciancaglini. 1992. *El octavo circulo: Crónica y entretelones de la Argentina menemista.* Buenos Aires: Planeta.

Chang, Eric, and Miriam Golden. 2007. "Electoral Systems, District Magnitude, and Corruption." *British Journal of Political Science* 37, no. 1: 115–37.

Chavez, Rebecca Bill. 2004. *The Rule of Law in Nascent Democracies: Judicial Politics in Argentina.* Stanford: Stanford University Press.

Cherashny, Guillermo. 1997. *Menem, Yabrán, Cavallo: Final abierto.* Buenos Aires: Solaris.

Chisari, Omar, Antonio Estache, and Carlos Romero. 1997. "Winners and Losers from Utility Privatization in Argentina: Lessons from a General Equilibrium Model." Policy Research Working Paper 1824, World Bank, Washington, D.C.

Chubais, Anatolii. 1993. "Remarks Delivered by Vice-Premier Anatolii Chubais at the International Institute for Applied System Analysis." July 9. Mimeo. Cited in Nelson and Kuzes, *Radical Reform in Yeltsin's Russia,* 158.

Chudnovsky, Daniel, Andrés López, and Fernando Porta. 1995. "New Foreign Direct

Investment in Argentina: Privatization, the Domestic Market, and Regional Integration." In *Foreign Direct Investments in Latin America*, ed. Manuel Agosín, 39–104. Washington, D.C.: Inter-American Development Bank.

Clark, Terry, Ernest Goss, and Larisa Kosova. 2003. *Changing Attitudes Toward Economic Reform During the Yeltsin Years*. New York: Praeger.

Clemens, Grafe, and Kaspar Richter. 2001. "Taxation and Public Expenditure." In *Russia's Post-Communist Economy*, ed. Brigitte Granville and Peter Oppenheimer, 131–72. New York: Oxford University Press.

Comisión Econónomica para América Latina y el Caribe (CEPAL). 2000. *Balance preliminar de las economías de América Latina*. Santiago de Chile: CEPAL.

Correa, Jorge. 1992. "Dealing with Past Human Rights Violations: The Chilean Case After Dictatorship." *Notre Dame Law Review* 67, no. 5: 1455–65.

———. 1999. "La Cenicienta se queda en la fiesta: El poder judicial chileno en la década de los 90." In *El modelo chileno: democracia y Desarrollo en los noventa*, ed. Paul Drake and Iván Jaksic, 281–315. Santiago: LOM.

Couso, Javier. 2005. "The Judicialization of Chilean Politics: The Rights Revolution That Never Was." In *The Judicialization of Politics in Latin America*, ed. Rachel Sieder, Line Schjolden, and Alan Angell, 105–26. New York: Palgrave Macmillan.

Dabrowski, Marek, Oleksandr Rohozynsky, and Irina Sinitsina. 2004. "Poland and the Russian Federation: A Comparative Study of Growth and Poverty." Mimeo, World Bank, Washington, D.C.

Dahse, Fernando. 1979. *Mapa de la extrema riqueza*. Santiago: Editorial Aconcagua.

Della Paolera, Gerardo, and Alan Taylor. 2001. *Straining at the Anchor: The Argentine Currency Board and the Search for Macroeconomic Stability, 1880–1935*. Chicago: University of Chicago Press.

Desai, Raj, and Sanjay Pradhan. 2005. "Governing the Investment Climate." *Development Outreach* 7, no. 2: 13–15.

Diamond, Larry. 2005. "Democracy, Development, and Good Governance: The Inseparable Links." Annual Democracy and Governance lecture, March 1, in Accra, Ghana.

Diamond, Larry, Marc Plattner, and Andreas Schedler, eds. 1999. Introduction to *The Self-Restraining State: Power and Accountability in New Democracies*, 1–12. Boulder: Lynne Rienner.

Diaz-Cayeros, Alberto, Federico Estevez, and Beatriz Magaloni. 2001. "Private Versus Public Goods as Electoral Investments: A Portfolio Diversification Model of Policy Choice." Paper prepared for the Citizen-Politician Linkages in Democratic Politics workshop, March 30–April 1, at Duke University, Durham, North Carolina.

Doig, Alan, and Robin Theobald. 2000. *Corruption and Democratization*. London: Frank Cass.

Dollar, David, and Aart Kraay. 2003. "Institutions, Trade, and Growth: Revisiting the Evidence." Policy Research Working Paper 3004, World Bank, Washington, D.C.

Dornbusch, Rudiger. 2001. *World Economic Trends* 4:1–29.

Dutz, Mark, and Maria Vagliasindi. 2000. "Market Selection, Regulatory Barriers, and Competition: Evidence from Transition Economies." Mimeo, European Bank of Reconstruction and Development, London.

Easterly, William. 2001. *The Elusive Quest for Growth: Economists' Adventures and Misadventures in the Tropics*. Cambridge: MIT Press.

Easterly, William, and Ross Levine. 2003. "Tropics, Germs, and Crops: How Endowments Influence Economic Development." *Journal of Monetary Economics* 50, no. 1: 3–39.

Easterly, William, Ross Levine, and David Rodman. 2003. "New Data, New Doubts: Revisiting 'Aid, Policies, and Growth.'" Working Paper 26, Center for Global Development, Washington, D.C.

Edwards, Sebastián, and Alejandra Cox Edwards. 1987. *Monetarism and Liberalization: The Chilean Experiment.* Cambridge, Mass.: Ballinger.

Elliot, Kimberly, ed. 1997. *Corruption and the Global Economy.* Washington, D.C.: Institute for International Economics.

European Bank for Reconstruction and Development (EBRD). 1999. *Transition Report 1999.* London: European Bank for Reconstruction and Development.

Fazio, Hugo. 1997. *Mapa actual de la extrema riqueza en Chile.* Santiago: LOM.

Feld, Lars, and Stefan Voigt. 2003. "Economic Growth and Judicial Independence: Cross-Country Evidence Using a New Set of Indicators." *European Journal of Political Economy* 19, no. 3: 498–527.

Ferejohn, John. 1986. "Incumbent Performance and Electoral Control." *Public Choice* 30, no. 3: 5–25.

———. 1999. "Accountability and Authority: Toward a Theory of Political Accountability." In *Democracy, Accountability, and Representation,* ed. Adam Przeworski, Susan Stokes, and Bernard Manin, 131–53. New York: Cambridge University Press.

Ferreira Rubio, Delia, and Matteo Goretti. 1998. "When the President Governs Alone: 1997. The Decretazo in Argentina, 1989–93." In *Executive Decree Authority,* ed. John Carey and Mathew Soberg Shugart, 33–61. New York: Cambridge University Press.

———. 2000. "Executive-Legislative Relationship in Argentina: From Menem's Decretazo to a New Style?" Paper prepared for the Argentina 2000: Politics, Economy, Society, and International Relations annual conference, May 15–17, at the Oxford University.

Ffrench-Davis, Ricardo. 2002. *Economic Reforms in Chile: From Dictatorship to Democracy.* Ann Arbor: University of Michigan Press.

Fillipov, Petr. 1994. "Korrptsioner-drug mafiozi." *Delevoi Mir* 14 (February 21–27): 19.

Fischer, Stanley. 1998. "The Russian Economy at the Start of 1998." Press release, January 19, International Monetary Fund, Washington, D.C.

———. 2001. "Exchange Rate Regimes: Is the Bipolar View Correct?" *Finance and Development* 38, no. 2: 18–21.

Fischer, Ronald, Rodrigo Gutiérrez, and Pablo Serra. 2002. "The Effects of Privatization on Firms and on Social Welfare." Documentos de Trabajo 131, Centro de Economía Aplicada, Universidad de Chile.

Fish, Steve. 1998. "The Determinants of Economic Reform in the Post-Communist World." *East European Politics and Society* 12, no. 1: 31–78.

Foxley Alejandro. 1983. *Latin American Experiments in Neoconservative Economics.* Berkeley and Los Angeles: University of California Press.

Frankel, Jeffrey, and David Romer. 1999. "Does Trade Cause Growth?" *American Economic Review* 89, no. 3: 379–99.

Freeland, Chrystia. 2000. *Sale of the Century: Russia's Wild Ride from Communism to Capitalism.* New York: Crown Business.

Friedman, Milton. 1962. *Capitalism and Freedom*. Chicago: University of Chicago Press.

Gaddy, Clifford, and Barry Ickes. 1998. "Russia's Virtual Economy." *Foreign Affairs* (September–October): 53–67.

Gaidar, Yegor. 1999. *Days of Defeat and Victory*. Seattle: University of Washington Press.

Galleguillos, Nibaldo. 1999. "The Politics of Judicial Reform in the Democratic Transition: An Analysis of the Chilean Case." *Ciencia Ergo Sum* 5, no. 3: 239–48.

Garay, Alberto. 1991. "Federalism, the Judiciary, and Constitutional Adjudication in Argentina: A Comparison with the U.S. Constitutional Model." *Inter-American Law Review* 22, no. 2–3: 161–202.

Geddes, Barbara. 1994. *Politician's Dilemma: Building State Capacity in Latin America*. Berkeley and Los Angeles: University of California Press.

George, Alexander, and Andrew Bennett. 2005. *Case Studies and Theory Development in the Social Sciences*. Cambridge: MIT Press.

George, Alexander, and Timothy McKeown. 1985. "Case Studies and Theories of Organizational Decision Making." *Advances in Information Processing in Organizations* 2:21–58.

Gerchunoff, Pablo, and Guillermo Cánovas. 1995. "Privatización en un contexto de emergencia económica." *Desarrollo Económico* 34 (January–March): 483–512.

Gerchunoff, Pablo, and Germán Coloma. 1993. "Privatization in Argentina." In *Privatization in Latin America*, ed. Manuel Sánchez and Rossana Corona, 251–99. Washington, D.C.: Inter-American Development Bank.

Gibson, Edward, and Ernesto Calvo. 2000. "Federalism and Low-Maintenance Constituencies: Territorial Dimensions of Economic Reform in Argentina." *Studies in Comparative International Development* 35, no. 3: 32–55.

Gil, Federico. 1996. *The Political System of Chile*. Boston: Unwin Hyman.

Goldman, Marshall. 2003. *The Piratization of Russia: Russian Reform Goes Awry*. London: Routledge.

———. 2008. *Petrostate: Putin, Power, and the New Russia*. New York: Oxford University Press.

Goldsmith, Arthur. 2005. "How Good Must Governance Be?" Paper prepared for The Quality of Government: What It Is, How to Get It, Why It Matters conference, November 17–19, at the Göteborg University, Sweden.

Gómez, Gastón ernales. 1999. "Algunas ideas críticas sobre la jurisdicción constitucional en Chile." In *La jurisdicción constitucional chilena ante la reforma. Cuadernos de Análisis Jurjjídico 41*, Santiago: Universidad Diego Portales.

Gordillo, Augustín. 1996. *Después de la reforma del estado*. Buenos Aires: Fundación de Derecho Administrativo.

Gould, John. 2003. "Out of the Blue? Democracy and Privatization in Postcommunist Europe." *Comparative European Politics* 1:277–311.

Granville, Brigitte. 2001. "The Problem of Monetary Stabilization." In *Russia's Post-Communist Economy*, ed. Brigitte Granville and Peter Oppenheimer, 93–130. New York: Oxford University Press.

Greskovits, Béla. 1998. *The Political Economy of Protest and Patience: East European and Latin American Transformations Compared*. Budapest: Central European University Press.

Grupo Sophia. 2001. "Gasto en funcionarios políticos, funcionarios temporarios y legisladores." Documento de Trabajo, Buenos Aires.

Guislain, Pierre. 1997. *The Privatization Challenge: A Strategic, Legal, and Institutional Analysis of International Experience.* Washington, D.C.: World Bank.

Gustafson, Thane. 1999. *Capitalism Russian-Style.* New York: Cambridge University Press.

Haber, Stephen, ed. 2002. "Introduction: The Political Economy of Crony Capitalism." In *Crony Capitalism and Economic Growth in Latin America: Theory and Evidence,* xi–xxi. Stanford: Hoover Institution Press.

Hachette, Dominique, and Rolf Lüders. 1993. *Privatization in Chile: An Economic Appraisal.* International Center for Economic Growth. San Francisco: ICS Press.

Haggard, Stephan. 2000. *The Political Economy of the Asian Financial Crisis.* Washington, D.C: Institute for International Economics.

Hall, Robert, and Charles Jones. 1999. "Why Do Some Countries Produce so Much More Output per Worker than Others?" *Quarterly Journal of Economics* 114:83–116.

Handelman, Stephen. 1995. *Comrade Criminal: Russia's New Mafiya.* New Haven: Yale University Press.

Hanke, Steve, and Kurt Schuler. 1994. *Currency Boards for Developing Countries: A Handbook.* San Francisco: Institute for Contemporary Studies Press.

Harris, Clive. 2003. "Private Participation in Infrastructure in Developing Countries: Trends, Impacts, and Policy Lessons." World Bank Working Paper 5, World Bank, Washington, D.C.

Havrylyshyn, Oleh, and Thomas Wolf. 1999. "Determinants of Growth in Transition Countries." *Finance and Development* 36, no. 2: 1–6. Washington, D.C.: International Monetary Fund.

Hayek, Friedrich von. 1944. *The Road to Serfdom.* Chicago: University of Chicago Press.

———. 1978. *New Studies in Philosophy, Politics, Economics, and the History of Ideas.* London: Routledge and Kegan Paul.

———. 1979. *Law, Legislation, and Liberty: The Political Order of a Free People.* Vol. 3. Chicago: University of Chicago Press.

Healey, John, and Mark Robinson. 1992. *Democracy, Governance, and Economic Policy: Sub-Saharan Africa in Comparative Perspective.* London: Overseas Development Council.

Hedlund, Stefan. 1999. *Russia's "Market" Economy: A Bad Case of Predatory Capitalism.* London: UCL Press.

Heidenheimer, Arnold, ed. 1970. *Political Corruption: Readings in Comparative Analysis.* New Brunswick, N.J.: Transaction Books.

Held, David, and M. Koenig-Archibugi, eds. 2005. *Global Governance and Public Accountability.* Oxford: Blackwell.

Hellman, Joel. 1998. "Winners Take All: The Politics of Partial Reform in Postcommunist Transition." *World Politics* 50 (January): 203–34.

Hellman, Joel, G. Jones, and David Kaufmann. 2000. "Measuring Governance, Corruption, and State Capture: How Firms and Bureaucrats Shape the Business Environment in Transition Economies." *World Bank Policy Research Working Paper* 2312, World Bank, Washington, D.C.

Hellman, Joel, and David Kaufmann. 2001. "Confronting the Challenge of State Capture in Transition Economies." IMF Finance and Development 38, no. 3: 1–6.

———. 2002. "Far From Home: Do Foreign Investors Import Higher Standards of

Governance in Transition Economies?" World Bank Draft Paper, Washington, D.C., http://ssrn.com/abstract=386900.

Helmke, Gretchen. 2002. "The Logic of Strategic Defection: Court-Executive Relations in Argentina Under Dictatorship and Democracy." *American Political Science Review* 96, no. 2: 291–303.

Hendley, Kathryn. 1997. "Legal Development in Post-Soviet Russia." *Post Soviet Affairs* 13, no. 3: 228–51.

Hessel, Merek, and Ken Murphy. 2004. "Stealing the State, and Everything Else: A Survey of Corruption in Postcommunist World." Working Paper, Transparency International, Berlin, Germany, http://www.transparency.org/working_papers/ hessel.

Hilbink, Lisa. 1999. "Legalism Against Democracy: The Political Role of the Judiciary in Chile, 1964–1994." Ph.D. diss., University of California at San Diego.

Himes, Susan, and Martine Millet-Einbinder. 1999. "Russia's Tax Reform." *OECD Observer* 215 (November): 26–30.

Hoffman, David. 2002. *The Oligarchs: Wealth and Power in the New Russia.* New York: PublicAffairs.

Holmes, Leslie. 2006. *Rotten States? Corruption, Post-Communism, and Neoliberalism.* Durham: Duke University Press.

Hornbeck, J. F. 2003. "The Financial Crisis in Argentina." Congressional Research Service Report, Washington, D.C.

Hough, Jerry. 2001. *The Logic of Economic Reform in Russia.* Washington, D.C.: Brookings Institution Press.

Huneeus, Carlos. 2006. *The Pinochet Regime.* Boulder: Lynne Rienner.

Huntington, Samuel. 1968. *Political Order in Changing Societies.* New Haven: Yale University Press.

Hutchcroft, Paul. 1998. *Booty Capitalism: The Politics of Banking in the Philippines.* Ithaca: Cornell University Press.

Inter-American Development Bank (IDB). 1999. Argentina Country Paper, Inter-American Development Bank, Washington, D.C.

———. 2000. *Development Beyond Economics.* Baltimore: Johns Hopkins University Press.

———. 2007. "Nationalization for the Poor?" *Ideas for Development in the Americas* 13 (May–August): 1–12.

International Monetary Fund (IMF). 1997a. *Good Governance: The IMF's Role.* Washington, D.C.: International Monetary Fund.

———. 1997b. *Survey* 26, no. 11: 169–84.

———. 2004. *Report on the Evaluation of the Role of the IMF in Argentina, 1991–2001.* Washington, D.C.: International Monetary Fund.

———. 2005. *Report on the Observance of Standards and Codes—Fiscal Transparency Module.* Washington, D.C.: International Monetary Fund.

Jacob, Jeffry, and Thomas Osang. 2007. "Institutions, Geography, and Trade: A Panel Data Study." Paper prepared for the 2006 Midwest International Economics and Economic Theory meeting, October 13–15, at Purdue University, West Lafayette, Indiana.

Jain, Arvind. 2001. "Corruption: A Review." *Journal of Economic Surveys* 15:71–121.

Johnson, Simon, Daniel Kaufmann, and Andrej Shleifer. 1997. "The Unofficial Economy in Transition." Brookings Papers on Economic Activity 2. Washington, D.C.: Brookings Institution.

Johnson, Simon, Daniel Kaufmann, and Pablo Zoido-Lobatón. 1999. "Corruption, Public Finance, and the Unofficial Economy." Policy Research Working Paper 2169, World Bank, Washington, D.C.

Johnston, Michael. 2005. *Syndromes of Corruption: Wealth, Power, and Democracy.* Cambridge: Cambridge University Press.

Jones, Mark. 1997. "Evaluating Argentina's Presidential Democracy: 1983–1995." In *Presidentialism and Democracy in Latin America: Rethinking the Terms of the Debate,* ed. Matthew Shugart and Scott Mainwaring, 259–99. New York: Cambridge University Press.

Jones, Mark, and Wonjae Hwang. 2005. "Provincial Party Bosses: Keystones of the Argentine Congress." In *Argentine Democracy: The Politics of Institutional Weakness,* ed. Steve Levitsky and Maria Victoria Murillo, 53–88. University Park: Pennsylvania State University Press.

Jones, Mark, Sebastian Saiegh, and Pablo Spiller. 2002. "Amateur Legislators-Professional Politicians: The Consequences of Party-Centered Electoral Rules in a Federal System." *American Journal of Political Science* 46, no. 3: 356–69.

Jones, Mark, Pablo Sanguinetti, and Mariano Tommasi. 2000. "Politics, Institutions, and Fiscal Performance in a Federal System: An Analysis of the Argentine Provinces." *Journal of Development Economics* 61:305–33.

Kahler, Miles. 2004. "Defining Accountability Up: the Global Economic Multilaterals." *Government and Opposition* 39:132–258.

Kang, David. 2002. *Crony Capitalism: Corruption and Development in South Korea and the Philippines.* New York: Cambridge University Press.

Kaufmann, Daniel, Aart Kraay, and Massimo Mastruzzi. 2007. "Growth and Governance: A Rejoinder." *Journal of Politics* 69, no. 2: 570–72.

———. 2008. "Governance Matters VII: Governance Indicators for 1996–2007." Policy Research Working Paper 4654, World Bank, Washington, D.C.

Kaufmann, Daniel, Aart Kraay, and Pablo Zoido-Lobatón. 1999. "Governance Matters." Policy Research Working Paper 2195, World Bank, Washington, D.C.

———. 2002. "Governance Matters II: Updated Indicators for 2000/01." Policy Research Working Paper 2772, World Bank, Washington, D.C.

———. 2004. "Governance Matters III: Governance Indicators for 1996–2002." Policy Research Working Paper 3106, World Bank, Washington, D.C.

Keech, William. 2007. "Economic Politics in Latin America: Rethinking Democracy and Dictatorship." Duke University, manuscript.

Keefer, Philip. 2002. "DPI2000 Database of Political Institutions: Changes and Variable Definitions." Washington, D.C.: World Bank.

———. 2003. "Democratization and Clientelism: Why Are Young Democracies Badly Governed?" Mimeo, World Bank, Washington, D.C.

Keohane, Robert, and Joseph Nye. 2001. "Democracy, Accountability, and Global Governance." Paper prepared for the Conference on Globalization and Governance, March 23–24, at the University of California San Diego, La Jolla, California.

Keynes, John Maynard. 1936. *The General Theory of Employment, Interest, and Money.* New York: Harcourt Brace.

Khakamada, Irina. 1993. "Biudzhet-94: Peresmotr opasen, korrektivy neobkhodimy." *Moskovskie Novosti* 19 (May): 8–15.

Khan, Mushtaq, and Jomo Kwame Sundaram, eds. 2000. *Rents, Rent-Seeking, and Economic Development: Theory and Evidence in Asia.* New York: Cambridge University Press.

Klebnikov, Paul. 2000. *Godfather of the Kremlin: Boris Berezovsky and the Looting of Russia.* New York: Harcourt.

———. 2004. "The 100 Richest Russians." *Forbes* (July 23), http://www.forbes.com/2004/07/14/04russialand.html.

Klugman, Jeni, and Sheila Marnie. 2001. "Poverty." In *Russia's Post-Communist Economy,* ed. Brigitte Granville and Peter Oppenheimer, 445–74. New York: Oxford University Press.

Knack, Stephen. 2001. "Aid Dependence and the Quality of Governance: Cross-Country Empirical Tests." *Southern Economic Journal* 68, no. 2: 310–29.

Knack, Stephen, and Philip Keefer. 1995. "Institutions and Economic Performance: Cross-Country Tests Using Alternative Institutional Measures." *Economics and Politics* 7:207–27.

Kornai, Janos. 1992. *The Socialist System: The Political Economy of Socialism.* Princeton: Princeton University Press.

Krueger, Anne. 1974. "The Political Economy of the Rent Seeking Economy." *American Economic Review* 64:291–303.

———. 2002. "Why Crony Capitalism Is Bad for Economic Growth." In *Crony Capitalism and Economic Growth in Latin America: Theory and Evidence,* ed. Stephen Haber, 1–23. Stanford: Hoover Institution Press.

———. 2004. "Meant Well, Tried Little, Failed Too Much: Policy Reforms in Emerging Market Economies." Remarks at the Roundtable Lecture at the Economic Honors Society, March 23, at New York University.

Krusell, Per, and José Victor Ríos-Rull. 1996. "Vested Interests in a Theory of Growth and Stagnation." *Review of Economic Studies* 63:301–29.

Kuczynski, Pedro-Pablo, and John Williamson, eds. 2003. *After the Washington Consensus.* Washington, D.C.: Institute for International Economics.

Kunicova, Jana, and Susan Rose-Ackerman. 2005. "Electoral Rules and Constitutional Structures as Constraints on Corruption." *British Journal of Political Science* 35, no. 4: 573–606.

Kurtz, Marcus. 1999. "Chile's Neo-Liberal Revolution: Incremental Decisions and Structural Transformation, 1973–89." *Journal of Latin American Studies* 31 (May): 399–427.

Kurtz, Marcus, and Andrew Schrank. 2007. "Growth and Governance: Models, Measures, and Mechanisms." *Journal of Politics* 69, no. 2: 538–54.

Kydland, Finn, and Edward Prescott. 1977. "Rules Rather than Discretion: The Inconsistency of Optimal Plans." *Journal of Political Economy* 85, no. 3: 473–92.

Lagos, Marta. 2007. "Democracy Is Latin America's Second Independence: Evidence from the Latinobarometro." Paper presented at the James A. Baker III Institute for Public Policy, Rice University, Houston, Texas, October 5.

Llanos, Mariana. 2001. "Understanding Presidential Power in Argentina: A Study of the Policy of Privatization in the 1990s." *Journal of Latin American Studies* 33, no. 1: 67–99.

———. 2002. *Privatization and Democracy in Argentina: An Analysis of President-Congress Relations.* London: Palgrave Macmillan.

La Porta, Rafael, Florencio Lopez-de-Silanes, Andrei Shleifer, and Robert Vishny. 1999. "The Quality of Government." *Journal of Law and Economic Organization* 15:222–79.

Larkins, Christopher. 1998. "The Judiciary and Delegative Democracy in Argentina." *Comparative Politics* 30:423–43.

Larraín, Felipe, and Raúl Labán. 1997. "From the Military to Democracy: Two Decades of Chilean Economic Policies." Development Discussion Paper 612, Harvard Institute for International Development, Harvard University.

Larraín, Felipe, and Andrés Velasco. 1990. "Can Swaps Solve the Debt Crisis? Lessons from the Chilean Experience." Princeton Studies in International Finance 69. Princeton: Princeton University.

Latinobarometro. 2003. *Summary Report: Democracy and Economy.* Santiago de Chile: Latinobarometro.

———. 2004. *Resumen: Una década de mediciones.* Santiago de Chile: Latinobarometro.

———. 2005. *A Decade of Public Opinion.* Santiago de Chile: Latinobarometro.

———. 2007. *Informe 2007.* Santiago de Chile: Latinobarometro.

Laver, Michael, and Kenneth Shepsle. 1999. "Government Accountability in Parliamentary Democracies." In *Democracy, Accountability, and Representation,* ed. Adam Przeworski, Susan Stokes, and Bernard Manin, 279–96. New York: Cambridge University Press.

Leff, Nathaniel. 1964. "Economic Development Through Bureaucratic Corruption." *American Behavioral Scientist* 8, no. 3: 8–14.

Levitsky, Steven. 2003. "From Labor Politics to Machine Politics: The Transformation of Party-Union Linkages in Argentine Peronism." *Latin American Research Review* 38, no. 3: 3–66.

Lieberman, Evan. 2005. "Nested Analysis as a Mixed-Method Strategy for Comparative Research." *American Political Science Review* 99, no. 3: 435–52.

Loveman, Brian, and Elizabeth Lira. 2000. *Las ardientes cenizas del olvido: Via chilena de reconciliación política: 1932–1994.* Santiago: LOM.

Lushin, Andrei, and Peter Oppenheimer. 2001. "External Trade and Payments." In *Russia's Post-Communist Economy,* ed. Brigitte Granville and Peter Oppenheimer, 261–300. New York: Oxford University Press.

MacIntyre, Andrew. 2001. "Institutions and Investors: The Politics of the Economic Crisis in Southeast Asia." *International Organization* 55, no. 1: 81–122.

Mainwaring, Scott, and Christopher Welna, eds. 2003. *Democratic Accountability in Latin America.* New York: Oxford University Press.

Majul, Luis. 1993. *Los Dueños de la Argentina: La cara oculta de los negocios.* Buenos Aires: Planeta.

———. 1994. *Los dueños de la Argentina II: Los secretos del verdadero poder.* Buenos Aires: Planeta.

Manin, Bernard, Adam Przeworski, and Susan Stokes. 1999. "Elections and Representation." In *Democracy, Accountability, and Representation,* ed. Adam Przeworksi, Susan Stokes, and Bernard Manin, 29–54. New York: Cambridge University Press.

Manzetti, Luigi. 2003. "Political Manipulations and Market Reform Failures." *World Politics* 55 (April): 315–60.

Marcel, Mario. 1989. "La privatización de empresas en Chile, 1985–88." *Notas Técnicas* 125, CIEPLAN.

Marín, Gustavo, and Patricio Rozas. 1988. *Los grupos tradicionales y la crisi: El caso chileno.* Buenos Aires: Nueva América.

Martimort, David, and Stéphane Straub. 2006. "Privatization and Corruption." Mimeo, University of Toulouse.

Matus, Alejandra. 1999. *El libro negro de la justicia chilena.* Buenos Aires: Planeta.

Mauro, Paolo. 1995. "Corruption and Growth." *Quarterly Journal of Economics* 110, no. 3: 681–712.

———. 1997. "The Effects of Corruption on Growth, Investment, and Government Expenditure: A Cross Country Analysis." In *Corruption in the Global Economy*, ed. Kimberly Elliott, 83–107. Washington, D.C.: Institute for International Economics.

———. 1998. "Corruption and the Composition of Government Expenditure." *Journal of Public Economics* 69, no. 2: 263–79.

———. 2004. "The Persistence of Corruption and Slow Economic Growth." Staff Paper 51, International Monetary Fund, Washington, D.C.

McCubbins, Matthew, and Thomas Schwartz. 1984. "Police Patrols Versus Fire Alarms." *American Journal of Political Science* 28:165–79.

McFaul, Michael. 2001. *Russia's Unfinished Revolution: Political Change from Gorbachev to Putin.* Ithaca: Cornell University Press.

McFaul, Michael, and Kathryn Stoner-Weiss. 2008. "The Myth of the Authoritarian Model: How Putin's Crackdown Holds Russia Back." *Foreign Affairs* 87, no. 1: 68–84.

Medina, Luis Fernando, and Susan Stokes. 2007. "Monopoly and Monitoring: An Approach to Political Clientelism." In *Patrons, Clients, and Policies: Patterns of Democratic Accountability and Political Competition*, ed. Herbert Kitschelt and Steven Wilkinson, 68–83. New York: Cambridge University Press.

Mehrez, Gil, and Daniel Kaufmann. 1999. "Transparency, Liberalization, and Financial Crises." Policy Research Working Paper 2286, World Bank, Washington, D.C.

Milanovic, Branko. 1996. "Nations, Conglomerates, and Empires: The Tradeoff Between Income and Sovereignty." Policy Research Working Paper 1675, World Bank, Washington, D.C.

———. 1998. *Income, Inequality, and Poverty During the Transition from Planned to Market Economy.* Washington, D.C.: World Bank.

Miller, Jonathan. 1997. "Judicial Review and Constitutional Stability: A Sociology of the U.S. Model and Its Collapse in Argentina." *Hastings International and Comparative Law Journal* 21, no. 1: 113–30.

———. 2001. "Evaluating the Argentine Supreme Court Under Presidents Alfonsín and Menem. 1983–1999." *Southwestern Journal of Law and Trade in the Americas* 7, no. 2: 369–433.

Mishler, William, and Richard Rose. 2001. "What Are the Origins of Political Trust? Testing Institutional and Cultural Theories in Post-Communist Societies." *Comparative Political Studies* 34, no. 1: 30–62.

Mo, Pak Hung. 2001. "Corruption and Economic Growth." *Journal of Comparative Economics* 29:66–79.

Molinelli, N. Guillermo, Valeria Palanza, and Gisela Sin. 1999. *Congreso, presidencia y justicia en Argentina: Materiales para su studio.* Buenos Aires: CEDI/Fundación Gobierno y Sociedad.

Monckeberg, María Olivia. 2001. *El saqueo de los grupos económicos al estado chileno.* Santiago: Ediciones B.

Montecinos, Verónica. 2003. *Economic Policy Making and Parliamentary Accountability in Chile.* Geneva: United Nations Research Institute for Social Development.

Montinola, Gabriella, and Robert Jackman. 2002. "Sources of Corruption: A Cross-Country Study." *British Journal of Political Science* 40, no. 2: 570–602.

Morgenstern, Scott, and Luigi Manzetti. 2003. "Legislative Oversight: Interests and Institutions in the United States and Argentina." In *Democratic Accountability in Latin America*, ed. Scott Mainwaring and Christopher Welna, 132–69. New York: Oxford University Press.

Morris, Stephen. 1991. *Corruption and Politics in Contemporary Mexico.* Tuscaloosa: University of Alabama Press.

Moser, Nat, and Peter Oppenheimer. 2001. "The Oil Industry: Structural Transformation and Corporate Governance." In *Russia's Post-Communist Economy*, ed. Brigitte Granville and Peter Oppenheimer, 301–24. New York: Oxford University Press.

Muhlenbrock, Gisela von. 1996. "Discretion and Corruption: The Chilean Judiciary." *Crime, Law, and Social Change* 25, no. 4: 335–51.

Mulgan, Richard. 2003. *Holding Power to Account.* New York: Palgrave Macmillan.

Murillo, Maria Victoria. 2002. "Political Bias in Policy Convergence: Privatization Choices in Latin America." *World Politics* 54 (July): 462–93.

Natale, Alberto. 1993. *Privatizaciones en privado: El testimonio de un protagonista que desnuda el laberinto de las adjudicaciones.* Buenos Aires: Planeta.

Nellis, John. 1999. "Time to Rethink Privatization in Transition Economies?" *Finance and Development* 36, no. 2: 1–6.

Nelson, Lynn, and Irina Kuzes. 1995. *Radical Reform in Yeltsin's Russia: Political, Economic, and Social Dimensions.* Armonk, N.Y.: M. E. Sharpe.

Nino, Carlos. 1993. "On the Exercise of Judicial Review in Argentina." In *Transition to Democracy in Latin America: The Role of the Judiciary*, ed. Irwin Stotzky, 3–22. Boulder: Westview.

North, Douglass. 1990. *Institutions, Institutional Change, and Economic Performance.* New York: Cambridge University Press.

———. 1994. "Economic Performance Through Time." *American Economic Review* 84, no. 3: 359–68.

North, Douglass, and Robert Paul Thomas. 1973. *The Rise of the Western World: A New Economic History.* New York: Cambridge University Press.

Nye, Joseph. 1967. "Corruption and Political Development: A Cost-Benefit Analysis." *American Political Science Review* 61, no. 2: 417–27.

Nystèn-Haarala, Soili. 2001. *Russian Law in Transition: Law and Institutional Change.* Helsinki: Kikimora Publications, Aleksanteri Institute.

O'Donnell, Guillermo. 1999. "Horizontal Accountability in New Democracies." In *The Self-Restraining State: Power and Accountability in New Democracies*, ed. Andreas Schedler, Larry Diamond, and Marc Plattner, 29–51. Boulder: Lynne Rienner.

Olson, Mancur. 1965. *The Logic of Collective Action: Public Goods and the Theory of Groups.* Cambridge: Harvard University Press.

———. 1982. *The Rise and Decline of Nations.* New Haven: Yale University Press.

Oppenheimer, Andres. 1996. *Bordering on Chaos: Guerrillas, Stockbrokers, Politicians, and Mexico's Road to Prosperity.* New York: Little, Brown and Company.

Orenstein, Mitchell. 2001. *Out of the Red: Building Capitalism and Democracy in Post-Communist Europe.* Ann Arbor: University of Michigan Press.

Organization for Economic Cooperation and Development. 2004. *Competition Law and Policy in Chile: A Peer Review.* Paris: OECD.

Ostrom, Elinor. 1990. *Governing the Commons: The Evolution of Institutions for Collective Action.* New York: Cambridge University Press.

Panizza, Ugo, and Mónica Yañez. 2006. "Why Are Latin Americans Unhappy About Reforms?" Mimeo, Inter-American Development Bank, Washington, D.C.

Paredes Molina, Ricardo, José M. Sánchez, Ricardo Sanhueza, and Leonardo Letellier. 1998. *Autonomia de las instituciones gubernamentales de Chile.* Washington, D.C.: Inter-American Development Bank.

Parente, Stephen, and Edward Prescott. 1999. "Monopoly Rights: A Barrier to Riches." *American Economic Review* 89:1216–33.

Payne, Mark, Daniel Zovatto, Fernando Carrillo Flórez, and Andrés Allamand Zavala. 2002. *Democracies in Development: Politics and Reform in Latin America.* Washington, D.C.: Inter-American Development Bank and the International Institute for Democracy and Electoral Assistance.

Persson, Torsten, Gerard Roland, and Guido Tabellini. 1997. "Separation of Powers and Political Accountability." *Quarterly Journal of Economics* 112:1163–202.

Persson, Torsten, Guido Tabellini, and Francesco Trebbi. 2003. "Electoral Rules and Corruption." *Journal of the European Economic Association* 1, no. 4: 958–89.

Peruzzotti, Enrique, and Catalina Smulovitz, eds. 2006. *Enforcing the Rule of Law: The Politics of Societal Accountability in Latin America.* Pittsburgh: University of Pittsburgh Press.

Petrazzini, Ben. 1995. "Telephone Privatization in a Hurry." In *Privatizing Monopolies: Lessons from the Telecommunications and Transport Sectors in Latin America,* ed. Ravi Ramamurti, 108–46. Baltimore: Johns Hopkins University Press.

Petrecolla, Alberto, Alberto Porto, Pablo Gerchunoff, and Guillermo Canovas. 1993. "Privatization in Argentina." *Quarterly Review of Economics and Finance* 33:67–93.

Pharr, Susan, and Robert Putnam, eds. 2000. *Disaffected Democracies: What's Troubling the Trilateral Countries?* Princeton: Princeton University Press.

Piñera, José. 1990. *La revolución laboral en Chile.* Santiago: Editorial Zig Zag.

Pistor, Khatarina, and Andrew Spicer. 1996. "Investment Funds in Mass Privatization and Beyond: Evidence from the Czech Republic and Russia." Development Discussion Paper 565, Harvard Institute for International Development, Harvard University.

Prebisch, Raúl. 1950. *Theoretical and Practical Problems of Economic Growth.* New York: United Nations Commission for Latin America.

Przeworski, Adam. 1991. *Democracy and the Market: Political and Economic Reforms in Eastern Europe and Latin America.* New York: Cambridge University Press.

———. 2004. "Institutions Matter?" *Government and Opposition* 39, no. 2: 527–40.

Putzel, James. 2002. "Developmental States and Crony Capitalists." In *Rethinking Development in East Asia: From Illusory Miracle to Economic Crisis,* ed. Pietro Masina, 189–222. Richmond, Surrey: Curzon Press.

Pye, Lucian. 1997. "Money and Politics and Transition to Democracy in East Asia." *Asian Survey* 37, no. 3: 213–28.

Reddaway, Peter, and Dmitri Glinski. 2001. *The Tragedy of Russia's Reforms: Market Bolshevism Against Democracy.* Washington, D.C.: United States Institute for Peace Press.

Rehren, Alfredo. 2002. "Clientelismo político, corrupción y Reforma del estado en Chile." In *Reforma del estado. Dirección pública y compras públicas II,* ed. Salvador Valdés Prieto. Santiago: Centro de Estudios Públicos.

———. 2004. "Political Corruption in Chilean Democracy." *Harvard Review of Latin America* (Spring): 13–15.

Remington, Thomas. 2001. *The Russian Parliament: Institutional Evolution in a Transitional Regime, 1989–1999*. New Haven: Yale University Press.

Remington, Thomas, Steve Smith, and Moshe Haspel. 1998. "Decrees, Laws, and Inter-Branch Relations in the Russian Federation." *Post-Soviet Affairs* 14, no. 4: 287–322.

Remmer, Karen, and Erik Wibbels. 2000. "The Subnational Politics of Economic Development: Provincial Politics and Fiscal Performance in Argentina." *Comparative Political Studies* 33, no. 4: 419–51.

Rezk, Ernesto. 2000. *Federalism and Decentralization under Convertibility: Lessons from the Argentine Experience*. Cordoba: National University of Cordoba.

Rigoli, Orlando Juan. 2000. *Senado S.A.: Una maquinaria en funcionamiento*. Buenos Aires: Planeta.

Ritzen, Jo, William Easterly, and Michael Woolcock. 2000. "On 'Good' Politicians and 'Bad' Policies: Social Cohesion, Institutions, and Growth." Policy Research Working Paper 2248, World Bank, Washington, D.C.

Rivera-Batiz, Francisco. 2007. "Democracy, Governance, and Economic Growth: Theory and Evidence." Mimeo, Department of Economics, Columbia University, New York.

Robinson, James, and Thierry Verdier. 2003. "The Political Economy of Clientelism." Discussion Paper 3205, Centre for Economic Policy Research, http://ssrn.com/abstract = 303185.

Rodan, Garry. 2004. "Neoliberalism and Transparency: Political Versus Economic Liberalism." Mimeo, Murdoch University, Perth.

Rodden, Jonathan, and Marta Arretche. 2003. "Legislative Bargaining and Distributive Politics in Brazil: An Empirical Approach." Paper prepared for discussion at Yale University.

Rodríguez-Boetsch, Leopoldo. 2005. "Public Service Privatisation and Crisis in Argentina." *Development in Practice* 15, nos. 3–4: 302–15.

Rodrik, Dani. 1997. "Democracy and Economic Performance." Unpublished paper, Harvard University.

———. 1999. "Where Did All the Growth Go? External Shocks, Social Conflict, and Growth Collapses." *Journal of Economic Growth* 4, no. 4: 385–412.

———. 2006. "Goodbye Washington Consensus, Hello Washington Confusion? A Review of the World Bank's Economic Growth in the 1990s: Learning from a Decade of Reform." *Journal of Economic Literature* 44, no. 4: 973–87.

———. 2007. *One Economics, Many Recipes: Globalization, Institutions, and Economic Development*. Princeton: Princeton University Press.

Rodrik, Dani, Arvind Subramanian, and Francesco Trebbi. 2004. "Institutions Rule: The Primacy of Institutions over Geography and Integration in Economic Development." *Journal of Economic Growth* 9, no. 2: 131–65.

Roeder, Philip. 1994. "Varieties of Post-Soviet Authoritarian Regimes." *Post-Soviet Affairs* 10 (January–March): 61–101.

Rose, Richard, William Mishler, and Christian Haerpfer. 1998. *Democracy and Its Alternatives: Understanding Post-Communist Societies*. Baltimore: Johns Hopkins University Press.

Rose-Ackerman, Susan. 1996. "The Political Economy of Corruption: Causes and Consequences." Public Policy for the Private Sector Note 74, World Bank, Washington, D.C.

————. 1999. *Corruption and Government: Causes, Consequences, and Reform.* New York: Cambridge University Press.

Rupnik, Jacques. 2007. "From Democracy Fatigue to Populist Backlash." *Journal of Democracy* 18, no. 4: 17–25.

Saavedra, Eduardo, and Raimundo Soto. 2004. "Toward a Modern State in Chile: Institutions, Governance, and Market Regulation." Working Paper 57, Latin American Institute of Doctrine and Social Studies at Georgetown University, Washington, D.C.

Saba, Roberto. 2000. "Regulatory Policy in an Unstable Legal Environment: The Case of Argentina." In *Regulatory Policy in Latin America: Post-Privatization Realities,* ed. Luigi Manzetti, 257–79. Miami: North-South Center Press at the University of Miami.

Sachs, Jeffrey. 1993. *Poland's Jump to the Market Economy.* Cambridge: MIT Press.

————. 2003. "Institutions Don't Rule: Direct Effects of Geography on Per Capita Income." Working Paper 9490, National Bureau of Economic Research, Cambridge, Massachusetts.

Sachs, Jeffrey, and Katharina Pistor. 1997. "Introduction: Progress, Pitfalls, Scenarios, and Lost Opportunities." In *The Rule of Law and Economic Reform in Russia,* ed. Jeffrey Sachs and Katharina Pistor, 1–22. Boulder: Westview.

Samuels, David, and Richard Snyder. 2001. "The Value of a Vote: Malapportionment in Comparative Perspective." *British Journal of Political Science* 31:651–71.

Sawers, Larry. 1996. *The Other Argentina.* Boulder: Westview.

Schacter, Mark. 2001. "When Accountability Fails: A Framework for Diagnosis and Action." *Isuma* (Summer): 134–37.

Schady, Norbert. 2000. "The Political Economy of Expenditures by the Peruvian Social Fund. FONCODES. 1991–95." *American Political Science Review* 94, no. 2: 289–304.

Schamis, Hector. 2002. *Re-Forming the State: The Politics of Privatization in Latin America and Europe.* Ann Arbor: Michigan University Press.

Schedler, Andreas, Larry Diamond, and Marc Plattner, eds. 1999. *The Self-Restraining State: Power and Accountability in New Democracies.* Boulder: Lynne Rienner.

Schmitter, Philippe. 1999. "The Limits of Horizontal Accountability." In *The Self-Restraining State,* ed. Andreas Schedler, Larry Diamond, and Marc F. Plattner, 59–62.

————. 2004. "The Ambiguous Virtues of Accountability." *Journal of Democracy* 14, no. 4: 47–60.

Schneider, Friedrich, with Dominik Enste. 2002. "Hiding in the Shadows: The Growth of the Underground Economy." *Economic Issues* 30. Washington, D.C.: International Monetary Fund.

Seligson, Mitchell. 2002. "The Impact of Corruption on Regime Legitimacy: A Comparative Study of Four Latin American Countries." *Journal of Politics* 64 (May): 408–33.

Shepsle, Kenneth. 1991. "Discretion, Institutions, and the Problem of Government Commitment." In *Social Theory for a Changing Society,* ed. Pierre Bordieux and James Coleman, 245–63. Boulder: Westview.

Shleifer, Andrei, and Maxim Boycko. 1993. "The Politics of Russian Privatization." In *Post-Communist Reform: Pain and Progress,* ed. Olivier Blanchard et al., 37–80. Cambridge: MIT Press.

Shleifer, Andrei, and Daniel Treisman. 2000. *Without a Map: Political Tactics and Economic Reform in Russia.* Cambridge: MIT Press.

Shleifer, Andrei, and Robert Vishny. 1993. "Corruption." *Quarterly Journal of Economics* 108:599–617.

———. 1998. *The Grabbing Hand: Government Pathologies and Their Cures.* Cambridge: Harvard University Press.

Shugart, Matthew, and John Carey. 1992. *Presidents and Assemblies.* Cambridge: Cambridge University Press.

Shugart, Matthew, Erika Moreno, and Brian Crisp. 2002. "The Accountability Deficit in Latin America." In *Democratic Accountability in Latin America,* ed. Scott Mainwaring and Christopher Welna, 79–131. New York: Oxford University Press.

Siavelis, Peter. 2000a. *The President and Congress in Postauthoritarian Chile: Institutional Constraints to Democratic Consolidation.* University Park: Pennsylvania State University Press.

———. 2000b. "Disconnected Fire Alarms and Ineffective Police Patrols: Legislative Oversight in Postauthoritarian Chile." *Journal of Interamerican Studies and World Affairs* 42, no. 1: 71–98.

Silva, Eduardo. 1996. *The State and Capital in Chile: Business Elites, Technocrats, and Market Economics.* Boulder: Westview.

Singh, Anoop, Agnès Belaisch, Charles Collyns, Paula De Masi, Reva Krieger, Guy Meredith, and Robert Rennhack. 2005. *Stabilization and Reform in Latin America: A Macroeconomic Perspective on the Experience Since the Early 1990s.* Occasional Paper 238, International Monetary Fund, Washington, D.C.

Smarzynska, Beata, and Shang-Jin Wei. 2000. "Corruption and Composition of Foreign Direct Investment: Firm-Level Evidence." Policy Research Working Paper 2360, World Bank, Washington, D.C.

Solnick, Steve. 1998. *Stealing the State: Control and Collapse in Soviet Institutions.* Cambridge: Harvard University Press.

Solomon, Peter. 1992. "Legality in Soviet Political Culture: A Perspective on Gorbachev's Reforms." In *Stalinism, Its Nature and Aftermath: Essays in Honor of Moshe Lewin,* ed. Nick Lampert and Gabor Ritterspoon, 244–60. London: Macmillan.

———. 1995. "The Limits of Legal Order in Post-Soviet Russia." *Post-Soviet Affairs* 11, no. 2: 89–114.

Soros, George. 1998. *The Crisis of Global Capitalism: Open Society Endangered.* New York: PublicAffairs.

Spiller, Pablo, and Mariano Tommasi. 2003. "The Institutional Foundations of Public Policy: A Transactions Approach with Application to Argentina." *Journal of Law, Economics, and Organization* 19, no 2: 281–306.

———. 2007. *The Institutional Foundations of Public Policy in Argentina: A Transactions Cost Approach.* New York: Cambridge University Press.

Stark, David, and Lázló Bruszt. 1998. *Postsocialist Pathways.* New York: Cambridge University Press.

Stavrakis, Peter. 1993. "State-Building in Post-Soviet Russia: The Chicago Boys and the Decline of Administrative Capacity." Occasional Paper 254, Kennan Institute for Advanced Russian Studies, Washington, D.C.

Stiglitz, Joseph. 2002. *Globalization and Its Discontents.* New York: Norton.

Stokes, Susan. 2005. "Perverse Accountability: A Formal Model of Machine Politics with Evidence from Argentina." *American Political Science Review* 99, no. 3: 315–26.

Stone, Randall. 2002. *Lending Credibility: The International Monetary Fund and the Post-Communist Transition*. Princeton: Princeton University Press.

Summers, Lawrence. 1998. "Russia in 1998: Building a Pluralist Market Economy." Address by Lawrence Summers, U.S. Deputy Secretary, April 1, at the U.S.-Russia Business Council, Washington, D.C.

———. 2000. "International Financial Crises: Causes, Prevention, and Cures." *American Economic Review* 9 (May): 1–16.

Tanzi, Vito, and Hamid Davoodi. 1997. "Corruption, Public Investment, and Growth." Working Paper 97/139, International Monetary Fund, Washington, D.C.

Teichman, Judith. 2001. *The Politics of Freeing Markets in Latin America: Chile, Argentina, and Mexico*. Chapel Hill: University of North Carolina Press.

———. 2004. "The World Bank and Policy Reform in Mexico and Argentina." *Latin American Politics and Society* 46, no. 1: 39–46.

Thames, Frank. 2000. "Patronage and the Presidential Critique: Budget Policy in the Fifth Russian State Duma." *Demokratizatsiya* 8, no. 1: 34–56.

Tikhomirov, Vladimir. 2000. *The Political Economy of Post-Soviet Russia*. New York: St. Martin's Press.

Tommasi, Mariano, Sebastián Saiegh, and Pablo Sanguinetti. 2001. "Fiscal Federalism in Argentina: Policies, Politics, and Institutional Reform." *Economia* 1 (Spring): 147–201.

Tornell, Aaron, and Andres Velasco. 1992. "The Tragedy of the Commons and Economic Growth: Why Does Capital Flow from Poor to Rich Countries?" *Journal of Political Economy* 1:157–211.

Treisman, Daniel. 1999. *After the Deluge: Regional Crises and Political Consolidation in Russia*. Ann Arbor: University of Michigan Press.

Tulchin, Joseph, and Ralph Espach, eds. 2000. *Combating Corruption: Anti-Corruption Policies in Latin America*. Boulder: Lynne Rienner.

Tullock, Gordon. 1967. "The Welfare Costs of Tariffs, Monopolies, and Theft." *Western Economic Journal* 5:224–32.

United Nations Conference on Trade and Development (UNCTAD). 2007. *World Investment Report*. New York: United Nations.

United States Congress House Speaker's Advisory Group on Russia. 2000. *Russia's Road to Corruption: How the Clinton Administration Exported Government Instead of Free Enterprise and Failed the Russian People*. Washington, D.C.

Urbiztondo, Santiago, Daniel Artana, and Fernando Navajas. 1997. *La autonomia de los entes reguladores argentinos*. Buenos Aires: FIEL.

Valdés, Juan Gabriel. 1995. *Pinochet's Economists: The Chicago School in Chile*. Cambridge: Cambridge University Press.

Valenzuela, Arturo. 1977. *Political Brokers in Chile: Local Government in a Centralized Polity*. Durham: Duke University Press.

Veigel, Klaus. 2009. *Dictatorship, Democracy, and Globalization: Argentina, 1973–2001*. University Park: Pennsylvania State University Press.

Verbitsky, Horacio. 1991. *Robo para la corona: Los frutos proibidos del árbol de la corrupción*. Buenos Aires: Planeta.

———. 1993. *Hacer la corte: La construcción de un poder absoluto sin justicia ni control*. Buenos Aires: Planeta.

Vergara, Pilar. 1981. "Las Transformaciones de las funciones Económicas del estado en Chile bajo el Régimen Militar." *Colleción Estudios Cieplán* 5 (July): 117–54.

————. 1985. *Auge y caída del neoliberalismo en Chile*. Santiago: FLACSO.

Vidal, Armenado. 1995. *El Congreso en la trampa*. Buenos Aires: Planeta.

Waller, Michael, and Victor Yasmann. 1995. "Russia's Great Criminal Revolution: The Role of the Security Services." *Journal of Contemporary Criminal Justice* 11, no. 4: 276–97.

Wampler, Brian. 2004. "Expanding Accountability Through Participatory Institutions: Mayors, Citizens, and Budgeting in Three Brazilian Municipalities." *Latin American Politics and Society* (Summer): 73–99.

Waterbury, John. 1976. "Corruption, Political Stability, and Development: Comparative Evidence from Egypt and Morocco." *Government and Opposition* 11, no. 4: 426–45.

Webster, William H. 1997. *Russian Organized Crime: Global Organized Crime Project*. Washington, D.C.: Center of Strategic and International Studies.

Wedel, Janine. 2001. *Collision and Collusion: The Strange Case of Western Aid to Eastern Europe, 1989–1998*. 2nd ed. New York: Palgrave Macmillan.

Wei, Shang-Jin. 1999. "Corruption in Economic Development: Beneficial Grease, Minor Annoyance, or Major Obstacle?" Policy Research Working Paper 2444, World Bank, Washington, D.C.

————. 2001a. "Corruption and Globalization." Policy Brief 79. Washington, D.C: Brookings Institution Press.

————. 2001b. "Domestic Crony Capitalism and International Fickle Capital: Is There a Connection?" *International Finance* 4, no. 1: 15–45.

Weingast, Barry. 1997. "The Political Foundations of Democracy and the Rule of Law." *American Political Science Review* 91:245–63.

Weir, Fred. 2004. "Kremlin versus the Oligarchs." *The Nation* (November 28): 21.

Weller, Christian, and Laura Singleton. 2003. "Reining in Exchange Rates: A Better Way to Stabilize the Global Economy." Briefing Paper 131, Economic Policy Institute, Washington, D.C.

Weyland, Kurt. 1998. "The Politics of Corruption in Latin America." *Journal of Democracy* 9, no. 2: 108–21.

Williamson, John. 1990. "What Washington Means by Policy Reform." In *Latin American Adjustment: How Much Has Happened*, ed. John Williamson. Washington, D.C.: Institute for International Economics.

————. 1994. *The Political Economy of Policy Reform*. Washington, D.C.: Institute of International Economics.

Williamson, Oliver. 1986. *Economic Organization: Firms, Markets and Policy Control*. New York: New York University Press.

Woods, Ngaire. 2006. *The Globalizers: The IMF, the World Bank, and Their Borrowers*. Ithaca: Cornell University Press.

World Bank. 1994. *Good Governance: The World Bank Experience*. Washington, D.C.: World Bank.

————. 1995. *Bureaucrats in Business*. New York: Oxford University Press.

————. 1995. *World Development Report: The State in a Changing World*. New York: Oxford University Press.

————. 1998. *Assessing Aid: What Works, What Doesn't, and Why*. New York: Oxford University Press.

————. 2001. *World Development Report 2000/2001: Attacking Poverty*. New York: Oxford University Press.

———. 2003. World Development Report 2003. New York: Oxford University Press.

———. 2005. *Economic Growth in the 1990s: Learning from a Decade of Reform.* Washington, D.C.: World Bank.

———. 2007. *East Asia 10 Years After the Financial Crisis.* Washington, D.C.: World Bank.

World Economic Forum. 2004. *The Global Competitiveness Report 2003–2004.* New York: Oxford University Press.

Yeltsin, Boris. 2000. *Midnight Diaries.* New York: PublicAffairs.

Yergin, Daniel, and Thane Gustafson. 1993. *Russia 2010—and What It Means to the World.* New York: Random House.

Yergin, Daniel, and Joseph Stanislaw. 1998. *The Commanding Heights: The Battle Between Government and the Marketplace That Is Remaking the Modern World.* New York: Simon and Schuster.

Yotopoulos, Pan. 1989. "The (Rip)Tide of Privatization: Lessons from Chile." *World Development* 17, no. 5: 683–702.

Zagha, Roberto, Gobind Nankani, and Indermit Gill. 2006. "Rethinking Growth." *Finance and Development* 43, no. 1: 1–6.

Zahler, Roberto. 1980. "Monetary and Real Repercussions of Financial Opening Up to the Exterior. The Case of Chile, 1974–1978." *CEPAL Review* 10:127–53.

Zarazaga, Carlos. 2006. "Argentina's Unimpressive Recovery: Insights from a Real Business Cycle Approach." Working Paper 0606, Federal Reserve Bank of Dallas, Texas.

Zettelmeyer, Jeromin. 2006. "Growth and Reforms in Latin America: A Survey of Facts and Arguments." Working Paper WP/06/210, International Monetary Fund, Washington, D.C.

Index